lonely 🌏 planet

Washington, Oregon & the Pacific Northwest

T0286923

Vancouver Island p330

Vancouver p300

Northwestern Washington & the San Juan Islands p86

Seattle, p56

Eastern Washington p150

Washington Cascades p132

Olympic Peninsula & Washington Coast p110

Columbia River Gorge p212

Portland, p166

The Willamette Valley p194

Central & the Oregon Cascades p226

Eastern Oregon p284

Oregon Coast p244

Ashland & Southern Oregon p268

Margot Bigg, Bianca Bujan, Brandon Fralic, Leslie Hsu Oh, Alex Leviton, Michael Kohn, Britany Robinson, Amy Sung

CONTENTS

teriyaki salmon,
Vancouver (p301)

Elk, Southern
Oregon (p269)

Surfer, Whidbey Island (p102)

Toolkit

Storybook

LEON WERDINGER/ALAMY STOCK PHOTO ©

Breitenbush Hot Springs (p204)

WASHINGTON, OREGON & THE PACIFIC NORTHWEST
THE JOURNEY BEGINS HERE

I must admit, I spent much of my life taking the Pacific Northwest for granted. Growing up in the region, I never truly appreciated how fortunate we were to be living among groves of towering evergreen trees, never more than a few miles from a wooded trail or a crystalline creek. Even as a confirmed city slicker, it never struck me as anything out of the ordinary to be awoken by the hoot of an owl or to spot deer grazing on the side of the road, mere miles from downtown Portland. It wasn't until I began traveling extensively around the world that I realized I hailed from a magical part of North America, where nature is not only omnipresent but also – to a large extent – honored. I've fallen in love with the Pacific Northwest, and I hope that you'll find this region as enchanting as I do.

Margot Bigg

@margotbigg

Margot is a travel writer and editor specializing in Oregon and India travel. She was born and mostly raised in Portland.

My favorite experience
is soaking in the geothermal waters of **Breitenbush Hot Springs** (p204). Every time I visit this wooded off-grid getaway, I feel both energized and at peace.

WHO GOES WHERE

Our writers and experts choose the places which, for them, define the Pacific Northwest.

LIJUAN GUO/SHUTTERSTOCK ©

My favorite experience is picnicking in **Granville Island** (p319). I pop into the public market for snacks, stroll the wooden boardwalk to Ron Basford Park, and settle in for a quiet picnic with harbor views.

Bianca Bujan

@bitsofbee

Born and raised in Vancouver, Bianca loves to share the best things to see, do and eat in her city.

TOMAS NEVESELY/SHUTTERSTOCK ©

Of all the iconic road trips in Washington, the scenic summer drive to **Artist Point** (p94) continues to draw me back. Heather-lined paths lead to expansive views of the North Cascades. I love staying until sunset for the magical alpenglow and stargazing.

Brandon Fralic

@beersatb

Brandon is a travel writer and beer columnist based in Bellingham.

CHECUBUS/SHUTTERSTOCK ©

The first time I sunk my toes into the sand at **Ruby Beach** (p114), I was 10. My mom held my hand tight as the white-capped waves broke at our feet. Ten years later, I would lose her to liver cancer. I appreciate returning to this place where I can still find her.

Leslie Hsu Oh

@lesliehsuoh

Lesie Hsu Oh is an award-winning writer and photographer.

BJORN BAKSTAD/GETTY IMAGES ©

The kitsch of Bavarian **Leavenworth** (p136) adds to the town's appeal. You can go snowshoeing or hiking during the day in some of the most beautiful, peaceful mountains on earth, and return in the evening for a schnitzel, German lager and to ride the alpine coaster.

Alex Leviton

@alexleviton

Alex teaches from her home on Bainbridge Island.

SAMUEL HOWELL/SHUTTERSTOCK ©

The drive over Belknap Crater from Sisters is an otherworldly experience I look forward to when **Highway 242** (p243) opens up after its long winter slumber. Once on top of the crater it's not too hard to imagine what it would be like to walk on the moon. Peering out at the landscape from fortress-like Dee Wright Observatory seals the surreal experience. Dropping down to the other side of the Cascades, an obligatory hike to Proxy Falls and its cool waters brings me back to the best that earth can offer.

Michael Kohn

@michaelkohnSF

Michael has contributed to over 25 Lonely Planet since 2004. He currently calls Central Oregon home and covers public lands and the environment for the Bend Bulletin.

TRISTANBNZ/GETTY IMAGES ©

Driving the **Rogue-Umpqua Scenic Byway** (p283) is a dreamy escape, but also an intimate interaction with the landscape. I get lost in my own thoughts as I trace the snaking Umpqua River; thick forests press against the road, then fall back to reveal stark burn areas and distant peaks. It's the perfect place to comtemplate the resilience and delicacy of nature.

Britany Robinson

@britseeingstars

Britany Robinson is a writer and editor living in Portland, Oregon, with her family.

PHILLIP WISE/SHUTTERSTOCK ©

CONTRIBUTING WRITERS

Amy Sung
Amy contributed to the Seattle chapter. A native Pacific Northwesterner, Amy is happiest when eating satisfying and mind-opening food (and writing about it).

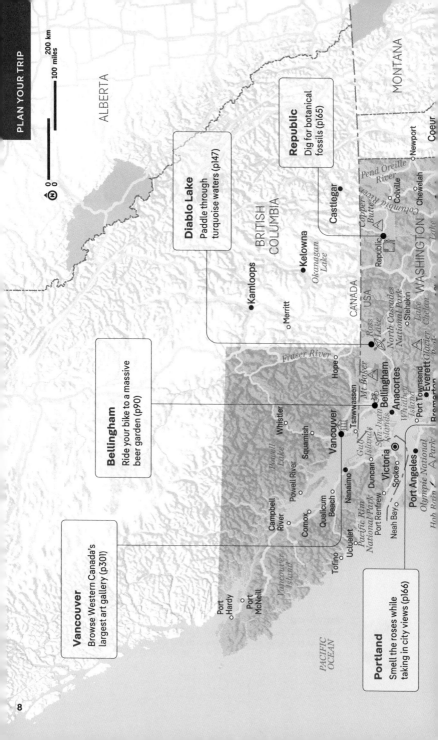

Vancouver
Browse Western Canada's largest art gallery (p301)

Bellingham
Ride your bike to a massive beer garden (p90)

Diablo Lake
Paddle through turquoise waters (p147)

Republic
Dig for botanical fossils (p165)

Portland
Smell the roses while taking in city views (p166)

ALBERTA

BRITISH COLUMBIA

CANADA   USA

WASHINGTON

MONTANA

200 km
100 miles

Kamloops

Merritt

Kelowna
Okanagan Lake

Castlegar

Republic

Copper Butte

Colville   Chewelah

Pend Oreille River

Newport

Coeur

Columbia River

Pacific Rim National Park

Tofino

Ucluelet

Port Renfrew

Neah Bay

Port Angeles

Olympic National Park

Hoh Rain

Port Hardy

Port McNeill

Vancouver Island

Campbell River

Powell River

Powell Lake

Comox

Qualicum Beach

Nanaimo

Duncan

Victoria

Sooke

Whistler

Squamish

Gulf Islands

San Juan Islands

Tsawwassen

Vancouver

Fraser River

Hope

Ross Lake

North Cascades National Park

Stehekin

Lake Chelan

Mt Baker

Bellingham

Anacortes

Whidbey Island

Port Townsend

Everett

Bremerton

Glacier Peak

PACIFIC OCEAN

8

Eagle Cap Wilderness
Hike through one of the remotest parts of Oregon (p297)

Cannon Beach
Spot tufted puffins congregating on a sea stack (p255)

Detroit Lake
Soak in Breitenbush's geothermal waters (p204)

Bend
Visit the last Blockbuster video store on earth (p230)

IDAHO

NEVADA

Boise

Nampa

Moscow

Pullman

Dayton

Walla Walla

Joseph

Halfway

Pendleton

La Grande

Baker City

Ukiah

John Day

Strawberry Mountain Wilderness

Seneca

Steens Mtn

Burns Junction

McDermitt

Owyhee

Jordan Valley

Moses Lake

Potholes Reservoir

Ellensburg

Yakima

Naches

Richland

Kennewick

Umatilla

Lake Wallula

Arlington

Columbia River

OREGON

Burns

Crane

Malheur Lake

Harney Lake

Ontario

Lake Owyhee

The Dalles

Hood River

Madras

Prineville

Bend

Newberry National Volcanic Monument

Summer Lake

Summer Lake

Lake Albert

Lake Abert

Goose Lake

Lakeview

Alturas

Mt Rainier National Park

Mt Rainier

Mt St Helen's National Volcanic Monument

Mt St Helen's

Mt Adams

Mt Hood

Mt Jefferson

Three Sisters

Sisters

Three Sisters Wilderness

Mt Bachelor

Cascade Lakes

La Pine

Crater Lake

Crater Lake National Park

Upper Klamath Lake

Klamath Falls

Merrill

Tacoma

Olympia

Aberdeen

Ocean Shores

Grays Harbor

Long Beach

Astoria

Seaside

Longview

Cannon Beach

Manzanita

Tillamook

Vancouver

Portland

Oregon City

Newberg

McMinnville

Lincoln City

Depoe Bay

Newport

Yachats

Florence

Oregon Dunes National Recreation Area

Reedsport

Charleston

Coos Bay

Bandon

Port Orford

Gold Beach

Brookings

Salem

Albany

Corvallis

Eugene

Springfield

Roseburg

Grants Pass

Jacksonville

Medford

Ashland

Yreka

Mt Shasta

CALIFORNIA

PACIFIC OCEAN

Willamette River

9

HAPPY TRAILS

It should come as no surprise that hiking is a popular pastime among Pacific Northwesterners and visitors alike. The region is rich with natural areas, with an enormous network of well-maintained trails suitable for hikers of varying ages and abilities. And while you can go for a hike through the trees within the limits of virtually all of the region's big cities, you're never more than a short drive from massive swaths of nearly untouched nature.

Rain Ready

It's always wise to be prepared for rain, particularly outside of the summer months. Always pack lightweight waterproof gear with you.

Offline Maps

Many hiking areas in the Pacific Northwest are located out of cell-phone coverage range, so it's wise to have a printed map with you.

Leash Laws

Many hiking areas allow dogs, provided they remain on a leash. These rules are designed to protect wildlife – please respect them.

④
⑤
③   ②
①

BEST HIKING EXPERIENCES

Check out the waterfalls along the aptly named **① Trail of Ten Falls** (p201), a popular 7.2-mile-long loop trail in Oregon's Silver Falls State Park.

Challenge yourself with a hike up the **② Chief Joseph Summit Trail** (p299) in Eastern Oregon's Eagle Cap Wilderness.

Hike up **③ Dog Mountain** (p224) on the Washington side of the Columbia River Gorge for spectacular views over the region.

Take a 4-mile (round-trip) hike through evergreen forests to **④ Fragrance Lake** (p95) in Washington's Larrabee State Park.

Explore the ancient Hoh Rain Forest in the Olympic National Park with a trek along the **⑤ Hoh River Trail** (p117).

FRANCESCO VANINETTI PHOTO/GETTY IMAGES ©

Terwilliger Hot Springs (p204)

NATURAL SPAS

Few things soothe sore muscles better than a hot springs soak. Fortunately for weary hikers in the Pacific Northwest, this geothermally active region has plenty. Expect a mix of developed hot springs resorts that require reservations and natural pools that cost next to nothing to visit, all with steaming, mineral-rich waters.

Wear or Bare?

While you're always welcome to wear a swimsuit, be aware that many of the region's hot springs are clothing-optional.

Remember to Hydrate

Sitting in hot water can dehydrate you, so it's a good idea to bring a (non-glass) water bottle with you whenever you soak.

BEST HOT SPRINGS EXPERIENCES

Rejuvenate your sore muscles with a soak at ❶ **Sol Duc Hot Springs** (p116) in Olympic National Park.

Experience the geothermal sauna and pools at Detroit's off-grid ❷ **Breitenbush Hot Springs** (p204).

Stay at the ❸ **Lodge at Hot Lake Springs** (p000) in La Grande and enjoy a free soak at their hot pools, or buy a soaking pass for the day.

Take a short hike to Oregon's ❹ **Terwilliger Hot Springs** (p204), with its four terraced pools.

Soak in geothermal water in the middle of the forest at Oregon's ❺ **Bagby Hot Springs** (p204).

BRING THE KIDS

Although the Pacific Northwest doesn't have much in the way of theme parks, it offers something that many kids – and their parents – may find even better: beautiful natural areas full of opportunities for educational discovery plus more than a handful of magnificently fun urban attractions where silliness is celebrated, no matter your age.

Junior Rangers

Many national parks have Junior Rangers programs designed to get kids interested in nature. You can learn more online or at park visitor centers.

Time it Right

Some urban kid-friendly attractions have adults-only hours in the evening, so it's wise to check carefully before planning your visit.

Restaurant Tips

Dining in the Pacific Northwest is a casual fare, and while kids' menus aren't super common, children are welcome at most restaurants.

BEST EXPERIENCES FOR KIDS

Graffiti the walls with lasers or play in an illuminated ball pit at the immersive ❶ **Hopscotch Portland** (p187).

Soar above the trees at ❷ **Crater Lake ZipLine** (p282), which offers a regular zipline course and one for smaller kids.

Add a Bavarian twist to your world of make-believe in ❸ **Leavenworth** (p136), a timber town that was revamped in the 1960s to resemble a Black Forest village.

Dig for 48-million-year-old fossils at Republic's ❹ **Stonerose Interpretive Center and Eocene Fossil Site** (p165).

Browse for handcrafted toys at Vancouver's ❺ **Kids Market** (p318).

BY THE SEASHORE

One of the Pacific Northwest's biggest draws is its magnificent beaches, but don't expect to do a lot of swimming and sunbathing if you make the journey for yourself. A day in this consistently cool part of the region is more likely to include long hikes through coastal forests, drives to scenic overlooks and strolls along the sand. Add to the mix walkable towns loaded with boutiques and seafood stops and you're in for quite a treat.

Tide Pools

Tide pooling is a popular low-tide activity in the Pacific Northwest, but remember to look, not touch – and never remove creatures from their pools.

Orca Season

You can see whales throughout the year along the Pacific Coast, but orca sightings peak between late spring and early fall.

Bundle Up

Pacific Northwest coastal beaches tend to be chilly and windy, so make sure to pack warm layers, even in the summertime.

BEST SEASIDE EXPERIENCES

Grab your binoculars and look for puffins nesting on ❶ **Haystack Rock** (p256), Oregon's most-recognizable monolith, on Cannon Beach.

Head to the Oregon Coast during low tide to see the ❷ **Neskowin Ghost Forest** (p256), the remnant stumps of a Sitka spruce forest that once stood where there's now only beach.

Hike to the top of the sea cliffs at ❸ **Rosario Head** (p99) in Fidalgo Island's Deception Pass State Park.

Take a 12-mile drive along the scenic ❹ **Samuel H Boardman State Scenic Corridor** (p266) on Oregon's South Coast.

Watch surfers and spot whales at ❺ **Long Beach** (p349) in Vancouver Island's Pacific Rim National Park Reserve.

ON THE WATER

If there's one thing you're sure to see in the Pacific Northwest (besides trees), it's water – and we don't just mean giant raindrops. The region is rich in waterways, from powerful rivers to calm lakes and reservoirs. Best of all, you don't have to be an avid outdoors person to take advantage of the region's aquatic abundance, as there are plenty of boating and rafting operators ready to take travelers of all abilities out for a float.

Early-Summer Swims

Exercise extra caution when swimming in lakes and rivers during the early summer months – many are fed by glaciers and remain dangerously cold until late summer.

Clear Kayaks

Plenty of outfitters across the Pacific Northwest offer kayaking tours aboard crystal-clear kayaks, which give the best water views imaginable.

Lifejackets

Lifejacket laws vary by state/province, but it's wise to have one per person on all watercraft.

BEST EXPERIENCES ON THE WATER

Join a marine biologist on a whale-watching tour in Oregon's **❶ Depoe Bay** (p257), known for its summer resident whales.

Spend a day rafting the lower **❷ Deschutes River** (p225) near Maupin, Oregon.

Get up close to the crystalline waters of Crater Lake at **❸ Cleetwood Cove** (p280), the only spot on the lake where visitors can access the shore.

Go boating on the **❹ Skagit River** (p147) in the Washington Cascades – during the cooler months, you're likely to spot resident bald eagles.

Take a guided boat trip out onto the aquamarine waters of Washington's **❺ Diablo Lake** (p147), or bring your own kayak for a self-directed adventure.

CYBERNESCO/GETTY IMAGES ©

Butchart Gardens (p338)

URBAN OUTDOORS

No matter where you are in the Pacific Northwest, nature is never far away. That even goes for the region's largest cities, where massive trees and snow-clad mountains form a part of urban skylines. Whether you're up for a hike or just a bit of forest bathing, you'll find plenty of ways to experience the outdoors in the city.

Public Transportation

You can easily get to natural areas in all of the region's main cities by relying on public transportation alone.

On the Right Foot

Many of the region's urban parks have trail systems, but don't expect them all to be paved – although trails are generally maintained, they're often made of compacted dirt.

BEST URBAN OUTDOORS EXPERIENCES

Stroll among plants from around the world at Victoria's ❶ **Butchart Gardens** (p338).

Take in oceanfront views from Vancouver's ❷ **Stanley Park** (p310).

Head west to visit Seattle's ❸ **Lincoln Park** (p82), for lovely views for miles.

Wander through ❹ **Portland Japanese Garden**, located inside sprawling Washington Park (p183).

Watch surfers ride artificial river waves on the Deschutes River at ❺ **Bend Whitewater Park** (p230).

WHIMSICALLY WONDERFUL

The Pacific Northwest has long had a reputation for being a little unconventional, attracting artists, writers and people who think a little differently to its shores. This means that you'll find more than a few quirky shops and galleries, amusing roadside attractions, and art installations designed to make you question your notions of reality.

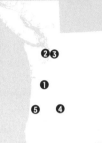

Northwest Trolls

In 2023 Danish artist Thomas Dambo erected six gargantuan trolls in publicly accessible locations across the Pacific Northwest, namely in Portland, Seattle, Vashon, Issaquah and on Bainbridge Island.

Keep Portland Weird

Portland is proudly quirky, with the 'Keep Portland Weird' bumper stickers to prove it, but this popular tagline actually originated in Austin, Texas.

Come As You Are

People in the Pacific Northwest are used to eccentricity. If you like wearing costumes just for the heck of it, you'll be right at home.

BEST WHIMSICAL EXPERIENCES

Sip tea while listening to live piano performances at Portland's ❶ **Rimsky-Korsakoffee House** (p188), in a historic home that's full of surprises.

Leave your mark in the form of a chewing gum wad at ❷ **Seattle's Gum Wall** (p66), a grossly popular selfie spot.

Experience the subterranean side of Pendleton with an ❸ **underground tour** (p288) of Prohibition-era whiskey bars and opium dens.

Rent a DVD at the ❹ **last Blockbuster** (p232) in Bend, the only remaining branch of the once-ubiquitous video store chain.

See a bog full of carnivorous cobra lilies at the Oregon Coast's compact ❺ **Darlingtonia State Natural Site** (p261).

BEER & BREWERIES

While the Pacific Northwest is celebrated for coffee and wine, there's another equally loved beverage keeping locals and visitors satiated: beer. Pacific Northwesterners have been brewing beer since the middle of the 19th century, but it wasn't until the 1980s that craft beer came on the scene in a major way. Today, this region – which also happens to be where the bulk of US hops are grown – is a destination for beer lovers, with breweries found in communities big and small.

Seasonal Brews

Many PNW craft breweries come out with seasonal ales, often to commemorate different holidays. Some also run special editions that are only available at their breweries.

McMenamins Breweries

The McMenamins chain operates brewpubs, historic hotels and music venues with a mildly hippie aesthetic and reliably consistent food and beer across Oregon and Washington.

Liquor Laws

While you can buy booze in Washington grocery stores, Oregon and British Columbia shoppers can only buy beer and wine (extra restrictions apply in BC).

BEST BEER EXPERIENCES

Take a tour of Bend's celebrated ❶ **Deschutes Brewery Tasting Room & Beer Garden** (p233), located in the Old Mill District.

Sample craft beers on tap at ❷ **Terminal Gravity Brewing** (p295) in the Eastern Oregon town of Enterprise.

Learn about the history of brewing by following the BC Ale Trail through Vancouver's recently revitalized ❸ **Brewery Creek** (p323).

Grab a pint at ❹ **Bale Breaker & Yonder Cider Taproom** (p800), located in the middle of a sprawling family-run hops farm in Walla Walla.

Pair Kulshan Brewing Company's beers with food-truck fare at Bellingham's ❺ **Trackside Beer Garden** (p91), which hosts the annual April Brews Day beer festival.

ARTISTIC ENDEAVORS

The Pacific Northwest has long been a haven for artists. The region's abundance of natural beauty has inspired many a creative soul, while galleries, performing arts venues and even the sides of buildings have provided outlets for the artists among us to express themselves. The region is also replete with museums that showcase everything from Indigenous arts to contemporary creations – you'll find these not only in major cities, but also in off-the-beaten-path spots in this expansive area.

Glass Art

Seattle is a hub for glass arts, as you can see for yourself at Chihuly Garden and Glass or by attending the annual Refract Glass Festival.

Portland Street Art

The sides of many Portland businesses are decorated with brightly colored murals. You can learn where to find them through the Portland Street Art Alliance (pdxstreetart.org).

Art Downtown

On Wednesdays and Fridays throughout the summer, local artists create and sell their works at Lot 19 on 855 West Hastings in downtown Vancouver.

BEST ARTS EXPERIENCES

Devote an afternoon to checking out the temporary and permanent exhibits on display at the six-story ❶ **Portland Art Museum** (p171), Oregon's largest and oldest art museum.

Join theater lovers at Ashland's Allen Elizabethan Theater, home of the ❷ **Oregon Shakespeare Festival** (p274).

Stroll through the outdoor art installations at Seattle's ❸ **Olympic Sculpture Park** (p67) while taking in views of the Olympic Mountains in the distance.

Take in the extensive collection of art and ephemera at Spokane's Smithsonian-affiliated ❹ **Northwest Museum of Arts and Culture** (p161).

Explore room after room of art from around the world at the sprawling ❺ **Vancouver Art Gallery** (p307).

REGIONS & CITIES

Find the places that tick all your boxes.

Vancouver Island

CHARMING COMMUNITIES AND WILDERNESS WONDERS

A garden-rich big city, beautiful beaches and Indigenous cultural attractions make this massive BC island an ideal place to slow down and appreciate the natural world.

p330

Vancouver

GREEN CITY BY THE SEA

Towering skyscrapers are overshadowed by spectacular mounts in this multicultural city, where the arts and the outdoors receive equal appreciation.

p300

Northwestern Washington & the San Juan Islands

PRISTINE PARKS, ISLANDS AND COASTAL TOWNS

This quieter part of Washington is characterized by forested islands, great seafood, fantastic beer and plenty of opportunities for year-round recreation.

p86

Olympic Peninsula & Washington Coast

DRIFTWOOD-STREWN COASTLINES, RAINFORESTS AND SNOWCAPPED PEAKS

You're never far from a sandy beach – or an ancient rainforest – in the westernmost part of Washington.

p110

Vancouver
Island   Vancouver
p330   p300

Northwestern
Washington &   Seattle
the San Juan   p56
Islands, p86

Olympic   Washington
Peninsula &   Cascades
Washington   p132
Coast, p110
              Columbia
Portland, p166 River Gorge
              p212

The Willamette   Central &
Valley, p194   the Oregon
                 Cascades
The Oregon   p226
Coast
p244   Ashland &
              Southern
              Oregon
              p268

Portland

UNCONVENTIONAL FROM THE BEGINNING

Independent restaurants and gorgeous parks and gardens will compete for your attention in Oregon's unabashedly quirky big city.

p166

The Oregon Coast

FOREST-FRINGED BEACHES AND ARTSY COMMUNITIES

With seashores lined with windswept trees and dozens of artsy beach towns, Oregon's coastal reaches prove that you don't need sunshine to have a great time at the beach.

p244

Seattle

A GEM OF A CITY, SURROUNDED BY BEAUTY

Incredible museums, sprawling parks, great music and a global dining scene are just some of the things to experience in this lively city.

p56

Washington Cascades

MOUNTAINS, GLACIAL LAKES, POWER-NAPPING VOLCANOES

Alpine adventures and epic views await in this mountainous region, home to both Mt Rainier and Mt St Helen's.

p132

Columbia River Gorge

AMERICA'S FIRST SCENIC ROUTE

Waterfalls, fruit orchards, outdoor adventure and unbelievably gorgeous views characterize this river-straddling region on the Oregon–Washington border.

p212

Eastern Washington

BUCOLIC FARMS, WINERIES AND RUGGED NATURE

Geological wonders compete with massive swaths of agricultural land in this gloriously remote part of the Evergreen State.

p150

Eastern Washington p150

Eastern Oregon p284

The Willamette Valley

HISTORIC TOWNS AND BEAUTIFUL VINEYARDS

Wine tasting takes center stage in this vineyard-filled region, but there's plenty to experience beyond the pinot.

p194

Central Oregon & the Oregon Cascades

OREGON AT ITS HIGHEST

With year-round opportunities for outdoor adventure and a characteristically dry climate, this high desert region will have you questioning everything you thought you knew about Oregon weather.

p226

Ashland & Southern Oregon

BLUE SKIES OVER VOLCANOES AND VINEYARDS

An internationally renowned theater scene, fantastic wine and the sapphire waters of Crater Lake draw travelers to this sunny part of the Beaver State.

p268

Eastern Oregon

RUGGED COUNTRY AND FRONTIER TOWNS

Expansive grasslands, untouched swaths of wilderness and frontier towns that have never given up their Wild West vibes set Oregon's least-populous region apart.

p284

Best of the Pacific Northwest

Allow: 11 days
Distance: 1103 miles

While you'd need months to explore all of what the Pacific Northwest has to offer, this itinerary gets you familiar with the highlights including three national parks, four major cities and over a thousand miles worth of scenic landscapes.

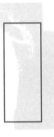

① VANCOUVER ⏱3 DAYS

Start your journey in Vancouver (p301). Check out the art at the Vancouver Art Gallery and the Bill Reid Gallery of Northwest Coast Art, stroll Gastown plus Stanley Park, then shop for culinary treats on Granville Island, before hopping on a ferry to Vancouver Island.

② VICTORIA ⏱2 DAYS

Ferries drop passengers at Swartz Bay, but most people prefer to make the BC capital city – Victoria (p334) – their base. There's plenty to see here: from visiting Fan Tan Alley in historic Chinatown to wandering among the fragrant flora of the historic Butchart Gardens.

🔙 *Detour: Hikers could consider a day trip to Potholes Provincial Park, named for its numerous rock pools.*

Gastown (p306), Vancouver

DAN BRECKWOLDT/SHUTTERSTOCK ©

③ PORT ANGELES ⏱1 DAY

Ferry from Victoria to Port Angeles. It's then a short drive to Olympic National Park, celebrated for its massive old-growth rainforests and miles of hiking trails. Visit the Hoh Rain Forest (p117) and Sol Duc Hot Springs (p116).

④ SEATTLE ⏱2 DAYS

Make Seattle (p56), Washington's biggest city, your next stop. Don't miss the installations at the Olympic Sculpture Park, the music-industry ephemera at the Museum of Pop Culture and the breweries in the Ballard neighborhood.

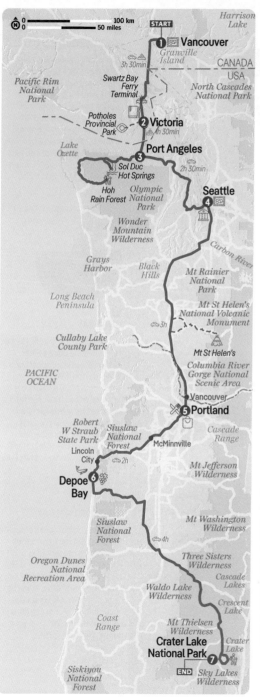

START

1 Vancouver

3h 30min

Granville Island

Harrison Lake

CANADA
USA

Pacific Rim National Park

Swartz Bay Ferry Terminal

North Cascades National Park

Potholes Provincial Park

2 Victoria
1h 30min

Lake Ozette

3 Port Angeles

Sol Duc Hot Springs

2h 30min

Hoh Rain Forest

Olympic National Park

4 Seattle

Wonder Mountain Wilderness

Grays Harbor

Black Hills

Carbon River

Mt Rainier National Park

Long Beach Peninsula

Mt St Helen's National Volcanic Monument

3h

Cullaby Lake County Park

Mt St Helen's

PACIFIC OCEAN

Columbia River Gorge National Scenic Area

Vancouver

5 Portland

Robert W Straub State Park

Siuslaw National Forest

McMinnville

Cascade Range

Lincoln City

2h

Mt Jefferson Wilderness

6 Depoe Bay

Siuslaw National Forest

4h

Mt Washington Wilderness

Oregon Dunes National Recreation Area

Three Sisters Wilderness

Cascade Lakes

Waldo Lake Wilderness

Crescent Lake

Coast Range

Mt Thielsen Wilderness

Crater Lake National Park

Crater Lake

END

Sky Lakes Wilderness

Siskiyou National Forest

---

⑤ PORTLAND ⏱ 2 DAYS

Continue to Portland (p166) where you'll find an excellent dining scene, beautiful parks – many filled with rose bushes – and the world's largest independent bookstore, Powell's Books.

➤ *Detour: Between Seattle and Portland, Mt St Helens (p279) is a great place to stretch your legs while learning about the 1980 volcanic eruption.*

⑥ DEPOE BAY ⏱ 1 DAY

Drive through the Willamette Valley wine country; pick up a bottle of pinot in McMinnville (p201). Stop in Lincoln City (p257) to see the glassblowers in action before continuing to Depoe Bay (p257) where you can take a whale-watching cruise or try your luck from the shore.

⑦ CRATER LAKE ⏱ 1 DAY

Make Crater Lake National Park (p279) your final stop to see the deepest lake in North America. You can drive around the entirety of the crater or hike down to the lake on the Cleetwood Cove Trail, which leads to the only swimming area in the park. For a special treat, sign up for a boat tour of the lake.

Coastal Cruising

Allow: 6 days

Distance: 552 miles

Take in spectacular views as you make your way up along the forested coastal cliffs of Hwy 101, from the California–Oregon border clear up to the Olympic Peninsula in Washington. Expect adorable towns, historic attractions, pristine hiking areas and mile upon mile of gorgeous sea-facing scenery.

Samuel H Boardman State Scenic Corridor (p266)

NICK FOX/SHUTTERSTOCK ©

❶ PORT ORFORD ⏱1 DAY

Drive along the Samuel H Boardman State Scenic Corridor (p266) – arguably the most beautiful stretch of the Oregon Coast – stopping at the Natural Bridges and Arch Rock along the way. Continue to Humbug Mountain State Park (p267) for a hike before driving up to Port Orford (p267), where you'll spend your first night.

❷ COOS BAY ⏱1 DAY

Head north to the Historic Hughes House in Cape Blanco State Park (p265) to learn about life in Oregon in the 1890s. Continue to Bandon (p265) to check out art installations fashioned from upcycled sea waste (pictured above) and sample products made from local cranberries. Finish in Coos Bay (p262) after a pit stop at Shore Acres State Park (p262).

❸ NEWPORT ⏱1 DAY

Continue up the coast, stopping to check out the carnivorous cobra lilies preserved at the Darlingtonia State Natural Site (p261) along the way. From here, it's a 10-minute drive to the Sea Lion Caves (p261), where you can see wild Steller sea lions in huge numbers. Wrap up your day in Newport (p258).

CYNTHIA LIANG/SHUTTERSTOCK ©

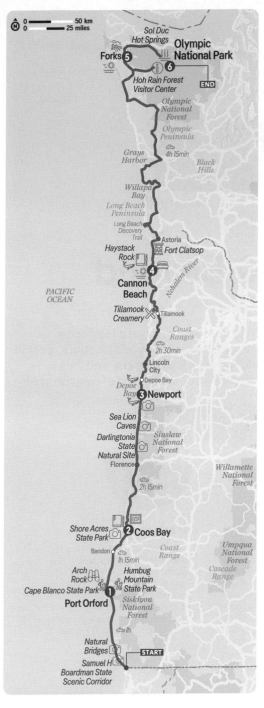

4

CANNON BEACH ⏱ 1 DAY

From Newport, it's just a short drive to Depoe Bay (p257), where you can take a whale-watching expedition. Continue to Lincoln City (p257) to hunt colorful glass floats hidden along the shore for beachcombers to find. Then go for cheese tasting at the Tillamook Creamery before checking into a hotel in Cannon Beach (p255).

5

FORKS ⏱ 1 DAY

Take a walk over to Cannon Beach's Haystack Rock before continuing north to Fort Clatsop (p250), where the Lewis and Clark expedition spent a winter. Continue to the Victorian city of Astoria (p250) for lunch before crossing the Columbia River into Washington. Drive up Hwy 101 to the town of Forks (p121), a convenient spot to spend the night.

6

OLYMPIC NATIONAL PARK ⏱ 1 DAY

Devote your final day to exploring the Olympic National Park (p114). Drive from Forks to the Hoh Rain Forest Visitor Center (p117) to see a gorgeous grove of ancient moss-covered maples. Then head over to Sol Duc Hot Springs (p116) for a soak.

29

Seattle (p56)

ITINERARIES

Seattle & Beyond

Allow: 6 days   **Distance:** 488 miles

You don't have to journey far from Seattle to get a feel for the wonders of Washington. In less than a week, you'll be able to behold the towering stratovolcano that is Mt Rainier and spend time in cute, forested communities, while still having a bit of time for urban adventures.

1 SEATTLE ⏱ 2 DAYS

Spend your first couple of days in Seattle (p56). Visit Downtown's Pioneer Square for an underground tour of the city's subterranean side and lively Pike Place Market (pictured above). Don't miss the Seattle Center, home to many of the city's most celebrated attractions, including the Space Needle, the Pacific Science Center, the Museum of Pop Culture and Chihuly Garden and Glass.

2 MT RAINIER ⏱ 1 DAY

Wake up bright and early and head to Mt Rainier National Park (p141) for a day of alpine adventure. Hike the Sourdough Ridge Trail (p143) for great views of the Emmons Glacier (p143), largest glacier in the contiguous United States. Book a campsite, or a coveted room at one of the park's two hotels, or stay at one of the many spots in Ashford near the Nisqually Entrance.

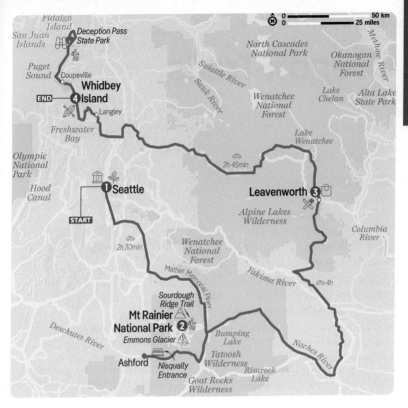

PLAN YOUR TRIP

ITINERARIES

❸ LEAVENWORTH ⏱1 DAY

Head deep into the Cascades until you reach
Leavenworth (p136), which was transformed in the
1960s to resemble the American idea of a typical
Bavarian town. Fill up on pretzels at the Bavarian
Bakery or grab beer and bratwurst at München
Haus. Don't leave town before seeing the massive
collection of nutcrackers at the Nutcracker
Museum or petting adorable reindeer.

❹ WHIDBEY ISLAND ⏱2 DAYS

Spend your last couple of days unwinding on
Whidbey Island (p102), a popular Puget Sound
getaway for Seattleites. Here you'll find compact
local villages such as historic Coupeville and
adorable Langley and lots of kayaking spots. On the
northern tip of the island and on neighboring Fidalgo
Island (p98), Deception Pass State Park (pictured
above; p99) offers miles of hiking trails and beautiful
views out over the water.

ITINERARIES

Oregon Trails

Allow: 7 days
Distance: 533 miles

See some of the natural and cultural features for which Oregon is known on a road trip through the entire state. Visit vibrant cities and magnificent natural areas, driving along gorgeous coastlines, through ancient forests, past rolling vineyards and clear over to the edge of the deepest freshwater lake in the country.

Willamette Valley vineyards (p201)

JENNIFER LARSEN MORROW/SHUTTERSTOCK ©

❶
PORTLAND ⏱ 2 DAYS

Fly or drive into Portland (p166) to visit highlights such as Washington Park and the Lan Su Chinese Garden. While you're in town stop by Powell's City of Books to check out the Rare Book Room, plus the city's many restaurants and food carts, before heading out on your Oregon adventure.

❷
ASTORIA ⏱ 1 DAY

On your third day, head west to Astoria (p250) where the Columbia River meets the Pacific Ocean. Check out the house where much of cult classic *The Goonies* was filmed (pictured above), before heading to Fort Stevens State Park (p253) to see the wreck of the *Peter Iredale*.

❸
MCMINNVILLE ⏱ 1 DAY

Next, head to McMinnville (p201), a major hub for the Willamette Valley wine industry. You may want to stop along the way in smaller wine towns such as Carlton and Yamhill, where you'll find wineries galore specializing in pinot and chardonnay.

➥ *Detour:* Take a detour to Ecola State Park (p255) for gorgeous views of the Oregon Coast.

WILLIAM DOWNS PHOTOGRAPHY/SHUTTERSTOCK ©

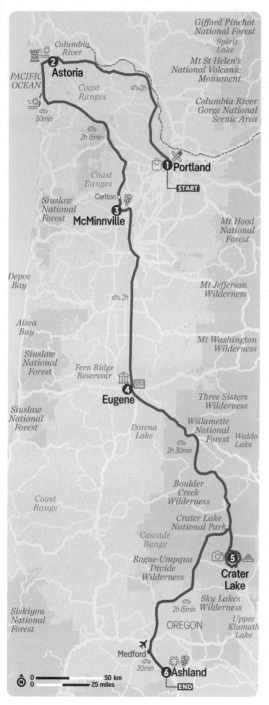

❹ EUGENE ⏱1 DAY

Although Eugene (p206) is often overshadowed by bigger and busier Portland, this mid-sized university city has tons to offer with fewer crowds. Browse the huge collection at the Jordan Schnitzer Museum of Art, or visit the kid-friendly Museum of Natural and Cultural History. Don't miss the chance to meet the resident birds at the Cascades Raptor Center (p208).

❺ CRATER LAKE ⏱1 DAY

The following morning head to Crater Lake National Park (p279), the only national park in Oregon. The park's cobalt-hued lake can be seen from numerous viewpoints along Rim Dr – or join a boat tour out to Crater Lake's Wizard Island.

❻ ASHLAND ⏱1 DAY

Spend your final day in Ashland (p272), set in bucolic hills and best known for the Oregon Shakespeare Festival (April through October). Theater fans won't want to miss a performance, while oenophiles should consider a wine-tasting tour to the nearby Applegate Valley. The nearest airport to Ashland is in Medford, a 20-minute drive away.

WHEN TO GO

While the Pacific Northwest has plenty to offer year-round, the best time for outdoor exploration is summer and early fall.

Outdoor exploration is a big part of the Pacific Northwest experience, but sometimes the weather gets in the way. Summers range from gloriously warm to stiflingly hot, but even on days when the sun is at its most powerful, the region's abundance of trees means that shade is rarely far away. Warm weather generally extends well into fall before quickly shifting into a cool season with gray skies and plenty of precipitation that continues well into the spring. The result: long skiing and snowboarding seasons but less-than-ideal conditions for traipsing through the forest – unless you make like a Pacific Northwesterner and load up on waterproof gear.

During the summer months, accommodations prices soar, particularly in tourism hot spots. For the best rates-to-weather ratio, consider coming in September, when temperatures are still warm, but kids in the area have gone back to school.

⊚ I LIVE HERE

SPRING BLOOMS INTO SUMMER

Winemaker Dave Specter is the owner of Bells Up Winery in Newberg, Oregon. @bellsupwinery

June and July – late spring/ early summer – in the Willamette Valley is my absolute favorite time of the year. The weather is beautiful and the vineyards are beginning to truly leaf out after several months of dormancy. The flowering redbud trees, wildflowers and crimson clover are also in bloom. It's an absolutely stunning time to experience the region. Admittedly, it can also be allergy season, so plan accordingly.

Forest fire

FIRE SEASON

Forest fires are an increasing issue in the Pacific Northwest, particularly in the late summer. Burn bans are common during high-risk periods, so if you plan to camp, you may not be allowed to have a campfire.

Weather Through the Year (Portland)

JANUARY	FEBRUARY	MARCH	APRIL	MAY	JUNE
Average daytime max: 47°F	Average daytime max: 51°F	Average daytime max: 57°F	Average daytime max: 61°F	Average daytime max: 68°F	Average daytime max: 74°F
Days of rainfall: 16	Days of rainfall: 15	Days of rainfall: 16	Days of rainfall: 14	Days of rainfall: 12	Days of rainfall: 8

RAIN CHECK

There's no denying that much of the Pacific Northwest can be a rainy place – it's the magic ingredient that keeps the forests lush and emeraldine, particularly in the more populated regions west of the Cascade Mountains. Always be prepared for showers, even in summer.

Major Festivals

Portland Rose Festival (p172) Portland's primary city fest harkens in summer in the City of Roses with carnival rides, live entertainment, dragon boat races, and daytime and after-dark parades. **June**

Oregon Country Fair (p206) You don't need to drop out to be in at this festival in Veneta, near Eugene. Started in 1969, it evokes the ethos of the flower-power era with music, puppet parades, and lots of food and crafts. **July**

Bumbershoot Held annually at the Seattle Center (p69) over the Labor Day Weekend, this major international music festival attracts big-name bands and music fans from around the world. **September**

Sisters Folk Festival (p240) The Central Oregon city of Sisters fills with song every fall when this festival comes to town, bringing with it seven stages featuring a mix of established and up-and-coming acts. **September/October**

I LIVE HERE

LATE SUMMER IN VANCOUVER

Adam Middleton is Executive Chef at Arc Restaurant at the Fairmont Waterfront in Vancouver.

My favorite season in Vancouver is late summer when our rooftop garden at the Fairmont Waterfront is in full swing, busy with bees, fragrant with flowers, and full of herbs, figs, tomatoes, cucumbers and zucchini flowers – all perfect for our summer menu.

Fairmont Waterfront (p312)

Local Events & Celebrations

Winthrop Balloon Roundup (p148) Brightly colored hot-air balloons soar above Washington's snowy Methow Valley during this annual event, which coincides with peak cross-country skiing season. **March**

Skagit Valley Tulip Festival (p101) Tiptoe through a rainbow of beautiful blooms at this festival in Mt Vernon, Washington. While the chance to visit tulip fields is the big draw, there's plenty more to do, including rummage sales, a street fair and a parade. **April**

Mt Angel Oktoberfest (p201) The Oregon town of Mt Angel honors all things Bavarian at the annual Oktoberfest. Along with requisite beer and sausage vendors, the festival features all kinds of events, including wiener dog races. **September**

Holiday Lights at Shore Acres State Park (p249) Witness a massive display of twinkling fairy lights as you stroll through manicured gardens overlooking the Pacific Ocean. **December**

SNOW DAYS

While people living in mountainous and eastern parts of the Pacific Northwest are used to snow, more than a dusting can cause a small panic in western parts of the region, where snow often turns into ice instead of melting.

	JULY	AUGUST	SEPTEMBER	OCTOBER	NOVEMBER	DECEMBER
Average daytime max:	81°F	81°F	76°F	64°F	53°F	46°F
Days of rainfall:	3	5	7	11	16	17

LEFT: THINAIR28/GETTY IMAGES ©; FAR RIGHT: CINEMATIC/ALAMY STOCK PHOTO ©

Hiking, Mt Rainier National Park (p141)

GET PREPARED FOR THE PACIFIC NORTHWEST

Useful things to load in your bag, your ears and your brain.

Clothes

Rain gear No matter when you visit the Pacific Northwest, you should be prepared for the possibility of rain, especially if you plan to spend a lot of time outdoors. A water-resistant jacket with a hood is essential.

Layers Hoodies are part of the de facto Pacific Northwest uniform, and some sort of sweater or sweatshirt is a must-have, even in the hot summer months, when nighttime temperatures can dip quite a bit. They're also a boon for visits to coastal regions, when strong winds can add a serious chill to otherwise balmy days.

Manners

Communication in the Pacific Northwest is less direct than in other parts of the country, and bluntness can be seen as brash. The flip side of this is that passive-aggressive speech is common.

This part of the country is **very casual**, and flashy displays of wealth are considered vulgar.

Shoes Comfort is a priority for people in the Pacific Northwest, and while fancy dinners dictate nice shoes, you're better off packing casual athletic shoes or boots that can withstand a bit of rain and dirt.

📖 READ

Snow Falling on Cedars
(David Guterson; 1994)
Murder mystery dealing
with anti-Japanese
sentiments in the PNW
after Pearl Harbor.

**Sometimes a Great
Notion** (Ken Kesey;
1964) Novel about
loggers in a small
Oregon Coast town
during a mill strike.

Ramona the Pest
(Beverly Cleary; 1968) A
timeless children's novel
recounting the antics
of a young Portlander
starting kindergarten.

Twilight (Stephenie
Meyer; 2005) First in a
series of young-adult
vampire novels set in the
small Olympic Peninsula
town of Forks.

Words

'The Coast' refers to the coastal regions of Oregon and Washington. People don't call it 'the Shore' and while some people use 'beach' to denote the region, the term is usually used specifically to mean a stretch of sand flanking the Pacific Ocean.

'Filbert' is another word for hazelnut, particularly in Oregon, where around 99% of the nation's filberts are produced.

'Food cart' might mean a rolling cart serving snacks in much of the country, but in the Pacific Northwest – and especially in Portland – the term is used to denote what people elsewhere call 'food trucks.'

'Food cart pods' are collections of food carts, usually occupying old parking lots. Most have common seating areas and restrooms.

'Jojos' are what Pacific Northwesterners call potato wedges. You'll find them in the hot deli sections of convenience stores across the region.

'Pre-funk' is a term for a get-together before an event or party (akin to pre-game). It likely stems from 'pre-function.'

'Rack' (of beer) refers to a 24-pack of beer, also known as a 'case' of beer in other parts of the country.

'Spendy' is a common way to say 'expensive.' While people in other parts of the country might say 'pricey,' this term is much more common in the Pacific Northwest.

'Sunbreak' is a term used to describe brief periods of sun on otherwise cloudy or rainy days.

🎬 WATCH

The Goonies (Richard Donner; 1985) Cult film about a group of Oregon Coast kids searching for pirate's treasure.

Leave No Trace (Debra Granik; 2018) Film adaptation of novel *My Abandonment* about a father and daughter living in Portland's Forest Park.

Prefontaine (Steve James; 1997) Biographical film about the short life of Oregon's celebrity runner Steve Prefontaine.

Sleepless in Seattle (Nora Ephron; 1993) A much-loved romantic comedy with Tom Hanks and Meg Ryan set in Seattle.

🎧 LISTEN

Are You Experienced
(The Jimi Hendrix
Experience; 1967)
The debut album of
one of Seattle's most
celebrated musicians of
all time.

Nevermind (Nirvana;
1991) The seminal album
that shot Nirvana, and
the Seattle grunge scene,
to international fame.

Peak Northwest (Jamie
Hale and Vickie Connor;
2019) Pacific Northwest
travel podcast with an
outdoor slant.

Timber Wars (Aaron
Scott; 2020) Oregon
Public Broadcasting
radio show recounting
the conflict between
environmentalists and
loggers in the 1990s.

Glacier Peak Wilderness (p143), Pacific Crest Trail

TRIP PLANNER

THE PACIFIC CREST TRAIL

Extending along the crests of the Sierra and Cascade Mountains, from the California–Mexico border clear up to the Washington–Canada border, the Pacific Crest National Scenic Trail (PCT) is the most legendary hike on the West Coast. Here's what you need to know about exploring the Pacific Northwestern parts of this legendary trail.

The Long & Winding Trail

ON THE TRAIL

While some people attempt to hike the entire 2650-mile trail in one go, many hikers opt to tackle it piece-by-piece, often over multiple years. Others do what's known as 'flip-flopping,' starting in the middle of a segment, heading in one direction, and then returning and going in the opposite direction. Many of the more popular hiking and backpacking trips in the Pacific Northwest are along segments of the trail, and if you go on a summer hike in the Cascades, you might end up encountering a few PCT hikers.

OREGON

Most people who have hiked the entire PCT will tell you that the Oregon section is the easiest stretch, with relatively little elevation change compared to other more challenging sections. It starts in Southern Oregon near the Siskiyou Summit and continues through the Cascade Range and over to the Columbia River, before crossing into Washington over the Columbia River via the Bridge of the Gods.

WASHINGTON

The Washington segment of the PCT starts where the Oregon section leaves off, stretch-

While most people who hike the entire length of the PCT start in Southern California in late April or at the beginning of May, the Oregon and Washington segments require a later start due to cooler temperatures. If you plan to cover both states, July is a good month to get going, though you may run into snow in some higher-elevation areas. August is an even safer bet, particularly in parts of Washington where the snow doesn't melt until the end of July – just be prepared for potential heat waves.

ing from the Bridge of the Gods up to the border with British Columbia (though many people continue into Canada in order to access the nearest road, Hwy 3, about an 8-mile walk beyond the border). Be prepared for plenty of elevation gain and challenging ascents once you cross the border, especially once you get into the remote North Cascades National Park, where snow and rain are the norm, even during much of the summertime.

Shorter Hikes

You don't have to be a hardcore hiker to experience a bit of the PCT for yourself. There are plenty of great hikes that can easily be braved in a day. Washington's **Indian Heaven Trail** near Stevenson is a short but challenging option. This 6.2-mile out-and-back hike passes along beautiful alpine lakes. In Oregon, the 11.2-mile out-and-back hike up to **Jefferson Park via Park Ridge** is a favorite, taking day hikers and backpackers up past huckleberry bushes to Russell Lake, which spreads out just below the perpetually snowcapped Mt Jefferson.

PREPARING FOR YOUR JOURNEY

Getting ready for the PCT takes a lot of work for even the most experienced backpackers. You'll need to read up on what to expect, obtain maps and camping gear, figure out your food plans, and find yourself a great pair of shoes or boots. If possible, ask someone else who has hiked the trail recently to mentor you; the Pacific Crest Trail Association (PCTA) is a particularly good place to start.

Permits

● If you're going to hike 500 or more miles on the PCT in one go, you'll need to obtain a **PCT Long-Distance Permit**. The permit will allow you to camp along the way, without having to obtain individual permits in different areas on your trek.
● If you're finishing off in Canada, you'll need to apply for the **Canada PCT Entry Permit**, which will allow you to enter the country legally. If you're a US citizen, you won't need your passport to enter Canada, but you'll need it to get back into the States.
● Day hikers and those going on short backpacking trips should also check any permits they may need. Overnight trips generally require permits, and many of the trails in Oregon's Mt Jefferson, Mt Washington and Three Sisters wilderness areas require day hikers to obtain a **Central Cascades Wilderness Permit** before setting out.
● Pack snacks. Items as simple as peanut-butter sandwiches and an apple stuffed in your bag will save time, money and stress.

WAYNE H. BAUER/SHUTTERSTOCK ©

Mt Jefferson and Jefferson Park

KEVIN SCHAFER/GETTY IMAGES ©

Lake Chelan, Stehekin

TRIP PLANNER

STEHEKIN

On the edge of the North Cascades National Park sits Washington's remotest community: Stehekin. This quiet lakefront getaway is surrounded by massive old-growth forests and towering peaks, but its real charm lies in the fact that you'll need a bit of gumption to visit, as it's only accessible on foot or by boat or plane.

Where No Roads Lead

THE STEHEKIN EXPERIENCE

Stehekin draws in intrepid travelers who want to trade in urban traffic and noise for a quiet time away in the woods. It's a particularly popular spot for hiking, kayaking, horseback riding and fly fishing, but many people just come to relax while taking in the majestic views.

There are a few places to eat in Stehekin, but most visitors – at least those staying at campgrounds or in cabins with kitchens – end up doing a bit of cooking during their stay. Cash is king in Stehekin, and while the hotels here do accept credit cards, some shops only take cash or check. There are no ATMs in Stehekin, so make sure to bring enough cash to last you.

GETTING AROUND

You won't be able to take your car over to Stehekin, but you can rent an off-road vehicle once you're in town. Many people prefer to get around by bike, and rentals are available from **Discovery Bikes** near the dock at Stehekin Landing. There's also a red shuttle bus that plies up and down the road that connects the boat landing with the **High Bridge** trailhead on the opposite end of town, making stops along the way – including at the beloved **Stehekin Pastry Company**, a favorite place for cakes

Although people visit Stehekin year-round, and ferry service is available throughout the year, it is very much a summer destination. The summer months offer great weather, with highs around 70°F (21°C) or 80°F (26°C) from June to September, and less likelihood of rain than in the cooler months. Just be prepared to book accommodations well in advance, as places are generally in high demand this time of the year. If you plan to hike in, you'll have the most pleasant weather in July and August, but it's wise to contact the National Parks Service for up-to-date information about trail conditions (and snow) before you set out.

and sweet treats. The shuttle usually runs every hour to every 90 minutes during the summer high season.

WHERE TO STAY

There are quite a few accommodations options in Stehekin, ranging from private cabins with self-catering facilities to campgrounds. There are also two major hotels. The concessionaire-run **North Cascades Lodge** is the most convenient option if you're coming by boat, as it's located right across from the dock. It offers a mix of guest rooms and cabins with kitchens, the latter of which are available year-round. Around 9 miles up the road from the dock, **Stehekin Valley Ranch** has a mix of lodge accommodations, regular and tented cabins, and wooden trailers with bathrooms. Meals and transportation are included.

GETTING TO STEHEKIN

There are no roads to Stehekin, which means that unless you have access to a private plane, you'll need to either hop aboard a boat or visit on foot.

Getting There by Boat
● There are two ferry companies that offer service to Stehekin: Stehekin Ferry and Lake Chelan Boat Company. Both depart from in or near the city of Chelan and offer round-trip or one-way service. Lake Chelan Boat Company also offers day tours; ideal if you want to pay a quick visit to Stehekin but can't commit to an overnight stay.
● You can also bring your own boat to Stehekin and dock it at one of 15 federally managed boat docks in town. If you go that route, you'll need to obtain a Lake Chelan Federal Dock Site Permit ahead of time. Permits are available at the Chelan Ranger District Office and at select shops in Chelan, Manson and Wenatchee.

Getting There on Foot
● If you'd rather approach the remote community on foot, you can take the Cascade Pass Trailhead from near the town of Marblemount to High Bridge, on the western end of Stehekin, and catch a shuttle bus into the main part of town. The hike is around 23 miles long. Backcountry permits are required.

JON LOVETTE/GETTY IMAGES ©

Cycling, Stehekin

JIM FISCHER/GETTY IMAGES ©

Pinot noir grapes, Willamette Valley (p195)

TRIP PLANNER

WINE REGIONS OF THE PACIFIC NORTHWEST

Although the Pacific Northwest's wine countries have long been eclipsed by their better-known counterparts in California, the region offers fantastic opportunities for wine tourism. The climate here is remarkably diverse, ideal for growing cool- and warm-weather varietals alike, and many of the top wine destinations are but a short jaunt from Seattle or Portland.

Major Wine Destinations

THE WILLAMETTE VALLEY, OREGON

Oregon's oldest and largest wine region, the Willamette Valley is home to rough-ly two-thirds of the state's wineries. This American Viticultural Area (AVA) extends from Portland clear down to just south of Eugene and encompasses 11 smaller sub-AVAs. The area is particularly known for its pinot noir, but you'll find all sorts of wine in the region, from muscadet to bubbly. The Willamette Valley has a particularly well-developed infrastructure for visitors, with all sorts of lodging accommodations and wine-centric restaurants, particularly in areas such as Newberg, Dundee, Carlton and McMinnville. It's also a popular desti-nation for shorter wine-focused day trips from Portland.

THE UMPQUA VALLEY, OREGON

South of the Willamette Valley, the sce-nic Umpqua Valley has been producing wine since the 1880s, and the state's first pinot noir was planted here back in 1961. Today, this diverse region produces both cool- and warm-weather varietals, from pi-not and riesling to tempranillo and syrah.

Summer is the most popular season for wine tasting in the Pacific Northwest, when the weather is generally warm and dry enough to sit out on tasting patios and take in the views, though visitors to some parts of Eastern Washington might find the slightly cooler spring and fall months more favorable.

Harvest season generally takes place in September or October, and while most wineries keep their tasting rooms open during this time, the presence of slow-moving farm machinery on area roads can make getting between wineries a slow pursuit at times. Note that while many wineries are open throughout the year, many close during the slower winter months.

The Umpqua Valley's slightly removed location makes this region an excellent choice if you want the Oregon wine experience without the crowds of the better-known Willamette Valley.

THE ROGUE VALLEY, OREGON

Near the border with California, Southern Oregon's Rogue Valley AVA has fewer wineries than many of the other wine-growing regions in the Pacific Northwest, but what it lacks in quantity it makes up for in quality. Oregon's first official winery was established in the valley back in 1873, unsurprising given the relatively warm and dry climate in this part of the state. You'll find all sorts of varietals in the area, from cabernet to sangiovese (and, yes, lots of pinot – you're still in Oregon, after all). A great place to get a taste of this region's wine scene is in the little historic town of Jacksonville, just outside of Ashland, where you'll find plenty of small tasting rooms within an easy walk of one another.

WINE-TASTING ETIQUETTE

Make reservations in advance
● While some wineries do take walk-ins when they have availability, many operate on a reservations-only basis. Most have reservation platforms on their websites, making it easy to book. Of course, if you happen to drive by a winery and want to stop in, it's fine to do so, but don't expect it to be open.

It's OK to use your dump bucket
● Most wineries furnish dump buckets so that guests can pour out any extra wine they don't want to drink. Nobody will be offended if you only take a sip of each pour and then toss out the rest, whether it's because you don't want to drink too much or simply don't like a particular wine.

Don't wear perfume
● Wine tasting involves plenty of sniffing, and the aromas of other people's perfume or scented lotion can make it difficult to accurately taste a wine.

Buying a bottle or two is appreciated
● Although almost all wineries charge pour fees, tastings are designed to get customers familiar with wines in hopes that they will become customers. While you should never feel obligated to make a purchase, if there's something you enjoyed, it's courteous to pick up a bottle.

Applegate Valley wine country (p277)

THE COLUMBIA VALLEY, OREGON & WASHINGTON

Nearly all of the wine grapes grown in Washington hail from the massive Columbia Valley AVA, which is spread over 11 million acres. Spanning across Central and Eastern Washington, the region is known for its diverse soil and its remarkably dry and sunny days. This AVA encompasses a number of smaller AVAs. The largest of these is the Yakima Valley, the first wine-growing region in the Pacific Northwest to gain federal recognition and one of the only areas in the state where you'll find more white plantings than red (chardonnay and riesling are the region's local stars). Walla Walla, Washington (which is also known for producing its own variety of sweet onions), is another popular stop for wine lovers, with loads of wineries and a historic downtown full of tasting rooms and restaurants.

THE COLUMBIA GORGE, OREGON & WASHINGTON

Right next to the Columbia Valley, straddling the Columbia River on the Oregon–Washington border, the Columbia Gorge AVA is noteworthy for its diversity of microclimates, and you'll find a mix of warm-weather and cool-climate wines in the area, from pinots to riesling. Many of the tasting rooms are found in and around

INTI ST CLAIR/GETTY IMAGES ©

Wine tasting, Walla Walla (p154)

Best of the Rest	AMATERRA WINERY	AMAVI CELLARS	COPPERBELT WINES
	Urban winery just outside of downtown Portland featuring an upscale restaurant with gorgeous views and a countryside ambience.	Walla Walla, Washington, estate winery with gorgeous views and certified sustainable growing practices.	Family-run winery in the tiny Snake River AVA on the Oregon–Idaho border producing everything from sparkling to port-style wine.

the city of Hood River, which is equally known as a hub of windsurfing and for its apple and pear industries.

PUGET SOUND, WASHINGTON

Extending from south of Seattle clear up to the border with British Columbia, the Puget Sound AVA is characterized by a cool maritime climate that makes it ideal for pinot noir and riesling. Despite its size, the region is home to just a few of the state's vineyards, but many of its wineries, most of which bring their grapes in from the Columbia Valley or from out of state. Although Seattle has a fair few wineries, the bulk of the region's tasting rooms are found in the city of Woodinville, just outside of Seattle, where there are over 130 wineries spread across four official wine districts.

VANCOUVER ISLAND, BRITISH COLUMBIA

People have been producing wine on Vancouver Island since the 1920s, and some of the earliest wines made on the island were crafted from loganberries. The majority of the vineyards on Vancouver Island are in and around the Cowichan Valley, though you'll find quite a few wineries within a short drive of Victoria. Some of the most popular varietals produced on the island include pinot gris and pinot noir, chardonnay, gewürztraminer, ortega and Maréchal Foch.

THE OKANAGAN VALLEY, BRITISH COLUMBIA

Over three-quarters of the vineyards in British Columbia are located in the Okanagan Valley, east of Vancouver. The condi-

PLANNING YOUR TIME

Day Trips
● There are plenty of wineries within easy day-trip distance of major cities. If you're in Seattle, the city of Woodinville – about a 20-mile drive northeast of downtown – is a great option, with over 130 wineries across four wine districts. Those staying in Portland can easily make a day trip down to the Willamette Valley (p195) or up to the wineries in the Columbia River Gorge (p212).

Winery Stays
● If you want to spend multiple days immersed in all things wine, you may prefer to base yourself in a wine region instead. Winery stay options include the Inn at Desert Wind near Prosser, Washington – which offers adobe-style rooms that look like they could have been plucked straight out of New Mexico – and the Silo Suites B&B at the Willamette Valley's Abbey Road Farm, a small guesthouse housed in a trio of converted grain silos.

tions in this part of the province are ideal for wine production, and a huge range of varietals are produced here, from merlot and cabernet sauvignon to riesling and pinot gris. The wines from this area are known to have a good amount of natural acidity, owing to warm daytime temperatures and contrastingly cool nights.

DOE BAY WINE COMPANY
Orcas Island, Washington, bottle shop offering daily flights from Pacific Northwest wineries along with special tasting events.

EYRIE VINEYARDS
Pioneering McMinnville, Oregon vineyard specializing in estate-grown pinots and chardonnay.

RED LILY VINEYARDS
Kid-and dog-friendly winery with picnic tables and Spanish-inspired wines on Southern Oregon's Applegate River.

STAVE & STONE
Winery and tasting room near Hood River, Oregon, with indoor and outdoor seating and great views of Mt Hood.

45

Seafood meal

THE FOOD SCENE

The cuisine of the Pacific Northwest draws from the region's incredible diversity of freshly farmed, caught and foraged ingredients.

Pacific Northwest cuisine is known for its blend of European-style cooking techniques and local, seasonal ingredients, and while you'll definitely find plenty of dishes that fit such a bill – especially in the realm of fine dining – the region offers so much more. Here you'll find culinary influences from across the globe, and many of the best restaurants in the region specialize not in the smoked salmon, truffles and huckleberry-infused food for which the region is known, but in cuisine with its roots in foreign lands. Asian cuisines are particularly popular, especially in bigger cities such as Vancouver, Seattle and Portland where there are sizable Chinese, Japanese, and Vietnamese American communities. Mexican and Mexican-fusion food is also incredibly popular, but the authenticity varies pretty widely. You'll also find that going out to eat is a fairly casual affair in this neck of the woods, and even in high-end establishments, you're more likely to spot a pair of blue jeans than a white tablecloth.

Local Bounty

Many restaurants in the Pacific Northwest take pride in sourcing their ingredients locally, and this sustainable, locavore approach is a big selling point for many visitors. If you go to a fine-dining spot in any big city in the region, you're almost guaranteed to learn about the providence of at least some of the ingredients on your plate, and many chefs rely nearly exclusively on

Best Pacific Northwest Dishes

GRILLED CHINOOK SALMON
Among the tastiest types of salmon on the market.

DUNGENESS CRAB
While many prefer this steamed, it's also great in crab cakes.

WALLA WALLA SWEET ONION RINGS
Elevate your onion ring experience with this Washington variety.

MINT IMAGES/GETTY IMAGES ©

produce sourced from nearby farms. Fortunately, this is very easy to do, as the Pacific Northwest is characterized by rich, fertile soil and various microclimates that lend themselves to decent agricultural diversity. The region's many waterways and easy access to the Pacific Ocean make it a great place to get fresh seafood, too, while the abundance of dank woodlands means that locally foraged mushrooms – including chanterelles, morels and king boletes – make a regular appearance on local menus. Oregon in particular is known as a hub for truffle foraging, but the tasty fungi can actually be found across the entire region.

Vegans & Vegetarians

Vegan and vegetarian dining come easy in much of the Pacific Northwest, particularly in larger cities. Both Portland and Victoria have long been heralded as global hubs for plant-based dining, and even non-vegan restaurants in the city generally have a few meat-free dishes on the menu. Seattle and Vancouver also have plenty of options, and even many of the region's smaller and mid-sized cities have vegan restaurants (or omni restaurants that can whip something up).

Many smaller communities in the region have Thai restaurants, which are great for vegans in a pinch – just make sure they hold the fish sauce. It's also a good idea to download the Happy Cow app, where you can search for user-submitted reviews of veg-friendly dining options based on your location.

BITE OF SEATTLE, CC0, VIA WIKIMEDIA COMMONS ©

FOOD & WINE FESTIVALS

Oregon Truffle Festival Truffles (the fungi type, not the chocolates) and the dogs that sniff them out take center stage at this annual Eugene event.

Bandon Cranberry Festival (p265) Cranberries are honored with a parade, live entertainment and a cranberry-eating contest at this annual event on the Oregon Coast.

Dine Around & Stay in Town Over 50 Victoria-area restaurants showcase their finest offerings at this annual celebration of the city's culinary scene.

Alt Wine Fest (July) Try everything *but* pinot noir at this annual showcase of Oregon wine, beyond the best-known varietal.

Bite of Seattle (July) Sample food and drinks from Seattle's restaurants and watch cooking and eating competitions, all while listening to live entertainment at this massive annual event.

CHRIS RYAN PHOTO/GETTY IMAGES ©

Baked polenta and goat cheese dish, Portland (p166)

Bite of Seattle

BANNOCK	SEATTLE-STYLE HOT DOG	MARIONBERRY PIE	NANAIMO BARS	APLETS & COTLETS
A staple bread commonly found in Indigenous cuisines in BC.	Served in a pretzel bun with sautéed onions and cream cheese.	Try piping-hot pie filled with Oregon's own breed of berries.	BC's no-bake delights unite chocolate, custard and coconut graham.	Chewy apple and apricot candies inspired by Turkish delight.

Local Specialties

From the Land

Hazelnuts The bulk of US hazelnuts are grown in Oregon, where they're also called filberts. Try them roasted as a crunchy snack or drizzled in sweet chocolate.

Truffles These pungent fungi grow in abundance throughout the Pacific Northwest, including four native species: the Oregon brown, black, winter white and spring white truffle.

Apples Both Washington and Oregon are major apple producers. Try the Cosmic Crisp apple, which was originally developed by Washington State University researchers.

Marionberries Named for Oregon's Marion County, this blackberry cultivar was developed at Oregon State University.

Rainier cherries This Washington State University cultivar is known for its yellowish hue and its tanginess.

From the Waters

Albacore tuna Caught off the Washington and Oregon

Hazelnuts

coasts, this fish is available fresh and abundantly in the second half of the summer.

Dungeness crab This sweet-tasting crab is found in abundance all along the northwestern coast from winter through summer.

Salmon The Pacific Northwest is salmon country, with five species found in the region's waters. The Chinook salmon is Oregon's state fish.

Oysters These shellfish are found in great numbers in the Pacific Northwest, particularly in Washington's coastal regions.

MEALS OF A LIFETIME

Kann (p188) Watch James Beard Award–winning chef Gregory Gourdet in action at this live-fire Haitian restaurant in Portland.

Published on Main (p323) Taste the bounty of British Columbia at this high-end Vancouver favorite, which relies on locally sourced and foraged ingredients to create dishes that are as beautifully presented as they are tasty.

Taylor Shellfish Oyster Bar (p71) You'll be hard-pressed to find fresher oysters than those served at this Northwest Washington spot, which offers oyster lovers a 'tide to table' experience at their waterfront picnic area.

THE YEAR IN FOOD

SPRING
The first sign of spring in the Pacific Northwest is the appearance of daffodils, quickly followed by a surge in local produce such as asparagus, rhubarb, herbs and leafy greens.

SUMMER
Summer is the high season for produce in the Pacific Northwest, and it's the best season for berry-picking. This is also when Washington's famous Walla Walla sweet onions are ready.

FALL
Squash, apples and pears are ripe for the picking come autumn. This is also when grapes for wine production are usually harvested (and, if you're in Southern Oregon, cranberries).

WINTER
You'll have access to local produce year-round in the Pacific Northwest, with the winter months favoring potatoes, rutabaga, brussels sprouts and carrots. Dungeness crab season starts in December.

MATT CAREY/GETTY IMAGES ©

Salmon, Seattle (p56)

CHENG FENG CHIANG/ISTOCK ©

David Lam Park (p314), Vancouver

THE OUTDOORS

Old-growth forests, wild waterways, grandiose mountains and magnificent coastlines offer an irresistible array of possibilities for outdoor adventure.

The Pacific Northwest has been celebrated for its seemingly endless outdoor opportunities, and many people visit – or even move to – the region to take advantage of its abundance of natural wonders. While much of the Pacific Northwest is blanketed in forest, making it ideal for hiking, mountain-biking and camping adventures, you'll also find arid high deserts, vast prairies, expansive lakes and rivers, and hundreds of miles of rugged coastline.

Walking & Hiking

Many people come to the Pacific Northwest specifically to hike, and it's perhaps the most popular outdoor activity in the region, particularly from late spring through early fall. The options are seemingly endless, from short, wheelchair- and stroller-friendly routes on paved trails to multiday backpacking routes that are sure to test the endurance of even the most hardcore of hikers. The Pacific Crest Trail passes through both Oregon and Washington, and while you'll need to take plenty of time off – and train – if you want to cross the entire region, hiking small sections is a great way to immerse yourself in the wilder parts of the region. The Oregon Coast Trail is another favorite among long-distance hikers, passing along gorgeous stretches of coastline, much of it flanked by forests. While some of the region's most pristine stretches of natural beauty, such as Ore-

---

Get Out & Play

ROCK CLIMBING
Hit the crags at Smith Rock State Park (p238), considered the birthplace of American sport climbing.

KITEBOARDING
Try your hand at kiteboarding in Hood River (p219), a major hub for the sport (and for windsurfing).

MOUNTAINEERING
Grab your crampons and join the 10,000-odd climbers who attempt to summit Mt Rainier (p143) every year.

FAMILY ADVENTURES

Spend a day at the beach in Vancouver's **Stanley Park** (p310), where there are a few good sandy beaches. Second Beach is a particularly great option for kids, and has a grassy playground and a pool.
Take a wild ride down the twists and turns of an alpine coaster

at Washington's **Leavenworth Adventure Park** (p138).
Dig for (and take home) botanical fossils at the **Stonerose Interpretive Center** and it's **Eocene Fossil Site** (p165), a 47-million-year-old shale deposit in Eastern Washington.

Feed fish while learning about their importance at the **Wizard Falls Fish Hatchery** (p241) in Central Oregon.
Wander among life-size dinosaurs at the **Prehistoric Gardens** (p267), an educational roadside attraction in the Oregon Coast forest.

gon's Eagle Cap Wilderness, require long drives, there are plenty of hikes within easy reach of – or even within – major cities. You can walk (or cycle) along Vancouver's Stanley Park Seawall, wander the wooded trails in Seattle's Lincoln Park, or take a 30-mile trek along the Wildwood Trail in Portland's Forest Park.

Cycling

Cyclists are sure to feel right at home in the Pacific Northwest. Many of the region's cities – including Victoria, Bellingham, Seattle, Portland and Eugene – are famously

bike-friendly, with designated cycle lanes and good driver awareness about how to share the road. Lopez Island in the San Juans is also a particularly great place to get in the saddle, and you're just as likely to see cyclists as drivers while you're on the island.

Skiing & Snowboarding

While the Pacific Northwest is better known for its rain than its snow, it's actually a fantastic place for skiing and snowboarding. Vancouver Island has Mt Washington, while Washington state's ski destinations include Mt Baker – just over an hour's drive from Bellingham – and the more remote Methow Valley, the site of the largest cross-country ski area in North America. Oregon's Mt Hood is equally notable for its extra-long ski season, which often runs through the end of May, and its proximity to Portland, a mere 90-minute drive away. Mt Bachelor, a 20-minute drive from the Central Oregon city of Bend, also has a remarkably long snow season and is a hit with families and skiers of all abilities. Many of the region's ski destinations transform into havens for hikers and mountain bikers in the summer months, when the snowpack melts and clears the way for miles of trails.

BEST SPOTS

For the best outdoor spots and routes, see the map on p52.

RUSS HEINL/SHUTTERSTOCK ©

Mt Washington (p346), Vancouver Island

WHITE-WATER RAFTING
Experience the powerful rapids of the Rogue River (p276) on a guided rafting trip.

SURFING
Catch a wave – or watch the pros compete – at Cox Bay Beach (p349), Tofino's primary spot for surfing.

KAYAKING
Rent a kayak or bring your own to the Victorian town of Fairhaven (p92) on Bellingham Bay.

OHV RIDING
Hop aboard an off-highway vehicle (OHV) for a sandy thrill ride at the Oregon Dunes National Recreation Area (p261).

ACTION AREAS

Where to find Washington, Oregon and the Pacific Northwest's best outdoor activities.

0 0
100 miles
200 km

Cycling

1. South Bay Trail (p90)
2. Lopez Island (p109)
3. Phil's Trail, Bend (p233)
4. Historic Columbia River Highway (p222)
5. Mt Emily Recreation Area (p295)
6. Galloping Goose Trail (p342)

Skiing/Snowboarding

1. Mt Washington (p346)
2. Mt Baker (p96)
3. Methow Valley (p149)
4. Mt Hood (p221)
5. Mt Bachelor (p235)

National Parks

1. Pacific Rim National Park Reserve (p352)
2. North Cascades National Park (p146)
3. Mt Rainier National Park (p141)
4. Olympic National Park (p114)
5. Crater Lake National Park (p279)

IDAHO

NEVADA

OREGON

CALIFORNIA

PACIFIC OCEAN

Kayaking/Canoeing

1. Telegraph Cove (p355)
2. Fairhaven (p92)
3. Whidbey Island (p104)
4. Coldwater Lake (p145)
5. Hosmer Lake (p236)
6. Wallowa Lake (p296)
7. Spring Creek (p282)

Walking/Hiking

1. Eagle Cap Wilderness (p297)
2. Stanley Park Seawall (p310)
3. Forest Park (p179)
4. Lincoln Park (p82)
5. Oregon Coast Trail (p253)
6. Columbia River Gorge waterfall corridor (p222)
7. Hoh Rain Forest (p117)

53

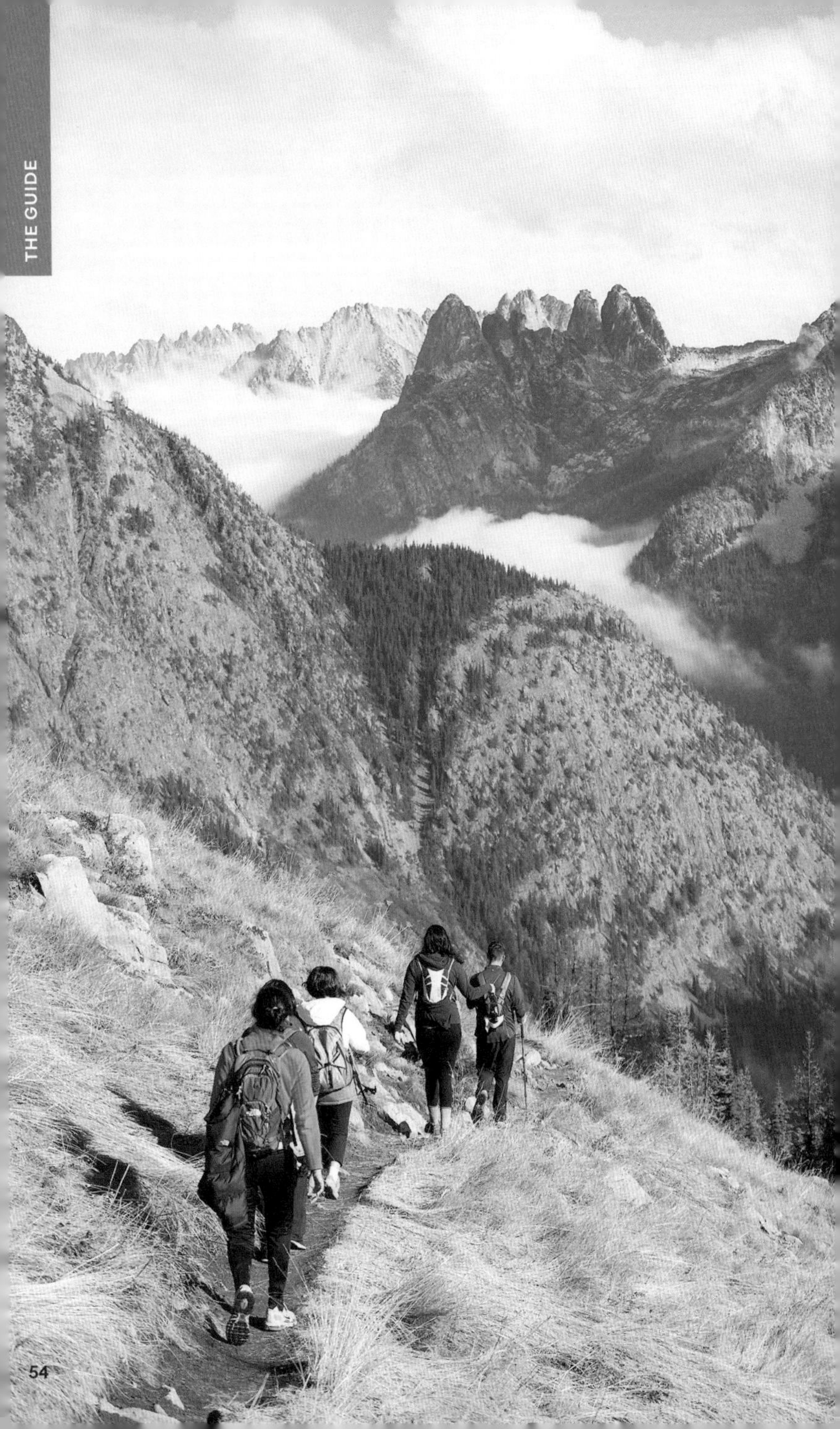

THE GUIDE

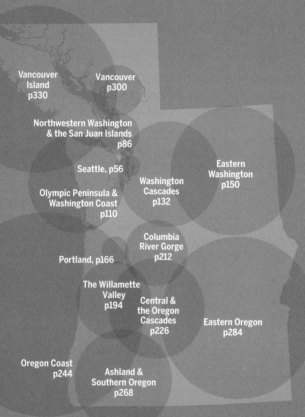

Vancouver
Island
p330

Vancouver
p300

Northwestern Washington
& the San Juan Islands
p86

Seattle, p56

Eastern
Washington
p150

Olympic Peninsula &
Washington Coast
p110

Washington
Cascades
p132

Columbia
River Gorge
p212

Portland, p166

The Willamette
Valley
p194

Central &
the Oregon
Cascades
p226

Eastern Oregon
p284

Oregon Coast
p244

Ashland &
Southern Oregon
p268

Chapters in this section are organised by hubs
and their surrounding areas. We see the hub as
your base in the destination, where you'll find
unique experiences, local insights, insider tips
and expert recommendations. It's also your
gateway to the surrounding area, where you'll
see what and how much you can do from there.

Heather Maple Pass Loop (p146), North Cascades National Park

Seattle

A GEM OF A CITY SURROUNDED BY BEAUTY

A rapidly growing city with cultural, culinary and artistic attractions against a backdrop of mountains and water, Seattle combines innovation with the beauty of nature.

With the Puget Sound to the west and the Cascade Mountains to the east, Seattle is surrounded by stunning scenery and within it, a melting pot of cultures. On a clear day, you can see Mt Rainier towering over the city (if you want to speak like a local say: 'the mountain's out today,' if it is a nice, clear day out). There are also plenty of parks and green spaces where you can enjoy the outdoors.

The city has a vibrant arts scene, with numerous museums, galleries and theaters showcasing local talent. Music is also a big part of Seattle's culture, with a rich history of jazz, grunge and indie rock. There are plenty of live-music venues throughout the city, as well as an annual music festival in September called Bumbershoot that draws thousands of visitors.

The food scene here is a notable one. Sustainable and local eating are high on the list at many Seattle restaurants: fresh seafood, artisanal coffee, and locally made craft beer and liquor take the spotlight. There's also cuisine from a wide variety of cultures throughout the city. From Laotian and Vietnamese to Chinese, Japanese, Ethiopian, Indian, Lebanese and Turkish, there are specialties within specialties to explore. And don't forget dessert. Seattleites' love of ice cream and soft serve is strong – no matter the weather.

Seattle is a unique and special city. Whether you're interested in nature, culture or cuisine, you're sure to find something that appeals.

BRIAN LOGAN PHOTOGRAPHY/SHUTTERSTOCK ©

THE MAIN AREAS

GOLDILOCK PROJECT/SHUTTERSTOCK ©

Left: Stoup Brewing (p81), Ballard; Above: Pike Place Market (p66), Downtown

Find Your Way

The layout of Seattle is fairly straightforward, with I-5 running straight down the middle, dividing most of the city's neighborhoods into a two-column grid. Many of the main neighborhoods are reachable by the city's Link light-rail train. Otherwise, bus, car or bike – depending on where you're staying – are options.

FROM THE AIRPORT

Since the Link light-rail train system was built in 2003, travelers have a convenient option outside bus, taxi cabs or rideshare services. You can get from the airport to Downtown in just under 40 minutes with trains coming every eight to 10 minutes. Ticket prices vary depending on where you're going, but they won't be more than $3.50.

0   2 km
0   1 mile

University District p76

Fremont/Wallingford p78

Ballard p80

Queen Anne p68

Capitol Hill p71

Downtown p65

Pioneer Square p73

Chinatown-International District p73

Ravenna Park

Green Lake

Woodland Park

Portage Bay

Gas Works Park

Lake Union

Lakes View Cemetery

Lakeview Cemetery

Volunteer Park

Seattle Asian Art Museum

Cal Anderson Park

Kiwanis Memorial Park

Ballard Locks

Space Needle

Olympic Sculpture Park

Elliott Bay Park

Elliott Bay

Pike Place Market

Smith Tower Observatory

Occidental

Wing Luke Museum

Puget Sound

Bainbridge Island

Bainbridge & Vashon Islands
p84

Harbor Island

West Island Waterway

Harbor Island Waterway

West Waterway

East Waterway

Duwamish River

West Seattle
p82

Lincoln Park

Blake Island State Marine Park

Blake Island

Vashon Island

CAR

Most neighborhoods are within a 10- to 30-minute drive from each other, though driving time can increase during rush hour. While there are parking lots and some free two-hour parking streets throughout the city, be prepared to pay meters either with a credit card or via the Pay by Phone app.

TRAIN

The Link light-rail train system is another great transportation option for those visiting Seattle. It connects Downtown to the airport and other major areas of the city, providing a fast and convenient way to get around. The trains are modern and comfortable, making for a smooth ride.

BUS

The Seattle Metro bus system is an affordable way to explore the city. With routes that cover all major attractions and landmarks, it's easy to get around without the hassle of driving or navigating unfamiliar streets. Visitors can easily navigate popular attractions like Pike Place Market, the Space Needle and the waterfront.

Space Needle (p69)

Seattle Great Wheel (p67), Downtown

Plan Your Time

In a city known for its coffee, start your day at a local coffee shop before sampling the diverse flavors of Seattle. Plan your days by geography to avoid covering the same ground.

In a Rush

Start in **Pioneer Square** (p62). Take the **Underground Tour** (p63) for a history lesson and go to the top of **Smith Tower** (p63) for city views. Next, **Pike Place Market** (p66) for food and souvenirs. Ride the **Seattle Great Wheel** (p67) then head north to **Olympic Sculpture Park** (p67) for more views and sculptural art outdoors. Finally, visit **Seattle Center** at the base of the **Space Needle** (p69).

With a Week

Check out **Capitol Hill** (p71), where there are plenty of eats and drinks, and visit **Volunteer Park** (p71) and **Seattle Asian Art Museum** (p71). Head to **Ballard** (p80) for breweries and distilleries and the **Ballard Locks**. Make time to canoe at the **University of Washington** (p76) and head to Fremont/Wallingford to visit the **Fremont Troll** (p78). Finally, get to **West Seattle** (p82) for a panoramic city view.

Seasonal Highlights

SPRING	SUMMER	FALL	WINTER
The **Cherry Blossom Festival** is in late March/early April. Trees are in bloom at the University of Washington.	Seattle in all its glory, with locals swimming in Lake Washington and kayaking Portage Bay. **Gay Pride** is celebrated all summer.	It starts to get dark and dreary around October, but the fall foliage in some areas makes sweater weather more tolerable.	Snow shuts the city down. Avoid taking cars or buses downhill and don't be surprised if you see locals sledding or skiing.

Pioneer Square

ART & HISTORY IN SEATTLE'S 'FIRST NEIGHBORHOOD'

Known as Seattle's 'first neighborhood,' the Indigenous land that is currently known as Pioneer Square is rich in history seen through the architecture of its buildings, relics of the past and the brick roads throughout. Before it was established in the early 1850s, Djijila'letc or 'little crossing-over place,' as Pioneer Square was originally known, was occupied by the ancestors of today's Duwamish and Suquamish people. Chief Si'ahl or Seattle, led the Duwamish and Suquamish peoples in helping white settlers homestead in the area, only to be pushed out in 1865. Still, Pioneer Square went on to represent the birthplace of diversity in Seattle, with Seattle's second Black resident establishing a hotel there and Chinese and Japanese communities supporting the city's development in the late 1800s. Today, fun shops, art galleries and restaurants dot the streets of Pioneer Square, and the neighboring International District is home to many Asian restaurants and stores.

HIGHLIGHTS
1 Occidental Square
2 Smith Tower Observatory

EATING
3 Darkalino's

SHOPPING
4 fruitsuper
5 Hometeam

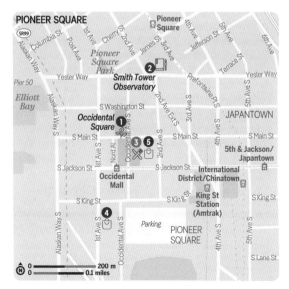

Bill Speidel's Underground Tour

Explore the original streets of Seattle

A popular tour for tourists and locals alike, this underground tour reveals subterranean streets that existed before Seattle as we know it was rebuilt after the Great Seattle Fire in 1889. The fire burned a 30-block radius of what was then the heart of the city and marked the beginning of the end of wooden buildings, which is why you see so many brick and stone buildings in Pioneer Square today. Mix in a little humor and you have a recipe for a fun and educational activity.

Bill Speidel's Underground Tour

Smith Tower Observatory

An alternative to the Space Needle

Built in 1914, Smith Tower is Seattle's first skyscraper and was the tallest building west of the Mississippi until 1931. You can ride up the now-modernized Otis Elevator Company elevators, which were reportedly among the last on the West Coast to use elevator operators, to the 35th floor. Here, a wrap-around deck for 360-degree views of the city and Puget Sound, a speakeasy-inspired bar serving cocktails and small plates, and a 'wishing chair' can be found. The wishing chair is said to have been a gift from China's Empress Dowager Cixi, and legend has it that those who are single and sit in the chair will be married within a year.

Smith Tower

Occidental Square

A quaint people-watching square

Located in the heart of Pioneer Square, Occidental Square is a charming place to relax and unwind, especially during the warmer months when people catch up at tables outside restaurants, wine bars and cafes, and kids – and adults – are playing the games provided in the park, like ping-pong or bocce ball. Tall London plane trees provide shade on the classic red-brick road that's closed off to cars, and the square is surrounded by historic buildings, including the Pioneer Building. In the winter, the trees are strung with lights, making it a festive place for photos. If you're visiting in early December, there is usually a holiday market and a free small ice-skating rink set up for one weekend.

Gallery open for the First Thursday Art Walk

WHERE TO SHOP

Bon Voyage Vintage
A true vintage shop, this picker's delight has been around for over a decade and carries clothing and accessories from every decade from the 1950s onwards.

Velouria
At this charming boutique clothing and accessories shop you can expect to find a carefully curated selection of unique pieces including US- and Canadian-made clothing, handmade jewelry, and other locally crafted apothecary and home goods. Velouria also donates 2% of its sales to a different nonprofit organization every month.

MORE IN PIONEER SQUARE

The New Pioneer Square
Art galleries and experiences

Fine art galleries sprinkle Pioneer Square in a higher concentration than other neighborhoods in the city, and there are an increasing number of shows dedicated to bringing new artists to the forefront of the local arts scene. Galleries have also made way for pop-up exhibits and artist-led events, adding to a change that Seattle as a whole has been experiencing.

To soak up the atmosphere here and make like a local, head first to **Darkalino's** – an Italian restaurant with a sneaker shop called **Hometeam** inside. Here DJs spin music every week while people enjoy handmade pastas and cocktails. Another nearby small business shop, **fruitsuper**, also combines unique experiences and events with shopping and art. Created by a local design studio of the same name, the boutique shop carries a selection of everyday items from more than 160 independent designers. Within the venue there is a wine shop and tasting room dedicated to wines from **Foundry Vineyards** in Walla Walla, while crafting workshops and art shows are held monthly. Pick up some gifts, or a bottle of Washington wine, to bring back home.

If you're there on the first Thursday of the month check out **First Thursday Art Walk**, a day when all galleries open their doors with new shows, and art lovers flow freely from one gallery to the next. While this art walk is one of the longest running in the country, beginning in the 1980s, Pioneer Square's art scene is still evolving in the aftermath of the pandemic, with some galleries and restaurants closing and others opening.

WHERE TO ENJOY A COCKTAIL

Damn the Weather
American gastropub using seasonal ingredients and serving craft cocktails in a wood and brick interior. $$

Bad Bishop
Craft cocktail bar with playful American comfort food, like corndogs and mac 'n' cheese. $$

Ohsun Banchan Deli & Cafe
Casual gluten-free eatery with Korean classics using quality ingredients and Korean-inspired cocktails. $$

Downtown

PIKE PLACE MARKET AND SIGHTS TO SEE

In pre-pandemic times, the tall buildings that make up Downtown Seattle were filled with office workers and the streets were bustling with cars, retail stores and foot traffic. These days it's slowly coming back, thanks to initiatives such as Seattle Restored, a city-funded program that activates empty storefronts with retail pop-ups and art installations from local entrepreneurs, artists and manufacturers in an effort to reinvigorate the area. There are also many of the traditional attractions, notably Pike Place Market, that bring tourists and locals to the area to enjoy the vendors, restaurants and views, the Seattle Art Museum and the Olympic Sculpture Park. Traffic is still at its peak throughout Downtown, but thankfully it's a walkable area with two Link light-rail stations (Westlake and University St). Some streets don fairly steep hills, so depending on where you're going be prepared to scale a few.

> ☑ **TOP TIP**
>
> The Westlake Link light-rail station will bring you to the heart of Downtown's shopping area and is straight up the street from Pike Place Market. University St will drop you in the central business district of Downtown – the Central Library and Seattle Art Museum are just a few blocks away. It's also the nearest stop to get to the piers and the Seattle Great Wheel.

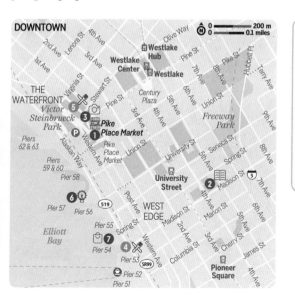

HIGHLIGHTS
1. Pike Place Market

SIGHTS
2. Central Public Library
3. Post Alley

EATING
4. Ivar's
5. Pink Door

ENTERTAINMENT
6. Seattle Great Wheel

SHOPPING
7. Ye Olde Curiosity Shop

Pike Place Market

One of Seattle's most iconic landmarks

Considered perhaps the most-popular must-see attraction in Downtown Seattle, or all of Seattle for that matter, Pike Place Market is a bustling marketplace that has been around since 1907. Visitors can wander through the stalls and sample fresh produce, local honey and other local delicacies. The fish counter still throws fish, as it has for decades, and the **Athenian Seafood Restaurant & Bar**, where a scene in *Sleepless in Seattle* was filmed, serves cold beer in frosted beer mugs, alongside plates of fish and chips and bowls of clam chowder. The seat where Tom Hanks sat is clearly marked for fans. Cross the cobblestone road to the Corner Market building where more shops, restaurants and food counters can be found, and head to Oriental Mart, a family-run 18-seat Filipino lunch counter that's been there since the 1970s. Despite being a 2020 James Beard Award winner, don't expect to find a website online or a menu when you're there. Instead, you'll see a wall of handwritten signs with rules on how to – or how not to – order (do order the salmon *sinigang* if it's not sold out). Beyond food, Pike Place features handmade crafts and fresh and dried floral bouquets aplenty – a productive place for souvenirs. Don't forget the lower level of the main market, where there are upwards of 100 more shops.

The market is also home to the famous **Gum Wall**, which is literally what it sounds like – a colorful wall of chewing gum wads that visitors have contributed to over time. It's a unique and quirky attraction that has become a popular photo spot for tourists.

TO GO OR NOT TO GO: THE ORIGINAL STARBUCKS

Marking the inception of the iconic coffeehouse chain in 1971, the original Starbucks still sits in Pike Place today. While historically significant, the site commands long lines for tourists but the coffee shop itself varies very little from most other Starbucks locations. If you're a die-hard fan, pay the storefront a visit, snap a photo outside, then use that saved waiting time to travel 0.8 miles to the **Starbucks Reserve Roastery** on Capitol Hill, where you'll find more of an experience with coffee-tasting flights, a retail shop, two levels of coffee roasting and packaging operations in plain sight, and more.

Gum Wall

From Architecture to the Puget Sound
Wide-spanning sightseeing

Whether you're passionate about architecture, art or majestic views of the Puget Sound and Olympic Mountains, you can experience it all Downtown.

Embark on a walking tour of Downtown by starting at the **Central Public Library**. Marvel at the 11-story glass and steel structure capable of housing 1.45 million books designed by world-renowned architect Rem Koolhaas and Seattle-based LMN Architects.

A 10-minute walk west will bring you to the piers, lined with dining options that come with a view, including **Ivar's**, famous for its clam chowder. Grab a cup, along with some fish and chips, and sit outside by the water – just know the seagulls will want some fries, too.

On the same pier, check out **Ye Olde Curiosity Shop** that's part souvenir shop, part museum and has been around since 1899. You can expect to find things like shrunken heads and mummies alongside Native American art and a plethora of oddities and gifts.

Continue the fun by hopping on the **Seattle Great Wheel**, a 157ft-tall Ferris wheel on the water's edge. On weekend nights, the wheel is a light show using 500,000 LED lights.

And last but not least, make your way to Pike Place Market and grab a drink and a bite at the **Pink Door**, a local favorite. Located in the quaint **Post Alley** just half a block up from the main market corridor, you'll feel as though you've been transported to Italy. Sit outside on the patio for a view, or enjoy cabaret and trapeze performances inside while you dine on lasagna that will melt in your mouth.

BEST ART DOWNTOWN

Seattle Art Museum
An attraction for art enthusiasts visiting Downtown Seattle, featuring a diverse collection of contemporary and classic art from around the world, including paintings, sculptures and installations.

Olympic Sculpture Park
If you're looking for a serene escape amid the tall buildings, head to the Olympic Sculpture Park at the edge of the Downtown area. Admire the stunning views of the Olympic Mountains and Puget Sound while strolling through the outdoor art installations. Don't miss the iconic *Eagle* sculpture by Alexander Calder and *Waves* by Richard Serra.

Frye Art Museum
More specifically located on First Hill, which is part of Downtown, this museum showcases modern and contemporary art. Admission is free, and there's a great gift shop.

 WHERE TO SEE LIVE MUSIC

Benaroya Hall
See the Seattle Symphony Orchestra and other acts. Talks with artists and thought leaders are held here, too.

Showbox
Founded in 1939, this venue can hold around 1100 concert-goers. Past acts include Duke Ellington and Pearl Jam.

Paramount Theater
With close to 3000 seats, this venue is a historic and iconic venue that hosts diverse entertainment events.

Queen Anne

OLD MANSIONS AND CITY VIEWS

☑ TOP TIP

Take a drive on Queen Anne Blvd, an approximately 4-mile loop and a designated Seattle Landmark, to see expansive views of the city and its surroundings, as well as some mansions along the way.

Perched high on a hill, Queen Anne is a charming neighborhood with a rich history. Named after the Queen Anne style of architecture, which is prevalent in the area, the community is situated on a hill that offers stunning views of the city and surrounding areas. While the neighborhood is primarily residential, small businesses, local shops and cafes line Queen Anne Ave N. The area is also home to several popular parks, including Kerry Park and Queen Anne Blvd, which offers sweeping vistas of the city skyline.

HIGHLIGHTS
1 Space Needle

SIGHTS
2 Kerry Park

ENTERTAINMENT
3 KEXP's Gathering Space
4 Climate Pledge Arena
5 SIFF Cinema Uptown

The Space Needle/Seattle Center
Elevated views, immersive experiences

Perhaps one of the most well-known markers of Seattle's skyline, the Space Needle sits slightly north of Downtown's cluster of skyscrapers in the lower Queen Anne neighborhood. It's located at Seattle Center, a 74-acre area of entertainment originally built for the 1962 World's Fair. Taking the elevator up to enjoy 360-degree views of the city at the Space Needle is a popular activity. Beyond going all the way up to the top, visitors can be entertained and educated at many experiences located at the base of the Space Needle, including the Pacific Science Center, the Museum of Pop Culture, McCaw Hall (home to the Seattle Opera), and the Chihuly Garden and Glass.

If you're in for a full day, start at the **Pacific Science Center**, where you can wander through hands-on exhibits of science and technology and experience a laser show at the laser dome. The **Museum of Pop Culture** is a must-visit for music lovers, with exhibits dedicated to legendary musicians and bands, but it also features exhibitions on movies and television. Even if you don't feel like committing to going in, you can enjoy the colorful and unique architecture of the building, designed by Frank Gehry to emulate the rock and roll experience. Finally, end your day with a calm stroll through the **Chihuly Garden and Glass**, where you can view the large-scale glass sculptures and gardens created by world-renowned artist Dale Chihuly. It's the perfect day out for culture, art and science enthusiasts alike.

A DOODLE OF AN IDEA

Inspired by a broadcast tower in Stuttgart, Germany, that featured a restaurant at the top, Seattle hotel executive Edward E Carlson, also a chief organizer of the 1962 World's Fair, drew a napkin doodle in 1959 of what would become the now-iconic Space Needle. Opening on the first day of the 1962 World's Fair, the 605ft-tall observation tower that quickly became synonymous with Seattle's skyline offers a 360-degree view of the city and beyond – and you guessed it, features a revolving restaurant at the top that offers a unique dining experience paired with panoramic vistas of the city and its surroundings.

Space Needle and the Museum of Pop Culture

THE LAY OF THE LAND

The Queen Anne neighborhood is generally divided into two parts – Upper Queen Anne and Lower Queen Anne, the latter of which is sometimes referred to as Uptown these days (but not by longtime Seattleites). **Lower Queen Anne** sits closer to Downtown and is home to the sites that frequent many 'Things-to-do-in-Seattle' lists, including shops, restaurants and the SIFF movie theater. **Upper Queen Anne** is more residential and where you'll find the mansions, small shops and Queen Anne Blvd views.

JON BILOUS/SHUTTERSTOCK ©

Kerry Park views

MORE IN QUEEN ANNE

Shared Experiences of Enriching Entertainment

Movies, music and sports, oh my

To spend a day in Queen Anne, start by getting a sense of where you are by heading to **Kerry Park** to see a postcard-worthy view of Seattle's skyline and surrounding mountains that's hard to get from anywhere else in the city. It's a small 'park,' if you want to call it that, and is more of a viewpoint where you can see the city as it appears in the television sitcom *Frasier,* as the view from his apartment, and also in the cult classic movie *10 Things I Hate About You*.

If you're a movie buff, head from there down the hill to **SIFF Cinema Uptown**, a cultural gem and a quaint place to catch a movie with historic architecture and state-of-the-art technology. The theater also hosts a variety of film festivals and special events throughout the year, most notably the annual **Seattle International Film Festival**, usually in late May or early June. Movie lovers can expect to see the latest international releases and arthouse films here.

Then tap into the music lover in you and immerse yourself in the music scene local to Seattle and beyond at **KEXP's Gathering Space**. The world-renowned nonprofit radio station is dedicated to promoting new and emerging artists from around the world and the gathering space features a coffee shop, art and space to lounge while seeing the DJs hard at work. Next door, sports fans can catch a game or event at the newly built **Climate Pledge Arena**, home to Seattle's NHL team, the Kraken. It's hard to miss the Space Needle from there, too, which makes for a great photo opportunity.

 ## WHERE TO EAT IN QUEEN ANNE

Paju
A small and simple space that serves modern takes on Korean dishes. $$

Taylor Shellfish Oyster Bar
Washington shellfish company with a few city oyster bars. This one has a close-up Space Needle view. $$

Toulouse Petit
A Cajun-Creole restaurant with food, decor and ambience inspired by New Orleans. $$

Capitol Hill

GOOD FOOD AND INCLUSIVE NIGHTLIFE

Just east of Downtown, Capitol Hill is a vibrant and progressive neighborhood known for its diverse community, artistic culture and thriving nightlife. Since the 1950s, the neighborhood has been a LGBTIQA+ community center. In the '90s it was the center of Seattle's influential grunge culture. In addition to its cultural offerings, vintage shops, independent boutiques, restaurants, coffee shops, bars, gay clubs and music venues, Capitol Hill is also home to a variety of green spaces including Cal Anderson Park, and the 50-acre Volunteer Park where you can also find the Seattle Asian Art Museum and the Conservatory – where plant enthusiasts can view thousands of plant species. For those interested in history and architecture, the Harvard-Belmont Historic District, which Volunteer Park sits in, is home to a collection of beautiful mansions and homes that date back to the early 1900s. Bruce Lee fans can also stop by Lake View Cemetery next to the park to visit his grave.

☑ **TOP TIP**

Pike and Pine Sts, as well as Broadway, are where the bulk of the restaurants, shops and bars are. Still, some gems are to be found on the surrounding streets, like Melrose Ave and Summit Ave, which feature quaint brick apartment buildings, small restaurants and coffee shops, and independently owned shops.

ICE CREAM

Perhaps it's because it offers a bright spot in the seemingly never-ending dark months of the winter, but despite the dreary weather most months of the year, Seattle loves its ice cream. You can find two of the city's most popular ice-cream shops on Capitol Hill: **Molly Moon's Ice Cream** and **Frankie & Jo's**. Molly Moon's is a Seattle staple, known for creative and delicious flavors made with locally sourced ingredients. It's also well known among locals for its strong values with free health care for employees working a 20+-hour week. Frankie & Jo's offers plant-based ice cream with gluten-free options.

MORE IN CAPITOL HILL

Eat & Drink Your Way Around
Taste the rainbow on Capitol Hill

For a day of eating and drinking, Capitol Hill establishments cater to a diverse range of tastes and budgets. Start the day with coffee or tea and a good read. Check out **Little Oddfellows** at Elliott Bay Book Co and **Ada's Technical Books & Cafe**, which offers vegetarian food alongside science-minded literature.

For a bite on-the-go, try **Yalla**, a walk-up window that serves some of the best Middle Eastern wraps in town. Every wrap is worth trying, and make sure to try the fermented hot sauce.

Hot Mama's Pizza makes a reliable New York–style slice with the perfect crispy crust, and is one of very few, if not the only, to serve a pesto slice. And of course, **Dick's Drive-In** on Broadway has almost 70 years of burger-slinging experience, with a favorite being the Dick's Deluxe burger.

Unless you're vegetarian or vegan, you can't go to Seattle and skip a platter of freshly shucked Pacific Northwest oysters.

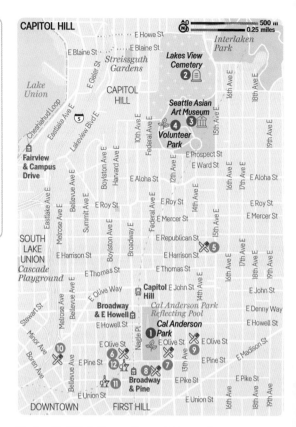

HIGHLIGHTS
1 Cal Anderson Park
2 Lake View Cemetery
3 Seattle Asian Art Museum
4 Volunteer Park

EATING
5 Ada's Technical Books & Cafe
6 Hot Mama's Pizza
7 Karachi Cowboy
8 Little Oddfellows
9 Spinasse
10 Taylor Shellfish Oyster Bar

DRINKING & NIGHTLIFE
11 La Dive
12 Linda's Tavern

Taylor Shellfish Oyster Bar, which supplies many restaurants throughout the city and has been farming oysters since 1890, has a tiny outpost on Capitol Hill so if you have a larger group, check out its Queen Anne or Pioneer Square locations.

Then for a proper dinner that's special-occasion-worthy without the stuffiness of fine dining, head to **Spinasse**, where rustic Northern Italian is done right. Pasta is handmade and a classy ambience cozies up next to attentive service. Cap off your day with a visit to renowned bars like **Linda's Tavern**, a divey Seattle original open since 1994 (and reportedly where Kurt Cobain was last seen before his death); **La Dive**, a natural wine bar with non-alcoholic options and 'Chambongs;' or **Canon**, an award-winning cocktail bar with an extensive menu of classic and modern cocktails presented in creative ways.

WHERE TO DRINK COFFEE

Victrola Coffee Roasters
Laid-back, no-frills coffee shop that focuses on great coffee. Multiple city locations yet the coffee is consistent.

Espresso Vivace
Serving some of the city's best espresso since 1988; founder David Schomer is credited with bringing latte art to the US.

Caffe Vita
Local favorite since 1995, its drinks are consistent across locations – Capitol Hill has its flagship coffee shop.

Chinatown-International District

AUTHENTIC EATS AND LONG-STANDING RESTAURANTS

Located just south of Downtown and east of Pioneer Square, Seattle's International District, or 'the ID' as locals call it, was home to the city's first Asian American immigrants. Today, a community of Chinese, Japanese, Korean, Filipino and Vietnamese businesses can be found here, primarily restaurants, shops and museums. You can also browse shops selling everything from handmade crafts to traditional clothing and accessories. Pay a visit to Uwajamaya, one of the larger Japanese grocery stores in the area that also has a large housewares section and bookstore, Kinokuniya.

☑ TOP TIP

The bulk of the International District sits on the west side of 12th Ave, near the sports stadiums; however, Little Saigon is on the east side between 12th and Rainier Aves. The homeless population is concentrated on King St under the I-5 overpass (between 8th and 12th Aves) and on 12th Ave, between Jackson and Weller Sts.

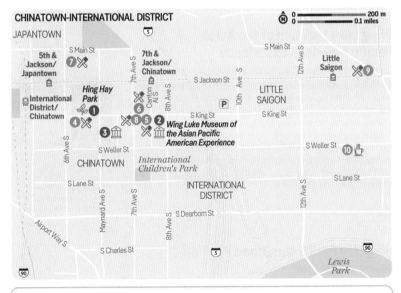

CHINATOWN-INTERNATIONAL DISTRICT

HIGHLIGHTS	SIGHTS	EATING	
① Hing Hay Park	③ Seattle Pinball	④ Fort St George	⑧ Tai Tung
② Wing Luke Museum	Museum	⑤ Harbor City	⑨ The Boat
of the Asian Pacific		⑥ Jade Garden	**DRINKING & NIGHTLIFE**
American Experience		⑦ Maneki	⑩ Hello Em Viet Coffee

Seattle Pinball Museum

Seattle Pinball Museum

Nostalgic journey

Unlike traditional museums, the Seattle Pinball Museum is a sort of interactive haven that allows visitors to play a vast collection of pinball machines spanning decades. With a nostalgic journey through vintage and modern games, it's a hands-on exploration of gaming history. The museum's mission is to preserve and share the joy of pinball, making it an engaging destination for enthusiasts and casual visitors alike, offering a unique blend of entertainment and nostalgia in the International District.

TOP LEFT: DAVID TONELSON/SHUTTERSTOCK ©; BOTTOM RIGHT: RITU MANOJ JETHANI/SHUTTERSTOCK ©

Wing Luke Museum of the Asian Pacific American Experience

Celebration of Asian Pacific American history

The Wing Luke Museum celebrates Asian Pacific American history with innovative exhibits, vividly narrating stories of resilience, identity and community contributions. The museum's namesake, Wing Luke, was the first Asian American elected to public office in the Pacific Northwest. Housed in historic buildings, the museum encourages personal exploration through interactive displays and contemporary art installations. One of its exhibits is the Bruce Lee story. Guided tours are available.

Wing Luke Museum of the Asian Pacific American Experience

Hing Hay Park & the Grand Pavilion

Vibrant cultural hubs

Hing Hay Park and the Grand Pavilion offer a blend of cultural richness and serene landscapes for visitors. Hing Hay Park welcomes visitors with traditional Chinese architecture, lush gardens and community events. The Grand Pavilion, a focal point of the neighborhood, hosts performances, festivals and gatherings, and is a great spot to be immersed in the area's diverse heritage.

You can explore the park's tranquil corners, adorned with public art, or engage in cultural celebrations, gaining an appreciation for Seattle's multicultural identity.

Harbor City

MORE IN CHINATOWN-
INTERNATIONAL DISTRICT

A Taste of Seattle's Asian American Community

Small businesses reawaken to feed the masses

Seattle's International District boasts a number of dining establishments that have stood the test of time by offering authentic cuisine in laid-back, unassuming environments. If you're looking to eat you'll find dim sum, pho, bubble tea, dumplings, sushi, a variety of bakeries and more. The pandemic hit many of the small businesses in the area hard, but many are back up and running with the support of locals and tourists alike.

Begin in the east end of the neighborhood, dubbed Little Saigon for its concentration of Vietnamese eateries. Hit **The Boat** (which housed the original Pho Bac Sup Shop), a James Beard Award finalist with a focus on chicken rice. Next, **Hello Em Viet Coffee** pours Vietnamese-style coffee drinks (with modern twists like egg foam), or try **Saigon Deli**, a reliable go-to for a quick and delicious banh mi to go – it's one of the few still under $7.

On the western edge of the neighborhood by the light-rail station you'll also find pho spots scattered throughout, plus Chinese and Japanese options including two of the city's oldest restaurants within blocks of each other: **Tai Tung** for Chinese food and **Maneki** for Japanese. For one of the more popular choices for dim sum in the area head to **Harbor City** or **Jade Garden**. Finally, for no-frills Japanese comfort food, or *yōshoku* cuisine, head where the locals go for a stiff drink, *doria* and the special spaghetti with meat sauce and garlic mayo, at **Fort St George**. It's located on the 2nd floor of an old office building that also houses a retro video-game store.

BEST ASIAN BAKERIES

Fuji Bakery
This Japanese French bakery makes handcrafted pastries – and *malasadas* (doughnuts) – with Japanese flavors. **$**

Yummy House Bakery
A Hong Kong–style bakery selling pastries and buns, as well as cakes with fresh fruit and light and airy frosting. **$**

Hood Famous Bakeshop
A Filipino bakery and coffee shop that also serves savory breakfast dishes by day; it's a cocktail bar with Filipino bar food by night. **$$**

 WHERE TO EAT DUMPLINGS

Szechuan Noodle Bowl	Dough Zone Dumpling House	Mike's Noodle House
Mom-and-pop casual eatery. Crave-worthy veggie dumplings and possibly the best green-onion pancake in the city. **$**	Casual, modern Chinese chain specializing in *jian bao* (fried dumplings), soup dumplings, noodles and other classics. **$$**	While more of a noodle than dumpling house, the wontons and dumplings in the noodle dishes satisfy any cravings. **$**

University District

YOUTHFUL ENERGY AND WATER ACTIVITIES

☑ **TOP TIP**

While you can park on campus, there's street parking to be found just outside campus whether it's in the surrounding neighborhood or close to the central street University Ave (or 'the Ave'), with most of the off-campus action. The Link light-rail also has a station here, which will drop you at Husky Stadium.

The University District, otherwise known as 'U-District,' surrounds the University of Washington (called 'U-Dub' by locals). The campus has stunning historical architecture and is famous for its cherry blossom trees – planted in the form of a 'W' in the Quad – which visitors flock to in spring. Other highlights include quintessentially Seattle cafes, affordable restaurants and two great museums. On the east side is a mid- to higher-end outdoor shopping mall called University Village (or 'U-Village') with larger retail stores like Everlane, Warby Parker, Apple, Madewell and Parachute. Some local restaurants, like Ba Bar and Rachel's Ginger Beer, are also here, along with national and international chains such as Din Tai Fung and Shake Shack. Beyond shopping, eating and a beautiful campus, the area is surrounded by water, touching both Portage and Union Bays, as well as Lake Washington. Locals (and visitors) enjoy kayaking and stand-up paddleboarding on the waters.

MORE IN UNIVERSITY DISTRICT

Educational Exploration On & Off Campus

Art, artifacts and nature

The University District has offerings for lifelong students of art and nature. The University of Washington campus features two museums: the **Henry Art Gallery**, a contemporary art gallery home to a vast collection of thought-provoking installations and sculptures from artists all over the world, and the **Burke Museum of Natural History & Culture**, which houses artifacts of natural history and anthropology of the Pacific Northwest and beyond, including exhibits on Native American culture and geological history.

If you're looking for a serene experience in springtime, head over to the nearly 90-year-old Yoshino cherry-blossom trees in the **Quad**. The sheer volume of the pink and white blooms are a sight to see and draw large crowds during the **Cherry Blossom Festival** in late March/early April.

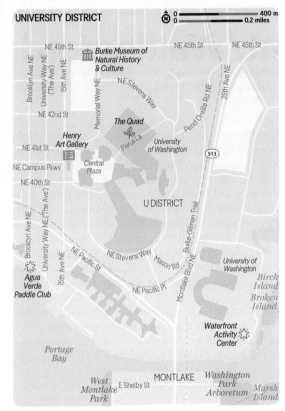

UNIVERSITY DISTRICT

0 — 400 m
0 — 0.2 miles

NE 45th St
Burke Museum of Natural History & Culture
NE Stevens Way
NE 42nd St
The Quad
Henry Art Gallery
Pierce La
University of Washington
513
Central Plaza
NE 41st St
NE Campus Pkwy
NE 40th St
Brooklyn Ave NE
University Way NE (The Ave)
15th Ave NE
Memorial Way NE
25th Ave NE
Pend Oreille Rd NE
U DISTRICT
Burke-Gilman Trail
Agua Verde Paddle Club
NE Pacific St
NE Stevens Way
Mason Rd
NE Pacific Pl
Montlake Blvd NE
University of Washington
Birch Island
Broken Island
Waterfront Activity Center
Portage Bay
West Montlake Park
E Shelby St
MONTLAKE
Washington Park Arboretum
Marsh Island

For a more active adventure, the **Waterfront Activity Center** by Husky Stadium offers reasonably priced canoe and kayak rentals on Lake Washington. You can take in the views of the lake and the arboretum and experience the city from a different perspective. If stand-up paddleboarding is more your thing, **Agua Verde Paddle Club** offers rentals, along with kayaks, and also features a casual and lively Mexican restaurant with waterfront tables.

Finally, if you're looking for some shopping, delicious dining and nightlife, **University Avenue** is the place to go with its trendy shops, lively bars and unique restaurants.

BULLDOG NEWS & CAFE

In an age where people say 'print is dead,' it's very much alive at Bulldog News. Located on University Ave since 1983, this newsstand has an impressive collection of magazine titles covering the walls of the shop (reportedly over 800). Mainstream or obscure, big and glossy or artsy zines, the variety and volume of magazines that can be found here is unmatched, and they come from all over the world. Pay this newsstand a visit if you have an appreciation for print. Grab a coffee at the coffee stand and stay awhile to peruse the whole collection.

WHERE TO EAT LIKE A COLLEGE KID

Aladdin Gyro-Cery & Deli
Long-standing eatery slinging gyros, shawarma rolls and kebab sandwiches til 2:30am. Vegetarian options, too. $

Agua Verde Paddle Club & Cafe
Not the cheapest Baja-style Mexican, but you get quite a view with your tacos. $$

Thai Tom
A longtime local favorite, this tiny space literally fires up hot Thai dishes with speed and flavor. $

Fremont/Wallingford

ECLECTIC CHARM AND CURIOUS ATTRACTIONS

☑ TOP TIP

If you want to hit the main attractions in the Fremont/ Wallingford area, like Theo Chocolate, the Fremont Sunday Market, the Fremont Troll and Gas Works Park, these stops are all within a mile of each other and are walkable. Other destinations in these areas might be better visited with a car or bike if you don't have a lot of time to kill.

The Fremont and Wallingford areas sit north of the heart of the city, across the bridges over Lake Union and Portage Bay. These areas are known for their eclectic charm, lively atmosphere and community-driven spirit. Fremont (declared the 'Center of the Universe' in 1991 by a group of residents and business owners) is home to the iconic Fremont Troll, a public art installation under the Aurora Bridge. This neighborhood is also known for quirky shops, delicious restaurants and fun events such as the annual Solstice Parade and the new Fremont Dungeness Festival.

Wallingford is a more laid-back, quieter neighborhood, also with a strong sense of community. It is home to the beautiful Gas Works Park, a former gasification plant turned public park with outstanding views of Lake Union, the Space Needle and some of the Downtown skyline. Wallingford has a variety of cozy cafes, local breweries and vibrant murals.

MORE IN FREMONT/WALLINGFORD

Indulge Your Inner Child
Awaken the senses with the weird and wonderful

While Pike Place has the Gum Wall, Fremont and Wallingford might take the cake for fun and quirky attractions in Seattle.

The **Space Rocket**, a towering sculpture that has become a popular symbol of the neighborhood, bears Fremont's coat of arms and telling motto *De Libertas Quirkas* or 'Freedom to be Peculiar.' Nearby is a solid example of that motto – the 'Center of the Universe' sign, which was put up in a rogue act in 1991 and has become a beloved landmark. The sign points people to the **Fremont Troll**, which lives under the Aurora Bridge about a mile east. Before heading there, satisfy your sweet tooth at **Theo Chocolate**, an artisanal chocolate factory focused on ethical sourcing that offers chocolate-making tours and samples.

For a scenic spot to enjoy a picnic or let out some energy on a playground while enjoying stunning views of the city, visit

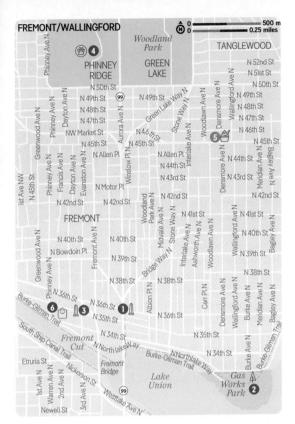

FREMONT/WALLINGFORD

SIGHTS
1 Fremont Troll
2 Gas Works Park
3 Space Rocket
4 Woodland Park Zoo

EATING
5 Molly Moon's Homemade Ice Cream

SHOPPING
6 Theo Chocolate

THE FREMONT TROLL

Located under the north end of the Aurora Bridge, the Fremont Troll is a whimsical sculpture created in 1990 by a group of local artists as part of a Fremont Arts Council competition aimed at enhancing the freeway underpass, which had previously been a neglected dumping ground. The troll, constructed from concrete, rebar and wire, stands at an impressive 18ft tall and features a playful expression as it clutches a Volkswagen Beetle in its left hand. Visitors love climbing on its hands and taking photos.

Gas Works Park. This former gas plant turned park offers plenty of green space, as well as picturesque views of Lake Union and the Seattle skyline.

Further north in Wallingford, you can find **Woodland Park Zoo**, home to an array of creatures, from big cats and bears to penguins and primates. With plenty of interactive exhibits and educational programs, it's a great place to spend a day with family or friends.

Finally, no trip to Fremont or Wallingford is complete without a visit to **Molly Moon's Homemade Ice Cream**. This location was the first of this local favorite and offers a rotating selection of inventive flavors, from honey lavender to balsamic strawberry, all made with organic and locally sourced ingredients.

 WHERE TO EAT SEAFOOD

Manolin
Fresh seafood in a classy but comfortable space with bright flavors reminiscent of coastal Latin American vacations. $$

RockCreek Seafood & Spirits
Full-service restaurant with dishes sourced from ethical fisheries. Designed like an upscale fishing lodge. $$$

Local Tide
Small casual eatery with seafood classics like fried oysters, and outliers like black-cod *kasuzuke*. $$

Ballard

SCANDINAVIAN ROOTS, SHIPS, SALMON & BEER

Located to the northwest of Downtown Seattle, the Ballard neighborhood has a Scandinavian heritage and a deep connection to Seattle's maritime history. Visitors can learn more about each by visiting the Nordic Museum – which showcases the history and culture of the Nordic region, including exhibits on Vikings, Sami culture and contemporary Nordic art – and the Hiram M Chittenden Locks (otherwise known as the Ballard Locks), a popular attraction that allows boats to move between the Puget Sound and the Ship Canal, traveling from salt water to fresh. The fish ladder here is open to the public and offers a unique opportunity to watch salmon migrate upstream. The neighborhood also has a lively and eclectic mix of restaurants, bars and shops, including Sonic Boom Records and many others that are locally owned and operated. A brewery district has emerged in recent years, and live-music venues draw bands of note.

GOLDEN GARDENS

Golden Gardens is a serene and stunning beach park where you can bask in the breathtaking views of the Puget Sound and Olympic Mountains. The park has a clean and well-kept sandy beach, fire pits, a playground and a casual food stand open during summer when the beach is filled with people picnicking, playing volleyball or just taking in the views. But parking spots are hard to come by. While the cold waters of the Puget Sound might feel good on the hottest of summer days, it borders on being too cold for most. On the north end of the beach, you'll find a green lawn space if you need a break from the sand, as well as a freshwater marsh.

MORE IN BALLARD

Sip & Swig Local Brews & Liquors
Ballard is brimming with breweries and distilleries

Seattle's Ballard neighborhood has a high concentration of local breweries and distilleries, making it an efficient way to try a variety of local craft breweries and spirits. In fact, it has an official **Ballard Brewery District**.

Begin your tour at **Big Gin Distilling** for handcrafted gin made with locally sourced botanicals, since it will be beer and cider from here on out. The tasting room features single tastes, flights and cocktails, and you can purchase a bottle to take home. Next, cross the Ballard Bridge to **Bale Breaker & Yonder Cider Taproom**, which makes ciders with fresh, locally sourced ingredients in a variety of flavors. If it isn't raining, its outdoor space is easily one that visitors love to pass time in, complete with fire pits and Adirondack chairs.

For a nice transition from cider to beer, walk about one block to **Fair Isle Brewing**, which specializes in farmhouse-style

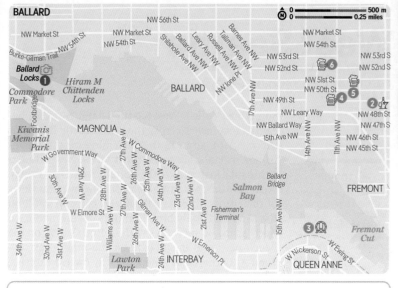

HIGHLIGHTS
1 Ballard Locks

DRINKING & NIGHTLIFE
2 Bale Breaker & Yonder Cider Taproom
3 Big Gin Distilling
4 Fair Isle Brewing
5 Lucky Envelope Brewing
6 Stoup Brewing

ales, or saisons, using traditional brewing methods and local ingredients. This small-batch brewery features a rustic setting and serves its beers in elegant stemmed wine glasses. Next, head three blocks north to **Stoup Brewing** (where the head brewer is a former forensic scientist). It has a long list of beers, from classic IPAs to experimental brews, in a setting that is reminiscent of drinking in your friend's glorified beer-making garage. And if you have one more beer in you, walk over to **Lucky Envelope Brewing** – a great stop for those looking for something a little different. It offers a wide variety of beers that are 'culturally inspired,' including some that are brewed with Asian ingredients and flavors such as Szechuan peppercorns.

☑ TOP TIP

While Ballard has its own brewing district, if drinking isn't your thing, there are plenty of sights to see. Between the shops and restaurants on Ballard Ave to the Ballard Locks and Golden Gardens, you could easily spend a full day in Ballard.

 ## WHERE TO WATCH LIVE MUSIC

Sunset Tavern
Intimate live-music venue in Ballard with a loyal following, featuring a diverse range of artists.

Tractor Tavern
Cozy Ballard music spot in a historic building with devoted patrons and eclectic performances.

Ballard Locks
In the summer, visitors can enjoy free outdoor concerts featuring local and regional artists with a scenic backdrop.

West Seattle

THE CITY SKYLINE FROM THE SAND

Sometimes called 'West Seattle Island' by locals because most have to cross the West Seattle Bridge or the water to get to it, this charming neighborhood blends urban with small-town vibes. Nestled on a peninsula just across the water from Downtown, West Seattle's Alki area has postcard-worthy views of the city skyline. At Alki Beach you can stroll on the sand and enjoy breathtaking sunsets, and it's a lively scene on nice days with in-line skaters on the beach path and flashy cars on the main drag. Beyond Alki, there are independently owned eateries, from cozy coffee shops to classy – but not uptight – restaurants with everything from handmade pasta to local seafood. The area's rich history can be explored at the Log House Museum or the Duwamish Longhouse & Cultural Center. And Lincoln Park has miles of hiking trails and beautiful waterfront views.

MORE IN WEST SEATTLE

Shopping Small

Small local businesses, including vinyl

If you're looking for some retail therapy before or after you get to **Alki Beach Park** for your dinner by the water, head up to California Ave – West Seattle's main drag – where you'll find coffee shops, bars, independent shops and local boutiques. One of the best places to start your shopping adventure is at the **West Seattle Junction**, a hub of activity and commerce that's been around for over a century. You'll find everything from vintage clothing to handmade jewelry, and there are plenty of cafes and restaurants to grab a bite between browsing.

Music lovers should make sure to stop by **Easy Street Records**, a beloved local record store that's been around since the 1980s. Browse its extensive collection of vinyl and CDs, grab a coffee at the cafe, and enjoy live music performances on the stage.

For those looking for unique skin-care products and housewares, stop at **Spruce Apothecary**, which also features a spa

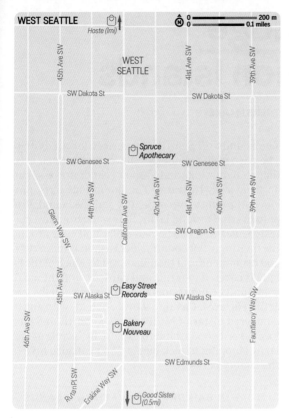

WEST SEATTLE

Hoste (1mi)

WEST
SEATTLE

45th Ave SW

41st Ave SW

39th Ave SW

SW Dakota St

SW Dakota St

 Spruce
Apothecary

SW Genesee St

SW Genesee St

Glenn Way SW

44th Ave SW

California Ave SW

42nd Ave SW

41st Ave SW

40th Ave SW

39th Ave SW

SW Oregon St

45th Ave SW

Easy Street
Records

SW Alaska St

SW Alaska St

Fauntleroy Way SW

46th Ave SW

Bakery
Nouveau

Rutan Pl SW

Erskine Way SW

SW Edmunds St

Good Sister
(0.5mi)

---

where you can book a facial for some relaxation. Another local retail and spa favorite is BIPOC-owned **Good Sister**, which carries lifestyle goods and offers inclusive services. For a little bit of everything, **Hoste** has a selection of vintage clothes and modern items. You'll also find carefully curated items for every facet of your life, from self care to pantry to home and decor. If you're in the mood for a sweet treat, don't miss **Bakery Nouveau**. This award-winning bakery has a wide selection of pastries, breads and desserts, all made from scratch. By choosing to support small businesses, you'll not only find one-of-a-kind treasures, but you'll also be helping to support the local economy and community.

WEST SEATTLE FARMERS MARKET

One of the few year-round farmers markets in Seattle, the West Seattle Farmers Market is a great place to experience the city's food scene and support local farmers and vendors. The market is held every Sunday from 10am to 2pm and features an array of fresh produce, artisanal goods and delicious food options. You can find everything from organic fruits and vegetables to handcrafted cheeses and baked goods as well as food trucks and stands serving hot meals, snacks and drinks. Make sure to bring a tote bag so that you can really blend in.

 ## WHERE TO EAT SEAFOOD BY THE BEACH

Driftwood
Elegant beachfront seafood restaurant using local fish, meat and produce. Its interesting cocktails use local produce. $$$

Harry's Beach House
The West Seattle outpost of Harry's Fine Foods with more seafood options than its Capitol Hill counterpart. $$

Spud Fish & Chips
An iconic no-frills destination for fish and chips that has been around since 1935. $

Bainbridge & Vashon Islands

SCENIC FERRY AND FARMERS MARKETS

☑ **TOP TIP**

Catch the Bainbridge Island ferry or the Vashon Island water taxi from Pier 50, near Pioneer Square. Travelers are beholden to the ferry and water-taxi schedules, so plan accordingly. Depending on the day and time, there can be a line for cars to drive onto the ferries and when it's busy, you might have to wait for the next ferry.

The islands off Seattle are perfect for a day trip. The pace of life is notably slower and calmer, even though Bainbridge and Vashon Islands are less than an hour away by water. The Bainbridge ferry provides stunning views of Seattle and the Sound. Prepare to stroll around lazily, tour waterfront taverns, taste wines, and maybe rent a bike and cycle around the invitingly flat countryside. Vashon is more rural and countercultural than Bainbridge. Much of the island is covered in farms and gardens, and the small community centers double as commercial hubs and artist enclaves. Cascade views abound, with unencumbered vistas of Mt Rainier and north to Baker. Vashon is a good island to explore by bicycle or car, lazily stopping to pick berries. You can also hike in the county parks.

MORE IN BAINBRIDGE & VASHON ISLANDS

Farmers Markets Grow Community

The islands' hearts beat on summer Saturdays

Island farmers markets feel different than city farmers markets – the intimacy of the small-town feel, the excitement about the community, and people's willingness to slow down and chat are just part of it.

Both Bainbridge and Vashon hold weekly farmers markets in the warmer months, so if you're visiting in the late spring, summer or early fall months, timing your visit to fall on a Saturday will allow you to see the islands' celebrating their communities of farmers and makers. These markets offer a unique opportunity to experience the local culture and taste some of the best produce the area has to offer.

The **Vashon Island farmers market**, located downtown, is a small but lively one where friendly vendors are eager to share their stories and knowledge about their products, ranging from fresh produce to flowers to eggs. The island

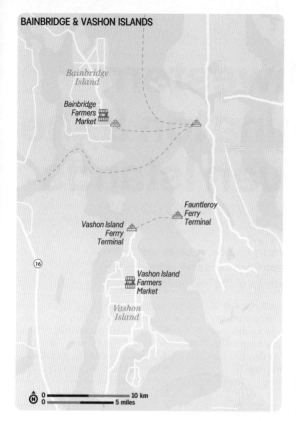

Bainbridge Island

Bainbridge Farmers Market

Fauntleroy Ferry Terminal

Vashon Island Ferry Terminal

16

Vashon Island Farmers Market

Vashon Island

0   10 km
0   5 miles

BEST PLACES TO EAT ON VASHON ISLAND

May Kitchen + Bar
Authentic Thai food is served in an intimate setting featuring intricately carved wood decor. **$$**

Zamorana
It has a great wet burrito and housemade salsa. Authentic Mexican served with a friendly smile. **$$**

Pop Pop Bottle Shop
Craft beer and a curated wine list at this family-friendly teriyaki shop connected to an ice creamery. **$$**

has a rich agricultural history, so it's likely that the vendors are the farmers themselves. Artisanal goods like handmade soaps and candles that make great gifts for friends and family back home can also be found.

The **Bainbridge Island farmers market**, on the other hand, is larger with around 40 vendors, but offers a slightly calmer atmosphere. Situated in a picturesque location by the water, the market provides stunning views of the surrounding area while you browse the stalls. Here, you'll find a wide variety of organic vegetables and herbs, as well as baked goods, crafts, and locally made wine and cider.

WHERE TO EAT ON BAINBRIDGE ISLAND

Ba Sa Restaurant
Modern Vietnamese made with locally sourced ingredients, in an elegant setting. **$$**

Proper Fish
Casual spot serving British-style fish and chips, complete with minted peas and thick-cut fries. **$$**

HiLife Chopsticks Stand
Quick and casual poke-by-the-pound and Japanese dishes like curry and rice. Also has sake, beer and Toki highballs. **$$**

Northwestern Washington & the San Juan Islands

PRISTINE PARKS, ISLANDS AND COASTAL TOWNS

A region spanning dreamy islands, endless waterways, fertile farmlands and snowy mountains, Northwestern Washington is the epitome of the Pacific Northwest.

North of Seattle, south of Canada and west of the Cascade Mountains, Washington's greatest hits are concentrated into a single archetypal region. Northwestern Washington has it all: hundreds of islands decorate the Salish Sea, connected by evergreen forests, farmlands and winding scenic highway to 10,781ft Mt Baker. Not to mention the abundant homegrown produce, seafood and locally brewed beer.

Bellingham is the Northwest's regional hub, a mainland city nestled between Seattle and Vancouver, BC. Once an industrial logging port and pulp mill site, its revitalized historic waterfront is now a public park, bike playground and seasonal beer garden – the most 'Bellingham' place imaginable in a city that typifies the greater Northwest. Bellinghamsters revere Mt Baker, a glaciated volca-

no known for its no-frills ski area and subalpine summer hikes.

Further west, Fidalgo and Whidbey Island stretch south into Puget Sound. These drive-on islands, connected to the mainland by bridges and ferries, act as transition zones between frantic city life and chilled-out island time. Plentiful parks and public lands entice city folk with beaches, seaside trails and copious campgrounds.

Perhaps the Northwest's most sought-after destination, the contested San Juan Islands might have ended up in Canada had the notorious Pig War played out differently. Nationality aside, the islands of San Juan, Orcas and Lopez are melting pots of Northwest arts, culture and farm-to-table foods. From leisurely whale-watching to oyster-slurping, time has a way of slowing down in the islands.

LIJUAN GUO/GETTY IMAGES ©

THE MAIN AREAS

BELLINGHAM
Bike-friendly, beer-loving bayside city.
p90

ANACORTES
Seaside port town and trails.
p98

WHIDBEY ISLAND
Pastoral parks and farms.
p102

SAN JUAN ISLANDS
Emerald islands, marine life and epic sunsets.
p105

NORTHWESTERN WASHINGTON & THE SAN JUAN ISLANDS

EDMUND LOWE PHOTOGRAPHY/SHUTTERSTOCK ©

Left: Orca (p105), San Juan Islands; Above: Chuckanut Drive (p95)

Find Your Way

Stretching some 100 road miles from Whidbey Island to the US–Canada border, Northwestern Washington is made up of mainland port towns, coastal cities and the San Juan Islands – all connected by the Salish Sea.

CAR

Driving a car is the best way to get around. Traffic is relatively breezy, parking is generally easy to find (passes required for state parks and national forests), and you can drive onto the ferries.

BOAT

Getting out on the salt water is an essential Northwestern Washington experience. Take a scenic ferry ride from Anacortes to the San Juan Islands, join a whale-watching cruise, or go sailing in Bellingham Bay.

Bellingham, p90

Spend your time on the water, in the mountains or sipping craft beer by the bay in outdoorsy Bellingham.

Anacortes, p98

Explore artsy Anacortes' historic streets and seaside trails before hopping on a ferry to the San Juan Islands.

San Juan Islands, p105

Experience a slower pace of life in an archipelago where marine wildlife, historic parks and farm-to-table dining are among the countless charms.

Whidbey Island, p102

Discover easily accessible Whidbey Island, 169 sq miles of dramatic vistas, pastoral landscapes and fascinating history between Seattle and the San Juans.

Lime Kiln Lighthouse (p107), San Juan Island

Plan Your Time

Northwestern Washington balances its laid-back lifestyle with active, outdoor adventures. Take your time exploring, especially while on 'island time' in the low-key San Juans.

Pressed for Time

Choose **Bellingham** (p90)or the **San Juan Islands** – not both. In Bellingham, cruise along **Chuckanut Drive** (p95), go paddling or sailing in **Fairhaven** (p92) and walk the downtown waterfront at **Waypoint Park** (p90). For San Juan Islands day trips, choose just one island to maximize your time. **San Juan Island** (p105) and **Orcas** (p108) offer the most bang for your buck.

A Weeklong Stay

Spend a day hiking or skiing at **Mt Baker** (p94), sample local produce at **Skagit Valley** farms (p101) and explore the beaches of **Deception Pass State Park** (p99). Take a hike in **Anacortes** (p98) before ferrying to the San Juan Islands. Watch for whales at **Lime Kiln Point State Park** (p107), then survey the Salish Sea from Orcas Island's **Mt Constitution** (p109).

Seasonal Highlights

SPRING	SUMMER	FALL	WINTER
Daffodils and tulips bloom in the **Skagit Valley** during spring – one of the best times to visit, despite the rain.	Wonderful weather, whale-watching opportunities in the islands and seasonal hiking trails at **Mt Baker**.	Harvest season, fall colors, and the return of rain means shorter days and dwindling crowds.	Winter can be dark and wet, but prices fall during low season and the snow is legendary at **Mt Baker**.

Bellingham

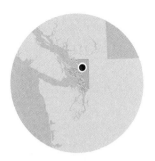

GETTING AROUND

Bellingham is best navigated by car, with plenty of paid parking downtown and in Fairhaven. Walkers and cyclists will encounter some hills, but it's easy to get around the urban centers by foot or bike. Local Whatcom Transportation Authority buses run frequently between downtown and Fairhaven.

☑ **TOP TIP**

Consider bringing (or renting) a bike to get around Bellingham, where bike lanes and parking are widely available. The 2.5-mile, cyclist-friendly South Bay Trail connects downtown Bellingham to Fairhaven. From there, the mostly flat Interurban Trail runs south for 6 miles above Chuckanut Dr to Larrabee State Park.

A bayside college town between Vancouver and Seattle, Bellingham (population 95,960) is undeniably influenced by its metropolitan neighbors. Yet this urban hub of Northwest Washington strikes a rare balance between big-city variety and small-town charm. You'll find a melting pot of regional attractions here, from coffee shops and breweries on nearly every corner to abundant seafood, live music and outdoor adventures.

Historically home to the Lummi people, Bellingham Bay attracted settlers in the 19th century due to its abundant natural resources. Those same resources – namely ancient forests and waterways – attract residents and recreationists to this day. Hikers, pedalers and paddlers embrace Bellingham's Cascade Mountain foothills and Salish Sea shoreline.

For all of its active pursuits, Bellingham is surprisingly laid-back. You can easily spend an entire day lounging in seaside parks, strolling historic streets, or tasting your way around town. This choose-your-own-adventure destination can be savored at any speed.

Bikes & Beer by the Bay

A microcosm of Bellingham life

Bellingham's downtown waterfront opened to the public in 2018 with the creation of **Waypoint Park**. Sea-starved locals dip their toes in the salt water at this rocky urban beach where Whatcom Creek empties into Bellingham Bay. The nearby **Acid Ball** – a 430,000lb pulp mill vessel – reminds parkgoers of the waterway's industrial past.

Dredging of the Whatcom Waterway led to heavy industrial development in Bellingham in the early 1900s. Pulp and tissue mills boomed on the waterfront for decades, supporting the economy but cutting off public access to Bellingham Bay. The last mill shuttered in 2007, leaving behind a century of contamination. After a $35 million environmental cleanup

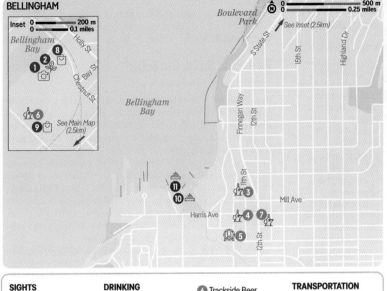

BELLINGHAM

Inset

Bellingham Bay

Boulevard Park

See Inset (2.5km)

Bellingham Bay

See Main Map (2.5km)

Harris Ave

Mill Ave

SIGHTS
1 Acid Ball
2 Waypoint Park

DRINKING & NIGHTLIFE
3 Avenue Bread - Fairhaven
4 Fairhaven Poke
5 Fairhaven Stones Throw Brewery

6 Trackside Beer Garden
7 The Black Cat

SHOPPING
8 Granary Building
9 Portal Container Village

TRANSPORTATION
10 Bellingham Cruise Terminal/Ferry Terminal Long-Term Parking
11 Community Boating Center

project, the Port of Bellingham is actively redeveloping and restoring access to this former industrial site.

Stop by the historic **Granary Building** for coffee, ice cream or a glass of mead. Then stroll southwest along Granary Ave to the **Portal Container Village**. A bustling seasonal destination from late spring through early autumn, the Portal's main attractions are its bike park and beer garden. It doesn't get more Bellingham than this. Bring your bicycle (or rent one from onsite Sun-E-Land Bikes) to ride the free, public pump track. While most Portal businesses close during winter, the pump track is open year-round.

Adjacent to the bike park is Kulshan Brewing's 25,000 sq ft **Trackside Beer Garden**. Families sprawl out on Trackside's massive lawn to watch live music during the summer months. Various vendors – from food and drink to putt-putt golf –

 WHERE TO SLEEP IN BELLINGHAM

Heliotrope Hotel
Comfy rooms and huge communal lawn in renovated 1950s inn. Artsy, outdoorsy, oh-so-Bellingham. **$$**

Hotel Leo
Modern and historic hotel rooms in downtown Bellingham, plus theater, library and Prohibition-era bar. **$$$**

Fairhaven Village Inn
Charming harbor-view and village-view rooms in the highly walkable Fairhaven district. **$$**

BEST BREWPUBS IN BELLINGHAM

Otherlands Beer
Cozy cafe serving European-inspired street food alongside rustic lagers and saisons. Don't miss the indulgent weekend brunch menu. **$$**

El Sueñito Brewing
Super-satisfying tamales and tacos complement sessionable brews at this inclusive and Mexican-owned brewery. Expect a line on weekends. **$$**

Structures Brewing
Bellingham's legendary IPA brewer offers drive-in-style burgers and fried chicken sandwiches at its Old Town location. **$$**

Aslan Brewing
Aslan pairs house-made beer with fusion flavors at two downtown locations. The brewpub is best for groups and families; head to the Depot for a quieter experience. **$$**

Larrabee Lager Co.
Wash down some of the best pizza in town with traditional German-inspired lagers at this community beer hall. **$$**

operate out of shipping containers in the shadow of towering digester tanks. Some of Bellingham's biggest annual events take place here, including the April Brews Day beer festival and Northwest Tune-up – a bike, music and beer fest held in July.

Paddles, Sails, Sin & Gin
Salty adventures in Fairhaven

Best known for its handsome brick buildings, relaxed restaurants and walkable historic blocks, Fairhaven is a Victorian-era dream district. But don't be fooled by its prim and proper facade – these cobblestone streets were once teeming with brothels, saloons and all kinds of colorful characters. Founded by 'Dirty Dan Harris' in 1883, Fairhaven has some salty tales to tell. Learn more about the town's seedy history on a 'Sin and Gin' walking tour with the **Good Time Girls**.

These days, Fairhaven is more laid-back and respectable. Perched above Bellingham Bay with easy access to the Chuckanut Mountains, the south-side district is Bellingham's unofficial outdoor adventure hub.

Follow Harris Ave west to get out on the water. If you have your own gear, Marine Park's popular beach is the best launching spot for paddleboards and kayaks. The nearby **Community Boating Center** offers affordable rentals and paddling trips for all experience levels. Their summer bioluminescence paddles are simply magical and should be booked well in advance. **Moondance Sea Kayaking** runs guided tours – from evening paddles to multiday trips – launching from Fairhaven and Larrabee State Park.

If sailing is more your speed, book a cruise on the 160ft **Schooner Zodiac**. Built as a private yacht in 1924, this century-old vessel hosts brunch and dinner sails, beer cruises and multiday San Juan Island adventures. Another good option is **San Juan Cruises**, whose narrated whale-watching tours guarantee a sighting. They offer everything from beer, wine,and dinner sailings to a tufted puffin bird-watching cruise. Schooner Zodiac and San Juan Cruises both depart from the **Bellingham Cruise Terminal** in Fairhaven.

 WHERE TO DINE & DRINK IN BELLINGHAM

The Black Cat
'Le Chat Noir' serves classic cocktails and bistro fare from its 3rd-floor perch in the historic Sycamore Building. **$$**

Fairhaven Poke
High-quality Hawaiian-style poke bowls, best enjoyed to-go at Fairhaven Village Green or the local brewery. **$**

Stones Throw Brewery
Constructed from shipping containers with a variety of covered outdoor seating. **$**

Beyond Bellingham

Langley
Blaine • Abbotsford
Drayton • Lynden Maple Falls
Harbor
Ferndale •
Mt Baker
Bellingham
Fairhaven •
Bow

From hiking and skiing at Mt Baker to scenic drives along the Salish Sea, day trips abound around Bellingham.

Bellingham is defined by its access to the outdoors. To fully experience these diverse landscapes and waterways, you'll want to get out of the city. Head east on Hwy 542 toward Mt Baker – the North Cascades' landmark volcano – for legendary winter snowfall and sublime summer hiking. By traveling northwest from Bellingham, you'll end up in Blaine, Semiahmoo and Birch Bay. These Salish Sea destinations offer waterfront parks and fresh seafood away from the big city. Finally, cruise south from Fairhaven along scenic Chuckanut Dr. Soaring island views are the highlight of this historic highway, cut from sea cliffs some 200ft above the water. Not to mention the beaches, forested trails and abundant eateries.

GETTING AROUND

You'll need a car to get around outside of Bellingham. If visiting state parks, bring a Discover Pass for parking. National forests require a separate Northwest Forest Pass. Purchase one-day or annual parking passes at ranger stations, outdoor retailers and some grocery stores.

☑ TOP TIP

Whether heading to the mountains or the beach, savvy Northwesterners always dress in layers. Check the forecast and plan accordingly.

DENE MILES/SHUTTERSTOCK ©

Heather Meadows and Table Mountain, Mt Baker Ski Area (p96)

UPPER LEFT STATE PARKS

Two Washington State Parks grace the northwest corner of Whatcom County. The northernmost, **Peace Arch Historical State Park**, is right on the US–Canada border. You'll drive through it to cross into British Columbia. Walk across manicured lawns for a photo op with the Peace Arch itself – a 67ft symbol of peaceful relations constructed in 1921. Just don't wander too far north without a passport.

South of Blaine and Semiahmoo, **Birch Bay State Park** is one of Washington's finest beach parks with 8255ft of saltwater shoreline. Locals spend hours (or days) at the sprawling beach picnicking, swimming and camping.

Check the Washington State Parks website before your trip for camping reservations, hours and parking pass requirements.

Drayton Harbor

TIME FROM BELLINGHAM: **30 MINS**

Seaside and seafood from Blaine to Semiahmoo

Just a half-hour drive from Bellingham, **Blaine** and **Semiahmoo Spit** are worth a day trip for some leisurely seaside exploration. Originally inhabited by the Semiahmoo people, the lands encircling Drayton Harbor developed in the mid-19th century as fishing and canning industries took hold. The harbor remains a commercial fishing hub and seafood destination to this day.

Begin your tour in the tiny border town of Blaine – the last I-5 exit before crossing into Canada. Free street parking is available along tree-lined Peace Portal Dr and at nearby **Marine Park**. The park's pleasant walking paths lead to an impressive waterfront playground, plus views north to White Rock, BC, and the Peace Arch border crossing.

Drayton Harbor is best experienced by getting out on the water. Seasonal ferry rides run from Blaine Harbor Marina to Semiahmoo Spit. Hop on Washington's oldest foot-passenger ferry, the *Plover,* for a fun harbor tour. Built in 1944 to shuttle cannery workers across Drayton Harbor, the restored 17-passenger vessel runs 15–20-minute round-trip rides during summer weekends.

Once you reach the mile-long Semiahmoo Spit (also accessible by car), grab a bite at **Semiahmoo Resort** or walk the beach to **Semiahmoo Park**. Formerly dominated by the world's largest salmon cannery, the spit is now a vacation destination for birders, families and burned-out city folk. Check out the **Alaska Packers Association** cannery museum (open summer weekends only) for a self-guided historical tour.

Mt Baker

TIME FROM BELLINGHAM: **90 MINS**

A scenic drive to Artist Point

Summer at Mt Baker is spectacular. Subalpine trails lead through forests and wildflower meadows to glacier-clad mountain views. It's heaven for hikers, and road-trippers can enjoy the scenery without bringing boots or a backpack. Stock up on essentials in Bellingham, Maple Falls or Glacier before heading further east. The **Glacier Public Service Center** sells books, maps and required parking passes. Beyond Glacier, services (including cell-phone service) are very limited.

The 57-mile Mt Baker Scenic Byway begins near sea level in Bellingham and terminates at the mile-high **Artist Point** parking lot. This winding mountain road quickly leaves the city behind, transitioning from blueberry fields to old-growth forests. Built gradually in the late 1800s as a logging road,

WHERE TO EAT AROUND DRAYTON HARBOR

Drayton Harbor Oyster Co
Slurp the freshest tide-tumbled Pacific oysters from this restaurant's sunny harbor-view patio. **$$**

Bordertown Mexican Grill
Come for the fish tacos; stay for the quick, friendly service at this cheery takeout spot with outdoor seating. **$**

Packers Kitchen & Bar
Semiahmoo Resort's waterfront restaurant serves brunch and dinner, with local seafood and libations. **$$$**

Chuckanut Dr Scenic Byway – a roughly 22-mile serpentine route carved from the Chuckanut Mountains – begins in **1 Fairhaven**. Follow Hwy 11 south to **2 Woodstock Farm**, a historic estate perched over Chuckanut Bay. Woodstock offers peaceful trails and gorgeous saltwater views.

Continue south to **3 Larrabee State Park** for beach access, hiking and camping at Washington's first state park. The 4-mile round-trip hike to **Fragrance Lake** begins here. Prepare for 1000ft of climbing through evergreen forest to reach the lake.

From Larrabee State Park's Lost Lake parking lot, take the short trail to **Clayton Beach**. A pedestrian bridge spans the railroad tracks, leading to one of Washington's rare sandy beaches. Some of Chuckanut Dr's finest scenic viewpoints (and tightest turns) are south of Larrabee State Park. Stop at any of the pullouts for views across Samish Bay to the San Juan Islands. **4 Dogfish Point** is one of the best.

The bumpy road leading to **5 Taylor Shellfish Farms** is a must for oyster lovers. Operating as both a retail market and oyster bar, you can grab fresh seafood to go or enjoy a feast at Taylor's bayside picnic area.

Still hungry? A minor detour off the main route, **6 Edison** deserves a mention for its unusually high number of eateries per capita. A tiny artisan town, Edison is easily walkable. You can spend all day eating and drinking here, from highly sought-after baked goods at Breadfarm to housemade beer and cocktails at Terramar Brewstillery.

Returning to Chuckanut Dr from Edison, head back to Bellingham or continue south – through Skagit Valley flatlands – to the end of the drive in **7 Burlington**.

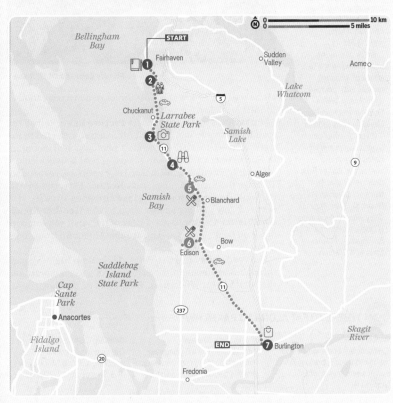

WORLD RECORD SNOWFALL

Mt Baker is a powder paradise in winter. Known for its world-record snowfall (1140in in the 1998–99 season), **Mt Baker Ski Area** was one of the first West Coast slopes to allow snowboarding. Today, it's all about no-frills skiing and snowboarding. The ski area operates only eight lifts, with no resort town or overnight accommodations to speak of. Lessons, rentals and food are available at White Salmon and Heather Meadows day lodges.

If you'd rather catch a ride than brave Mt Baker Hwy in the winter, the **Baker Bus** provides round-trip transportation to Mt Baker Ski Area. It runs daily when the ski area is open, with stops in Bellingham, Maple Falls and Glacier.

IMAGE SOURCE/GETTY IMAGES ©

Picture Lake and Mt Shuksan

Mt Baker Hwy is now the most direct route to recreation at 10,781ft Mt Baker.

Most visitors make a beeline for **Picture Lake**. Pull off the road for an iconic shot of 9131ft Mt Shuksan reflected in the waters. Sometimes called the most photographed mountain in North America, Shuksan's rugged appeal is undeniable.

The first 55 miles of Mt Baker Hwy are open year-round. To drive the final 2.5 miles from Heather Meadows to Artist Point – by far the road's most jaw-dropping stretch – visit between July and September. Stop by the **Heather Meadows Visitor Center** to get the lay of the land; you can peer down on Bagley Lakes and up at Table Mountain from an interpretive overlook.

The road ends at Artist Point. There's no highway pass through these mountains – just miles of national forest and the Mount Baker Wilderness. Walk south on the short, paved

WHERE TO EAT ALONG MT BAKER HWY

Wake 'N Bakery
'Get sconed' at the go-to spot for baked goods, breakfast burritos and trail snacks in Glacier. **$**

North Fork Brewery
Locals drive from Bellingham for North Fork's pizza and beer. Always packed, but worth the wait. **$$**

Graham's Bar & Restaurant
Old-fashioned pub in a 1906 building, serving Glacier off-and-on since the 1970s. **$$**

Artist Ridge trail for a panoramic overlook. A glaciated volcano, Mt Baker dominates the western skyline. Mt Shuksan rises to the east in North Cascades National Park, illuminated by alpenglow at sunset.

Choose Your Trail

Hiking around Mt Baker

Hikers can experience everything from a joyous jaunt to epic, multiday backpacking trips around Mt Baker. Several short hikes are accessible from the paved highway. **Horseshoe Bend Trail** is a forested, 3-mile round-trip walk along the Nooksack River, just outside of Glacier. Another easy hike, the **Bagley Lakes Trail** begins at Heather Meadows Visitor Center for a 2-mile lakeside loop among summer wildflowers.

A 1-mile lollipop loop, **Artist Ridge Trail** is the most popular hike on the mountain. Beginning at Artist Point, it climbs gently to Huntoon Point for incredible views of Mts Baker and Shuksan. **Chain Lakes Loop** begins from the same parking lot, showcasing a series of picturesque lakes along its 6.5-mile route.

Rough, unpaved forest roads branch off from Mt Baker Hwy to some of the best hiking trails in Washington. Bring a high-clearance vehicle to reach these. At a 7.5 miles round trip with 2500ft of elevation gain, **Yellow Aster Butte** is among the most sought-after. The 10.4-mile round trip up **Hannegan Peak** is another challenging route with 3100ft of elevation gain. Both trails pay off with 360-degree views of North Cascades peaks and valleys from over 6000ft in the sky.

Trails around Mt Baker are typically accessible between July and early October. Check with the Forest Service (fs.usda.gov/mbs) for road and trail conditions before setting out. A Northwest Forest Pass is required for parking at national forest trailheads.

ANNUAL EVENTS AT MT BAKER

Mt Baker hosts two big annual events during snow season. In February, snow-sports enthusiasts flock to the ski area to witness the **Legendary Banked Slalom** race. Started by 16 snowboarders in 1985, it's one of the sport's longest-running events and draws world-class competitors.

Every Memorial Day Weekend in May, the **Ski to Sea** race – a multisport team relay – begins at Mt Baker Ski Area and ends 93 miles away at Bellingham Bay. Racers compete in cross-country skiing and downhill ski/snowboard legs at Mt Baker before running and road biking down Mt Baker Hwy. First run in 1973, Ski to Sea is the largest one-day event in Whatcom County.

Anacortes

GETTING AROUND

Fidalgo Island and Anacortes are best reached by car. You can drive onto the island via Hwy 20 from the mainland or via the Deception Pass bridge from Whidbey Island. Skagit Transit buses run from Mt Vernon to Anacortes, La Conner, and the San Juan ferry terminal. Ferries depart daily from Anacortes to the San Juan Islands.

☑ TOP TIP

Art in all forms – from murals to music – is abundant throughout Anacortes. The city celebrates its local artists during the Anacortes Art Festival in August. Drawing some 90,000 visitors and spanning several city blocks, the fest features hundreds of art booths, plus gallery events and live entertainment.

Anacortes is the gateway to the San Juan Islands. Sometimes dismissed as a pass-through ferry port, the maritime city has evolved into a worthy destination of its own. Spend some time exploring Anacortes' attractive downtown, beautiful beaches and huckleberry-lined trails and you may just skip the ferry altogether.

Connected to the mainland by twin bridges, Anacortes is located at the northern end of Fidalgo Island. These lands were long inhabited by the Samish and Swinomish peoples before white settlers arrived. Railroad surveyor Amos Bowman founded Anacortes in 1879, naming the settlement after his wife, Anne Curtis. Anacortes showcases its history through colorful cutout murals by local artist Bill Mitchell; over 150 of them are displayed around town.

Despite decades of logging, fishing and oil refining, Fidalgo Island retains its natural beauty. Eagles soar overhead and harbor seals bob offshore. Exploring Fidalgo's parks and trails is an exercise in slowing down and transitioning to island life.

Seaside Parks & Trails

Exploring Fidalgo Island's public lands

From state and city parks to the 3000-acre **Anacortes Community Forest Lands** (ACFL), a sizable share of Fidalgo Island is public land. Hikers and park-goers are spoiled with easy access to the lakes, mountains and beaches of Anacortes.

Get the lay of the land at **Cap Sante Park**, a rocky knoll 200ft above sea level. A five-minute drive from downtown Anacortes, Cap Sante overlooks the marina and offers views east to Mt Baker. It's a serene spot for picnics and sunsets.

Follow Hwy 20 west, past the ferry dock turnoff, to **Washington Park** for beach access, camping and miles of hiking trails. Driving the one-way loop – with its numerous pullouts

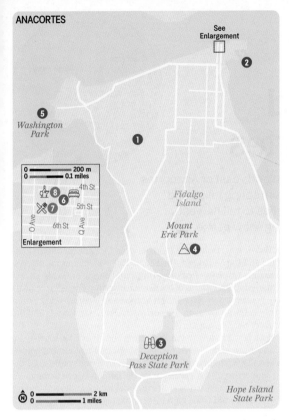

ANACORTES

See Enlargement

Washington Park

Fidalgo Island

Mount Erie Park

Deception Pass State Park

Hope Island State Park

Enlargement

0 — 200 m
0 — 0.1 miles

4th St
5th St
6th St
O Ave
Q Ave

0 — 2 km
0 — 1 miles

---

and viewpoints – affords west-facing views of the San Juan Islands.

South of Anacortes, 1273ft **Mt Erie** is the island's high point. Drive (or hike) to the top for bird's-eye views of Fidalgo and Whidbey islands. Trails from Mt Erie connect to sister peak Sugarloaf and nearby Whistle Lake – a popular summer swimming hole. Be aware that the confusingly numbered ACFL trail system is nearly impossible to navigate without a map. Print a map from the City of Anacortes website, or purchase one from the visitor information center in town to get around.

Fidalgo Island shares its most famous park with Whidbey Island. Linked by the iconic Deception Pass bridge, both islands are home to the sprawling **Deception Pass State Park**. On the Fidalgo side, stop by **Rosario Head** for a short walk to epic sea cliffs. Hike or drive from Rosario to Bowman Bay, a picturesque picnic area and boat launch. Trekking south from Bowman Bay leads to Lottie Point and Lighthouse Point – scenic sea bluff trails through evergreen forest and Pacific madrone.

SIGHTS

1 Anacortes Community Forest Lands North
2 Cap Sante Park
3 Deception Pass State Park
4 Mt Erie
5 Washington Park

SLEEPING

6 Majestic Inn & Spa

EATING

7 GERE-a-DELI

DRINKING & NIGHTLIFE

8 Brown Lantern

WHERE TO EAT & SLEEP IN ANACORTES

GERE-a-DELI
Bustling breakfast and lunch spot known for its loaded deli sandwiches, soups, salads and desserts. **$**

Brown Lantern
Exposed-beam ale house serving Anacortes since 1933. Extensive pub grub menu featuring local beer and wine, cocktails, and classic fish and chips. **$$**

Adrift Restaurant
Satisfy your seafood cravings with Adrift's Dungeness crab cakes, gluten-free fish tacos, and burgers made with wild cod, salmon, or oysters. **$$**

Majestic Inn & Spa
Centrally located boutique hotel in a restored 1890 hardware store building. During summer, take the elevator to its impressive rooftop lounge for drinks and dining. **$$$**

Beyond
Anacortes

The Skagit Valley farmlands east of Anacortes delight year-round, from spring tulips and bountiful summer berries to fall harvest festivities and wintering snow geese.

☑ **TOP TIP**

Expect traffic if visiting Skagit Valley during the spring Tulip Festival. Go early, late or during weekdays to avoid crowds.

A thriving agricultural region between Cascade Mountain foothills and the Salish Sea, the Skagit Valley is famous for flowers. Dazzling displays of colorful tulips and sunny daffodils attract hundreds of thousands of tourists each spring. These fertile fields are bookended by riverside Mt Vernon and channel-side La Conner – gateway towns to Anacortes, the San Juan Islands and the greater Skagit Valley.

Both historic downtown Mt Vernon and charming, touristy La Conner are highly walkable with shops and restaurants galore. The valley's namesake Skagit River – Washington's only major river supporting all five species of Pacific salmon – flows through Mt Vernon, giving life to the entire region. Visit the valley's abundant farmstands and fields for a taste of the region in every season.

Skagit Valley Tulip Festival

Skagit Valley

TIME FROM ANACORTES: **25 MINS** 🚗

Farms, food & flowers through the seasons

Between La Conner and Mt Vernon, the lower Skagit River Valley thrives in every season. Visit its fertile farms for spring tulips, bountiful summer berries, fall harvest festivities and wintering snow geese.

During spring, flowers reign supreme in Skagit Valley. The season kicks off in March with **La Conner Daffodil Festival**, a celebration of bright yellow blooms. In April, the famous **Skagit Valley Tulip Festival** draws massive crowds to the rural roads between La Conner and Mt Vernon. Visit one of the ticketed display gardens for the best experience. Both **Roozengaarde** and **Tulip Town** burst with colorful tulip fields and offer endless photo opportunities.

In summer and autumn, Skagit Valley farms produce abundant fruits and veggies. Over 90 different crops are grown in Skagit County, including blueberries, raspberries, strawberries and potatoes. Taste your way across the valley with farm visits – from produce stands to pumpkin fields.

Overflowing with local produce, flowers and 'immodest' ice-cream cones, **Snow Goose Produce** – an open-air country market – is an essential stop. **Schuh Farms** offers u-pick berry fields during summer, plus smoothies, milkshakes and pies made with their own fruit. During autumn, Schuh Farms transitions into a pumpkin patch with hayrides and harvest activities.

Winter is slow season in the valley, but there are still reasons to visit. Tens of thousands of migratory snow geese winter in the flats around **Fir Island** between October and April. These literal snowbirds spend summers at Russia's Wrangel Island, some 3000 miles away. Bring long lenses and binoculars to spot their flocks among the fields.

SKAGIT VALLEY BREWS

Locally brewed beer is the beverage of choice in Skagit Valley. One of America's most celebrated lager brewers, **Chuckanut Brewery**, operates from a barn-red production facility and beer garden at the Port of Skagit. Skagit Valley College runs a brewing academy and tasting room next door at **Cardinal Craft Brewing**. And just down the street, **Garden Path Fermentation** uses barrel-aging and blending techniques to create unique oak-fermented brews.

Anacortes Brewery and **La Conner Brewing** have served classic Northwest beer in the valley since the mid-1990s. In downtown Mt Vernon, several breweries are within walking distance of one another. Start at **District Brewing**, an IPA-centric riverside brewpub housed in a historic theater. Pick up an ale trail passport (skagit-farmtopint.com) to discover the rest.

 ## WHERE TO EAT IN SKAGIT VALLEY

Skagit Valley Food Co-op
Natural groceries and cafe with fresh sandwiches, salads and smoothies in downtown Mt Vernon. $

La Conner Brewing
Brewpub serving West Coast–style beer and wood-fired pizza. If full, try nearby sister restaurant, The Firehall. $$

Calico Cupboard
Legendary local bakery and cafe chain. Treat yourself to a mountainous cinnamon roll or savory all-day breakfast. $$

Whidbey Island

GETTING AROUND

Whidbey is 58 miles long, from the Deception Pass bridge that connects to Fidalgo Island to the Clinton–Mukilteo ferry. That ferry connects Whidbey with Mukilteo on the mainland – just north of Seattle and Edmonds – about every half-hour. Mid-island, another ferry runs west from Coupeville to Port Townsend on the Olympic Peninsula every 1½ hours; reservations are taken and highly recommended in high season.

☑ TOP TIP

Whidbey Island has ample opportunities to get onto (or into) the water. Many rental houses and lodgings on Whidbey Island come with an assortment of watercraft – kayaks, canoes, paddleboards etc. You can also rent gear or take a guided tour or class with Whidbey Island Kayaking (whidbeyislandkayaking. com). Paddleboards, too!

Unspoilt Whidbey Island is the big spoon to Camano Island's little spoon, pastorally cradling the coast but attached in the north via the dramatic Deception Pass bridge. The oft-visited iconic steel marvel is breathtakingly juxtaposed over dark, rumbling seas, precariously placed in between impossibly steep forested cliffs. (Afraid of heights? Arrive via the gentle Mukilteo–Clinton ferry, located 45 minutes north of Seattle.)

As the fourth longest island in the continental US, the narrow terrain means unending beaches for kayaking, kiting or sea-glass foraging. In the north is Oak Harbor with its nearby (very loud!) naval air station. Southern Whidbey is far more rural and artsy, filled with 100-year-old farms and farm stands (so many farm stands!) and the postcard-worthy towns of Coupeville (the second oldest town in Washington) and Langley. Both are filled with shops, restaurants and art galleries. Plus, with relatively flat terrain, Whidbey is a road-tripper's or bicyclist's paradise.

Just bring earplugs.

Day-Tripping Whidbey Island

Drive through rural history

After arriving via the **Deception Pass** bridge, wave at the city of Oak Harbor as you drive through to **Ebey's Landing National Historic Reserve**. The first of its kind, the area preserves beaches, trails and the historic farmlands dating back to the 19th century. Wander the area's Kettle Trail, or stop by the beach (Discovery Pass required), where you can see a peek of the iconic **Admiralty Head Lighthouse**. At Fort Casey, you can hear the fighter jets from the Naval Air Station Whidbey Island overhead as you climb around the cannons and barracks, some dating back to 1897. Walk the Prairie Ridge Trail to see namesake settler Jacob Ebey's original home. The Ebeys arrived in the Pacific Northwest by way of the Oregon Trail (the pioneer wagon route, not the video game), and built the house

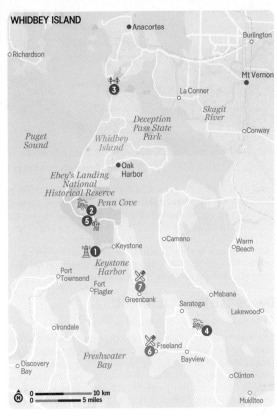

WHIDBEY ISLAND

- Anacortes
- Burlington
- o Richardson
- Mt Vernon
- La Conner
- *Skagit River*
- *Deception Pass State Park*
- *Puget Sound*
- *Whidbey Island*
- oConway
- Oak Harbor
- *Ebey's Landing National Historical Reserve*
- Penn Cove
- oCamano
- Warm oBeach
- oKeystone
- *Keystone Harbor*
- Port oTownsend
- Fort oFlagler
- Greenbank
- oMabana
- Saratoga o
- Lakewoodo
- oIrondale
- *Freshwater Bay*
- Freeland
- Bayview
- o Discovery Bay
- oClinton
- Mukilteo

0 — 10 km
0 — 5 miles

SIGHTS
1 Admiralty Head Lighthouse
2 Coupeville
3 Deception Pass Bridge
4 Ebey's Landing National Historic Reserve
5 Langley

EATING
6 Gordon's on Blueberry Hill
7 Greenbank Farm

in the 1850s. For sweeping views across the strait of San Juan de Fuca, hike the 3.2-mile Bluff Loop Trail.

Within the boundaries of the reserve is the fishing village of **Coupeville**, the second-oldest European-founded settlement in Washington. Peruse the galleries and shops, admire the Victorian architecture, or take a stroll on the antique pier. Then head to Greenbank Farms for pie; the restored farm now houses a cafe, cheese shop and art galleries along with an educational garden and pond, and several hiking trails. The next adorable village is **Langley**, where a postcard-worthy seafront downtown hosts shops and restaurants (the Braeburn serves delicious

CASCADES ROAD TRIPS

Although the terrain is radically different, the entire length of Whidbey Island holds up the western end of the mountainous **Cascade Loop Scenic Byway** (p146), one of the United States' most beautiful road trip destinations.

WHERE TO STAY ON WHIDBEY

Captain Whidbey Inn
As if an old salty dog ship's captain from 1907 turned himself into a cozy, quirky waterfront lodge. $$

Deception Pass State Park
Even with over 300 camping spaces, the views mean you need to book *now*. $

Blue Fox Drive-In Theater
Come for a movie (or three), and stay the night in your car, tent or camper. $

Deception Pass State Park bridge

WHIDBEY'S MOST DISTINCTIVE SPOTS

Kayaking
Launch from Clinton, Coupeville, Deception Pass State Park or any number of beaches for sea-to-mountain views. BYO kayak, rent one, or join a guided tour with Whidbey Island Kayaking.

Skein and Tipple
A skein's length from the Clinton ferry is a sustainable yarn store by day, hidden speakeasy with creative tipples by night. Their Fatter Elvis mixes banana liqueur with a peanut butter whiskey float.

The Blue Fox Drive-in Theater
Since 1959 locals have snuggled up for a double- (or triple-) feature. With a snack bar, arcade and go-kart track for kids and kids-at-heart. Camping options available.

comfort favorites on a quiet back patio). For dinner, stop by **Gordon's on Blueberry Hill** for local Penn Cove mussels and clams or squash hushpuppies and admire the view of the bay below. And, all the while, keep an eye out for the dozens of farm stands, large and small, that dot the entire island. From tiny family stands selling the area's dahlia flowers or berries to large markets selling produce, ice cream or meat, these stands help preserve the Whidbey way of life.

Deception Pass State Park

Breathtaking bridge and state park

As you witness the chaos and beauty of the churning waters below the bridge, you wouldn't know Deception Pass – the region, the bridge and the surrounding state park – is a microcosm of the history of the West Coast. That abundance of sea life (including the Pacific Northwest's beloved salmon) and rich soil across the island helped create a thriving population of Coast Salish peoples, including the Skagit and Snohomish. Captain George Vancouver missed the pass the first time round in 1792, and named it 'Deception Pass.'

In the 1930s Deception Pass became a ward of both the Civilian Conservation Corps (CCC) and the Works Progress Administration (WPA), President Franklin Roosevelt's New Deal projects that put millions of unemployed to work on public projects. While many visitors simply stop at the bridge, the peaceful 4134-acre park below has three lakes and over 15 miles of picturesque coast. The bridge (1935) actually came after the state park (1922), and you can still see remnants of the state park's past in CCC-built buildings (including an interpretative center about the New Deal projects on the Fidalgo side) and the **Cornet Bay Retreat Center**.

 FARMERS MARKETS ON WHIDBEY

Bayview Farmers Market
In Langley on Saturdays 10am to 2pm. Sells fresh produce and amazing food, plus artists, musicians and entertainment.

Coupeville Farmers Market
Also 10am to 2pm on Saturdays, located right in town and sells Whidbey produce, seafood, locally made soaps and crafts.

Tilth Farmers Market
The farm hosts a market on Sundays (11am–3pm), with activities for kids and a wide selection of organic produce.

San Juan Islands

Near the top of every Pacific Northwest bucket list are the San Juan Islands, an emerald archipelago made up of 172 named isles and reefs. Time slows down in the San Juans. Public lands preserve miles of shoreline and marine wildlife habitat here. Whale-watching from land is commonplace and sunsets are sublime.

There are no traffic lights to speak of in the San Juan Islands. No big box stores or chain restaurants. Just rural roads, pastoral farmlands and fiercely local businesses. Islanders are largely self-sustaining, relying on farming, fishing and tourism to support their economy.

Just four San Juan Islands are accessible by Washington State Ferries. San Juan Island, Orcas and Lopez are the main islands, while Shaw (the smallest and least populated) is typically skipped due to its lack of attractions. It's easy to spend several days – or even a lifetime – on a single island in the San Juans. Many residents have done just that.

Whale-Watching by Land & Sea

San Juan Island marine life

The most populous and developed of the islands, **San Juan Island** (also known by the name of its port town, Friday Harbor) is ground zero for whale-watching. Begin your journey in Friday Harbor with a trip to the **Whale Museum**. Opened in 1979, the museum's whale skeletons, videos and fascinating genealogy board tell the story of the endangered southern resident orcas (killer whales).

The most environmentally friendly way to see whales and other sea mammals is from land. The Whale Trail (thewhaletrail.org), a collection of over 100 shore-viewing sites along the Pacific Coast, designates a handful of viewing sites on San

GETTING AROUND

Most visitors travel to the San Juan Islands from Anacortes via Washington State Ferries. San Juan, Orcas, Lopez and Shaw are ferry-accessible. Make vehicle reservations online well before your trip. Passengers can also walk or bike onto the ferry, or fly with several airlines.

Once you reach the islands, it's easiest to get around by car. Many travelers bring bikes or rent them on-island. San Juan Transit and the Friday Harbor Jolley Trolley offer transportation to popular stops on San Juan Island. In Friday Harbor, Susie's Mopeds rents e-bikes, mopeds, and adorable two-seater 'scoot coupes' for cruising in style.

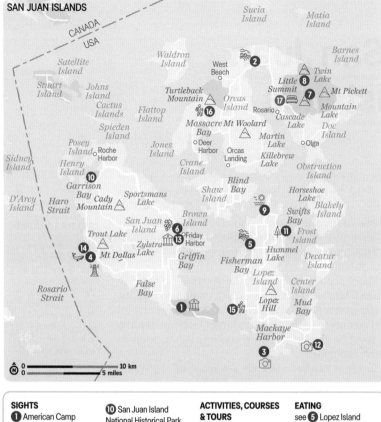

SAN JUAN ISLANDS

0   10 km
0   5 miles

SIGHTS
1 American Camp
2 Eastsound Village
3 Iceberg Point
4 Lime Kiln Lighthouse
5 Lopez Village
6 Madrone Cellars
7 Moran State Park
8 Mt Constitution
9 Odlin Park
10 San Juan Island National Historical Park
11 Spencer Spit State Park
12 Watmough Head
13 Whale Museum

ACTIVITIES, COURSES & TOURS
14 Lime Kiln State Park
15 Shark Reef Sanctuary
16 Turtleback Mountain Preserve

SLEEPING
see 5 Edenwild Inn
see 5 Lopez Islander Resort
17 Otter's Pond B&B

EATING
see 5 Lopez Island Creamery
see 5 Setsunai

SHOPPING
see 5 Lopez Village Market

WHERE TO SLEEP ON SAN JUAN ISLAND

San Juan County Park Campground
These 20 campsites between Lime Kiln and Roche Harbor are in high demand. **$**

Bird Rock Hotel
Central, Friday Harbor hotel within walking distance of the ferry dock. Some of the 15 rooms share bathrooms. **$$**

Roche Harbor Resort
Upscale options from historic cottages and Hotel de Haro rooms to luxe multi-bedroom homes and condos. **$$$**

Juan Island. **Lime Kiln State Park** (also known as 'Whale Watch Park') is one of the best places in the world to view orcas from land. Visit between May and September (and bring binoculars) for a chance to see southern resident orcas offshore.

From the park's rugged and rocky west-facing shoreline, scan the deepest channel in the San Juans. Haro Strait is home to gray whales, humpbacks, transients (Bigg's killer whales) and minke whales in addition to orcas. Even if you don't spot any wildlife, sunsets are guaranteed. The iconic **Lime Kiln Lighthouse**, built in 1919, offers interpretive information and volunteer-run tours in season.

Consider joining a responsible whale-watching tour to increase your orca-spotting odds. **Western Prince Whale and Wildlife Tours**, the San Juans' oldest whale-watching company, specializes in adventurous open-air excursions. **Maya's Legacy Whale Watching** offers small group tours (up to 16 guests) with less exposure to the elements. **San Juan Safaris** caters to larger groups and offers several vessel options, including the double-decker cabin cruiser, *Osprey*. Tours are an excellent way to learn about marine wildlife – onboard naturalists provide identification and stewardship suggestions along the way.

A Beef over Bacon

San Juan Island's Pig War

In the mid-1800s, a territorial dispute between Great Britain and the United States escalated rather quickly when a pig was shot and killed. Both sides claimed the San Juan Islands thanks to wishy-washy language in the 1846 Oregon Treaty. After 12 years of joint occupation, the 'Pig War' resolved peacefully. The San Juan Islands were awarded to America, and the war's only casualty was a single pig.

Today, **San Juan Island National Historical Park** is divided into two units at opposite ends of the island. Visit the **American Camp** visitor center, opened in 2022, for an introduction to the park's complex human history. Take a historic walk among the officer's quarters and parade grounds or follow interpretive signs to relive the Pig War.

Beyond military history, American Camp is worth visiting for its access to nature. With some luck, you may spot red and black foxes frolicking in the fields. Sweeping prairie lands slope down to driftwood-strewn South Beach – another Whale Trail site. Walk Mt Finlayson's 1.8-mile seaside bluff trail for Strait of Juan de Fuca views.

At the north end of San Juan Island, **English Camp**'s peaceful trails lead to formal gardens and historic buildings beside

ROCHE HARBOR HISTORY

At the north end of San Juan Island, seaside Roche Harbor was once the largest lime producer in the Pacific Northwest. The company town was built by Tacoma and Roche Harbor Lime Company founder John S McMillin in 1886 to support his enterprise. The lime kilns, hotel and historic structures still stand today, restored and transformed into stylish Roche Harbor Resort. Brick-lined paths lead to three unique eateries – from casual, dockside Lime Kiln Cafe to formal McMillin's Dining Room.

McMillin and his family are memorialized north of Roche Harbor at the **McMillin Memorial Mausoleum** (also known as Afterglow Vista). This otherworldly open-air rotunda features six chairs surrounding a limestone table, each containing the remains of a McMillin.

WHERE TO EAT ON SAN JUAN ISLAND

Bakery San Juan
Freshly baked goods, pizza and sandwiches served to-go. Stock up for island adventures or eat on the deck. $

San Juan Island Brewing
Island-brewed beer and pizza served in a modern, lofty space. Show up early for a table at dinnertime. $$

Duck Soup
Farm-to-table fine dining in a wooded, pondside environment. Locally sourced, from seafood to cocktails. $$$

WINING & DINING ON THE SAN JUAN ISLANDS

Cole Sisson, owner of Doe Bay Wine Company (@doebay winecompany), shares some of his San Juan favorites.

Setsunai, Lopez Island
Owner Josh Ratza offers handmade noodles and eclectic bowls featuring fresh ingredients from local farms with Asian influences. Get there early and enjoy sake on the deck.

Otter's Pond B&B, Orcas Island
These beautiful guestrooms are located a short walk from Moran State Park and feature gracious hospitality plus excellent home cooking from Chef Amanda Zimlich.

Madrone Cellars, San Juan Island
This little tasting room is a can't-miss when in Friday Harbor. Owners Shaun and Amy Salamida make both cider and wine from island orchards and it's truly inspiring.

STEVE LAGRECA/SHUTTERSTOCK ©

Turtleback Mountain Preserve

Garrison Bay. Watch the video in the visitor center (an old barracks building) to learn about the territorial dispute and its peaceful resolution.

Rural Roads, Parks & Preserves

Exploring Orcas Island

The largest and most mountainous of the San Juan Islands, rugged **Orcas Island** is beloved for its natural beauty. Rural roads connect seaside hamlets, with parks and preserves taking up much of the island's 57 sq miles. **Moran State Park** alone is home to over 30 miles of forested trails leading to lakes, waterfalls and island views.

Stretch your post-ferry sea legs with a hike at **Turtleback Mountain Preserve**. Less crowded than Moran State Park, the quiet natural area protects Garry oak woodlands, grasslands, forests and wetlands. Hikers can access over 8 miles of serene trails here. Start at the south trailhead (off Wild Rose Lane) for the 2.9-mile Ship Peak loop trail. The multi-use north trailhead (off Crow Valley Rd) permits horses and mountain bikes on alternate days.

Head to Orcas Island's center, **Eastsound Village**, for lunch, some shopping and a walk about town. This is where the art-

 WHERE TO STAY ON ORCAS ISLAND

Rosario Resort	**Moran State Park Campground**	**Doe Bay Resort**
Waterfront dining, spa services, a marina and a museum at Robert Moran's 1904-built mansion. **$$$**	Campsites near Mountain Lake and Cascade Lake are the cheapest – and most scenic. **$**	A true wellness retreat, serene Doe Bay offers camping, yurts and cabins, plus outdoor soaking tubs. **$$**

sy community displays its wares, from island-made ceramics to wine, spirits and galleries. Visit the **Saturday Farmers Market** (May–September) to peruse products grown by Orcas Island farmers and crafted by local artisans.

A drive (or heart-pounding hike) to the 2409ft summit of **Mt Constitution** is the quintessential Orcas Island experience. Located in Moran State Park, the highest point in the archipelago is topped with a 52ft, fortress-like stone tower built by the CCC in 1936. Ascend its steps for 360-degree views over the Salish Sea.

In 2021 a summer visitor center opened atop Mt Constitution in celebration of the park's 100th anniversary. Visit to learn about Coast Salish history, the park's namesake donor, and the fascinating ecology and geology of Orcas Island.

A Scenic Ride or Drive

Cruising around Lopez Island

Life on 'Slow-pez' is considerably more laid-back than San Juan or even Orcas Island. Passing motorists offer a nonchalant Lopezian wave on the friendly isle, where you're likely to see nearly as many bikes as cars. **Lopez Island** is best for park-hopping, quiet camping, and escaping the crowds on a Sunday ride or drive. This island is particularly cyclist-friendly due to its relatively flat terrain and ample bike parking.

Swing by **Odlin Park** for waterfront camping and beach access just 1 mile from the ferry dock. Then head south on Fisherman Bay Rd to **Lopez Village**, the humble island hub. Stock up on snacks at the market, grab a coffee or ice cream, then continue down-island. At **Shark Reef Sanctuary**, the 1-mile, family-friendly loop trail through forest wetlands leads to a secluded shoreline with west-facing water views. You may even spot seals hanging out on the rocks.

Continue to the island's southern end for additional hiking and wildlife-spotting opportunities at **Iceberg Point** and **Watmough Head**. Finally, turn your wheels north to **Spencer Spit State Park**. Cyclists may prefer to avoid Center Rd – a 'heavy traffic area' by Lopez standards. Upon arrival at Spencer Spit, pick out a campsite or head to the beach. Dual sand spits form a unique lagoon here, great for wandering, bird-watching and soaking up the serenity of Lopez Island.

WHERE TO EAT & STAY ON LOPEZ

Lopez Island Creamery
Small-batch creamery started on Lopez in the early 1980s. Their scratch-made ice cream is an essential island experience. **$**

Vortex Organic Juice Bar & Cafe
Fresh, raw juices and smoothies plus wraps, bowls, and salads made with seasonal, island-grown ingredients. **$**

Lopez Islander Resort
Sure it feels dated, but that's part of the charm at this classic Lopez destination offering hotel rooms, vacation homes and RV camping. Come for seafood and stay for sunset at Islander Bar and Grill. **$$**

Edenwild Inn
Victorian-style rooms and cottages located centrally in Lopez Village. On-site bike and kayak rentals available. **$$$**

 WHERE TO EAT ON ORCAS ISLAND

Brown Bear Baking
French-inspired cafe specializing in croissants, Orcas Island farm egg quiche and croque monsieur. **$**

Buck Bay Shellfish Farm
Fresh seafood market, bistro and wine bar serving oysters, clams and more from a shellfish farm in Olga. **$$**

Matia Kitchen and Monti
Acclaimed Matia (reservations recommended) and sister restaurant Monti (walk-ins) from Eastsound's firehall. **$$$**

Above: Rialto Beach (p114), Olympic National Park; Right: Barred owl, Olympic National Park (p114)

Olympic Peninsula & Washington Coast

DRIFTWOOD-STREWN COASTLINES, RAINFORESTS AND SNOWCAPPED PEAKS

With the Pacific on the west and Strait of Juan de Fuca to the north, you'll find the earth's quietest place, diverse ecosystems and Indigenous culture.

The Olympic Peninsula, located in the northwestern part of Washington state, features a landscape dominated by mountains that are still being lifted from the depth of the sea. At nearly 8000ft above sea level, the tallest peak in the Olympic Mountain range, Mt Olympus, is protected by Olympic National Park, a UNESCO World Heritage Site and International Biosphere Reserve.

Within the national park's million acres, a variety of ecosystems thrive: mountains, hot springs, over 73 miles of wild coastline, one of the last surviving temperate rainforests and the quietest place on earth. The Olympic Peninsula is also home to seven Native American reservations, the world's largest unmanaged herd of Roosevelt elk, lavender farms and the last remnants of virgin unexplored wilderness.

The Washington coast stretches from the town of Ocean Shores (north side of Gray's Harbor) to Cape Disappointment, where the Columbia River flows into the ocean. Compared to the Olympic Peninsula, the Washington coast is less rugged.

While the weather in Olympic Peninsula and the Washington coast is generally unpredictable, the southwest averages about 140in of rainfall in the lowlands and over 200in in the mountains, while the northeast averages only 15in of precipitation per year. July and August usually experience less rain than other months; however, this is the peak season and will be crowded.

JAN ZOETEKOUW PHOTOGRAPHY/GETTY IMAGES ©

THE MAIN AREAS

OLYMPIC NATIONAL PARK	OLYMPIA	LONG BEACH PENINSULA
Hike mountains, rainforests and coastlines in a day.	Washington state capital and artesian wells.	Kite-flying capital of the United States.
p114	p123	p127

Find Your Way

The Olympic Peninsula is northwest of Seattle in the state of Washington. The Washington coast stretches 157 miles along the Pacific Ocean. Hwy 101 gives you access to both.

Olympic National Park, p114

This park protects ancient cedar trees, coastal wilderness and one of the last surviving temperate rainforests.

Olympia, p123

Not only is this the capital of Washington state, but also the center of artistic expression and a progressive community.

Long Beach Peninsula, p127

With 28 miles of continuous beach, you can fish, horseback ride, kayak and attend a major kite festival.

CAR

Hwy 101 is a two-lane, well-paved highway. It takes about three hours or 145 miles to drive from Port Angeles (northern Olympic Peninsula) to Aberdeen (southern Olympic Peninsula).

FERRY

Washington State Ferries operates Seattle to Bainbridge Island and Kingston; Edmonds to Kingston; or Coupeville on Whidbey Island to Port Townsend. From Port Angeles, you can also sail to Victoria, BC.

PAUL JONES/ALAMY STOCK PHOTO ©

Sol Duc Hot Springs (p116), Olympic National Park

Plan Your Time

The Olympic Peninsula and Washington coast offers a variety of outdoor activities that are dependent on tide schedules or the weather, such as beachcombing, tide pooling, bird-watching, clamming and fishing.

Pressed for Time

Stay in **Olympia** (p123) or **Forks** (p121) if you can't find lodging inside of **Olympic National Park** (p114). From Seattle, drive about one to two hours to Olympia by taking I-5 South. Then work your way around Hwy 101 and make sure you give yourself enough time to spend a few hours at a beach like **Ruby** (p114).

A Week or More

More time means you can spend a day or two in each of the three different ecosystems in **Olympic National Park** (p114), stay at more than one historic lodge in the park, and soak in three different mineral pools at **Sol Duc Hot Springs** (p116). If you are a fan of Stephenie Meyer's *Twilight* series, spend a day in **Forks** (p121).

Seasonal Highlights

SPRING	SUMMER	FALL	WINTER
Wildflowers are blooming but snow might still be present at higher elevations. It's less crowded.	The most popular time of the year to visit. Expect crowds, warm, dry weather, and plenty of wildlife.	Less rainy than spring and less crowded than summer, autumn offers photographers stunning fall foliage.	Winter is a great time for snowshoeing, snowboarding and dramatic scenes of stormy coasts.

Olympic National Park

GETTING AROUND

While there is public transportation available to Port Angeles and Neah Bay through Clallam Transit, the best way to get around Olympic National Park is by renting a car or driving your own. Be aware that if you are visiting during peak season, parking lots at visitor centers and beaches and trails do fill up.

☑ TOP TIP

Be sure to check the National Park Service's Olympic National Park sites for 'Current Road Conditions' and 'Trail Conditions' or call 360-565-3131. Hurricane Ridge Rd has had quite a few closures due to the Hurricane Ridge Day Lodge catching on fire on May 7, 2023.

Olympic National Park is a special place; you can hike 60 glaciers, taste the salt of the wilderness coast, and get caught in a downpour in the wettest rainforest in the continental US. It's also home to a storied history, with over 650 archaeological sites, some dating back 13,800 years ago, shedding light on indigenous peoples who hunted mastodons, deer and elk here. The Hoh, Jamestown S'Klallam, Lower Elwha Klallam, Makah, Port Gamble S'Klallam, Quileute, Quinault and Skokomish peoples harvested red cedar for their longhouses and canoes here, surviving off the sea and harvesting plants.

When Europeans settled in the area in the 18th century, natural resources began to dwindle due to logging, hunting and fishing. This led to environmentalists and conservationists recognizing the park's unique geology and establishing the Olympic National Monument in 1909. This in turn led to its designation as a national park in 1938, and then as a UNESCO World Heritage Site in 1981.

Photograph Tide Pools & Sea Stacks

Beaches of Olympic National Park

Olympic National Park protects about 73 miles of coastline in partnership with three national wildlife refuges and the Olympic Coast National Marine Sanctuary. Tide pooling is best at Kalaloch's Beach 4, Rialto Beach's Hole-in-the-Wall, Second Beach, Third Beach and Ruby Beach. When the tide rolls back, you might find anemones, wolf eels, barnacles, clams, sea snails, sponges, starfish, hermit crabs and seaweed competing and cooperating in pools, alcoves and basins of rocks.

Named after the red gem-like fragments in the sand, **Ruby Beach** is the most family-friendly and accessible beach in Olympic National Park. The parking lot is generous and the quarter-mile trail down to the beach is wheelchair accessi-

OLYMPIC NATIONAL PARK

HIGHLIGHTS
❶ Glines Canyon
Overlook

SIGHTS
❷ Kalaloch Beach

❸ Madison Falls
❹ Marymere Falls
❺ Rialto Beach
❻ Ruby Beach
❼ Shi Shi Beach

**ACTIVITIES, COURSES
& TOURS**
❽ Hoh River Trail
❾ Hole-in-the-Wall
❿ Hurricane Ridge Ski &
Snowboard Area

EATING
⓫ Lake Crescent Lodge
⓬ Roosevelt Dining
Room
⓭ Springs Restaurant

ble. You'll need to scramble over driftwood to reach the sandy beach, so you might want to hike down in a pair of shoes that are more protective than flipflops, then switch shoes when you reach sand. Photographers should plan extra time to shoot the sea stacks (column of rocks rising out of the sea) at sunrise and sunset.

Kalaloch Beach has a ranger station, campground and lodge that are open year-round. Park in the Kalaloch Campground lot to see the Tree Root Cave or Tree of Life, a spruce that looks like it's suspended in mid-air between two cliffs with all its roots exposed above an eroding riverbed.

Shi Shi Beach is furthest north and can only be reached via an 8-mile round-trip trail. Don't forget to purchase both a National Forest Pass and a Makah Recreation Pass (available in Neah Bay) since Shi Shi Beach is on Makah tribal lands.

ARTHURHPHOTOGRAPHY/SHUTTERSTOCK ©

Rialto Beach

EVERYTHING YOU NEED TO KNOW ABOUT TIDE POOLS

When to Go
The best time is during a 'minus tide' that's lower than normal; look up tides lower than 1ft via the National Oceanic and Atmospheric Administration.

Getting There
Start from Olympic National Park visitor centers. Consult topographic maps to find safe routes and tide charts to find low tide (usually once daily).

Footwear
Wear closed-toe non-slip shoes with traction. Test any rocks that appear slippery.

Respect the Environment
Don't touch anything inside the tide pools, and leave nothing behind when you leave.

Pet Care
Sharp stone, barnacles and mussels can cut your pet's paws and lead to infection.

Don't Mind the Cold?

Winter adventures in Olympic National Park

The winter is less crowded in Olympic National Park and arguably more beautiful; you can snap iconic shots of the landscape without worrying about cropping or erasing photobombs. Check the weather in each ecosystem. While you might find a light dusting of snow, the forests and coastlines rarely drop below freezing. Waterfalls and rivers also flow at high volumes because of the rain; the easiest ones to access are **Marymere Falls** and **Madison Falls**. Similarly, the coastlines are more dramatic in the winter with swells fueled by rain, wind and tides that crash relentlessly upon the shores, especially Rialto Beach. The **Hole-in-the-Wall** is about a 4-mile hike from the Rialto Beach parking lot. Make sure you make this trek at low tide.

Olympic National Park has one of the few remaining ski lifts operating inside a national park where you can downhill and cross-country ski, snowboard and snowshoe. At an elevation of 5242ft, **Hurricane Ridge Ski and Snowboard Area** has 10 trails, a terrain park and tubing. Be sure to check for road closures and equip your tires with chains. There are also plenty of trails that you can hike in the winter with or without snowshoes. Rangers recommend that you bring extra layers, waterproof jackets and pants, as well as emergency supplies including food, water and first aid gear. Wait in your

WHERE TO STAY IN OLYMPIC NATIONAL PARK

Lake Crescent Lodge
This National Register of Historic Places lodge was built in 1915 upon a glacially carved lake. **$$$**

Sol Duc Hot Springs Resort
In the northern section of the park, this resort features hot spring pools. **$$$**

Lake Quinault Lodge
This National Register of Historic Places, built in 1926, features the best restaurant in the park. **$$$**

car at the Heart O' the Hills entrance station if the parking lot at Hurricane Ridge is full. Leave your pets at home since they aren't allowed in buildings or on snow trails at Hurricane Ridge. Don't feed the Canada jays.

Winter is also a great time to see salmon returning from the ocean to spawn in the park's streams. The Quinault River is a great location to see returning sockeye salmon, usually in November or December.

The Quietest Place in the United States

The Hoh Rain Forest

According to Gordon Hempton, a sound recording expert of natural soundscapes, the quietest place in the United States (that he is willing to reveal publicly) is located in the **Hoh Rain Forest** of Olympic National Park. Hempton marked a spot on a moss-covered log at N 48.12885°, W 123.68234° measuring 1 sq in on April 22, 2005, in celebration of Earth Day. Hempton called it 'One Square Inch of Silence.' After many years of acoustic measurements, he concluded that this spot had the least amount of human-made noise pollution anywhere in the country.

Over the years, Hempton has defended this square inch from commercial airplanes as well as Navy Growlers (radar-jamming aircraft). He hopes to illustrate what scientists have already measured: noise can shorten your life. Noise pollution also decreases an animal's detection of prey. 'Silence creates an opening, an absence of self, which allows the larger world to enter into our awareness.'

Hike 3.2 miles up the **Hoh River Trail** from the visitor center above Mt Tom Creek Meadows. Find a Sitka spruce tree that you can walk through. That's the entrance to 'One Square Inch of Silence.'

Elwha River Dam Restoration

Dam removals and river restoration

The removal of the Elwha Dam and Glines Canyon Dam after decades of law suits and campaigns has inspired ecotourism projects globally. With the combined effort of the Lower Elwha Klallam Tribe and a host of US agencies and institutions, this is the largest ecosystem restoration project in National Park Service (NPS) history.

Today, you can visit the **Elwha Valley** in the central northern section of Olympic National Park, located about 11 miles southwest of Port Angeles. Be sure to check road conditions because sometimes vehicle traffic beyond Madison Falls parking

NATIONAL PARK PASSPORT & JUNIOR RANGERS

Visitor centers and shops in national parks sell a blue pocket-sized 'Passport to Your National Parks.' A rubber ink cancellation stamp with the name of the park and the date is available at visitor centers only. In case you miss the opportunity to stamp your passport, you can send a self-addressed envelope to the park requesting a cancellation stamp.

Parks that offer Junior Ranger booklets to kids may also have a cancellation stamp specific to the Junior Ranger. When your child completes their booklet, they receive a badge and are sworn in as Junior Rangers by a park ranger. Some rangers are willing to entrust this job to parents.

Log Cabin Resort RV and Campground
Located on the shores of Lake Crescent, this resort offers a mix of cabins and RV sites. $$

Kalaloch Lodge
The only lodging inside Olympic National Park with ocean-view rooms and easy access to the beach. $$$

Campgrounds
Reserve Fairholme, Hoh Rain Forest, Kalaloch, Mora, Sol Duc, Staircase and Log Cabin via recreation.gov. $

WHY I LOVE OLYMPIC NATIONAL PARK

Leslie Hsu Oh,
writer (@lesliehsuoh;
lesliehsuoh.com)

With the weight of a camera around our necks, my mother and I waded through glacier-carved lakes, caved, hiked and white-water rafted in nearly all the national parks in the United States before she died of cancer shortly before I turned 21. She left me with landscapes that are protected, woven with history and indigenous knowledge, where stories are trapped in rock layers and eroded in the earth. I can now bring my kids to Olympic National Park and walk in the footsteps of my past. We can close our eyes on windy days and hear my mother's laughter rippling through the trees.

lot can be flooded and only pedestrians and cyclists can use the Olympic Hot Springs Rd.

There are both self-guided and guided tours of major landmarks: **Glines Canyon Dam removal site**, Madison Falls, the riverfront of the Elwha, and the river delta at the mouth of the Elwha River flowing into the Strait of Juan de Fuca. The **Glines Canyon Overlook** offers views of what's left of the Glines Canyon Dam and exhibits on the Elwha River restoration. Stop at Elwha River Bridge or **Madison Falls Trailhead** to observe nature's resilience. You can also see human efforts such as replanting former lake beds and re-establishing native forests of Douglas fir, red alder, black cottonwood, western red cedar and Sitka willow. Revegetation is improving soil quality, creating habitats for wildlife, and preventing erosion. You can also kayak, canoe or raft sections of the Elwha River (class II-IV) but be sure to look up conditions and closures, especially around the former Elwha Dam Site.

Fishing is allowed but it's catch and release only. In the early 1900s, the construction of Elwha Dam and Glines Canyon Dam blocked anadromous fish, which are born in fresh water, mature in salt water and lay eggs in fresh water – including 11 varieties of salmon, native char, steelhead and sea-run cutthroat trout – from the upper reaches of the Elwha River for over a century. Because the salmon were blocked from swimming upstream, their predators, like bear, mink and river otters, also declined. Because no salmon carcasses decayed in the riverbeds, riverside vegetation was not being fertilized, and therefore cedar trees were starved. The dams also eroded riverbanks and flooded sacred sites belonging to the Lower Elwha Klallam Tribe.

In 1986 the tribe filed a motion to stop the relicensing of the dams because of the Treaty of Point No Point, which ceded tribal lands to settlers in exchange for the right to harvest fish. The tribe always had this legal standing to challenge the dams. What they didn't have was public support, which they gained by raising awareness during their annual **Canoe Journeys** (p126). With public support and partners like NPS and the US Fish and Wildlife Service, in 1992 the Elwha River Ecosystem and Fisheries Restoration Act authorized the US Department of Interior to assess the environmental impact of these dams. They concluded that both antique dams must be removed and the Elwha River ecosystem restored. In 2011 Elwha Dam was removed. Glines Canyon Dam was removed in 2014.

The recovery of this watershed can take from 30 to 100 years. The Olympic Park Institute hosted the Elwha Science Education project in order to connect Elwha kids to this watershed, send them to college, and hope some return home

 WHERE TO EAT IN OLYMPIC NATIONAL PARK

Roosevelt Dining Room
While your food is prepared, enjoy the view of Lake Quinault or wander the grand lawn. $$$

Springs Restaurant
An all-day menu features elk burger, roasted vegetables on French rolls, and fish and chips. $

Lake Crescent Lodge
Reservations recommended. Menu items include salmon, steak, fish and chips, chicken cutlet. $$

SCOTT HEANEY/SHUTTERSTOCK ©

Milky Way, Olympic National Park

as ecologists or scientists to study the restoration of this watershed, which is unique in that 87% of it is protected inside Olympic National Park and 3% is protected by the Lower Elwha Klallam Tribe.

What's fascinating is the scale of this ecosystem recovery, which involves fish and marine biologists, botanists, entomologists, geologists, ornithologists and students. These scholars and visitors alike have the rare opportunity to observe a 'living laboratory.' How will the salmon recolonize the river? How will releasing 100 years of sediment, sand and silt impact the river's turbidity or river geochemistry or coastal ecosystems?

Stargazing in the Park
Looking Up

The **Hurricane Ridge Astronomy Program** is free and includes a Master Observer or volunteer Dark Ranger who can point out planetary nebula M57 (also known as the 'Ring Nebula') and M31 (the Andromeda Galaxy). You can find a schedule at olympictelescope.com.

The best places to stargaze are Hurricane Ridge, Lake Crescent and Kalaloch Beach, where there are open skies and minimal light pollution. Remember to bring binoculars, red flashlight, water, gloves, hat and jacket, and dress in layers.

TRAILS WHERE PETS ARE WELCOME

Although service animals are permitted to accompany their owners anywhere in the park, other pets are limited to the following trails.

Peabody Creek Trail
Accessed via the Olympic National Park Visitor Center in Port Angeles.

Rialto Beach
Along the half-mile trail from the beach's parking lot to Ellen Creek.

Kalaloch Area
On the beaches between the Hoh and Quinault Reservations.

Madison Falls Trail
An impressive 60ft waterfall near the Elwha River.

Spruce Railroad Trail
On the north shore of Lake Crescent.

July Creek Loop Trail
On the north shore of Lake Quinault.

WHERE TO HIKE IN OLYMPIC NATIONAL PARK

Hoh River Trail
This 17.5-mile trek is flat for 13 miles, then steep until the end.

Rialto Beach and Hole-in-the-Wall
This 4-mile round trip starts at Rialto Beach parking lot and heads north along the beach.

Mount Storm King
Trailhead is next to Storm King Ranger Station and marked with the sign 'Marymere Falls Nature Trail.'

Beyond Olympic National Park

Cape Flattery, the furthest northwest point of the contiguous United States, is 70 miles to the west of Port Angeles' Olympic National Park Visitor Center.

Cape Flattery was named after Sir John Flattery, a Royal Navy officer. The Makah people believe that this is where First People emerged from earth. If you're feeling particularly adventurous, hike along the 1.2-mile out and back Cape Flattery Trail, which climbs steep terrain, sports narrow boardwalks and is dog-friendly (with a leash). Keep your eyes peeled for bald eagles, whales, and an incredible view of Tatoosh Island and the Cape Flattery Lighthouse. You can find accommodations, restaurants and stores at Neah Bay, which is a short drive away from Cape Flattery. Both are located on the Makah Indian Reservation. Neah Bay is small and remote but breathtaking with an abundance of fishing, beachcombing, bird-watching and camping opportunities.

GETTING AROUND

Unfortunately, there isn't reliable public transportation in the northwest point of the Olympic Peninsula. Driving your own car or renting one would give you the most flexibility of traveling between Olympic National Park and Forks and Cape Flattery, but always check road conditions and weather conditions. Be aware that cellular coverage may be spotty.

Once you have arrived at Forks or Neah Bay, walking and biking are perfectly reasonable.

☑ TOP TIP

You'll need a Makah Recreation pass to park at the Cape Flattery trailhead, which can be purchased at Makah Marina and the Makah Culture and Research Center.

ASHLEY HADZOPOULOS/SHUTTERSTOCK ©

Cape Flattery Trail

Neah Bay

TIME FROM OLYMPIC NATIONAL PARK: 1½ HRS

Discover the cultural heritage of the Makah

One mission of the **Makah Culture and Research Center** is to protect and preserve the linguistic, cultural and archaeological resources of the Makah Indian Nation. To this end, departments of the museum like the Makah Language Program develop curricula for Neah Bay Elementary and High School. Besides this, the center's mission is to educate tribal members and the public about Makah's culture, heritage and language, and its impressive displays include a scale model of a Makah village.

Set aside about two hours to enjoy the exhibits at the center, where you can learn about Makah's maritime heritage, including historic whaling and seal hunting practices and artistry, displayed in showcases, dioramas and full-sized replicas of canoes and a longhouse. The center also houses 300–500-year-old artifacts recovered from the Ozette Archaeological Site, which was exposed in a storm in the winter of 1969–70. Oral history and radiocarbon dates proved that a landslide occurred some five centuries ago, burying six longhouses and pre-contact wooden and wood-based artifacts.

The museum offers guided tours for about 15–24 people that range from 1½ to two hours; you can also hire someone to guide you on the Cape Flattery Trail or around local village sites or beaches. The museum also offers demonstrations of Makah basketry and carving, and lectures on Makah storytelling, fisheries management, forestry, history and tribal government. Contact 360-645-2711 if you would like to attend one of these workshops for $35 plus the cost of materials.

MAKAH CANOES

The Makah carve canoes out of western red cedar and add sails. Sails are rare among the indigenous peoples of the Pacific Northwest; however, the Makah are not the only tribe to use them. Traditionally the sails were made out of cedar-bark matting but nowadays they use canvas or synthetic fabrics. The Makah call these canoes *taholahs* and still rely upon them for Canoe Journeys (see p126), ceremonies, and sailing the Pacific Ocean or long distances. It demonstrates the sophistication of their navigation, maritime skills and trade practices.

Forks

TIME FROM OLYMPIC NATIONAL PARK: 35 MINS

Visit the home of the famous Twilight vampires

Forks is a great place to stay if you can't find lodging inside Olympic National Park. It is located on Hwy 101, bordered by the Pacific Ocean on the west, the Strait of Juan De Fuca on the north, and Olympic National Park to the east.

Historically, it was known as a logging town (find out more about that at the **Forks Timber Museum**) but once Stephenie Meyer set her *Twilight* series here in 2003, fans and cosplayers started moving in. Even though the movies weren't filmed here and Meyer never even visited this town until after her books were published, locals created a map directing visitors to what they think might be the home of Edward Cullen and his family of vampires (the **Miller Tree Inn**). On this map, you'll also find **Bella Swan's House** with her red truck

WHERE TO FISH IN THE OLYMPIC PENINSULA'S NORTHWEST POINT

Makah Marina	Shi Shi Beach	Tsoo-Yess River
Washington requires a saltwater license, while the Makah Tribe require a tribal fishing license.	Surf fishing is popular. A longer rod is recommended and a fishing license from Washington state.	Makah National Fish Hatchery releases millions of Chinook and coho salmon every spring.

4KCLIPS/SHUTTERSTOCK ©

Forks Visitor Imformation Center and Bella Swan's truck

RAIN OF TERROR HAUNTED HANGAR

Every Halloween, the Forks Police Foundation throws what is known as **Olympic Peninsula's most extreme Halloween Experience** in the Quillayute Airport hangar. For only $10 per person, you can try to make it through a haunted house that only 70% have had the nerve to complete. The hours are usually 7am to midnight during the month of October. Reviews say that every step is terrifying. Designers of the experience say they try to cloud visitors' senses of sight and hearing with darkness, music and screams. You might find a maze, stairwells, dark hallways, evil clowns, devils – or any other pant-wetting shock you could imagine.

parked in the driveway, Forks High School, Forks Community Hospital where Dr Cullen worked and Forks Outfitters where Bella used to work after school.

Every September, the Forks Chamber of Commerce organizes an immersive **Forever Twilight in Forks Festival** in celebration of Bella's birthday. Fans from all over the world can hang out with cosplayers who portray their favorite characters, and the town has even built the Rainforest Arts Center to accommodate the festival. Open year-round, it features the world's largest collection of props, motorcycles and costumes from the movies. Best of all, it's free and you are allowed to take photos.

Some 10ft of annual rainfall earned this town its slogan as the 'rainiest town in the contiguous United States.' But if you want to blend in with the locals, don't use an umbrella. Fun fact: it was this slogan that inspired Meyer to set her *Twilight* novels in Forks.

Olympia

The capital of Washington state is also known as the gateway to the Cascade Mountains, Mount Rainier National Park, Nisqually National Wildlife Refuge, Olympic National Park, Puget Sound and the Washington coast. Located at the southern tip of Puget Sound, halfway between Portland and Seattle, Olympia is a place where the wilderness meets free-spirited locals and artists like Kurt Cobain and Sleater-Kinney. The Squaxin, the Nisqually, and the Chehalis people have lived in this area for thousands of years. You can find their stories being told at the Hands On Children's Museum, the Chehalis Tribe Cultural Center, the Nisqually Tribe Cultural Center, and the Squaxin Island Museum Library and Research Center.

Experience-Oriented Community
Murals and random acts of poetry

You can tell the arts are important to Olympia just by walking around downtown, where you'll find 96 murals and random acts of poetry on the sides of buildings and traffic boxes. Near Olympia's **Farmers Market**, 700 Capital Way, where live musicians play Thursday to Sunday from April through October and on weekends or just Saturdays during the off season, words are inscribed on the bricks that appear only when they get wet. Located on the wall of the **Old School Pizzeria**, Abe Poulridge and Chris Ross painted the Super Hero Wall, which has 132 life-size characters. At the corner of State and Capital you'll find a 4000-sq-ft mural, commissioned by the Olympia-Rafah Solidarity Mural Project to celebrate the life of Rachel Corrie, an activist from Olympia who was murdered in Gaza in 2003.

If you're interested in creating your own art, try **InGenius! Local Artisan Gallery & Boutique's** 'create and sip' classes for tourists who are beginners to watercoloring, and Airbound Arts's aerial studio where you can train privately with an instructor or drop in for open gym.

GETTING AROUND

Olympia is about two hours' driving distance from airports in Seattle and Portland. The closest Olympic National Park visitor center (Kalaloch Ranger Station) is 2¼ hours away. If you're staying in downtown, Olympia, you probably won't need a car. Intercity Transit operates bus services in Olympia. Some buses have bike racks so you could rent one or try bike-sharing services. You can also take a train to Olympia through Amtrak Cascades. Olympic National Park is about an hour's drive from Olympia.

☑ **TOP TIP**

Celebrate the return of wild salmon from the ocean to the Deschutes River with printmaking, a scavenger hunt, problem-solving adventures, stone carvings and henna art in the Turnwater Falls Festival.

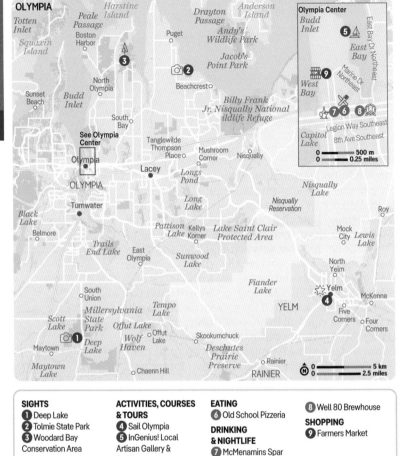

OLYMPIA

Olympia Center

SIGHTS
1 Deep Lake
2 Tolmie State Park
3 Woodard Bay Conservation Area

ACTIVITIES, COURSES & TOURS
4 Sail Olympia
5 InGenius! Local Artisan Gallery & Boutique

EATING
6 Old School Pizzeria

DRINKING & NIGHTLIFE
7 McMenamins Spar Café

8 Well 80 Brewhouse

SHOPPING
9 Farmers Market

A Unique Sailing School

Certification class or vacation

Sail Olympia was founded by a couple who combined their expertise in education with sailing. They developed a program that trains you on technical competencies of sailing while strengthening communication and partnering in your relationships.

 ## WHERE TO STAY IN OLYMPIA

Marie Bed & Breakfast
Organic, locally sourced meals with sourdough starter from 1897. Guests must be 17+. **$$**

Offutt Lake Resort
Family-owned campground offers cabins, RV sites, and restaurant and bar and boat rentals. **$**

Courtyard by Marriott Olympia
Spacious rooms with indoor pool, breakfast, gym, free parking. No pets allowed. **$**

In five days and four nights, you can either enjoy a luxurious vacation or work toward sailing qualifications on a 382 Dufour Grand Large with three private cabins. This boat features a 3-ton, 6ft-long keel, which means it will never capsize. Classes begin in Budd Inlet, where waters are calm and there is no ferry traffic or crowded marinas, then continue on to Sucia Island, Stuart Island, Roche Harbor and Orca Island. Reviews consistently say that this vacation is the kind you want to repeat.

The Secret Behind Olympia's Beer

'It's the water'

Although the Olympia Brewing Company with the slogan 'It's the water' closed in 2003, you can still taste beer made from Olympia's artesian waters at **Well 80 Brewhouse**. Today, they are still brewing beer from the well located at the back of their building. **McMenamins Spar Café** serves water and their own Spar Vodka from a well bubbling in their basement. No wonder there's a legend that says 'if you drink from any of the artesian wells in Olympia, you'll come back to the city.' For those who want to go straight to the source, the best-known Olympia artesian well runs 24/7 and is located between 4th Ave E and Jefferson St.

At one point, Olympia had more than 100 artesian wells. The source of this water, which scientists believe to originate from under the Cascade Mountains, is a subterranean reservoir located beneath downtown called the Turnwater Sand aquifer. The water filters naturally between sloping layers of bedrock and minerals.

Calling all Nature Buffs

Access to state-managed lands

With its network that now includes 142 parks and which predates the US National Park System, Washington state protects over 140,000 acres of land and attracts around 40 million visitors a year. Here are just a few that are located close to Olympia.

Woodard Bay Conservation Area provides wetland habitat for shorebirds and songbirds, harbor seals, river otters, bald eagles, a large maternity colony of bats, and one of the most significant heron rookeries in the state. It also protects mature second-growth forests. No dogs allowed.

If you're interested in a coastal salt marsh system, visit **Billy Frank Jr Nisqually National Wildlife Refuge**. Established in 1974, the refuge protects more than 275 migratory

WHAT I WANT PEOPLE TO KNOW

Willie Frank III, Nisqually Tribal Council Chairman, is the youngest to be elected to this position. His mother, Susan Crystal, a top health care advisor to Washington governors, passed away in 2001. His father, Billy Frank Jr, who devoted his life to protecting tribal treaty fishing rights, died in 2014. Willie continues their legacy while carving his own path.

'Everything that grows in Puget Sound is our medicine. We protect it with environmental education, wildfire mitigation, forest management, watershed planning, water quality programs, restoration, environmental assessments and salmon recovery programs. Learn about each tribal nation. Some have museums and cultural centers. Come experience our culture, dances, and stories.'

✂ WHERE TO EAT IN OLYMPIA

Well 80 Brewhouse	McMenamins Spar Café	San Francisco Street Bakery
Order beer-battered chicken bites with 'drive-in style tots' and play board games after eating. $	One of Olympia's oldest eateries and workers' favorite watering hole; McMenamins took over in 2007. $$	Fan favorites: black currant scone, lox sandwich with capers, marionberry pie. $

Puget Sound

INTERTRIBAL CANOE JOURNEYS

Since 1989 Indigenous Nations from Alaska, British Columbia, Oregon and Washington, along with Ainu, Hawaiian and Māori people have paddled along ancestral highways in an annual Intertribal Canoe Journey. Each year, a different nation hosts the event, with the Muckleshoot Journey gathering some 10,000 guests in 2023. Muckleshoot Tribal Chairman Jaison Elkins explained that the canoe journeys revitalize their culture. 'It's a display of unity. It's a display of strength, and it's a display of healing for our people.'

In 2025 the Lower Elwha Klallam Tribe will host. It will be 20 years since the tribe last hosted and the first time visitors can witness recovery from dam removals on the Elwha River. In 2026 Nisqually will host.

bird species that use it for migration, wintering or breeding. It also provides rearing and migration habitat for steelhead trout and several salmon species, and habitat for a variety of threatened and endangered species, especially those that thrive in fresh water (Nisqually River) and salt water (the Nisqually River Delta, which was designated a National Natural Landmark). It is considered the last unspoiled major estuary in Puget Sound. The refuge is open every day from sunrise to sunset.

A few miles south of the state capital, you can swim at two beaches on **Deep Lake** in **Millersylvania State Park**. Fishing, boating, hiking and biking are also options. If you prefer salt water over fresh water, then swim at **Tolmie State Park** (open from 8am to dusk in the summer). Be sure to check the local tide tables (high tide for more water, low tide for more beach). You can also walk through the Lacey Producer's District for a tasting.

McMenamins Passport

Keeping the past in the present

In the Pacific Northwest, the McMenamin brothers have made it their mission to 'keep the past in the present' by purchasing and operating historic bars, hotels, restaurants, gardens, soaking pools, breweries and movie theaters. In Olympia, get a taste for what this town was like in 1935 at the **Spar Café**.

Customers who purchase a $35 McMenamins passport can collect stamps from each location by completing a clue/task. Full sets of stamps in each region earn you free food, drinks or merchandise; by completing the whole passport you become a 'Cosmic Tripster' and earn even richer prizes including hotel stays and concert or movie tickets.

Long Beach Peninsula

Along the Washington coast, which stretches from Ocean Shores down to Cape Disappointment, there are charming towns with lighthouses and antique shops. On the southwestern tip of Washington state, there's a 28-mile-long beach with sand dunes and forests, arguably the longest in the world, where Columbia River enters the Pacific Ocean. In 2024 the City of Long Beach will commemorate its 100th anniversary. Snow Peak, the outdoor brand founded in Japan, will launch its first campground in North America in winter 2023, called 'Snow Peak Campfield Long Beach – a place for people to gather and experience the rejuvenating power of the outdoors.' It will provide accommodations options from a campsite where you bring your own gear to a Tent Suite that is set up with sleeping bags, pillows and chairs or a Jyubako Suite cabin with air-conditioning/heater and a private restroom, similar to its campfields in Hokkaido, Osaka, Kochi, Oita, Niigata.

GETTING AROUND

Long Beach Peninsula is a two-hour drive away from Olympia and 1½ hours to Aberdeen. If you are flying into Sea-Tac Airport and renting a car, then the drive to Long Beach Peninsula would take three hours.

☑ TOP TIP

Best time to visit would be in the fall and winter when there are fewer crowds and lodging rates are lower too. No camping, swimming or ATVs allowed on the beach. Driving on the beach is not recommended and there are motor vehicle prohibitions during razor clam season and April 15 through the day following Labor Day.

SEBASTIAN BRINKMAN/SHUTTERSTOCK ©

Lighthouse, Cape Disappointment

Wild Mushroom Celebration
Visit Long Beach for mushrooms between October 1 and November 15. The celebration includes foraging hikes with experts; experienced foragers sometimes pick their own, at their own risk, down Discovery Trail or at state parks.

Long Beach Razor Clam Festival
In April, there are two days of live music, an oyster-shucking contest, crab races, clam chowder taste-off competitions and razor clam digging lessons.

Washington State International Kite Festival
Every August since 1981, one of the largest and longest-running kite festivals and competition in North America happens here. More than 150,000 people attend and it's free.

Digging Razor Clams on Washington Beaches

Most sought-after shellfish

Razor clams are the most popular shellfish to harvest in Washington state. Because clams are not mobile and they don't fight back, all you need to do is look for a 'clam show' – the clam starts to dig, leaving a dimple or doughnut shape on the sand. When the clam withdraws its neck, it can also leave a clam show.

While razor clam digging can be enjoyed by anyone, be sure to check the Washington Department of Fish and Wildlife (WDFW) website on levels of marine toxins and domoic acid ingested by razor clams (wdfw.wa.gov/fishing/shellfishing-regulations/razor-clams#current). If toxins are detected, clamming season will be delayed or canceled.

WDFW posts a proposed digging schedule for public clam beaches each year (wdfw.wa.gov/places-to-go/shellfish-beaches); in 2023 this began on November 12. Diggers should check this site for information on which beaches are open. One to two hours prior to the listed low tide time is when you should start digging.

You will need to purchase a clamming license online (at fishhunt.dfw.wa.gov/login) or at one of 600 licensed vendors as long as you are 15 years old and older. You are also limited to 15 razor clams a day and must carry your own catch separately from anyone else. To dig for razor clams, you'll need a clam gun or clam shovel, clam rake, neoprene gloves, waders and a shellfish gauge (so you know which clams you can keep).

Horseback Riding with Panoramic Ocean Views

Riding on Long Beach Peninsula

Riding a horse on Long Beach Peninsula is a bucket-list item, because where else can you ride for 28 miles on a strip of sand with ocean views in every direction? Visitors can saddle up with regular rides offered by **Long Beach Horse Rides** and **West Coast Horse Rides** for $50.

Be prepared for your horse to fall into a single-file line initially to get onto the beach. After that, they will fan out and each horse will set their own pace. Sometimes they might get curious about something in the water and veer away from the group.

Sand can tire out horses quickly as they raise their hooves high with every step. You might consider steering your horse to the surf's edge because the firmer packed sand will give your horse more support. If this is the first time you have ever

 WHERE TO HIKE ON THE LONG BEACH PENINSULA

Lewis and Clark Discovery Trail
Find the replica where explorer William Clark carved his name on a cedar.

Long Beach Boardwalk
ADA-accessible and dog-friendly half-mile one-way oceanside walk through grass dunes.

Willapa Art Trail
Artwork designed and installed by University of Washington students tells the story of a stream restoration.

Horseback riding

tried to ride on sand, it's best to choose a time during a receding tide or a day when the sea is calm. Stay out of the water since waves can make a horse's footing unstable.

Be sure to tighten and adjust the helmet they supply; you don't want it to slide around when your horse is galloping, then fall forward across your eyes and blind you.

If you plan to bring your own horse, there are some rules to be aware of: do not ride on the sidewalks through town or the clam beds at low tide, stay on designated trails, announce your presence when you are behind another rider and then ask permission to pass. Long Beach Peninsula also has campgrounds that accommodate horses with pens and corrals.

THE WORLD'S LARGEST FRYING PAN

This iconic frying pan was commissioned by the Long Beach Chamber of Commerce in 1941 for their first annual Razor Clam Festival. Northwest Copper and Sheet Metal Works handcrafted it at 1300lb and measures 10ft wide and 20ft tall. That year, Chef Wellington W Marsh cooked a 9ft clam fritter in this pan for 20,000 people. Unfortunately, this pan began to rust over the years. Everett L Mosher, a retired fisherman, tried to restore the pan but he was only able to save the handle. The town recreated the rest of the pan with fiberglass and still uses it to cook clam fritters during the Razor Clam Festival.

Beyond
Long Beach
Peninsula

Stop off in Vancouver for a dose of local fur-trade history and entertainment galore in the ilani Hotel.

Poor old Vancouver. Often confused with its glamorous Canadian namesake or dismissed as Portland's ugly cousin, in fact the city's lack of star power is part of its charm. Few travelers go out of their way to visit, but those who do may be in for a pleasant surprise, with pioneer history, worth-the-trip restaurants and brewpubs, a weekend farmers market and the oldest surviving fort in the Pacific Northwest. And the city is definitely on the up thanks to a recent development project that's turned the waterfront into an evolving public space with restaurants, walking paths and river views. Just outside town, the ilani Hotel offers uniquely luxurious stays while celebrating the rich Cowlitz culture.

GETTING AROUND

In Vancouver, you can use the C-Tran bus system, but driving is still usually most convenient since you can park in the street in either paid or free parking zones. Uber and Lyft are also available. Use the MAX LIght Rail system to travel to Portland downtown.

☑ **TOP TIP**

The ilani Hotel hosts performances, live shows and concerts from stars like Ali Wong and Alanis Morissette; book tickets in advance.

STEVEN BALTAKATE SANDOVAL, CC BY-SA 4.0, VIA WIKIMEDIA COMMONS ®

ilani Hotel

Vancouver

Vancouver

TIME FROM LONG BEACH PENINSULA: 2 HRS

Fort, fur & riverside fun

Though far closer to Portland, Vancouver warrants an overnight trip from the Olympic Peninsula, not least for the chance to stay in the nearby, indigenous-owned **ilani Hotel**. This casino and hotel megacomplex will keep you entertained at night, so keep a day free to explore the town's historic sights and learn of the explorers and trappers who made their home here before indulging in wine, shopping and river walks.

Start at the **Vancouver National Historic Reserve**, a large complex walking distance from the center that comprises several points of interest including archaeological sites and museums with displays on the local fur trade as well as military and aviation history. Most impressive is the **Fort Vancouver Historic Site**, a reconstruction of a fort that served as the headquarters for the British Hudson Bay Company's western fur-trade operations.

A short stroll south takes you to areas on the Columbia River's northern shore that had been closed to the public for more than a century until an ongoing development project opened them up, beginning in 2018. The park at **Grant Street Pier**, with its distinctive monument designed to resemble the billowing sail of a passing boat, is a great place to start exploring the area's waterfront hotels, unique retail spaces and flagship restaurants. These include eight renowned wineries, the **Yard Milkshake Bar** (featured on *Shark Tank*), the **Headwaters Wall** interactive water play feature for kids, and a 2-mile paved path that's been voted one of the best river walks in the USA.

THE ILANI HOTEL

You'll feel lighter as soon as you walk inside the ilani Hotel, you feel lighter, with the copious sunlight instantly reducing anxiety and the blue carpeted hallways sparkling like the surface of a river with salmon running beneath. This hotel and casino complex is the perfect place to relax while soaking up some Indigenous culture.

The latter is evident throughout, in displays celebrating the Cowlitz worldview through formline art, contemporary works by Indigenous artists and in a Cowlitz Cultural Corridor with a multimedia display of the canoes used in the Canoe Journey. You'll also find an indoor-outdoor pool, fitness center, 19 restaurants, an entertainment facility featuring star talent and top-of-the-line kids' entertainment facilities.

Washington Cascades

MOUNTAINS, GLACIAL LAKES, POWER-NAPPING VOLCANOES

Famously admired as one of the most stunning collections of natural beauty on earth; wild but surprisingly accessible.

The Cascade Range mountains are the punk-rock teens of Washington state's geography – jagged and eruptive, filled with scenic bravado and rapidly changing peaks (geologically speaking, that is). In Washington, the Cascades (as they're known locally) have an outsized influence on the culture, personality and vibe of the entire state. A sizable portion of Washingtonians – even those living in Seattle, Tacoma or Spokane – moved here for these mountains.

If it can be done in the great outdoors – hike, climb (mountain, ice or rock), ski (downhill or cross-country), ride an alpine coaster – it can be done in the Cascades. You'll see hordes of outdoor enthusiasts with their ice axes and crampons flock here, but beginners are most welcome to hike, learn or just enjoy the scenery.

The entire range runs 700 miles from Lassen Peak and Mt Shasta in far Northern California to Washington's Mt Baker (with a quick foray into Canada's British Columbia). While the mountaintops and locations in this chapter aren't far as the crow flies, there are long roads in and out of each one. Add in traffic and wait times at entrance gates, it could take four to six hours (or more!) to drive between Mt Rainier and Mt St Helen's. Plan your visit accordingly!

A note: while Mt Baker is geographically in the Cascades, the skiing and hiking powerhouse can only be accessed through Bellingham (p90).

ROMAN KHOMLYAK/GETTY IMAGES ©

THE MAIN AREAS

LEAVENWORTH
Alpine vacation playground.
p136

MT RAINIER
Magical mountain.
p141

MT ST HELEN'S
In-your-face volcanology.
p144

NORTH CASCADES NATIONAL PARK
Glaciers, lakes and hiking.
p146

Left: Harry's Ridge Trail, Mt St Helen's (p144); Above: North Cascades National Park (p146)

Find Your Way

The Washington Cascades are long and narrow, so visitors usually pick one or two spots to focus on. Always check before heading out – you never know what might close a road: snow, landslides, wildfires, even volcanoes.

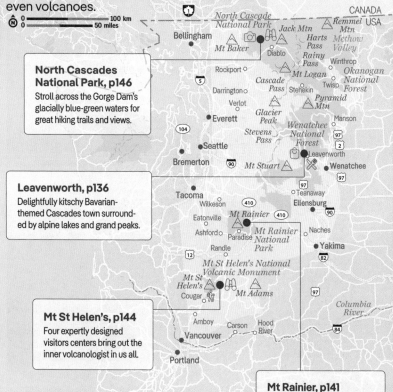

North Cascades National Park, p146
Stroll across the Gorge Dam's glacially blue-green waters for great hiking trails and views.

Leavenworth, p136
Delightfully kitschy Bavarian-themed Cascades town surrounded by alpine lakes and grand peaks.

Mt St Helen's, p144
Four expertly designed visitors centers bring out the inner volcanologist in us all.

Mt Rainier, p141
The prominent peak is on every WA license plate for a reason.

CAR
The most popular and easiest way to get around the Cascades is by car, as most trailheads and activities aren't accessible by public transportation. Trailhead parking areas can fill up as early as 8am or 9am.

HIKE
About 700 people thru-hike the 2600-mile Pacific Crest Trail each year, from the Mexican to the Canadian border. Sections cross near Mt Rainier National Park, North Cascades National Park and near the Methow Valley.

PUBLIC TRANSPORTATION
Amtrak's *Cascades* route stops surprisingly far from the actual mountains, though the *Empire Builder* route stops in Leavenworth. Buses only reach nearby towns. Don't pooh-pooh organized trips; fewer cars are better for the regional ecology.

Leavenworth (p136)

Plan Your Time

It takes hours to get from each mountain or destination to another –
when it's even possible to drive between them. In winter, snow shuts
down roads, sometimes until May or even June.

A Cascadian Weekend

There's nothing like a **Leavenworth** (p136) weekend during Oktoberfest, the winter lights or the bustling summer. And while we would encourage you to visit during the less-crowded weekdays, **Mt Rainier** (p141) really *is* all that. Only a few hours away is the more relaxed **Mt St Helen's National Volcanic Monument** (p144). Mt Rainier has 155 trails and Mt St Helen's has over 200 – a year of hikes!

A Week+ in the Cascades

Rent a cabin in the **Methow Valley** (p149) or **Leavenworth** (1360). Ski-bum it for a week, or in the summer, get a backcountry permit for the **North Cascades National Park's** (p146) turquoise glacial lakes. You don't need to do all 2600 miles, but pick a small section of the **Pacific Crest Trail** (p143) and challenge yourself.

Seasonal Highlights

SPRING

Can be cold, but prices drop. Beat the crowds in May when the **North Cascades Highway** opens.

SUMMER

Wildflowers explode on **Mt Rainier and Mt St Helen's**, and it's a good time to soak up the sun on **Lake Chelan**.

FALL

Fall colors everywhere. **Oktoberfest** in Leavenworth is a month-long celebration of food, beer and culture.

WINTER

Visit reindeer in **Leavenworth** and bald eagles in the **North Cascades**, or ski in the **Methow Valley**.

Leavenworth

☑ **TOP TIP**

Weekends can be beyond crowded – especially during events or summertime – but many places are closed Tuesdays and Wednesdays, so plan ahead. If you want to visit the reindeer farm or ride the alpine coaster, book well in advance. Beyond Main Street, you'll need a car.

WHY I LOVE LEAVENWORTH

Alex Leviton, writer

I love how each season in Leavenworth brings an entirely different experience: snowshoeing in winter, the river activities in summer and hiking almost year-round. My favorite time is autumn, as the leaves are gorgeous, I spent my last milestone birthday renting a vacation house there with friends, doing the Leavenworth Escape Room and eating our collective weight in schnitzel.

If you're coming to Leavenworth, put on your Bavarian-colored glasses (or carry your Bavarian-themed stein), appreciate 1960s-style tourism ingenuity, and embrace the kitsch.

Populated by the Wenatchi people for centuries, Leavenworth became a thriving timber town from the 1890s until a rerouted railroad changed their luck. To avoid becoming a ghost town, Leavenworth thought maybe some folks would appreciate the valley's incredible beauty. Whoa Nelly, were they – and the now million-plus visitors a year – right.

Visits to Leavenworth are seasonal: winter is snow sports and holiday lights; autumn brings Oktoberfest and fall leaves; summer bursts with sun-loving holiday-goers, hiking and the Leavenworth Summer Theater; and spring's melting snow means fewer tourists but cozier carriage rides.

Unlike much of the Cascades, Leavenworth is *gefüllt* with tourist services (most kid-friendly): activities, hotels, restaurants, wineries, shops, events. Are most of them Bavarian-themed? Oh, *ja*. Does that include architecturally ye olde shoppe flourishes, even at McDonald's and the town's hospital? *Natürlich*.

Bavarian-Themed Wonderland
Beer, brats, bakeries and books

Jump straight into the Bavarian theme at the **Bavarian Bakery**. In the 1990s Berthold Timmermann answered a job ad in the back of his German bakers' newspaper from the town of Leavenworth. The result is home-country recipes for delectable pastries, rye bread and pretzels. Head back to the pedestrianized town center and the **Nutcracker Museum**. We dare you not to become absolutely fascinated by the nonagenarian owner's Guinness Book of World Record–holding collection of 10,000+ nutcrackers (as well as 4000-year-old Indigenous nutting stones, Roman-era bronze nutcrackers and more).

LEAVENWORTH

Orchard St · Central Ave · Summit Ave · Ash St · Evans St · Whitman St · Sherbourne · Front Street Park · 9th St · 10th St · Commercial St · Main St · Division St · Front St · 13th St · 12th St · Commercial St · Lions Club Park · Front St · 8th St · Leavenworth Adventure Park (0.6mi) · Blackbird Island · Waterfront Park · Wenatchee River · E Leavenworth Rd

Chumstick Hwy · Leavenworth Reindeer Farm (0.4mi)

0 — 200 m
0 — 0.1 miles

SIGHTS
1 Greater Leavenworth Museum
2 Nutcracker Museum
3 Waterfront Park

4 Wenatchee River Institute

EATING
5 Andreas Keller
6 Bavarian Bakery
7 Colchuck's

8 Leavenworth Sausage Garden
9 München Haus

ENTERTAINMENT
10 Escape Room Leavenworth

11 Leavenworth Summer Theater

SHOPPING
12 A Book For All Seasons

Lounge over a bratwurst from the **Leavenworth Sausage Garden** or **München Haus** while flipping through one of Ellie Alexander's Leavenworth beer mystery novels (*The Pint of No Return* or *Death on Tap*) you bought from the perfectly curated **A Book For All Seasons**, which also features a huge collection of local naturalist books. Get out of the intense heat (June–August) or warm up (December–February)

WHERE TO EAT NON-GERMAN FOOD

Yodelin
Chic riverfront spot featuring bowls like artisanal bone broth, local salmon or Thai peanut and rice. **$$**

Wok About Mongolian Grill
Build-your-own stir-fry creations at this second-story restaurant with some of Leavenworth's best views. **$$**

Mana Organic
A multi-course sensory evening of locally foraged or farmed ingredients and culinary innovation. **$$$**

OUTDOORS LEAVENWORTH

From dozens of excellent hikes year-round to snowshoe, cross-country and skating tracks in winter and inner tubing, rock climbing and mountain biking in summer, Leavenworth is an excellent base for launching Cascadian adventures.

In town, **Der Sportsmann** store not only sells or rents just about anything you'll need, but every employee has an expert-level knowledge about the area. Their favorite hiking areas are **Colchuck Lake**, **Icicle Gorge** and the **Icicle Ridge** to **Fourth of July Creek Trail**. On leavenworth. org, find dozens of outfitters running everything from white-water rafting and inner-tubing trips (gear provided) to back-country horse-drawn sleigh rides and Nordic skiing.

with wine- and beer-tasting at **Icicle Brewing Company**, **Boudreaux Cellars** or **Icicle Ridge Winery**. Soak up a little quiet alpine nature with a walk around the **Wenatchee River Institute** and its educational trails and native plant garden, or head downstream from town to **Waterfront Park** to hike, stroll, swim or picnic.

Book your tickets now for the alpine coaster at **Leavenworth Adventure Park** (jokingly the most Bavarian thing in Leavenworth, built by Germans based on similar coasters in the German Alps). Heart-stoppingly placed on a granite ridge, it's got the best views in town. In the late afternoon, book a Bavarian- or alpine-themed escape room at **Escape Room Leavenworth**, go on a **Bavarian Walking Tour** or read about how to turn your town into Bavaria at the **Greater Leavenworth Museum** before dining on schnitzel, spaetzle or sauerkraut at **Andreas Keller** or **Colchuck's**.

In summer, catch a show at the **Leavenworth Summer Theater**, especially in the **Ski Hill amphitheater** with its view of the alpine mountains that feels like you might as well be in the real – er, original – Bavarian Alps town. Be sure to check out the majestic **Anderson Carriage Rides** draft horses in the fields on Ski Hill Dr along the way.

Cuddling Rudolph

Visit Leavenworth's reindeer farm

Dasher, Rudolph, Sven...few experiences beat being tickled by a reindeer's fuzzy little nose while feeding one of these majestic, gentle creatures.

The **Leavenworth Reindeer Farm** is owned and operated by the Hans Christian Anderson (no, not that one) family. Owners of the best carriage rides in town, the family patriarch joked one day about also starting a reindeer farm in Leavenworth. Fast forward past several attempts to import a herd (several airlines did not appreciate the irony of disallowing reindeer from flying), and now the herd of more than 50 helps educate and entertain visitors.

After a fun introduction, visitors get to feed the cuddly reindeer. Afterwards, buy souvenirs from the extremely well-stocked gift barn, or dine on difficult-to-find reindeer sausage (flown in from Alaska), wrapped in traditional Norwegian *lefse* bread. Starting in November, the farm truly – and literally – shines with holiday lights, snow...and photos with a special jolly guest.

 WHERE TO STAY IN LEAVENWORTH

Haus Rohrbach Pension	Obertal Inn	Sleeping Lady Mountain Resort
Adorable, reasonably priced Bavarian hotel near Ski Hill with homemade breakfast. $$	A good choice in the city center, it's also dog-friendly with a hot tub. $$	By cross-country skiing tracks; rustic-chic rooms/cabins, spa and restaurant. $$$

Beyond Leavenworth

Lake Chelan
Manson
Chelan
Stevens Pass
Winton
Chelan Falls
Entiat
Orondo
Leavenworth
Cashmere
Sunnyslope
Wenatchee

Just past Leavenworth, get a taste of Central Washington's 'rain shadow' high-desert climate – apple orchards, sun-worshipping Lake Chelan and tumbleweeds.

Before the Cascade Loop National Scenic Byway rounds its way back to the Methow Valley, you have a brief chance to set foot in Washington's arid agricultural region. The views here are more rolling hills and farmlands than jagged peaks and wilderness, but no less remarkable. Sleepy sagebrush (with their accompanying honest-to-goodness tumbleweeds) is juxtaposed with the life-giving bright green of apple and peach orchards, with a backdrop of mustard-yellow hills. The area around Wenatchee and Lake Chelan produces over 70% of the United States' apples. Yakima Valley produces almost as much of the nation's hop crop, helping Washington attain the rank of one of the top brewery states in the US.

☑ TOP TIP

Many locations require a Discovery Pass, National Park Pass or Northwest Forest Pass. Buy online or in local outfitters.

DAN LEWIS/SHUTTERSTOCK ©

Apple orchard near Wenatchee (p140)

WHAT'S UP WITH THE RAIN?

Washington has a love/hate/ignore relationship with its rain. While most Washingtonians worth their weight in flannel wouldn't be caught dead with an umbrella, those in Eastern Washington don't need them. The Cascades create a 'rain shadow,' keeping precipitation-producing clouds from reaching the arid shrubsteppes of Central and Eastern Washington. So, while Paradise on Mt Rainier and parts of the Olympic Peninsula can get 110in a year, Lake Chelan gets only 12in and Prosser (near Walla Walla's wine region) dries up with only 7in. (For reference, famously 'rainy' Seattle gets about 40in, about the same as Kansas City, Missouri.) Reason enough to visit Eastern Washington!

NEELIMA AYILAVARAPU/SHUTTERSTOCK ©

Lake Chelan

Lake Chelan

TIME FROM LEAVENWORTH: 1 HR

Sun, wine and family summer camp

California has its beaches, Jersey has its shore and Washington has Lake Chelan. Sun worshippers, water-sports enthusiasts and families with kids have been bringing their floaties, paddleboards, boats and jet skis to this 50-mile-long fjord-like glacial lake (the third deepest in the US) for generations. More recently, wine buffs and hikers have discovered the quieter side: Lake Chelan and the nearby (but unfortunately named) town of Manson host dozens of wineries. While the town of Chelan is in the arid rain shadow, the lake's westernmost point is deep in the Cascades. One of the most magical and secret spots in Washington is at the tip of this corner. Tiny Stehekin (p40) is only accessible by four-hour ferry, seaplane, or one very, very, very long hike.

Wenatchee

TIME FROM LEAVENWORTH: 30 MINS

Tranquility above the apple orchards

Ohme Gardens was founded in 1929 by Herman Ohme, the owner of an apple orchard in nearby Wenatchee who wanted to bring the beauty of the nearby Cascades closer to him. For 41 years, he and his wife Ruth created an oasis of pines, firs and native plants that overlooks the desert sagebrush of Washington's agricultural landscape. Natural stone paths and towering waterfalls wend their way from viewpoint to viewpoint. A peaceful spot between Leavenworth and Lake Chelan, it's next to **Stutzman Ranch**, one of the area's best u-pick farms for cherries, apples, peaches and more. Check thestutzmanranch.com for what's on, ahem, branch.

KID-FRIENDLY SPOTS IN CHELAN

Slidewaters
With 19 water-park attractions, inner tubing and the world's largest stationary wave, the lake views are almost secondary.

Wapato Point Cellars
A kid-friendly vineyard? Why, of course! In Manson, complete with playground and full-service restaurant.

Local Myth Pizza
Families flock to this popular pizzeria across from a lakefront park – perfect for picnics!

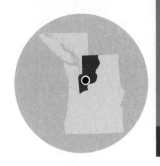

Mt Rainier

Visible for up to 300 miles, the prominent, mystical peak has been the grounding soul of Western Washington for millennia. Its original Puyallup name – Tahoma – means 'Mother of all waters.' Washingtonians buy houses based on their view of Mt Rainier.

Get a bit closer and the experience is no less mystical. In the short summer season, meadows are covered in every color of wildflower imaginable. Mountain goats march up the impossibly steep hillsides where huckleberries sprout. Waterfalls, glaciers, adorably cute marmots...the mountain is awash in nature.

Mt Rainier National Park is an exceedingly accessible destination, about two hours from Seattle or Portland. Yes, this can mean shoulder-to-shoulder weekend visits during the mountain's short summer season ('winter' road closures can last until July). But with 369 sq miles, Mt Rainier is spread out across a vast network of roads and trails, and nearby towns like Ashford have plenty of hotels, restaurants and provisions.

GETTING AROUND

Mt Rainier has four entrance gates. The most popular area, Paradise, is accessed by the southwest Nisqually entrance on Hwy 706 or the southeast Stevens Canyon via Hwy 12. The White River in the northeast is the only way to the Sunrise area and the tiny Carbon River entrance leads only to the northwest 'quiet corner' of the national park (both generally closed to cars October–June).

Driving between them can take upwards of four or five hours. Know your entrance point, expect delays on summer weekends, and check ahead on road conditions. It's possible to drive from the Nisqually and Stevens Canyon entrance through Paradise. Stevens Canyon closes October–June, but Nisqually stays open during winter daytime.

RENE FREDERICK/GETTY IMAGES ©

Mt Rainier

141

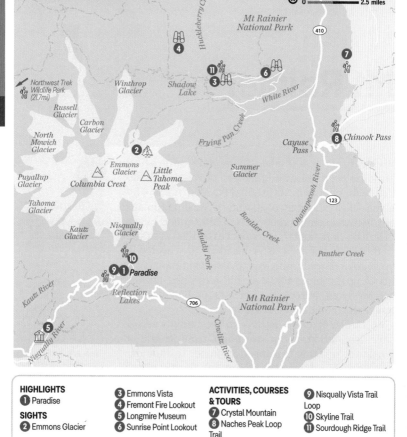

MT RAINIER NATIONAL PARK

Mt Rainier
National Park

410

Northwest Trek
Wildlife Park
(21.7mi)

Russell
Glacier

Winthrop
Glacier

Shadow
Lake

White River

Carbon
Glacier

North
Mowich
Glacier

Frying Pan Creek

Cayuse
Pass

Chinook Pass

Puyallup
Glacier

Emmons
Glacier

Little
Tahoma
Peak

Summer
Glacier

Columbia Crest

Ohanapecosh River

123

Tahoma
Glacier

Kautz
Glacier

Nisqually
Glacier

Boulder Creek

Panther Creek

Paradise

Mudily Fork

Kautz River

Reflection
Lakes

706

Mt Rainier
National Park

Nisqually River

Cowlitz River

0   5 km
0   2.5 miles

HIGHLIGHTS
1 Paradise
SIGHTS
2 Emmons Glacier

3 Emmons Vista
4 Fremont Fire Lookout
5 Longmire Museum
6 Sunrise Point Lookout

ACTIVITIES, COURSES & TOURS
7 Crystal Mountain
8 Naches Peak Loop Trail

9 Nisqually Vista Trail Loop
10 Skyline Trail
11 Sourdough Ridge Trail

Four Seasons Beauty

Mt Rainier from Paradise

☑ **TOP TIP**

Imagine how busy Mt Rainier is in the extremely short summer (around eight–10 weeks) season when the snow melts and the wildflowers bloom. Now: triple that. If you can't come on a weekday, plan on arriving by 9:30am (or after 3pm). Book camping months in advance at recreation.gov.

As the most glaciated peak in the contiguous US with unsurpassed beauty around every twist and turn, Mt Rainier is Western Washington's siren song for the power of nature to astound us.

Summer weekends may indeed mean entrance wait times of over two hours, and parking lots are jam-packed. But there are many ways to enjoy Mt Rainier even in high season if you plan ahead.

From mid-July through late August, wildflowers like lavender lupines, fiery orange paintbrush and snow-white avalanche lilies rave silently in the surrounding meadows. Late summer into early fall offers huckleberry picking, gorgeous autumnal colors, and the calls of elk bugling during their rutting season. In winter, as one of the snowiest place on earth (669in annually), the roads to Paradise are plowed on all but the most difficult days. Even if you're not fully kitted out, it's possible to go snowshoeing, tubing, skiing and hiking at **Crystal Mountain** (or just riding the scenic gondola). Try snowshoeing under the glaciers of the **Nisqually Vista Trail Loop** or on the **Skyline Trail**. In spring, melting snow creates rushing waterfalls and lowland hikes. It's a great time to visit the bison, wolves, bears and native Pacific Northwest animals at the **Northwest Trek Wildlife Park**.

Don't worry about schlepping equipment. There are well-stocked gear rental locations in Ashford before you hit the park, just west of the busy Nisqually entrance. The majority of visitors enter the park via this entrance. The first stop is the **Wilderness Information Center** and **Longmire Museum**. Learn about the mountain's history and ask about activities, hiking trails, snowshoeing locations or the **Mt Rainier Scenic Railroad**.

And then, welcome to **Paradise**. At 5400ft elevation, this small section of the park sees an astonishing 1.3 million visitors a year, here to stop by the visitors center, stay at the cozy **Paradise Inn**, or park (few spaces after 10am!) and take in the rip-your-face-off levels of beauty. During the summer, come during the week, before 9am or after 4pm, or be prepared for heavy crowds.

There are plenty of spots off the beaten track, too. Mt Rainier has over 150 trails, including short and easy loops, several wheelchair-accessible trails and the famed 93-mile cross-mountain **Woodland Trail**. To hike your own section of the PCT (Pacific Crest Trail), you can access it via the 3.5-mile-long **Naches Peak Loop Trail** at Chinook Pass.

Experience Alpine Grandeur

Mt Rainier from Sunrise

Some 1000ft higher than Paradise, the **Sunrise** area is secretly the favorite of many Washingtonians, and entered via the wending forested drive from the **White River** entrance (closed to cars for the very long winter). The view from the **Sunrise Point Lookout** is of not only Mt Rainier but the whole Washington Cascade chain, from Mt Baker to Mt Adams. Plus, the wildflowers, glaciers and the Mother of All Waters herself can be taken in with a little more breathing space.

Want to see the largest glacier in the continental US? Take a quick stroll to **Emmons Vista** – or a longer hike along the **Sourdough Ridge Trail** or **Glacier Basin Trail** – to marvel at **Emmons Glacier**. If you're feeling particularly hardy, try waking up at 3am or 4am for the 5-mile hike to the **Fremont Fire Lookout** to take in the sunrise.

CHOICEST SPOTS ON THE PACIFIC CREST

Award-winning narrative journalist and adventurer **Wudan Yan** (wudanyan.com) shares her favorite spots along the Pacific Crest Trail (PCT).

Goat Rocks & the South Cascades
Traveling north along the PCT, you'll get your first taste of the alpine environs of Washington: jagged peaks on the Cispus Pass climb, and a 2-mile ridge walk along the iconic Knife's Edge.

Alpine Lakes Wilderness
Like beads along a necklace, alpine lakes stud this 74-mile stretch. A slight detour to camp or swim at Spectacle Lake is worth it.

Glacier Peak Wilderness
Test your fortitude as you admire Washington's least-visited volcano. Catch your breath in the electric-green meadows, mountain passes or alpine lakes.

 WHERE TO EAT AROUND MT RAINIER

Wildberry Restaurant	Paradise Village	Crystal Mountain
Owned by the world record holder of the fastest ascent of Mt Everest. Burgers and Nepalese cuisine. $	The Ukrainian restaurant at this vacation village features pierogies, borscht and delectable pastries. $$	Take a gondola to dine at Washington's highest-elevation restaurant. $$

Mt St Helen's

GETTING AROUND

There is no public transit on Hwy 504, so you'll need a car for all locations.

☑ TOP TIP

To climb Mt St Helen's above 4800ft, you'll need a permit (available at recreation.gov). Only a few hundred permits are available per day so apply as soon as they're available: on the first day of the month before your climb (ie April 1 for a May 1–31 ascent).

In early 1980, one of the most geologically transformative events in modern history began. An intrusion of magma in the occasionally grumpy volcano set off a series of (relatively) small earthquakes, avalanches and mini-eruptions.

And then, at 8:32am on May 18, 1980, a 5.1-magnitude earthquake set off the largest debris landslide in recorded history (3.3 billion cu yards). By 3pm, the pent-up magma erupted. By 5pm, ash covered Spokane in complete darkness, 250 miles to the east.

What happened next? Who witnessed the eruption? What have we learned about nature's ability to bounce back since?

Mt St Helen's now has three (or four, depending on landslides or other events) visitor centers offering mountains of knowledge. Plus, the now-8366ft cratered volcano (1200ft were blown off in the blast) is covered in wildflowers in the spring, herds of grazing elk, and unsurpassed geological beauty.

A Volcanic Detour

Eighteen minutes off I-5

Visiting Mt St Helen's could be anything from a one-hour detour off the highway, or an adventurous multiday trek to the summit. For the detour, start at **Mt St Helen's Visitor Center**, open year-round. Walk inside a model of the volcano or through the chronology of events, watch a film about the eruption, or join in a mini-lesson in volcanology or ecology with a park ranger.

With more time (and filled up on gas, water and food), keep driving until you reach milepost 33 and the **Mt St Helen's Forest Learning Center**. Co-sponsored by the Weyerhaeuser lumber company, it's filled with interactive and kid-friendly exhibits, including a 'Discovery Room' with hands-on volcanic

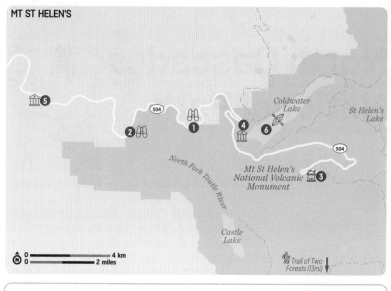

MT ST HELEN'S

SIGHTS
1. Castle Lake
2. Elk Rock
3. Johnston Ridge Observatory
4. Mt St Helen's Forest Learning Center
5. Mt St Helen's Visitor Center

ACTIVITIES, COURSES & TOURS
6. Coldwater Lake

rocks. The next two viewpoints – **Elk Rock** at milepost 37 and **Castle Lake** at milepost 40 – is when the statuesque, desolate beauty of the volcanic blast zone becomes most apparent.

Mt St Helen's has over 200 hiking trails – including the family-friendly and well-signposted **Trail of Two Forests** or **Birth of a Lake Trail**. And not much beats a kayak on **Coldwater Lake**, formed from the 1981 eruption. The lake has stayed pristine, with only human- and electric-powered crafts allowed.

If the **Johnston Ridge Observatory** at the end of Hwy 504 is still closed from landslides, stop at the equally informative **Science and Learning Center** at milepost 43. If you have several days (and a permit), Mt St Helen's is a peakbagger's delight. The summit climb itself is not terribly technical; but with strong winds (consider goggles!) and deep ash fields, it can take an entire day.

DOG-FRIENDLY CASCADES

Leavenworth
Dogs often welcome on trails and even inside sometimes, like the Doghaus Brewery.

National Parks
Dogs are mostly allowed on paved areas, with a few dog-friendly trails, including the PCT.

Mt Rainier
Dogs are welcome at nearby Crystal Mountain ski resort, including on the gondola.

Mt St Helen's
The volcanic ash of Mt St Helen's is especially dangerous for canine paws, but they are allowed at Coldwater Lake.

North Cascades National Park

GETTING AROUND

Be prepared! Inside the park, there are no gas stations, hotels or restaurants, and cell-phone service is spotty. Hwy 20 (the North Cascades Hwy) closes in winter between Newhalem and Mazama, when you'll need to drive around the southern routes to reach the Methow Valley. Always check for road conditions, even in summer, as wildfires or landslides can also shut down the area.

☑ **TOP TIP**

Wildfires sometimes close the area in summer. You can still reach much of the area, but plan your route carefully in every season. And be mindful of any burn bans!

Mt Terror. Mt Fury. Damnation Peak. Mt Triumph (phew!).

The North Cascades National Park is as infamous for its treacherous conditions as it is for its wild beauty. It's also famously the fifth-least-visited national park in the US, but this is a myth. True, only 30,000 folks officially apply for permits. But these are backcountry permits – for the mountaineers, PCT thru-hikers and leave-no-trace dispersed campers who bask in the solitude of one of the most majestically isolated national parks in the US.

However, the front-facing side of the park – the route along the Cascades Hwy 20 – is no less majestic, and the barrier for entry is far more accessible. One million visitors come to kayak the bright turquoise glaciated waters of the lakes (Diablo, Ross or Gorge), camp at the lakefront Colonial Creek Campground or sneak a peek at the foreboding peaks, deep forested valleys and exotic fauna that call this region home.

Alpine Beauty, Turquoise Waters

Driving the Cascades' scenic highway

The drive through the North Cascades National Park is one of the United States' most photogenic road trips, with more than 300 glaciers, peaks above 9000ft, and climbing, hiking and camping.

Just past the national park is **Washington Pass** overlook, where you can see the **Liberty Bell Mountain** spires, the sheer cliffs often dotted with rock climbers. The area's best hike, the secluded **Heather Maple Pass Loop**, is accessed via the **Rainy Pass** picnic area. Head through to access the 7.2-mile trail, which highlights the region, from wildflowers in the summer to brilliantly yellow larch trees in fall.

The **North Cascades Highway** is part of the Cascade Loop National Scenic Byway, circling from Whidbey Island (p102)

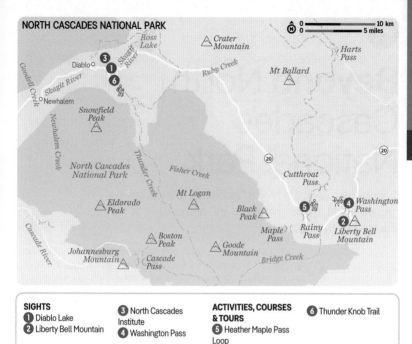

NORTH CASCADES NATIONAL PARK

0 — 10 km
0 — 5 miles

Ross Lake
Crater Mountain
Harts Pass
Diablo
Skagit River
Ruby Creek
Mt Ballard
Goodell Creek
Skagit River
Newhalem
Newhalem Creek
Snowfield Peak
North Cascades National Park
Thunder Creek
Fisher Creek
Cutthroat Pass
20
20
Eldorado Peak
Mt Logan
Black Peak
Washington Pass
Cascade River
Boston Peak
Maple Pass
Rainy Pass
Liberty Bell Mountain
Johannesburg Mountain
Cascade Pass
Goode Mountain
Bridge Creek

SIGHTS		ACTIVITIES, COURSES & TOURS	
❶ Diablo Lake	❸ North Cascades Institute	❺ Heather Maple Pass Loop	❻ Thunder Knob Trail
❷ Liberty Bell Mountain	❹ Washington Pass		

in the west to the Methow Valley (p149) in the northeast and then Leavenworth (p136). The whole loop takes several days.

Dam Fine Views

Exploring Diablo Lake

One of the most photographed spots in Washington is this impossibly turquoise lake surrounded by snowcapped peaks and emerald-green evergreens.

While **Diablo Lake**'s waters are ancient, the lake itself is not. That teal color is due to reflective 'glacial flour,' but the lake originated with the creation of the **Skagit River Hydroelectric Project** in 1917, bringing power to Seattle by 1924 via the Gorge Dam, Diablo Dam and Ross Lake Dam.

The best lake view is from the 3.6-mile **Thunder Knob Trail**, accessed through the park's **Colonial Creek Campground**. Kayaking the lake is otherworldly; if you didn't bring your kayak (no rentals available), the educational **North Cascades Institute** offers both lunchtime and afternoon **Diablo Lake Boat Tours**.

BALD EAGLE VIEWING

The center of Washington's bald eagle viewing is the **Skagit River** just west of the North Cascades National Park. At the **Skagit River Bald Eagle Interpretive Center** in Rockport's **Howard Miller State Park** (open weekends during bald eagle season, usually November-February), a resident Eagle Watcher will answer questions.

For closer view, **Skagit River Eagle Tours** (skagiteagles. com) goes daily for a three- to four-hour small-boat float to spot eagles during the busiest season.

Beyond North Cascades National Park

Continue on past the North Cascades to the rugged small towns and skiing and hiking trails of the Methow Valley.

With the most cross-country skiing tracks in the United States and backcountry views to match, the Methow Valley feels like the natural, populated extension of the North Cascades.

As you drive east along the Methow River, ponderosa pines turn into Wild West shrubsteppes. The largest town, Winthrop, has gone all-in on the theme; visitors flock here to walk along wooden boardwalks and visit cowboy-themed outfitters, or go on Western-themed horseback rides. In March, the Winthrop Balloon Roundup floats in, and July boogies with the Winthrop Rhythm and Blues Festival. Neighboring Twisp is where art colony meets the outdoors crowd, and one-road Mazama feels like the coolest summer camp ever, complete with in-town rock climbing.

Cross-country skiing, Methow Valley

Mazama

TIME FROM NORTH CASCADES NATIONAL PARK: **45 MINS**

Adventure in the Methow

Fill up on baguettes at the **Mazama Store**, the unofficial social headquarters for the outdoors world of Methow Valley. Grab locally made goodies, buy a map and plan your day, or pick your fellow travelers' brains for the best hiking, skiing or climbing spots.

Next door is **Goat's Beard**, full of outdoor gear for sale or rent, and the **Methow Valley Ski School and Rentals** has rental downhill and cross-country skis as well as group and private instruction. Or plan ahead and book a climbing, skiing or back-country trip with the **Mountaineers** (www .mountaineers.org). This beloved Pacific Northwest-based organization has a mission to explore and preserve the region's natural world. It offers reasonably priced, expert-led single or multiday trips to almost everywhere in the Cascades. Non-members welcome.

In the evenings, dine with your new friends under the mountains and stars at the **Mazama Public House**.

Methow Valley

TIME FROM NORTH CASCADES NATIONAL PARK: **45 MINS**

Ski, hike, climb the Methow

With more groomed Nordic and cross-country skiing trails than anywhere else in the United States (130 miles!), the Methow Valley is also sunnier, less crowded and at lower elevation than many of its more treacherously mountainous or volcanic Cascade neighbors (we're lookin' at you, Mt Rainier, Mt Baker and Mt St Helen's). Friends and families have been coming to the Methow for generations to cross-cross ski at **Methow Trails** in winter or bike or hike during summer. Dog-friendly!

THRIVING CREATIVE DISTRICTS

In tiny **Twisp**, where one-tenth of the population is a working artist, you can visit the 6-acre artist campus **TwispWorks** to buy arts and crafts, check out the gardens of native plants or natural dyes, or kick it with a pint at the **Old Schoolhouse Brewery.**

Twisp is one of a dozen (and counting) Washington Creative Districts. These officially designated locations celebrate how art, culture, food or history help a region thrive and flourish. The Districts get funding to grow their diversity, economy and creativity. Support artists (and the concept itself) in these communities, including Rainier Valley in Seattle (p56), Bainbridge Island (p84) or Chewelah.

WHERE TO SLEEP IN THE METHOW VALLEY

Inn at Mazama
Dog-friendly with a sauna; a quick walk to the Mazama Store. $$$

North Cascades Mountain Hostel
Great prices and convivial atmosphere in the center of Winslow. $

Twisp River Suites
Cool and quiet metal motel with leaded windows right in town. $$

Above: Vineyard, Walla Walla (p154); Right: Monroe St Bridge, Spokane (p161)

Eastern Washington

BUCOLIC FARMS, WINERIES AND RUGGED NATURE

Road trip country: where the Wild West meets the South of France, with a side of otherworldly geology.

Western Washington and the Cascades get most of the tourism glory, what with their fancy islands, snowcapped mountains and flashy cities. (And crowds.)

But for many city dwellers and international visitors, this mix of desert plains, rocky scablands, forested wilderness and pastoral rolling hills is like nothing they've ever seen. This is amber-waves-of-grain, this-land-is-your-land cowboy country, with swaths of sleepy sagebrush interspersed with lunar-looking geological marvels – and hundreds of sights, trails and activities in between.

Road-tripping was born for regions like this – u-pick farms, wine-tasting rooms and breweries in the middle of grapes-and-hops country; Wild West towns; fossil hunting (and hunting-hunting) and honest-to-goodness tumbleweeds. Plus, after visiting, you might just want to move here, to up-and-coming Spokane or friendly Walla Walla (often included on 'Best Small Cities in the USA' lists).

Eastern Washington is enormous (over 46,000 sq miles, the same size as Pennsylvania or North Korea). The Missoula Floods raged through here almost 15,000 years ago, leaving in their wake both geological formations and the rich, fertile soil that makes this one of the best natural farming regions in the world. The region grows over 70% of the nation's apples (and a good portion of its hops, apricots, wheat, barley and many other crops), and its abundant rivers provide some of the nation's best inner tubing.

© KINGWU/VW/GETTY IMAGES

THE MAIN AREAS

WALLA WALLA	NORTHEASTERN WASHINGTON	SPOKANE	COULEE CORRIDOR
Wine, food, farms and scenery.	Fossils, farms and foraging.	Waterfall inside big, gentle city.	Striking geological formations.
p154	p160	p161	p162

Find Your Way

With over double the land of Western Washington but one-fifth the population, getting around Eastern Washington takes a while. But this is a road-tripper's paradise, serviced by good roads, myriad farm stands and attractions, and dramatic scenery.

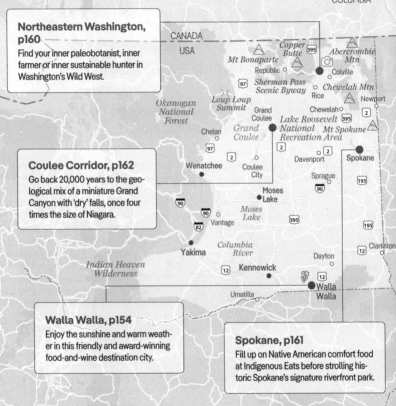

BRITISH COLUMBIA

Northeastern Washington, p160

Find your inner paleobotanist, inner farmer or inner sustainable hunter in Washington's Wild West.

Coulee Corridor, p162

Go back 20,000 years to the geological mix of a miniature Grand Canyon with 'dry' falls, once four times the size of Niagara.

Walla Walla, p154

Enjoy the sunshine and warm weather in this friendly and award-winning food-and-wine destination city.

Spokane, p161

Fill up on Native American comfort food at Indigenous Eats before strolling historic Spokane's signature riverfront park.

CANADA
USA

Mt Bonaparte
Copper Butte
Abercrombie Mtn
Republic
Colville
Sherman Pass Scenic Byway
Rice
Chewelah Mtn
Newport
Okanogan National Forest
Loup Loup Summit
Grand Coulee
Chewelah
Lake Roosevelt National Recreation Area
Mt Spokane
Chelan
Grand Coulee
Wenatchee
Coulee City
Davenport
Spokane
Moses Lake
Sprague
Moses Lake
Vantage
Yakima
Columbia River
Dayton
Clarkston
Indian Heaven Wilderness
Kennewick
Walla Walla
Umatilla

PUBLIC TRANSPORTATION

Cities are accessible by bus, but journeys can be infrequent and long (the once-daily Seattle to Walla Walla route is eight hours each way). There are no regional trains, though Amtrak's *Empire Builder* stops in Spokane.

CAR

Eastern Washington was built for road-tripping, with vast distances covered by well-maintained roads. The drive from Seattle to Walla Walla is over five hours; most destinations in the chapter are an hour or two apart.

0 — 100 km
0 — 50 miles

Rainier cherries

Plan Your Time

Eastern Washington is absolutely enormous, so you'll be able to visit one or two locations at most in a weekend. Plan your trip in advance.

Eastern Washington Weekend

Spend a day or two in **Walla Walla** (p154). Without a car, you could stay downtown and visit any number of dozens of wineries, restaurants and locally owned shops. With a car, add a **Coulee Corridor** (p162) day trip or, in summer, find a **u-pick farm** (p154) with Rainier cherries, berries or apricots.

Stay a Week

Head up to **Northeastern Washington** (p160), where you can do a walking day trip in up-and-coming **Spokane** (p161), hunt for fossils in **Stonerose** (p165), do an agritourism course on Slow Food farm living at **Quillisascut** (p164) or learn hunting or foraging at **Human Nature Hunting** (p164).

Seasonal Highlights

SPRING
While the rest of Washington is still thawing out, **Walla Walla** bursts with shades of green.

SUMMER
By June, u-pick farms open across the region, and the agricultural areas of **Northeastern Washington** shine.

FALL
Fall colors rival New England, especially around **Yakima** and in the gardens of **Manito Park** in **Spokane**.

WINTER
An icy beauty blankets the striking geological formations and rivers of the **Coulee Corridor** area.

Walla Walla

HOW TO FIND A U-PICK FARM

To pick Washington's beloved pink-yellow Rainier cherries – or apricots, apples, blueberries, even lavender – plan a trip around early summertime. Dozens of farms in and around Walla Walla (and Eastern Washington) have u-pick opportunities at their peaks. Try the following to find one for your visit.

Classifieds
Check out the back of the local newspaper. Bonus: info on events, culture, too.

Tourist Boards
Call or email before you even arrive to plan ahead.

Online
Larger farms list opening days on their websites, but some websites list all the u-pick farms for Washington.

Ask!
Spark a conversation with a local, or ask at shops or farm stands.

We're not gonna say it. Not gonna... 'Walla Walla; the town so nice, they named it twice.'

The town's local saying is true; Walla Walla is exceedingly welcoming. The downtown is small-town perfection, with two thriving universities, historic architecture in walkable neighborhoods, and a backdrop of grapevine-covered fields and hills of amber wheat. Plus, what award *hasn't* Walla Walla won recently? Its accolades include Best American Wine Region, 25 Cutest Main Streets, Prettiest Winter Towns and Friendliest Small Town in America.

The small city punches above its weight with great restaurants, picturesque farm stands and over 120 wineries broken into six stunningly beautiful tasting districts – most spread out over absolutely gorgeous rolling hills. With warmer weather and as one of the sunniest towns in Washington, Walla Walla is at its best on spring and fall weekends, during winery release weeks, and u-pick season for Rainier cherries and berries.

Wine Tasting in Walla Walla
Sip around the city

Situated atop the rich soil, basalt and deposited sediments of the Missoula Floods is the **Walla Walla Valley**, famed for its excellent grape-growing terroir for over 150 years. Cabernet sauvignon and Syrah reign supreme here, but merlot is a close third. Established as Washington's second AVA (American Viticultural Area) in 1984, there are now over 120 wineries in and around Walla Walla, broken into six different regions: Downtown, Airport, Westside, Eastside, Southside, and Oregon.

To get the most out of a wine-tasting adventure to Walla Walla, plan in advance. Leave the car and visit downtown (over 30 tasting rooms!) or check www.wallawalla.org for over a dozen private driver and group tour options, includ-

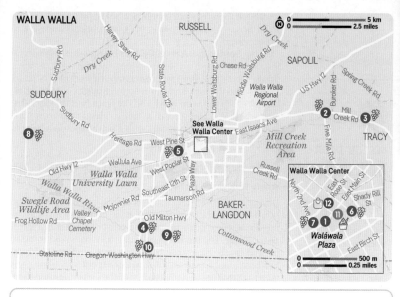

WALLA WALLA

HIGHLIGHTS&
1 Waláwala Plaza

SIGHTS
2 Abeja Winery
3 Aluvé

4 Amavi Cellars
5 Foundry Vineyards
6 House of Smith
7 Kontos Cellars

8 Long Shadows Vintners
9 Northstar Winery
10 Sleight of Hand Cellars

EATING
11 Pine Cone Creamery

SHOPPING
12 Showroom on Colville

ing winery tours by bicycle. Or, bring your own or rent bikes. Many wineries prefer or require that you book in advance, so do your research.

Downtown, off Main St, you'll find sixth-generation vintners **Kontos Cellars** or the award-winning rock 'n' roll **House of Smith**. Venture a little further for the funky **Foundry Vineyards**, with an enclosed patio and rotating collection of installations by nationally known artists.

It's worth the drive to the **Westside** for the gorgeous **Long Shadows Vintners**, where robust reds meet an impeccably designed tasting room with views of the Blue Mountains. Recently voted the single best tasting room in the United States.

The area near the **Airport** boasts up-and-coming wineries, including the inventive **Incubator**, where a rotating collection of a half-dozen start-up wineries create their origin stories.

Eastside wineries have some of the best views amid rolling hills and mountain vistas. Highlights include the small but gorgeous **Aluvé**, run by former Air Force pilots, and **Abeja**,

☑ TOP TIP

Visit on Thursday and Friday, or Sunday. Many restaurants and wineries close on some weekdays and some locations shut on Saturday (Walla Walla has a large Seventh Day Adventist population). Some wineries require or strongly prefer reservations. You'll need a car to get the most out of the area.

WHERE TO EAT IN WALLA WALLA

TMACS
Upscale, innovative cuisine with craft cocktails and delightful outdoor seating. $$

La Monarca
Popular with locals, the taco truck's Walla Walla taco features the famed eponymous sweet onions. $

AK's Mercado
Southeast Washington meets south of the border and the US South with tinga tacos or voodoo fries. $$

155

located in a century-old farmhouse beautiful enough to host weddings, with guest rooms, five-course meals and several white wines.

On the **Southside**, **Amavi Cellars** boasts sustainable farming practices (and is the rare winery outside of downtown that's open until 6pm) with gorgeous views from its patio. There's also the rock-and-roll-inspired **Sleight of Hand Cellars**, with its tunes on vinyl, and the large **Northstar Winery**, where you can reserve a spot to blend your own wine or do the 'cabana experience,' with a private outdoor cabana amid gorgeous rolling hill scenery.

Pedestrianized Food & Wine City Center
Where to begin

Downtown Walla Walla has won accolades for its revitalization efforts, and the efforts have made this small town in the middle of wheat fields feel like the convivial center of a European village. During the pandemic, the town voted to make permanent the pedestrianized city core, including **Waláwala Plaza** and the surrounding **Main Street**. Celebrate their efforts at this plaza, a microcosm of the surrounding region, including its Native communities. Waláwala means 'many small streams' in the Sahaptin language, and elements from Walla Walla's natural world are incorporated into the design, including colors from the local balsamroot sunflowers and pavers marking the streams below. With dozens of tables and benches, grab an ice cream from the **Pine Cone Creamery**, enjoy the sunny Walla Walla weather and people-watch off your wine-tasting tipsiness. On Saturday mornings from May to October, check out the **Downtown Farmers Market**, filled with bounty from this rich agricultural region. In November and December, it moves indoors to the artsy **Showroom on Colville**, filled with local shops, crafts and market goodies year-round.

BEST OUTDOOR ACTIVITIES IN WALLA WALLA

Bicycling
The rural backroads in and around Walla Walla are tailor-made for bicycling, especially around Bennington Lake – a great spot for kayaking or bird-watching – or head up to the nearby Blue Mountains to get your heart pumping.

Frog Hollow Farms
Feed the goats and pigs, shop for produce and locally made gifts, or add to your garden with the enormous selection of organic seeds and plant starts.

Hot-Air Balloon
Visit for the Walla Walla Balloon Stampede (second Sunday in May) or book a peaceful float above the hills year-round.

WHERE TO SLEEP IN WALLA WALLA

The GG
Period-designed rooms and possibly the country's most elaborate private vintage Louis Vuitton collection. **$$$**

The Finch
Motel rooms with modernized artist-designed spaces and Wednesday wine tastings. **$**

Marcus Whitman Hotel
In the heart of downtown, the historic Whitman's restaurant is as good as its Blue Mountain views. **$$**

Beyond
Walla Walla

In southeast Washington, you'll find vintage small towns, sprawling vineyards and hop fields, and prime inner-tubing.

If you haven't gotten your fill of bucolic wineries, deliciously fresh farm-grown fruit and veggies, and the meditative, rhythmic calm of road-tripping through mustard-yellow and sage-green rolling hills, then continue either west or north from Walla Walla.

Those three-hour waits just to get into Mt Rainier? Pshaw. You've got this wide-open countryside to yourself. From Yakima Valley's hops, inner tubing and small-town summer festivals to the area's farms, small towns and forests, the region is awash in ways to immerse yourself in the local culture. Make your own cheese at Monteillet Fromagerie, cut down a Christmas tree in Umatilla National Forest, or follow in the footsteps of Sacajawea.

GETTING AROUND

Although some hardy folks bicycle between wineries and other destinations near Walla Walla, a sturdy vehicle is essential for harvesting a Christmas tree. Rafting logistics can be quite complex (even with your own car and equipment), so outfitters are a great choice.

☑ **TOP TIP**

If you're floating down the Yakima, come prepared with double the water (and sunscreen) you think you'd need.

PHIL AUGUSTAVO/GETTY IMAGES ©

Hops vines, Yakima Valley

EVERY KID OUTDOORS

Are you in the fourth grade? Do you know someone who is? Great news: every fourth grader in the United States and their families receive free admission or a free annual pass (currently worth $80) to all National Park Service properties. Tell a friend; fewer than 1% of eligible families participate. Christmas tree permits are included, making Christmas-tree harvesting a most affordable, fun and family-friendly day out in the run-up to Yuletide.

Yakima River

Yakima River
TIME FROM WALLA WALLA: 1 HR

Inner-tubing the Yakima

As the cows moo from the riverbanks and fish jump in the waters below, you're on top of the world/water, floating your worries away. The Yakima River is outlandishly popular and tailor-made for floating, with over a dozen boat launch access points from **Cle Elum** to **Prosser**, all well marked along the river. Bring your own floaties or rafts (or rent or buy them nearby; there are dozens of locations, from gas stations to rental companies) or join a trip with a rafting outfitter.

MORE RIVER ADVENTURES

There's also great river rafting and inner tubing near **Leavenworth** (p136) and **Mazama** (p149). Bring your own tubes, or contact one of the dozens of outfitters that supply everything you'll need.

Dayton
TIME FROM WALLA WALLA: 40 MINS

Try your hand at cheese-making

For the experience of a lifetime, learn to make your own cheese with owners Joan and Pierre Louis of **Monteillet Fromagerie**. From four hours to two days on their stunningly gorgeous property, the absolutely delightful French-American couple will teach you each stage of the cheese-making process. Not just chèvre! Learn how to make hard cheese in a copper kettle the old-fashioned way, or how to stretch, cook and cut mozzarella. Tasting is encouraged throughout the course, and wine flows very, very freely. Check their website (monteilletcheese.com) to enquire about classes or to arrange your own small group course. Not ready for cheese school? Stop by the farmers markets in **Richland** (Fridays 9am–1pm) or **Walla Walla** (Saturdays 9am–1pm) in summer to buy some of their half-dozen delicious (pre-made) cheeses.

Umatilla National Forest

TIME FROM WALLA WALLA: 1 HR

Harvest your own Christmas tree

It's the day after Thanksgiving. The lower mountains are dusted with snow, but not too cold yet. You want an enjoyable family outing or a mini-adventure – maybe with some nature built in – that doesn't cost a lot, *and* helps the national forests of Washington thin their trees.

Well, have we got the activity for you! Welcome to the Christmas Tree Permit system, which, exactly as it sounds, means anyone with $5 (or $10, for the Mt Baker Snoqualmie Forest) and a decent set of wheels can depart from Walla Walla in the morning to return with a freshly cut festive prize by evening.

Be sure to come very, very well prepared. Permits are available starting in November, by which time the roads maybe already be icy and wet. Daytime temperatures are already starting to dip below freezing, and you might end up hiking for an hour in the most popular spots to find the right tree, so dress warmly. It goes without saying that you'll need a sturdy vehicle to reach the forest and to lug your prize back to town.

Permits are available in Umatilla and Washington's five other national forests, including Colville (near Kettle Falls) in east Washington; Okanogan-Wenatchee in north-central Washington; two in the Cascades (Gifford Pinchot and Mt Baker Snoqualmie); and the Olympic National Forest on the far-western peninsula. As long as you follow the rules and guidelines of each national forest, you are welcome to help the forest with their own version of Christmas trimmings. These rules may include only cutting trees that are a certain distance from either a main road or a campground, trying to choose one in a grouping of trees, cutting the entire tree and not just the top, and so on; call the local forest service office for detailed information,

SACAJAWEA GUIDES LEWIS AND CLARK

In early 1803 Thomas Jefferson proposed sending an expedition to explore the new Louisiana Purchase and Pacific Northwest. In 1804 Meriwether Lewis and William Clark headed out from St Louis, Missouri. They soon encountered Touissant Charbonneau and one of his wives, a pregnant 16-year-old Sacajawea of the Shoshone people. The expeditioneers' journals – saved from a rushing river by Sacajawea, now the mom of a three-month-old infant – later speaks of 'the warm and friendly Wallah Wallahs.'

You can visit the nearby towns of Clarkston in Washington and Lewiston in Idaho, or learn more about Sacajawea at the **Sacajawea Historical State Park and Interpretive Center** in **Pasco**, near the sacred confluence of the Columbia and Snake Rivers.

 WHERE TO SLEEP NORTH OF WALLA WALLA

Stella's Homestead
Riverfront cabins filled with loads of personality, charm and history at a 100-year-old family farm. $

Royal Block
Finnish design meets New York loft-style brick and PNW Douglas fir floors, above a hip wine bar. $$

Lewis and Clark Trail State Park Campground
On a river with secluded, wooded campsites and several tipis to rent. $

Northeastern Washington

GETTING AROUND

You'll need a car to get around. Quillisascut and Human Nature Hunting are minutes from each other near the Columbia River north of Lake Roosevelt, about 1½ hours north of Spokane. Stonerose is another hour's drive west.

At the furthest western edge of the Rocky Mountain foothills, Northeastern Washington is where the mountains meet the modern frontier. Ponderosa pines and rugged lakes and forests are home to grizzlies, moose and wolf packs, as well as back-country farmers and folks who know how to live off the land. From fishing and boating on Lake Roosevelt to bird-watching or hiking in the peaceful Colville National Forest, this is one of the US's last frontier country getaway spots (with a tiny fraction of the crowds of Mt Rainier).

The main city round these parts is Spokane, a once-thriving city reclaiming its past glory (with the architecture, foodie culture and sites to prove it). Beyond Spokane, find fossils in Republic, preserve the farm's strawberries or milk the goats at culinary-school favorite Quillisascut, or hunt or forage your own dinner at Human Nature Hunting.

☑ TOP TIP

If you're visiting the Stonerose Fossil Center in the hot summer, arrive as early as possible (it opens at 8am), bring plenty of water and retreat to the shady spots provided. Hats, gloves and long pants protect against the sun and rocky terrain.

As the biggest city in the intermountain northwest, Spokane has always played second fiddle to Seattle. But while the pandemic population dropped in Seattle, it grew in Spokane, and this once-sleepy destination is thriving. Most people drive through Spokane, but you won't regret a day dining, drinking and enjoying the city's proximity to nature.

Start at 1 **Atticus Gifts and Coffee** with a beverage and pastry, including a side order of gifts like art supplies or old books. Once well fueled, head 50ft north to 2 **Riverfront Park**, the jewel in Spokane's civic crown. Spend a few hours here, riding the gondola or the carousel, admiring the rushing waters and waterfall below, or walking the trails. Then head west through the park to River Park Square Mall and 3 **Indigenous Eats**, a Native-owned restaurant featuring Indian frybread.

Walk off lunch on your way to 4 **Northwest Museum of Arts and Culture**, 30 minutes west of the mall in the historic Browne's Addition neighborhood. The Smithsonian-affiliated MAC houses an extensive collection from the Plateau Indians, the 1898 Campbell House outfitted in period furnishings and decor, and a rotating collection of art.

A walk (or quick taxi) up the hill will bring you to the world-class 5 **Manito Park**. In addition to lilacs, roses and Japanese horticulture, there's a conservatory, dog parks and several playgrounds. After working up an appetite, 6 **Feast World Kitchen** is an ideal dinner stop with chefs from local refugee and immigrant communities shaking up the menu every month. Finally, stop in for a pint at 7 **Bark! Rescue Pub**, where you can cuddle kitties and puppies at the adjacent Humane Society, and then a nightcap under the glorious grandeur of 8 **Hotel Davenport**'s stained-glass ceilings.

The Coulee Corridor

The Ice Age, about 13,000 years ago. You're the Coulee Corridor in Eastern Washington, minding your own business, when whammo! Montana's ice dams break, sending a series of cataclysmic floods to cut otherworldly geological formations throughout your landscape. A few millennia later, the Missoula Floods have left this arid, sparsely populated region a road-tripper's Eden, home to some of Washington's most stunning hiking trails, campgrounds, bird-watching and lakes for fishing or kayaking.

1 Vantage

Before you hop on the Coulee Corridor coming from the west, stop in Vantage for a good vantage spot overlooking the mighty Columbia River from the **Wanapum Viewpoint**. Visit the **Ginkgo Petrified Forest State Park**, where lava flows mineralized local trees, creating Washington's official state gem: petrified wood.

The Drive: Jump on interstate Hwy 90 east, peeling off at Hwy 238, then Hwy 28. Stop in Soap Lake for lunch and to fill up on gas. Then continue on Hwy 17.

2 Sun Lake-Dry Falls State Park

The clear-water lake is surrounded by rocky outcroppings and Martian surfaces from the flood's path. Plus, the views of **Dry Falls** can't be beat. If you have

Sun Lake-Dry Falls State Park

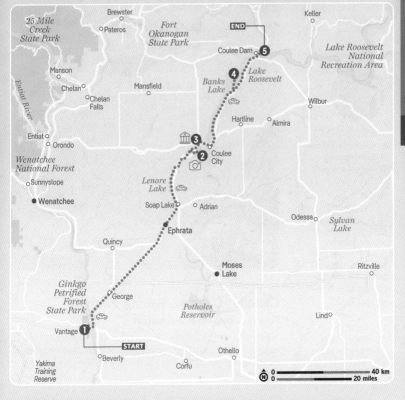

the time, stay a while: kayak under the cliffside rocky escarpments or camp under the Milky Way.

The Drive: Take the back way from the state park to Dry Falls itself, or continue on Hwy 17 to the Dry Falls Visitor Center.

3 Dry Falls Visitor Center

Look out for the brutalist architecture, ice cream truck and harrowing viewpoints over the 400ft-high dry waterfalls for this thoroughly engaging visitor center. Be sure to check out the exhibit on the **Blue Lake Rhino**. In 1935 hikers discovered this 15-million-year-old rhinoceros encased in basalt. Stop by the Burke Museum in Seattle's UW campus to see a replica.

The Drive: Continue northeast on Hwy 17, wave at Coulee City as you continue onto Hwy 2 and Hwy 155 past Banks Lake before turning left onto the Steamboat Rock peninsula.

4 Steamboat Rock State Park

A popular stopover for Native tribes as well as later settlers, the peninsular park is surrounded by sheer beauty. Families have been coming here for generations to camp, fish, kayak, swim at the warm-water beaches, enjoy the playgrounds and spot wild turkeys. Great ice cream at the concession stand.

The Drive: Keep heading up Hwy 155 along Banks Lake through the towns of Electric City and Grand Coulee until you reach the dam itself.

5 Grand Coulee Dam

A modern marvel when it was built in 1935, it's still the largest producer of hydropower in the US (powering two million homes). The west-side visitor center is chock full of info, and you can take a free tour behind the scenes. Stay at a nearby motel or RV park (or, better yet, camp back at Steamboat Rock) and watch the kitschy but enjoyably educational laser light show.

163

SEASONAL HUNTING & FORAGING

Bruce and Sarah McGlenn run **Human Nature Hunting** (www.humannature hunting.com).

Spring
People flock to Eastern Washington for morel mushroom season. Look in areas that have been burned recently, but do beware of toxic 'false' morels!

Summer
Look for serviceberries. Slightly nuttier and meatier than a blueberry, the trees and shrubs are found all over low elevations.

Fall
You can hunt your own wild turkey feast, especially around Colville.

Winter
In February and March, we teach courses on the Hood Canal. Or, do it yourself! Get a license, bring gear (oyster knife, gloves, container), and find a public beach to forage for shellfish.

GEORGE OSTERTAG/ALAMY STOCK PHOTO ©

Leaf fossil, Eocene Fossil Site

Canning, Cooking, Baking, Farming
Slow Food courses at Quillisascut

A long-time favorite of Seattle chefs, culinary students and foodie professionals, **Quillisascut Farm School for the Domestic Arts** (www.quillisascut.com) offers a Slow Living Autumn Gather and Food Lovers summer course for non-professionals. Spend four days (Thursday-Sunday) at this stunningly beautiful and peaceful farm, focusing on the intersection between nature, sustenance and creativity.

Learn to harvest the land, tend goats, dye natural fabrics, make preserves, bake bread. Farmers, cookbook authors and Slow Food experts Lora Lea and Rick make each meal almost entirely from the farm's harvest, and you're welcome to join in cooking as much as you'd like. Or as little: guests are welcome to journal, walk through the gardens or simply breathe in the fresh air. Courses run in late spring or early summer and October, and guests stay in comfortable rooms at the farm or in the hand-built caravan (or bring a tent to camp under the stars). Custom courses available for small groups.

 WHERE TO DRINK, EAT & STAY IN NORTHEASTERN WASHINGTON

Quartzite Brewery
A town gathering spot in the tiny Washington Creative District of Chewelah. **$**

18 North Bar and Grill
Across from Stonerose with delicious food, including top-rate biscuits and gravy. Airbnb upstairs! **$$**

Curlew State Park
Quiet camping 10 minutes from Stonerose. **$**

Hunting, Human Nature–Style
Sustainable hunting, foraging and survival courses

With a mission to 'heal and strengthen the bonds of humans and nature to the point we realize we are nature,' the family who run **Human Nature Hunting** (humannaturehunting.com) is helping us learn how to sustainably and ethically awaken our hunter-gatherer roots. On three- to five-day courses in spring and early summer, Human Nature provides very, very hands-on experience on hunting, foraging and survival skills from their hand-built cabin near **Kettle Falls**. In their stunningly gorgeous forested valley, pitch a tent, bring a camper or upgrade to a rustic cabin and enjoy three chef-cooked organic meals a day. For a less intense entry point into local food, nothing beats dining on newly foraged oysters and manila clams on their one-day shellfish foraging courses on the Olympic Peninsula in February and March.

Find Your Inner Paleobotanist
Fossil-hunting at Stonerose

Here's something you wouldn't have guessed: fossil-hunting is meditative. Maybe even a little addictive. Maybe it's in the thrill of rhythmically chiseling away at a thin piece of shale until – pop! – the rock splits apart to reveal an extinct ginkgo leaf not seen for 48 million years.

After the dinosaurs (by 15 million years) but before the Cascade mountain range (by about three million years) was the Eocene epoch, when the **Stonerose Interpretive Center** and its **Eocene Fossil Site** was the site of an ancient lake bed filled with fish, insects, leaves and plants. With some of the earliest fossils in the rose and maple family, Stonerose is a scientifically significant stop on the paleobotany circuit.

Stonerose is also the only organized spot in Washington to hunt for fossils. First visit the Stonerose Center, open year-round, to peruse local fossil finds with museum-quality details. When the digging site is open (May-October), rent a hammer and chisel and head up the hill. Practically everyone is guaranteed to find a fossil within an hour or so, but it's easy to spend a full day here. If you do come across a fossil of scientific importance – a new species, perhaps – they'll need to keep those findings. But diggers will get credit, including in scientific journals. Everyone gets to take their three best fossils home with them.

WHY I LOVE NORTHEASTERN WASHINGTON

Alex Leviton, writer (thethirdlayer.com)

As a city person, Northeastern Washington is radically different from anywhere I've ever lived, or even visited. I like having my assumptions of rural life challenged. Friends ditched their city jobs to start a sheep farm near Kettle Falls, and I get it. **Quillisascut** reminds me of Umbria, Italy, which I covered for a dozen years, and time spent at **Human Nature Hunting** is pure peace (I say this as a former vegetarian!). Whenever I'm here, I start looking for land or a cabin – near **Stonerose Fossil Site**, of course, to live out my inner paleobotanist fantasy. Plus, the nature is stunning, it's so serene, and I always see wildlife like marmot, deer and wild turkeys.

Portland

UNCONVENTIONAL FROM THE BEGINNING

Easy access to natural wonders and a world-class food scene makes this famously 'weird' city a great place to experience.

Portland started out as a port city, but its name has nothing to do with its position on the Willamette River and everything to do with a coin toss. The city's two founders wanted to name the city after his hometown. While the man from Maine won, Portland could have just as easily been called Boston. This 1843 penny toss was just the beginning of an unconventional way of doing things.

The city has taken great care in upholding an urban growth boundary that has forced developers to build up, not out. The benefits of that are reaped today: as long as traffic isn't bad you can easily cross the city in 20 minutes or so, while half an hour in a car can get you out into beautiful natural areas.

Although Portland has long been viewed as one of the most progressive cities in the US, it's not all roses. Well into the 20th century, Portland had blatantly discriminatory housing policies that prevented African Americans from owning homes in all but a handful of neighborhoods. Recent gentrification in these areas hasn't helped things and Portland is among the whitest big cities in the country. Although there are people of all backgrounds living here, Portland can feel more parochial than multicultural.

Portland's recent population boom has also played a significant role in shaping it into what many refer to as the 'new Portland.' The city began to get popular in the early 2000s when people caught wind of a little city in the Pacific Northwest where housing was affordable, the beer was good and nature was everywhere.

What once felt like a small town in disguise emerged as a destination in its own right. The culinary scene boomed and Portland began showing up on 'best places to live' lists. Portlanders no longer had to clarify that they were from *Oregon*, not Maine, when on vacation elsewhere in the US. And while growth has slowed recently, Portland has managed to hold onto its reputation as a bastion for hipsterism, natural beauty and exceptionally tasty food.

ARTYOORAN/SHUTTERSTOCK ©

THE MAIN AREAS

DOWNTOWN
The city's compact
urban heart.
p170

OLD TOWN/CHINATOWN
The gritty heart
of Old Portland.
p174

**THE PEARL DISTRICT &
NORTHWEST PORTLAND**
Upscale boutiques, a bookstore
and plenty of art.
p178

SEAN PAVONE/ALAMY STOCK PHOTO ©

Left: Portland Oregon sign, Old Town (p174); Above: Portland

SOUTHWEST PORTLAND
Countryside vibes
in the city.
p182

SOUTHEAST PORTLAND
Family fun and
culinary adventure.
p186

**NORTHEAST & NORTH
PORTLAND**
Artsy neighborhoods
with great dining.
p190

Find Your Way

Portland is compact and well planned. It's divided on an east–west axis by the Willamette River and between north and south by Burnside St. Street names are preceded by prefixes: NW, SW and S Portland are on the west side, while the east side encompasses SE, NE and N Portland. Burnside is prefixed by W or E.

0 — 2 km
0 — 1 miles

Portland International Airport

Willamette River

PORTSMOUTH

Northeast & North Portland
p190

Alberta Arts District

ROSEWAY

The Pearl District & Northwest Portland
p178

Forest Park

Hollywood Theatre

Oldtown/Chinatown
p174

Powell's City of Books

Lan Su Chinese Garden

Portland Chinatown Museum

Laurelhurst Park

International Rose Test Garden

Japanese Garden

Portland Art Museum

Oregon Historical Society Museum

Hopscotch Portland

Hoyt Arboretum

Washington Park

MT TABOR

World Forestry Center

Portland Japanese Garden

South Park Blocks

Discovery Museum

Oregon Zoo

Downtown
p170

Oregon Museum of Science & Industry

Southeast Portland
p186

Marquam Nature Park

Southwest Portland
p182

BROOKLYN

REED

HAYHURST

HILLSDALE

George Himes City Park

Ross Island

EASTMORE

CAR

Portland is car-friendly, and a vehicle is necessary for day trips. Download the Parking Kitty app to make paying for metered parking a breeze. The app meows at you when your time is running low.

PUBLIC TRANSPORTATION

Portland has a robust and bicycle-friendly public transportation network that includes buses, a light-rail network known as the MAX and modern streetcars (trams). The MAX is a convenient way to get between Portland International Airport (PDX) and Downtown.

Powell's City of Books (p179)

Plan Your Time

Explore artsy neighborhoods, hike through urban forests, find solace in global gardens and fill up on food cart fare.

A Whirlwind Day

Spend your morning in **Old Town/ Chinatown's** (p174) **Lan Su Chinese Garden** (p175). Grab lunch in the **Pearl District** (p178) and don't forget to stop by **Powell's City of Books** (p179) to browse the tomes. Wrap your day up with a stroll through the **Alberta Arts District** (p191), followed by a dip in the **Kennedy School's soaking pool** (p192).

Three Days to Explore

Devote your first day to visiting urban highlights such as the **Portland Art Museum** (p171) and **Powell's City of Books** (p179). Spend day two exploring scenic **Washington Park** (p183). On your final day, head to **Southeast Portland** (p186) to immerse yourself in art at **Hopscotch Portland** (p187) or science at the **Oregon Museum of Science and Industry** (p187).

Seasonal Highlights

SPRING	SUMMER	FALL	WINTER
Portland is at its most colorful in the (rainy) spring when flowers at local botanic gardens burst into bloom.	Hot temperatures and a break from the rain mean outdoor festivals and street fairs. Parks get busy.	Crisp air and shorter nights herald in the harvest season. Expect the rain to return.	Winters are relatively mild, but there's usually a late-season snowstorm that shuts the city down for a few days.

Downtown

THE CITY'S COMPACT URBAN HEART

☑ **TOP TIP**

Make the Portland Visitor Center on SW Harvey Milk St your first stop in Downtown Portland. Pick up brochures for local attractions, fill your water bottle and even charge your cell phone while you get tips from local experts on what to see, do and eat in the City of Roses.

On the western banks of the Willamette River, Downtown Portland is characterized by red-brick sidewalks, towering office buildings and plenty of green space. Downtown was once Portland's main commercial and shopping district, and while many of the people who used to work Downtown now operate from home offices, it's still a hub of activity. This is particularly the case in the summer months, when concerts, fun runs, cultural festivities and parades draw in big crowds. The bar and restaurant scene isn't too shabby either, particularly if you venture to the northwest corner of Downtown to an area that in recent years has been informally dubbed 'The West End.' Downtown is also where the vast majority of Portland's nicer hotels are located. As Downtown is Portland's main public transportation hub, it's the best place to base yourself if you're planning a car-free trip.

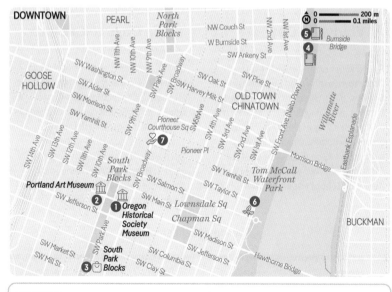

HIGHLIGHTS
1 Oregon Historical Society Museum
2 Portland Art Museum

3 South Park Blocks

SIGHTS
4 Governor Tom McCall Waterfront Park

5 Japanese American Historical Plaza
6 Mill Ends Park

7 Pioneer Courthouse Square

Portland Art Museum

The Northwest's oldest art museum

If you love the fine arts, you'll have plenty to keep you busy at the Portland Art Museum, the largest – and oldest – art museum in the state. Spread out over 112,000 sq ft, the museum hosts a mix of temporary and permanent exhibits showcasing art, photography and decorative objects from around the world. The museum's **Confederated Tribes of Grand Ronde Center for Native American Art** houses a huge collection of Indigenous art from across North America, spread across two floors.

Oregon Historical Society Museum

Portland Art Museum

Oregon Historical Society Museum

Learn about Oregon's roots

A great way to get familiar with the story of Oregon is by visiting the Oregon Historical Society Museum. Previous temporary exhibits have covered everything from the construction industry to carousels, while the permanent exhibit – Experience Oregon – tells the many stories of the people who shaped the state into what it is today, from the Indigenous Oregonians to early settlers. You can even see the penny that was flipped to determine Portland's name. If you're traveling with children don't miss the History Hub, an interactive exhibit that covers topics such as cultural diversity and discrimination through the lens of history.

South Park Blocks

Farmers markets and cultural institutions

Stretching from SW Salmon St clear through the Portland State University campus, the 12-block-long park known as the South Park Blocks forms one of the main arteries of Downtown's cultural scene. This leafy, statue-filled park is flanked by institutions such as the Arlene Schnitzer Concert Hall, the Portland Art Museum and the Oregon Historical Society, but it's best known as the site of the largest Portland **farmers market**, held on the southern end of the park every Saturday. While produce from local farms is the star of this year-round market, you'll also find food carts and bakers hawking their delights. A second, smaller market takes place on the northern end of the park on Wednesdays.

DOWNTOWN DINING WITH A LOCAL

Kimiko Matsuda, Multnomah Whiskey Library's Director of Culture, shares three of her favorite Downtown Portland restaurants. @kimi.ko__

MÂURICE
This lovely cafe is like a quick trip to Europe: a blend of French pastry technique and Scandinavian *fika* (the leisurely coffee break tradition). This tiny luncheonette is so special.

Tercet
A Portland-style fine-dining speakeasy. Want to surprise your sophisticated foodie friends? This seven-course tasting menu with wine pairing will be an experience that they will not forget.

Toki Restaurant
A great space, big windows and such a vibe! It has the best bibimbap and the Korean fried chicken will quickly become your favorite. The **Bao Burger** is not to be missed.

Portland's Living Room
The true center of town

Portland's self-declared 'living room,' **Pioneer Courthouse Square** – usually just called 'Pioneer Sq' or 'the Square' – is the de facto center of Downtown. This red-brick plaza serves as a public transit hub with MAX light-rail stops on its northern and southern perimeters. A semicircle of steps on the southern side of the square is a popular spot for people-watching, and there's a handful of food carts that cater to the office worker lunchtime crowd. Remember to look down: many of the tens of thousands of bricks that make up the square have been 'sponsored,' and bear the names of local Portlanders. The campaign is ongoing, and for a nominal fee you can have your name permanently etched in this central plaza.

While the square tends to be at its busiest during the summertime, when it plays host to all sorts of concerts and cultural events, it's very much a year-round attraction. Come during the holidays to witness the annual **Christmas tree lighting**, or visit in February when installations from the city-wide **Portland Winter Light Festival** illuminate the space.

Down by the River
Walk along the Willamette

Stretching for a mile and a half along the western banks of the Willamette River, **Governor Tom McCall Waterfront Park** (referred to simply as 'Waterfront' by most locals) is a great place to stroll if you want to experience Portland's greenery without having to leave Downtown. Waterfront hosts some of the city's biggest spring and summer events – including the Portland Cinco de Mayo Fiesta, the Waterfront Blues Festival and Portland Pride. It's also one of the main venues of the **Portland Rose Festival**, an annual community celebration that features multiple parades and a carnival – known as the CityFair – which takes over a section of the park for roughly two weeks.

North of the Burnside Bridge, the **Japanese American Historical Plaza** pays tribute to the Japanese Americans who were interred in prison camps during WWII, while reminding passersby of the protections they should have been afforded by the Bill of Rights. A hundred cherry trees line the plaza and their pretty pink blossoms draw in crowds when they bloom in early spring (March or April). A total of 13 **stand-**

 WHERE TO STAY IN DOWNTOWN

Hotel Rose
Clean, dog-friendly value-focused hotel with loaner bicycles, a gym and on-site parking. **$**

Kimpton RiverPlace Hotel
Elegant boutique property on the southern end of Waterfront Park where many rooms have river views. **$$$**

The Nines Hotel
High-end hotel housed in a converted department store building with plush, velvet-filled rooms. **$$$**

DAVEALAN/GETTY IMAGES ©

Governor Tom McCall Waterfront Park

ing stones decorate the plaza, including a centerpiece stone that lists the names of the 10 wartime internment camps in which Japanese Americans were imprisoned for no fault of their own. Other stones display art, poetry or political statements, and one bears the text of the Bill of Rights.

The World's Smallest Park

Here be leprechauns

While Portland has plenty of huge green spaces, it's also home to the smallest park in the world: **Mill Ends Park**. Spread out over a mere 452 sq in in a median strip on Downtown's Naito Parkway off SW Taylor, this Lilliputian delight traces its roots to 1946 when journalist Dick Fagan – who worked in the *Oregon Journal* office that overlooked the median – noticed an empty hole that had been dug for a light pole, but never filled. Fagan decided to plant flowers in the hole and began writing about it in a column called 'Mill Ends.' He used his column to tell stories of what he dubbed the 'World's Smallest Park,' most of them involving a group of leprechauns who lived in the park. He continued to delight Portlanders with his tales until his death in 1969, and in 1976 the magical little spot became an official park. Portland Parks and Recreation manages the park to this day. Take a walk over to the park and you'll see that it even has its own tiny sign, a scaled-down version of the official signs used at parks across the city. Portland has always been gloriously weird.

BEST SPOTS TO HEAR LIVE MUSIC

Crystal Ballroom
This historic ballroom turned concert venue features all the trappings of a traditional ballroom, down to its molded accents, crystal chandeliers and mildly bouncy floor. Despite the fancy ambience, the Crystal (as locals call it) generally hosts rock and electronic music shows.

Old Church Concert Hall
Occupying Downtown's oldest church building, this aptly named venue is known for its beautiful stained-glass windows and fantastic acoustics.

Arlene Schnitzer Concert Hall
Symphony fans love this concert hall (known simply as 'the Schnitz' in local parlance). It's the home of the Oregon Symphony and hosts a number of touring musicians throughout the year.

BEST PLACES FOR COCKTAILS IN DOWNTOWN

The Green Room
Emerald-hued cocktail bar with a stained-glass art deco ceiling and tasty tipples.

Fortune
Hotel bar with creative house cocktails, plus fortune-teller sessions every Friday.

Departure
Rooftop lounge with a view, serving sake cocktails chilled with giant ice cubes.

Old Town/Chinatown

THE GRITTY HEART OF OLD PORTLAND

As the oldest neighborhood in the city, Old Town/Chinatown has seen a lot. It was here where Portland's first buildings were erected and many of the city's earliest residents – including large groups of immigrants from China and Japan – once called the area home. Stroll through this small district and look up at the old red-brick buildings all around: you'll almost be able to envision what life was like here in the city's early days. That is until you look down again to see the neighborhood's equally characteristic piles of trash. Truth be told, Old Town/Chinatown – especially the part north of Burnside St – is not having its finest moment and it can be unsettling for first-time visitors to see somewhere in such a state of neglect. Still, this area is home to some of the city's most important historic attractions and you're unlikely to experience problems if you visit during the day.

☑ **TOP TIP**

Some Old Town cultural attractions, including a few of those highlighted in the following pages, keep their doors or gates locked at all times for security. At some attractions, you may have to knock on a door or ring a doorbell to be let in.

HIGHLIGHTS
1 Lan Su Chinese Garden
2 Portland Chinatown Museum

SIGHTS
3 Japanese American Museum of Oregon
4 Japantown
5 Skidmore Fountain

EATING
6 Voodoo Doughnut

DRINKING & NIGHTLIFE
7 Ground Kontrol Classic Arcade & Bar

OLD TOWN/CHINATOWN

Portland Chinatown Museum

Understand the Chinese immigrant experience

Deepen your understanding of what life was like for some of Oregon's earliest Chinese immigrants with a visit to the Portland Chinatown Museum. The museum's star attraction is its permanent exhibit, Beyond the Gate: A Tale of Portland's Historic Chinatowns. The exhibit tells the story of Chinatown's early development and the people who shaped it through information panels, old photos and beautifully presented displays of historic ephemera including a model of Chinatown's beloved – and now defunct – restaurant, Hung Far Low. The museum also has two additional spaces for temporary exhibits that focus on the stories and art of Chinese American Portlanders, past and present.

Lan Su Chinese Garden

Lan Su Chinese Garden

A Ming Dynasty delight

If you only have time to see one thing in Old Town/Chinatown make it Lan Su Chinese Garden. This glorious space, modeled after a traditional scholar's garden, was designed to inspire reflection and a sense of peace. Here you'll find walkways that wrap around a large pond filled with lilies, and a mix of indoor and outdoor spaces that include a two-story teahouse, an art room with live calligraphy presentations and a number of exquisitely fashioned pavilions, all crafted by Chinese artisans using materials sourced from Portland's sister city, Suzhou.

Although Chinatown is part of Portland's oldest neighborhood the garden is relatively new, opening to the public in 2000. However, this place of repose feels much, much older. It draws its inspiration from garden design from the Ming Dynasty (1368–1644 AD) and were it not for views of Portland's 'Big Pink' US Bancorp Tower and the subtle din of urban traffic, it could easily be mistaken for a portal to another world – and century.

Portland Chinatown Museum

DARCELLE XV SHOWPLACE

Old Town has been a popular nightlife spot for decades, and while clubs have come and gone over the years, one spot – Darcelle XV Showplace – has stood the test of time. This Portland institution was opened in 1967 by Walter Willard Cole, a local cultural icon and LGBTIQA+ rights activist who performed as Darcelle. At the time of his death in 2023, Cole was the Guinness World Records-certified oldest drag performer in the world. Although Darcelle is no longer with us, her memory is kept alive at the club through multiple drag performances per week – including a Sunday drag brunch. In July 2013, O'Bryant Square in Downtown was officially renamed Darcelle XV Plaza in her honor.

ARTYOORAN/SHUTTERSTOCK ©

Portland Saturday Market

MORE IN OLD TOWN/CHINATOWN

Japantown in Chinatown

A glimpse of historic Nihonmachi

Although Portland's Chinatown is well known, few people know that part of the neighborhood now known as Old Town/Chinatown was once Portland's Japantown (also called Nihonmachi). You can learn more about this oft-overlooked part of history at the **Japanese American Museum of Oregon**, which traces the lives of Japanese Americans in Oregon from the early wave of immigration in the late 19th century through the mass incarceration program during WWII – and beyond.

Getting Crafty

The hippiest markets(s) in the land

Before farmers markets were all the rage, many Portlanders would spend their Saturdays checking out the handicrafts and food booths at the **Portland Saturday Market** (which

WHERE TO EAT IN OLD TOWN/CHINATOWN

Xin Ding Dumpling House
Converted pub space serving food from across China, including dim sum, noodle dishes and dry hot pots. $$

Pine Street Market
Sleek, open-plan food court with a tap room and a smattering of food vendors. $$

Lechon
Upscale happy hour and dinner spot showcasing South American flavors with a Pacific Northwest twist. $$$

is, incidentally, also open on Sundays). Founded in 1974, it's the largest continuously operating open-air craft market in the United States, with booths extending from just next to the circa-1888 **Skidmore Fountain** on SW 1st and Ankeny all the way across to **Waterfront Park**, where live music performances are frequently staged. A second market, the **Portland Skidmore Market**, occupies an entire city block east of the Skidmore Fountain. While everything sold at the Saturday Market must be handcrafted, vendors at the Skidmore Market have a bit more liberty – and many sell imported goods from Central America and South Asia.

Portland's Doughnut Obsession
Good things come in pink boxes

If you see a late-night line around the block in most cities, you'll probably assume that people are waiting to get into an exclusive nightclub. In Portland, when people line up it's almost always for food, often of the sugary variety. If you happen to see such a scene unfold on SW 2nd and Ankeny, you'll know you're at **Voodoo Doughnut**. Founded in the early noughties by Tres Shannon – who rose to local prominence in the 1990s as a co-owner of all-ages post-punk club X-Ray Cafe – and his friend Kenneth Pogson, this doughnut shop was an early indicator of what Portland would become: a fast-growing hipster destination equally celebrated for its eccentricity and its fantastic food. The doughnut slingers gained early notoriety for selling doughnuts laced with NyQuil and Pepto-Bismol, and although health authorities put a quick stop to such shenanigans, many of their doughnuts are still far from conventional. Make sure to try the Voodoo Doll – a vaguely human-shaped jelly doughnut with a pretzel stake driven where its little heart would be – or the Diablos Rex, a simple chocolate cake doughnut adorned with a frosted pentagram. Don't want to wait in a long line? They have a branch across the river in NE Portland where the queues are usually shorter.

An Arcade for Adults
Perfect your pinball

Step back into another era of gaming at **Ground Kontrol Classic Arcade and Bar**, a two-story arcade full of video games that predate many of its patrons. Here you can discover games you may not have seen since childhood – think Mario Kart and Ms Pac-Man – all while filling up on nachos or sipping colorful cocktails. While this spot is definitely geared toward the 21-and-over set, kids are welcome until 5pm.

THE SHANGHAI TUNNELS

According to local legend, a network of underground tunnels runs below Old Town and all the way out to the banks of the Willamette River. Allegedly, these passageways were used to smuggle goods – and people kidnapped for enslavement on mercantile ships – between Old Town saloons and boats in the port. While these claims have never been substantiated, the rumors remain – and some tour operators offer visitors the chance to see the tunnels for themselves. But take this with a grain of salt: while Shanghai Tunnel tours can be a fun way to learn about Portland history and lore, you won't see any subterranean passages – just basements.

WHERE TO DRINK IN OLD TOWN/CHINATOWN

Kells Irish Pub
An Emerald Isle–inspired brewpub with a solid whiskey list plus a cigar lounge (a rarity in Portland).

Shanghai Tunnel Bar
A windowless subterranean bar with pinball and pool tables, plus cocktails, and beer on tap.

Raven's Manor
Celebrate the macabre at this spooky spot offering Halloweenesque cocktails and interactive experiences.

The Pearl District & Northwest Portland

UPSCALE BOUTIQUES, A BOOKSTORE AND PLENTY OF ART

☑ TOP TIP

The Portland Streetcar connects the Pearl District and Nob Hill with one another and with other destinations in Downtown Portland, making it easy to get around the area without having to rely on a car (or search for parking).

The Pearl District is one of the swankiest parts of town, despite its very apparent industrial roots. Although the area's landmark attraction, Powell's City of Books, opened here in 1971, it wasn't until the 1980s – when art galleries began to pop up in the neighborhood – that the Pearl District we know today began to take shape. By the late 1990s, many of the warehouses that dominate the area had been transformed into lofts and high-end offices. As a result, this a part of town looks quite different from elsewhere in Portland. And while you won't find much in the way of characteristic red brick and Victorian homes, you will find loads of high-end shops and restaurants. Head west to Nob Hill for similar shopping and dining experiences.

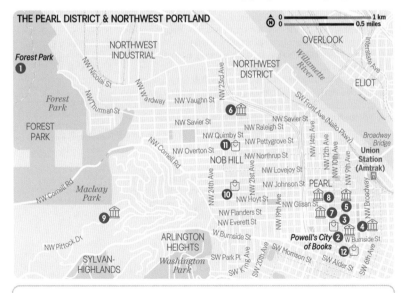

THE PEARL DISTRICT & NORTHWEST PORTLAND

HIGHLIGHTS
1 Forest Park
2 Powell's City of Books

SIGHTS
3 Blackfish Gallery
4 Blue Sky Gallery
5 Elizabeth Leach Gallery
6 Freakybuttrue Peculiarium
7 Gallery 114
8 J Pepin Art Gallery
9 Pittock Mansion

SHOPPING
10 Hip Hound
11 New Renaissance Bookshop
12 Tender Loving Empire

SANKAR RAMAN/GETTY IMAGES ©

Forest Park

Powell's City of Books

A block of books

If you're big on books, the chance to visit Powell's City of Books may have played a role in your decision to visit Portland. Occupying three floors and a full city block, Powell's touts itself as the largest independent new-and-used bookstore in the world. Books (and a smattering of gifts) are spread over nine color-coded rooms. It's a good idea to grab a store map when you enter to help get you oriented. Both new and used titles share the same shelf space, so you won't ever need to look in two places to find something. (Pro tip: if you find multiple used copies of a title, make sure to check the price of each, as they can range quite a bit.) Don't miss the Rare Book Room, which houses many of the oldest and most valuable books available at Powell's, including 1st editions and signed copies. Capacity is limited to 14 people at a time and you'll need to get a pass to enter.

Forest Park

Portland's urban forest

If you want to experience the grandeur of Oregon's forests but don't want to drive out to nearby Columbia Gorge, you're in luck: Portland has its own urban forest, just a few minutes' drive from the Pearl District. With over 80 miles of trails spread out over 5200 acres, Forest Park is big enough to rarely feel crowded, even if you hit up the popular **Wildwood Trail**, a 30-mile footpath that runs the entire length of the park, past an abandoned stone structure known as the Witch's Castle and into nearby Washington Park. While ambitious hikers and runners might brave the entire trail, most people just hike shorter segments.

WASHINGTON PARK

In the hills above Downtown in Southwest Portland, **Washington Park** (p183) is full of trails, grassy knolls and many of Portland's most popular attractions, including the International Rose Test Garden and the Portland Japanese Garden.

PRONOUNCING COUCH STREET

If a Portlander says you're pronouncing 'Couch St' wrong, we promise they're not pulling your leg. Despite spelling conventions that dictate that NW Portland's Couch St (and Couch Park) should be pronounced exactly like the synonym for sofa, the correct pronunciation is actually 'cooch.' While it may feel awkward – if not downright vulgar – to pronounce the name like this, pronouncing it any other way will quickly identify you as someone who has just rolled into town. Wondering why it's like this? The street was named for one of Portland's founders, a sea captain by the name of John Heard Couch, and that's how *he* said it. And what Captain Couch said, goes.

DORLING KINDERSLEY LTD/ALAMY STOCK PHOTO ©

First Thursday

MORE IN THE PEARL DISTRICT & NORTHWEST PORTLAND

First Thursday

Expose yourself to art

Art lovers descend on the Pearl District on the first Thursday of every month to visit galleries participating in the monthly First Thursday art walk, which has been taking place in the neighborhood since 1986. During this monthly event, most of the Pearl District's numerous art galleries stay open late – usually until around 8pm – enticing passersby with wine, snacks and – of course – art. It's also a popular night for art openings, and artists are often on hand for meet and greets.

If you want to see First Thursday for yourself, a good place to start is at the **J Pepin Art Gallery**, which focuses on 're-framing the perception of mental illness to be one of mental health.' Then continue around the corner to **Gallery 114**, an artist-owned-and-run collective with zero pretense. From here, you're only a few blocks from the **Elizabeth Leach Gallery**, one of the oldest galleries in the neighborhood. Continue to **Blackfish Gallery**, a cooperative gallery that's been around

WHERE TO EAT IN THE PEARL DISTRICT

Andina
Swanky spot offering seasonally inspired Peruvian fare and tasty pisco sours. **$$$**

Can Font
High-end Spanish dining with tapas and paella at dinnertime and creative egg dishes for brunch. **$$$**

Mediterranean Exploration Company
Showcases flavors of Greece and the Levant through meze and grilled-meat dishes. **$$**

since the 1970s, before wrapping your art walk up at the non-profit **Blue Sky Gallery**, which showcases photographic arts.

A Castle in the Clouds

Portland's stateliest home

Perched on a hilltop on the edge of Forest Park stands the **former mansion of Henry Pittock**, who made a name for himself as one of the first publishers of *The Oregonian* newspaper, which still exists to this day. The final residents moved out in the 1950s, and the mansion now operates as a museum, showcasing 23 rooms, including lounges, bedrooms and sleeping porches. While the home's ornate furnishings and gorgeous interiors alone merit a visit, the mansion also has exhibits and displays that give insight into what life was like in Portland in the early 1900s.

Although parking is available at the Pittock Mansion, many visitors opt to access it via a hike along Forest Park's Wildwood Trail (p179). If you don't want to pay to go inside, you can take in the views of the Portland skyline from the grounds free of charge.

Alphabet Soup

A stroll through Nob Hill

Sometimes referred to as the Alphabet District (streets in NW Portland are in alphabetical order), Uptown or simply Northwest, **Nob Hill** is where you'll find some of the fanciest boutiques in town. The bulk of shops and restaurants are located along NW 23rd Ave, though there are also plenty of places to part with your money along NW 21st Ave.

Start at the corner of NW 23rd and Glisan and head south stopping at **Tender Loving Empire** – an Oregon-centric gift shop with lots of handmade goodies – along the way. Continue for another block, where you'll find more tiny boutiques including **Ipnosi**, which sells pretty dresses and accessories, and **Hip Hound**, a pet accessory shop. You'll find plenty more shops and restaurants as you continue north to **New Renaissance Bookshop**, a massive metaphysical shop spread across two old houses. Once you've had your fill of crystals and incense, walk down to Thurman St and take a right, which will lead you to the **Freakybuttrue Peculiarium**, a museum/shop hawking all sorts of oddities. If you come in costume, they'll let you in for free.

BEST BREWERIES IN THE PEARL DISTRICT & NORTHWEST PORTLAND

Breakside Brewery
This spacious spot in NW's Slabtown mini-district features 16 taps of Breakside brews, some of which aren't available anywhere else.

Deschutes Brewery & Public House
The Portland outpost of this celebrated Central Oregon beer maker boasts a whopping 26 taps with a mix of classic and limited edition beers, including some Portland-only specials.

Lucky Labrador Quimby Beer Hall
Housed in a converted semi-truck warehouse, the NW location of this OG microbrewery serves a wide selection of stouts and ales and has plenty of pet-friendly outdoor seating.

WHERE TO EAT IN NOB HILL

Escape From New York Pizza
Portland's original pizza-by-the-slice spot serving cheesy New York–style pizza that's just begging to be folded. **$**

Top Burmese Burma Joy
Robots help servers bring out rich curries and fermented tea-leaf salads at this quirky Burmese joint. **$$**

Takibi
Sashimi and soba noodles at the US headquarters of Japanese outdoor company, Snow Peak. **$$**

Southwest Portland

COUNTRYSIDE VIBES IN THE CITY

☑ **TOP TIP**

A free shuttle runs through Washington Park and connects different attractions to the park's MAX light-rail Station (on the Blue and Red Lines) and to the #63 bus stop, which connects to Downtown Portland. If you're planning on visiting other parts of Southwest Portland, you're better off with a car.

Although Downtown is technically part of Southwest Portland, most residents use the term to refer to the areas that lie beyond the city center. Southwest's biggest draw is Washington Park, where you'll find many of Portland's top attractions, but it's certainly not all the quadrant has to offer. This is the part of town that will remind you that Portland was built in a forest, as its primarily residential neighborhoods are peppered with wooded parks, many with extensive networks of hiking trails. While not many visitors make it beyond Washington Park, there are lots of reasons why you should consider checking out this off-the-beaten-path part of town. Along with gorgeous parks – including Oregon's only urban state park – you'll find cute shops, an urban winery and some of the best views in the city – all just minutes from Downtown.

HIGHLIGHTS
1. Hoyt Arboretum
2. International Rose Test Garden
3. Oregon Zoo
4. Portland Japanese Garden
5. Washington Park
6. World Forestry Center Discovery Museum

DRINKING & NIGHTLIFE
7. Village Coffee

SHOPPING
8. Annie Bloom's Books
9. John's Marketplace
10. Multnomah Village
11. Thinker Toys

TRANSPORTATION
12. Portland Aerial Tram – Lower Terminal
13. Portland Aerial Tram – Upper Terminal

Washington Park
A park of many gardens

Just west of Downtown Portland (and a short MAX ride away), sits Washington Park, a hilly 410-acre park filled characterized by tree-lined trails, grassy open spaces and some of Portland's top attractions. If you come by light-rail, you'll end up at the southwestern corner of the park where three popular sights – the **Oregon Zoo**, the **Vietnam Veterans of Oregon Memorial** and the **World Forestry Center Discovery Museum** – are located. If you have to pick one, make it the Forestry Center, which features two floors of exhibits that cover topics ranging from the future of forests to forest fires to the logging industry. A short walk (or a one-stop ride on the park's free shuttle) will take you to the **Hoyt Arboretum**, a 'living museum' with around 2300 species of trees from around the world. From the arboretum, you can take a shuttle ride or hike along the Wildwood Trail to the **International Rose Test Garden**, where you'll have the chance to wander among over 10,000 blooming rose bushes representing more than 600 varieties, all while taking in fabulous views of the city. Up a small hill from this floral delight, the **Portland Japanese Garden** is considered one of the most authentic Japanese gardens outside of Japan and features bridge-crossed ponds, a teahouse, numerous stone features and lots of beautiful foliage – including cherry trees.

JAPANESE GARDEN DESIGN 101

Hugo Torii, Garden Curator at Portland Japanese Garden, introduces Japanese garden design.

Japanese gardens have evolved over the course of 1000 years, with each iteration reflecting the needs of a given time. This evolution has created a rich diversity of garden styles. They allow the visitor to experience Japanese culture and its emphasis on respecting nature and being in harmony with it. Whether a space is decorative like a raked gravel garden or more rustic like a tea garden, they provide a place to confirm our connection and find our distance with nature and in this, the opportunity to heal.

100 CHERRY TREES
You can see cherry blossoms for free at the Governor Tom McCall Waterfront Park **Japanese American Historical Plaza** (p172), where 100 cherry trees erupt into bloom every spring.

International Rose Test Garden

SOUTHWEST PORTLAND'S BEST VIEWS

Council Crest Park
A quick drive from Downtown via the posh West Hills will take you up to this small park. At 1073ft above sea level, it's the highest point in the city.

George Himes City Park
This wooded park is just one of many spots along SW Terwilliger Blvd where you can get great views of the city (but there are also plenty of pullouts along the road where you can park and take in the scenery).

International Rose Test Garden
Wander among the 10,000-odd rose bushes at this bloom-filled spot and take in quintessential postcard views of the Portland skyline, with Mt Hood in the distance.

POSNOV/GETTY IMAGES ©

Portland Aerial Tram

MORE IN SOUTHWEST PORTLAND

City Viticulture
Urban wine culture

Portland's proximity to Oregon's celebrated Willamette Valley wine country makes it tempting to take a day out of your schedule for a bit of wine tasting, but thanks to **Amaterra Winery** you can get a sense of the wine country experience without having to venture far. Straddling a vine-covered hillock in the West Hills, this spot feels very much like it's in the countryside, despite being less than 5 miles from Downtown. Drive up to the top of the hill where you'll have the option to dine on Pacific Northwest fare at the restaurant or do a wine tasting on a lower- level patio. Both spots offer fantastic views for miles. There's just one catch – you'll have to purchase a 'social membership' for $25, which you can apply to the purchase of two or more bottles of wine during your visit.

High Flying
Rise on the sky train

Linking the southernmost end of Portland's South Waterfront area with Marquam Hill – the site of the Oregon Health Sciences University (OHSU) – the **Portland Aerial Tram** af-

 WHERE TO EAT IN SOUTHWEST PORTLAND

Chart House
Long-standing European restaurant with steak, seafood and glorious city views. **$$$**

Cornell Farm Cafe
Casual brunch spot serving pastries, egg dishes and sandwiches on the grounds of a flower-filled nursery. **$$**

Yalla
Mediterranean smokehouse with an ever-evolving menu of meze, smoked meat dishes and creative desserts. **$$**

fords its passengers great views of the city without having to drive to one of Southwest's many viewpoints. The ride on this standing-room-only tram lasts around four minutes, and it moves slowly enough that it's easy to get decent photos of the city (provided you stand by one of the many windows). It's easiest to start at the bottom where there are direct connections to the Portland Streetcar.

Note: the tram was originally installed – much to the chagrin of those who live below it – to ferry students, patients and staff up to OHSU. While it's open to all, many locals use the tram to commute so it's a good idea to avoid rush hour, when you may have to wait to get on.

Into the Woods
Portland's only state park

Less than a 15-min drive from Downtown Portland will take you to **Tryon Creek State Natural Area**, the only state park in Oregon that's inside a metro area. Despite the park's proximity to the high-rise office towers of Downtown, it has all the attributes of a quintessential western Oregon forest, including miles of trails, beautiful old conifers and plenty of resident creatures from raccoons to barred owls. Tryon is a popular spot for hiking and jogging, and there are a few miles of equestrian-friendly trails (so watch where you step!). You can grab a trail map and fill your water bottle at the visitor center located at the far end of the parking lot.

Suburban Hamlet
A village in the city

Southwest's cutest place to window shop is undoubtedly **Multnomah Village**, named because it very much feels like its own little village. This tiny shopping district – spread over just a few blocks – is full of independent shops, many of which (such as **Annie Bloom's Books** and **Thinker Toys**) have been around for decades. Beer lovers should pay a visit to **John's Marketplace**, a medium-sized grocery store with an incredible selection of hard-to-find beers from around the world. If you're more of a coffee person, head to **Village Coffee**, a Lilliputian (and, refreshingly, wi-fi-free) coffee shop that caters primarily to residents of the neighborhood.

WHY I LOVE SOUTHWEST PORTLAND

Margot Bigg, Lonely Planet writer

I moved from Downtown to Southwest Portland when I was eight years old and while I've lived all over Portland – and the world – since, this quiet part of the city still has a special place in my heart. Although Southwest is not as walkable as other parts of town, the natural scenery is hard to beat, particularly if you're fond of trees. While it's not unusual to spot massive Douglas firs and fragrant western red cedars in backyards across the city, it's pretty much the norm in Southwest. Southwest may not be the most happening part of town, it's definitely the quietest.

WHERE TO SHOP IN SOUTHWEST PORTLAND

Annie Bloom's Books
Independent bookstore in Multnomah Village with helpful staff and a resident cat.

Peachtree Gifts
Colorful gift shop with quirky stocking stuffers, whimsical toys and a huge selection of greeting cards.

Washington Square Mall
Suburban mall with chain store, ideal for taking advantage of Oregon's lack of sales tax.

Southeast Portland

FAMILY FUN AND CULINARY ADVENTURES

☑ **TOP TIP**

Southeast Portland is very bike-friendly, with bicycle lanes on many major thoroughfares and lots of designated bike routes throughout the quadrant. Clinton St, which runs from east to west, is a particularly popular – and safe – street for cyclists, and gets considerably more bikes than cars.

If there's one part of town that really lives up to Portland's hipster stereotypes, it's Southeast. Once one of the city's more affordable areas, much of this quadrant has grown increasingly trendy. The area's landscape is a testament to its quick growth. While you can expect to see plenty of shiny new apartment buildings, most Southeast Portland neighborhoods are characterized by tree-lined streets with cute arts-and-crafts-style homes.

Southeast is a popular place for dining out, and while you'll find fantastic restaurants throughout this populated part of town, the highest density are located west of César E Chávez Blvd, with a particularly high concentration on three main thoroughfares: Division St, Belmont St and Hawthorne Blvd. While the food alone is reason enough to come to Southeast, there are also tons of parks and interactive attractions that are equally appealing to children and adults.

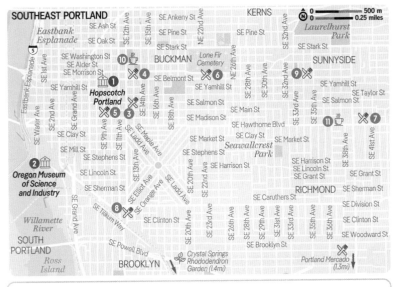

HIGHLIGHTS	EATING		DRINKING & NIGHTLIFE
1 Hopscotch Portland	3 Cartopia	6 Mirisiata	10 Rimsky-Korsakoffee House
2 Oregon Museum of Science and Industry	4 Fermenter	7 Next Level Burger	11 Tōv Coffee
	5 Hawthorne Asylum	8 Shoofly Vegan Bakery	
		9 Sweet Hereafter	

Oregon Museum of Science and Industry (OMSI)

Science is for everyone

This spacious science and technology museum offers hands-on permanent and special exhibits designed to get visitors of all ages excited about science. Check out the interactive labs focused on physics, chemistry, paleontology and insects or head to the **Natural Sciences Hall** to see displays on everything from geology to climate science. Visitors of all ages love the **Turbine Hall**, where an earthquake simulator allows you to experience the quake sensation, while young'uns can head to the **Curium**, a special area for those eight and under. Don't miss a tour of the decommissioned **USS Blueback**, the US Navy's final diesel-electric submarine, or take a trip into the night sky through a **Kendall Planetarium** show.

While children certainly are OMSI's target audience, visitors of all ages are welcome. If you feel awkward being the biggest kid around and you just want to enjoy the exhibits without worrying about stepping on tiny toes – and maybe have a drink – you can check out one of the themed monthly **OMSI After Dark** sessions, exclusively for the 21-and-over crowd.

Hopscotch Portland

Hopscotch Portland

Hop into a ball pit

If you want to relive your childhood memories of jumping into ball pits, while checking out lots of trippy, interactive art, head over to Hopscotch, an immersive sound-and-light installation space with Texan roots that launched its Portland branch in 2023. You can use lasers to spray paint make-believe graffiti, step into a kaleidoscopic world of colorful lights and infinite mirrors, or hop into another dimension on a **Quantum Trampoline**. Did we mention the ball pit? It's called **Diodic Daydream** and it replaces the rainbow of plastic balls of your youth with transparent, bubble-like orbs, illuminated by color-changing lights.

SHOPPING ON HAWTHORNE BOULEVARD

If you're in the market for creative souvenirs to take home (or just enjoy shopping), head to the stretch of SE Hawthorne Blvd between 34th Ave and César E Chávez Blvd. The strip has a high concentration of locally owned boutiques from **Presents of Mind** – a classic Portland spot selling cards and fun gifts – to **Gold Door Jewelry & Arts**, a great place to pick up folk art and jewelry from around the world. There's even an outpost of Downtown's famous **Powell's Books**. If you're a film buff, stick around to watch a flick at the **Bagdad Theater and Pub**, where you can sip on craft beer while watching the credits roll.

Rimsky-Korsakoffee House

ANOTHER BELIEVER, CC BY-SA 3.0, VIA WIKI COMMONS ®

MORE IN SOUTHEAST PORTLAND

A Mad Coffee Party

Curiouser and curiouser

Tucked away in an unmarked arts-and-crafts home behind a Plaid Pantry minimart, **Rimsky-Korsakoffee House** is easy to miss if you're not keeping an eye out for it. This classical music-themed coffee shop – among Portland's oldest – is notable not only for its rich desserts and live piano music but also for its oddball decor and mysterious tables that have been known to move, ever so slowly. Simply put: if you're at a round table and you set down your coffee, don't be surprised if it ends up in front of the person seated across from you. Maybe it's haunted!

Street Food Central

Outdoor dining at food cart pods

While Portland has plenty of great restaurants, the city is equally known for its food carts (aka food trucks). Most can be found in food cart 'pods', converted parking lots with common picnic-table dining spaces that house anywhere from four

 WHERE TO GO FOR A FANCY DINNER IN SOUTHEAST PORTLAND

Berlu
Cozy inner Southeast spot offering Vietnamese tasting menus whipped up from local produce. **$$$**

Kann
Award-winning restaurant by celebrity chef Gregory Gourdet featuring Haitian-inspired live-fire cooking. **$$$**

ASTERA
Intimate plant-based spot offering a multi-course chef's tasting menu and botanical cocktails and mocktails. **$$$**

to upwards of 20 carts. While you'll find food cart pods all over Portland, Southeast has a particularly high concentration. Two of the largest are **Cartopia** – famous for the poutine at long-standing food cart **Potato Champion** – and **Hawthorne Asylum**, a couple of blocks away. Just up the road, **Tõv Coffee** serves up Egyptian-style coffee, tea and sweets in a converted double-decker London bus. If you want to try food from across Latin America, head to the **Portland Mercado**, a hybrid market and food cart pod that showcases food from across the region.

Veggie Tables
Plant-based paradise

There's no denying that Portland is a foodie destination and even diners with more restricted diets will find plenty to eat here. The city is known among vegans for its plant-based dining scene (fun fact: one of the first commercially available veggie burgers, the Gardenburger, originated in the metro area). Spots to add to your itinerary include fast-food joint **Next Level Burger**, which serves up plant-based takes on burgers, nuggets and shakes, and **Fermenter**, where every dish on the ever-evolving menu has at least one fermented ingredient. For spicy Sri Lankan fare, head to worker-owned **Mirisiata**. If you're in the mood for desserts, let your sweet tooth lead you to the cinnamon rolls at **Shoofly Vegan Bakery**. For late-night pub bites and animal product–free cocktails, join the hipster crowds at **Sweet Hereafter**.

Secret Garden
Flowers, wildlife and crystalline waters

Sandwiched between a golf course and the campus of a liberal arts college, **Crystal Springs Rhododendron Garden** is a great place to get a nature recharge, without having to cross over to the woodsy west side of the Willamette River. Follow the gravel paths that meander through foliage and alongside massive **Crystal Springs Lake**. Maybe stop for a break at one of the park's many benches for a bit of wildlife-watching and – if you take the lead of the college kids who hang out here – canoodling. As the name suggests, rhododendrons are the star attraction here but even if you aren't in town when the flowers are in full bloom (usually in April and May), this 9.5-acre spot is still worth a visit, particularly if you're interested in watching resident waterfowl and nutria hang out on the water.

BEST PARKS IN SOUTHEAST

Laurelhurst Park
This massive park features paved walking paths, expansive green spaces and a duck pond. Summertime events include comedy nights, concerts and even silent discos – pop-up dance parties where participants groove to tunes transmitted to their headphones.

Mt Tabor Park
Take in sunset views from the summit of this dormant, wooded cinder cone that towers over southeast Portland.

Oaks Bottom Wildlife Refuge
This 163-acre park near the Willamette River provides a safe haven for birds and other aquatic critters plus a mix of hiking and hike/bike trails.

 WHERE TO SIP TEA IN SOUTHEAST PORTLAND

Tao of Tea	Portal Tea	Smith Teamaker Tea Bar
Sip lapsang souchong and listen to the rushing waters of the indoor fountain at this atmospheric teahouse.	A compact red caboose opens up to a spacious tea room with over 100 infusions on the menu.	Sample small-batch teas paired with macarons at this airy tasting room from a celebrated local tea company.

189

Northeast & North Portland

ARTSY NEIGHBORHOODS WITH GREAT DINING

☑ TOP TIP

Most of North and Northeast Portland is relatively flat, making it ideal for cyclists. Commercial streets such as Alberta St, Mississippi Ave and Williams Ave have free street parking, but spots can fill up quickly during the dinner hours so you might have to park your car on a residential side street and walk.

The northeastern part of Portland is divided into two sections: North and Northeast Portland. Here you'll find pretty parks – including sprawling Peninsula Park – as well as a few interesting historic sites including a 1920s movie theater and an old elementary school that's been converted into a hotel.

For many years, North and Northeast Portland were largely residential, but as the city has grown, and emerged as a major culinary destination, parts of these conjoined areas have become popular hubs for dining and drinking. This is particularly the case in historically Black areas such as Albina and in and around the Alberta Arts District.

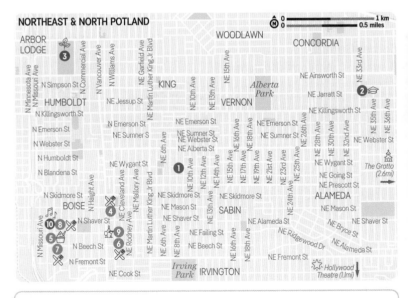

HIGHLIGHTS
1 Alberta Arts District

SIGHTS
2 McMenamins
Kennedy School

3 Peninsula Park

EATING
4 JinJu Patisserie
5 Kate's Ice Cream

6 Mamma Khouri's
7 Mississippi Pizza
8 UCHU Sushi & Fried
Chicken

DRINKING & NIGHTLIFE
9 Eem Thai BBQ &
Cocktails

ENTERTAINMENT
10 Mississippi Studios

Hollywood Theatre

Moving pictures

With an ornate façade that makes it look like something out of Candyland, Northeast Portland's Hollywood Theatre is hard to ignore. This Spanish Colonial–inspired building – clad with spiral pillars, Moorish-style archways and decorative domes – opened in the 1920s as a vaudeville and silent film theater. Today, the cinema primarily screens independent films in a 384-seat main auditorium, and in two smaller theaters. A 70mm projector adds to the vintage appeal. Hollywood Theatre also has a miniature cinema in Concourse C of Portland International Airport where transit passengers can watch shorts by Pacific Northwest filmmakers.

Hollywood Theatre

Alberta Arts District

Celebrate last thursday

The stretch of NE Alberta St between NE 12th and 32nd Aves, known as the Alberta Arts District, is one of Northeast Portland's biggest draws, and for good reason. This walkable stretch is loaded with cute boutiques, bars, restaurants and galleries, many of which have a bohemian bent. Black heritage markers tell an important piece of the story of this historically African American neighborhood and many businesses are decorated with colorful large-scale murals.

While the Alberta Arts District attracts crowds pretty consistently, its biggest draw is the monthly **Last Thursday** celebration, which emerged in the late 1990s as a countercultural alternative to the long-running First Thursday art walk in the Pearl District (p178). During this monthly event, artists and other vendors set up streetside tables to hawk their wares, street performers entertain the masses and local businesses keep their doors open late. Although Last Thursday happens throughout the year, it's far busier in the summer, when the street is also closed from traffic.

Restaurants, Alberta Arts District

191

McMenamins Kennedy School

OUTDOOR ACTIVITIES

Teresa Bergen, author of *Easy Portland Outdoors*, recommends these activities.
@teresa.bergen

Kayaking
Rent a kayak on the Columbia River to explore on your own, or take a four-hour basic skills class where you'll paddle over logs, play kayak tag and practice a wet exit (aka falling out) at Alder Creek Kayak, Canoe, Raft & SUP's Jantzen Beach store.

Swim or Disc Golf
A spray pad and shallow swim area make Blue Lake Regional Park heaven in summer for families with water-loving kids. Disc golfers will enjoy the world-class 18-hole course.

Smell the Roses
Peninsula Park is home to an English-style sunken rose garden, which is glorious in summer. It was designed by Frederick Law Olmsted, who designed New York's Central Park.

MORE IN NORTHEAST & NORTH PORTLAND

Back to Class
Soak in a converted schoolhouse pool

About half a mile from the eastern end of Alberta St, **McMenamins Kennedy School** is the place to stay if you've ever dreamt about spending the night in a school. Occupying a former elementary school that dates to 1915, this property offers rooms converted from classrooms that still retain original touches such as blackboards and cloakrooms. While the rooms are a big draw, the Kennedy School attracts plenty of Portlanders with its numerous bars and restaurants and its outdoor **hot-water soaking pool**, which you can soak in for a small fee (even if you're not staying in one of the rooms). There's even a **movie theater** in the school's former auditorium, where you can chow down on pizza and sip McMenamins' own craft beer while you gaze at the silver screen.

A Metropolitan Cave Shrine
Portland's urban sanctuary

Established in 1924, the **Grotto**, formerly known as the National Sanctuary of our Sorrowful Mother, is an outdoor shrine to

⚜ WHERE TO EAT IN NORTHEAST & NORTH PORTLAND

Kayo's Ramen Bar
Boise neighborhood spot specializing in clear-broth ramen (rather than the better-known *tonkotsu*-style). $$

El Nutri Taco
No-frills Mexican spot offering huge burritos, tacos and tortas – with plenty of meat-free and gluten-free options. $

Nepali Kitchen and Chai Garden
Beautiful garden cafe with little seating nooks, serving Tibetan *momos* (dumplings). $

Mother Mary at the base of – and atop – a basalt cliff. Although it's situated off a major thoroughfare in one of the less pretty parts of town, the Grotto does very much feel like a sanctuary, with tall trees and a beautiful Marian cave shrine housing a marble pietà. An elevator leads up to the cliff level of the sanctuary where there's a **botanic garden** with views over Mount St Helen's. Although the Grotto is Roman Catholic, it attracts people of all faiths – and non-religious people – particularly during the Christmas season and especially during the annual **Festival of Lights** when the shrine is illuminated with over two million colorful fairy lights.

Foodie Zone

Eat and be merry

In North Portland's **Albina** area, N Mississippi and N Williams Aves are home to some of the best places to eat in town. Mississippi Ave highlights include **UCHU Sushi & Fried Chicken** (perfect for groups of friends with wildly different preferences) and **Mississippi Pizza**, which offers cheap eats by the slice. If you visit during the summer, you can cool off with one of the plant-based concoctions at **Kate's Ice Cream**. This avenue is also home to **Mississippi Studios**, a celebrated indie music venue.

There's plenty more to eat just a half-mile away on N Williams Ave. If you like your food spicy and your cocktails strong, visit **Eem Thai BBQ & Cocktails**. For something milder, head to **Mamma Khouri's**, where you'll find a massive menu of Middle Eastern meze. If you have a sweet tooth, stop by **Jin-Ju Patisserie**, to check out its selection of croissants, tarts and chocolates.

A Rose is a Rose

A stroll through Peninsula Park

You can pretend you're in a scene from Alice in Wonderland at **Peninsula Park**, home to the city's first public rose garden. This symmetrical space features rows of rose bushes intercepted by grassy pathways, plus a giant fountain to add an extra dash of elegance (not that it needs it). There's also a huge field for picnicking, an old-fashioned bandstand if you need shade and a large playground with a splash pad for summertime play.

MAY YOUR WISHES COME TRUE

Portlanders love to set up whimsical displays in their front lawns. Some tether toy horses to sidewalk horse rings (loops found in sidewalks throughout town that were used in the pre-car era to hitch horses). Others build fairy gardens or free libraries. However, the most enchanting of Portland's sidewalk treasures is the **Wishing Tree** on the corner of NE 7th and Morris. At this interactive display, pedestrians are invited to write their wishes on tags (provided) and tie them to the tree. For an extra dose of magic, anyone making a wish should also read someone else's and hope that it comes true.

CITY OF ROSES

If roses are your thing, make sure to visit the **International Rose Test Garden** (p183) in Southwest's Washington Park, where you'll be able to admire around 10,000 bushes representing over 600 rose varieties.

WHERE TO SHOP IN NORTHEAST & NORTH PORTLAND

Blackthorn Mercantile
Mississippi Ave gift shop with home goods, gifts and a smattering of metaphysical supplies.

ECOVIBE
Alberta Ave home decor shop specializing in eco-friendly wares and houseplants.

GiftyKitty
Cat-themed shop on Mississippi Ave with plenty of artsy, feline-inspired creations by local artists.

Above: Willamette Valley vineyard (p201); Right: Goodpasture Bridge (p211)

The Willamette Valley

HISTORIC TOWNS AND BEAUTIFUL VINEYARDS

Cruise the highways and byways of the Willamette Valley, sampling some of the world's best wines while also exploring its forested mountains and historic towns.

The Willamette Valley and wine are synonymous – touring the vineyards to sample different vintages is a highlight of the region. But it's not all clinking glasses and wine-swirling sommeliers. Vineyard culture is just one part of what makes this swath of fertile land so special. In between wineries are a patchwork of charming towns that beckon with their stately brick buildings and colorful history. The foothills of the Cascades offer excellent hiking trails and waterfalls amid soaring Douglas fir trees and the occasional covered bridge. Eugene is a bastion of liberal attitudes with a vibrant student community and endless greenery. Corvallis, home of Oregon State University, is the ultimate college town where Beaver Nation filters into everything. And Salem may have a sleepy reputation but is filled with sights and museums that give insight into both Oregon's Indigenous people and the period of European settlement.

The Willamette Valley sits at the crossroads of multiple driving routes so whichever direction you're headed you are likely to see some of the area. It can be easy to jump on I-5 and zip through the area but the real charm of the valley is taking it slow on the back roads. Plan for a few extra days as the region's charms will reel you in for longer than you expect.

JAMIE HOOPER/SHUTTERSTOCK ©

THE MAIN AREAS

SALEM	EUGENE
Oregon State Capitol, museums.	Vibrant culture, athletics.
p198	p206

Find Your Way

The Willamette Valley, up to 40 miles wide and 120 miles long, covers a lot of territory. The region is mostly flat with wide open landscapes that are beautiful and well connected to other regions.

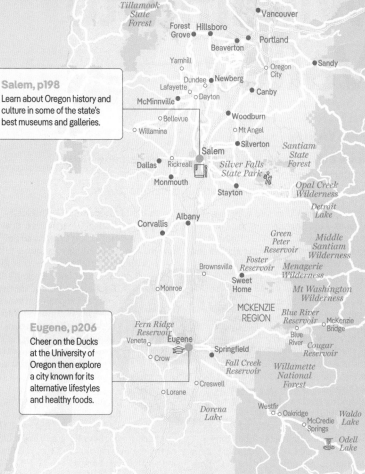

Salem, p198

Learn about Oregon history and culture in some of the state's best museums and galleries.

Eugene, p206

Cheer on the Ducks at the University of Oregon then explore a city known for its alternative lifestyles and healthy foods.

CAR

Getting around the valley by car can save a lot of time, especially if you are hopping between wineries. Good roads and I-5 allow for relatively quick access between towns and cities.

PUBLIC TRANSPORTATION

Amtrak trains connect the main cities in the valley, from Portland's Union Station to Eugene – bikes are allowed on trains. Cities in the valley are well connected to Portland by FlixBus. Oregon City and other suburbs have more frequent bus services.

Evergreen Aviation & Space Museum (p203), McMinnville

Plan Your Time

Exploring the Willamette Valley means spending time in sun-drenched vineyards and strolling historic towns. Thick forests and cascading waterfalls are never far away.

Short on Time

For a weekend of exploration, head to **McMinnville** (p201) where you can sample wines at tasting rooms and nearby vineyards. Check out the impressive **Evergreen Aviation & Space Museum** (p203) and make a stop in Salem to poke around the **Oregon State Capitol** (p198) and some museums. Mosey up to **Silver Falls State Park** (p201) for a hike and waterfall viewing.

Five Days in the Valley

On top of the two-day itinerary, make a stop in historic **Oregon City** (p203) for views of Willamette Falls. From here the **Bagby Hot Springs** (p204) make for a relaxing detour. Back in the valley, visit **Eugene** (p206) to look around the University of Oregon campus and experience its museums. Then head east to get a taste of the **McKenzie River** (p211) region.

Seasonal Highlights

SPRING	SUMMER	FALL	WINTER
Pleasant temperatures and blooming flowers make this one of the best times of year to travel. May is wine month in Oregon.	Festival season and hot temperatures make for invigorating trips to swimming holes in rivers.	Cool fall weather makes for easy and comfortable travel. Harvest season means full farm stands and grape crush events.	Cold weather and fewer farm-related events but prices are lower and it's a good time for college football and basketball.

197

Salem

Oregon's state capital flexes its political muscle with impressive government buildings, spacious gardens and museums. The Capitol building is fairly quiet except when protestors, and counter-protesters, descend on the complex. Salem can be a day trip from Portland but may also be used as a base for explorations of the Willamette Valley, thanks to its central location to nearby attractions. Walking around the center, looking at historic buildings and visiting its museums can take up the better part of a day. The pretty campus of Willamette University is also worth visiting. There are a handful of places that cater specifically for kids, including a riverfront park on the Willamette River and a carousel.

Capital Sights in Salem

Culture and history in Oregon's capital

Pedestrian-friendly Salem is a hub for the arts and local culture. Start at the **Oregon State Capitol**, the city's third government house; the first two burned down in 1855 and 1935

Oregon State Capitol

SALEM

Willamina-Salem Hwy
Willamette Park
Willamette River
Riverfront City Park
Minto Island Park
Civic Center

Front St NE
Commercial St NE
Liberty St NE
High St NE
Union St NE
Marion St NE
Center St NE
Chemeketa St NE
Court St NE
State St
Wilson Park
Capitol Mall

North Salem High School
Union St NE
Oregon State Hospital (1 mi)

Front St SE
Ferry St SE
Trade St SE
Commercial St SW
Liberty St SW
High St SW
Church St SE
Winter St SE

12th St NE
13th St NE
14th St NE
Court St NE

Oregon State Capitol

Willamette University

Ferry St SE
Trade St SE
Mill St SE

Pringle Park
Bellevue St SE
Mission St SE
Kearney St SE
Bush St SE
Owens St SE

Deepwood Estate
University St SE
12th St SE
13th St SE
14th St SE

Silver Falls State Park (23.6mi)

Enchanted Forest (6.5mi)

Bush's Pasture Park
Lee St SE
Tripp St SE

0 — 400 m
0 — 0.2 miles

HIGHLIGHTS
1 Oregon State Capitol

SIGHTS
2 Bush House Museum
3 Bush's Pasture Park
4 Hallie Ford Museum of Art
5 Riverfront Park
6 Willamette Heritage Center

respectively. The current structure is a 1938 Depression-era building topped by the famed 'Gold Man,' a 23ft-tall bronze statue painted with 11 ounces of gold leaf. Indoor visits are suspended until 2025 due to seismic retrofit work.

A block behind the Capitol is the **Hallie Ford Museum of Art**, one of the best private collections of art in the Northwest. History buffs will also want to visit the **Willamette Heritage Center**, a 5-acre complex of museums and historic buildings dating back to the mid-1800s, to get a hands-on feel for life in the pioneer West.

Bordering the south side of downtown is **Bush's Pasture Park**, a popular spot among locals for garden walks, with more than 2000 rose plants. Inside the park, the **Bush House Museum** is an 1878 mansion open for guided tours.

Don't miss **Riverfront Park**, located on a restored industrial wasteland that once housed mills and a junkyard. Today there is a carousel, a bike path and a beautiful pedestrian bridge over the Willamette River. Look for the Eco-Earth Globe, a reclaimed piece of industrial waste that once held acid and gas but is now a symbol of global peace.

OREGON STATE HOSPITAL

While hospitals aren't a typical feature on a city tour, the one in Salem is unique. The Oregon State Hospital was built in 1883 as a psychiatric hospital and continues to function today, making it one of the longest-running hospitals on the West Coast. It was a film location for *One Flew Over the Cuckoo's Nest*, starring Jack Nicholson.

Today, the campus contains a moving memorial to thousands of deceased patients whose remains were found in the basement. The on-site Museum of Mental Health tells the history of the facility, covering both the triumphs of mental health research and its dark past.

WHERE TO EAT IN SALEM

Wild Pear
Healthy soups, salads and sandwiches enjoyed in a French bistro atmosphere with art hung on bare brick walls. $

Yard Food Park
This culinary extravaganza is home to nearly 20 food carts, with barbecue, sushi, burgers, pizza and more. $

Noble Wave
The shrimp and grits at this Louisiana kitchen taste great, plus there's lots more, including fried alligator. $$

Beyond
Salem

From Salem, you can discover wineries, waterfalls, hot springs and historic sites that date back to the period before Oregon became a state.

GETTING AROUND

Getting around with your own wheels (car or bike) is the best way to explore. Public buses also connect the main towns and you can then rent a bike/e-bike to visit places of interest. Cherriots bus company serves the Salem area (with services to Silverton and Mt Angel), while Yamhill County Transit has routes from McMinnville (to Salem, Dundee and Newberg). Salem has an Amtrak train stop with service to Oregon City and Eugene.

Pick a day, pick a direction. Anywhere you go you'll find things to do within a short drive from Salem. Head southwest to Corvallis, the home of Oregon State University, to grab a pizza and explore this college town and campus. Travel north on I-5 to reach historic Oregon City, where pioneers traveling west ended their journey. In the foothills of the Cascades, you'll find hot springs, fast-flowing streams and thick forests. All around (but especially around McMinnville) there are wineries and tasting rooms where you can send your palate into viniculture bliss. While getting around by car is the quickest mode of transportation, traveling on two wheels is also a great way to explore the Willamette Valley's small towns.

MICHAEL WARWICK/SHUTTERSTOCK ©

Oregon State University, Corvallis (p204)

Silverton

TIME FROM SALEM: **25 MINS**

Churches and gardens galore

Willamette Valley takes its flower gardens seriously and one of the best examples is found at the **Oregon Garden**, located 16 miles east of Salem in Silverton. Here you can walk through 20 specialty gardens on 80 acres. Miles of pet-friendly walking trails make for good walking. In winter it hosts a delightful Christmas market and holiday light display. Don't miss the **Gordon House** next door, the only Frank Lloyd Wright-designed building in Oregon. It's open for guided tours.

Mt Angel

TIME FROM SALEM: **30 MINS**

European influences in the valley

Just five miles north of Silverton is Mt Angel, another unexpected discovery in the valley. Mt Angel grew up around several religious institutions including a monastery and seminary. Its early residents included a contingent of Benedictine monks from Switzerland and immigrants from Bavaria.

Because of its Germanic roots, Mt Angel has the largest **Oktoberfest** in the Pacific Northwest. The event, held in September, features yodelers, dancers, arts and crafts, and plenty of local beer and sausages.

Mt Angel's main street is lined with Bavarian-style storefronts and the local churches are true works of art. **St Mary Catholic Church** (1910) has a beautiful nave and murals.

Hidden in a forest on the edge of town, the **Mt Angel Abbey**, a Benedictine monastery, feels like a slice of Tuscany dropped into Oregon. There are guest quarters for those looking for a spiritual retreat and the theological library, designed by famed Finnish architect Alvar Aalto, is the largest of its kind in the Pacific Northwest. There's also a quirky museum here featuring a 2.5lb pig hairball, deformed calves and lots of taxidermy wildlife. In town you can stop by the **Benedictine Brewery**, operated by the monks.

Wines of McMinnville

TIME FROM SALEM: **35 MINS**

Tasting in the Oregon Wine Country

The first wineries in Oregon started in the 1850s but the Beaver state did not get serious about growing grapes until the late 1960s. One of the pioneers of the Oregon wine world was David Lett, who set up shop in the valley in 1965 and planted the area's first pinot noir vines, founding the famed **Eyrie Vineyards**. The Willamette Valley is now home to more than 700 wineries across 17,200 acres of land.

SILVER FALLS STATE PARK

Oregon's largest state park, **Silver Falls**, is 26 miles east of Salem and an easy day trip. The park offers good camping sites with showers and flush toilets. Waterfalls are a big attraction here and they are easily reached on a short walk. The famed **South Falls** (177ft) pours off a ledge, allowing you to walk behind it. The **Trail of Ten Falls** is a spectacular 7.2-mile moderate loop trail. Have a bathing suit and towel handy to swim in some of the pools. Kids may recognize the park upon arrival as some scenes from the film *Yogi Bear* were shot here. Whatever parts of the park you visit, arrive early to avoid the crowds – this place can get very busy.

WHERE TO STAY IN & NEAR SALEM

The Grand Hotel in Salem	Oregon Garden Resort	MaMere's Guest House
This modern hotel in downtown Salem is steps away from good restaurants and a short walk to the Capitol. $$	In Silverton, this place has clean and comfortable rooms in a peaceful area near the Oregon Garden. $$	Historic 1891 home in Monmouth. Rooms are cozy and a light breakfast is served on an outdoor patio. $$

WHERE TO DRINK

Paul Beck, owner of Willamette Wine Concierge (@willamettewineconcierge), shares his top winery recommendations.

The hills are dotted with small, sustainable vineyards, where you can enjoy world-class pinot noir, chardonnay and sparkling wine with genuine Oregon hospitality.

Granville Wine Co, Dundee
Ayla and Jackson are gracious hosts who love to share stories from growing up in the family vineyard.

Winter's Hill Estate, Dayton
Enjoy a beautiful setting overlooking the valley and choose from a variety of tasting flights including a wine and chocolate pairing.

Abbott Claim, Carlton
A must if you want a luxury feel with a private cave tasting.

Iterum Winery, Salem
A private wine and food pairing prepared by the winemaker.

JESS KRAFT/SHUTTERSTOCK ©

Vineyards, Dundee Hills

If there is a hub to the Willamette Valley wine industry, McMinnville is it. The city's business district, centered on 3rd St, has more than 10 tasting rooms. It's a great opportunity to sample the area's finest wines without having to get a car and drive between vineyards. In addition to wine, there are places to try craft beer and cider.

After a bit of downtown exploration and wine tasting, hit the road and visit a few wineries between McMinnville and Newberg. The McMinnville Area Chamber of Commerce has self-drive wine-tour maps. If you are just looking for a place to kick off a wine tour, try **Coeur De Terre Vineyard**, a beautiful and inviting vineyard where you'll learn a lot from the hosts on viniculture. **Stoller Family Estate** is another excellent stop – the 400-acre property in the Dundee Hills maintains high sustainability standards and has a state-of-the-art tasting room with a huge glass wall overlooking its vineyard.

 BEST PLACES TO EAT IN MCMINNVILLE

Sage
This casual eatery serves very good soups made from scratch, in-house bread and tasty salads. Great service. **$**

Horse Radish
Delightful Carlton restaurant specializing in artisan cheese plates, delicious sandwiches and soups. **$$**

Bistro Maison
This European-style restaurant in a converted home in McMinnville offers superb French cuisine. **$$$**

If you are behind the wheel and visiting wineries you'll need to practice taste and spit. If you'd prefer to kick back and let someone else do the driving (while you drink), there are a few local tour operators that can shuttle you around. Try **Grape Escape**, **Oregon Select Wine Tours** or **Valley Vineyard Tours**.

McMinnville Highlights

From parks to planes

Wine is just one part of McMinnville's appeal. While you are here, take some time to admire downtown, a fun place to hang out and soak in some of the historic brick architecture. **City Park**, which sits at one end of 3rd St, is a shady spot to wander when the weather heats up.

Try to time your visit to experience McMinnville's wacky **UFO Festival**, held annually since 1999, which features aliens parading down the street and a UFO symposium. The May festival is held in honor of a famous local UFO sighting on a nearby farm in 1950.

Do not leave McMinnville without stopping by **Serendipity Ice Cream** for a cone or some other treat. It's located in the lobby of the former Cook's Hotel, which opened in 1886. The player (self-playing) piano in the corner belting out old-time tunes is sure to delight.

The popular **Evergreen Aviation & Space Museum**, a few miles outside McMinnville, displays dozens of historic airplanes, helicopters and even some space capsules. The centerpiece of the museum is the **Spruce Goose**, the largest plane ever built. The massive plane was the brainchild of eccentric business tycoon Howard Hughes (portrayed by Leonardo DiCaprio in the film *The Aviator*). Right next to the Aviation & Space Museum sits the **Wings and Waves Waterpark**, another family-friendly attraction.

US history buffs may also want to travel to Newberg to visit the **Hoover-Minthorn House Museum**, the boyhood home of Herbert Hoover, the 31st president of the United States. The house is open Wednesday to Sunday in summer; call ahead if you want to visit outside these months.

Oregon City

TIME FROM SALEM: **45 MINS** 🚗

Final stop on the Oregon Trail

There was a time (two centuries ago) when Oregon City captivated pioneer lore. It was the last stop of the Oregon Trail and any settler wanting to file a land claim did so here. It was

THE FLOOD THAT WIPED OUT A TOWN

In the 1840s Champoeg, a town on the Willamette River near modern-day Newberg, had a bright future. The small settlement had a steamboat landing, a stagecoach office and a granary owned by the Hudson Bay Company. At the time, the status of the Oregon Territory was in dispute between the United States and the United Kingdom.

In 1843 settlers in Champoeg took matters into their own hands and voted to establish the first American government on the Pacific Coast. Alas, Champoeg was not destined to last long. In December 1861 floodwaters from the Willamette River devastated the town. Champoeg was abandoned but some of its original foundations remain in the **Champoeg State Heritage Area**. The area has a campground with good facilities.

BEST PLACES TO STAY IN MCMINNVILLE

The Vintages Trailer Resort
Just outside Dayton, this large RV resort offers retro glamping with Airstreams and camper vans. **$$**

Atticus Hotel
Luxurious hotel with ultra-modern decor and large rooms. Bikes are available for use by guests. **$$$**

Abbey Road Farm B&B
Nine miles from McMinnville, this stunning property is located on a working farm with roaming animals. **$$$**

CHILL OUT IN HOT SPRINGS

The geothermal activity of the Cascades bubbles up in hot springs in a number of locations east of the Willamette Valley. One of the best spots is the **Bagby Hot Springs** ($5, paid at the trailhead), located 55 miles southeast of Oregon City. From the parking lot, a 1.5-mile trail through dense forest ends at the springs. The rustic experience is amplified by the tubs, which are little more than hollowed-out logs.

Terwilliger Hot Springs ($10), aka Cougar Hot Springs, is located 55 miles east of Eugene. These hot pools also require a short hike and are picture-perfect. Both pools can get crowded, especially on weekends.

More developed pools are found at **Breitenbush Hot Springs**, 62 miles east of Salem.

the capital of the Oregon Territory for a stint and home to the first newspaper published west of the Rocky Mountains.

One of the attractions for early settlers was access to **Willamette Falls**, which provided power to run local lumber mills. The horseshoe-shaped falls are the largest waterfall by volume in the Northwest: 1500ft wide and 40ft high. For nearly two centuries the falls have been used to power local factories (mostly paper mills), the remains of which still sit on the opposite banks. Removal of the buildings is an ongoing process.

Begin a tour of the area at the **Oregon City Municipal Elevator**. The city was originally located along the river but when the town expanded to the upper cliffs an elevator was built to connect the two neighborhoods. The 1915 wooden elevator was replaced in the 1950s with the current concrete-and-steel structure.

Close to the top of the elevator, visit 713 Center St, location of the 1845 **McLoughlin House**, built by one of Oregon's founding fathers, John McLoughlin. Free tours are available. At 603 6th St, the **Stevens-Crawford House Museum** is a 1908 building with some original furniture and innovative features for the time, including electric light fixtures and central heating. For a more in-depth look at the local history, visit the **Museum of the Oregon Territory**, which contains, among other exhibits, a chunk of the Willamette Meteorite, the largest meteorite found in the US.

Corvallis

TIME FROM SALEM: **40 MINS** 🚗

College town vibes

Corvallis is a tidy, small city that is known primarily for being home to Oregon State University. Students make up around half of the city's population so in summer it can feel fairly quiet compared to the rest of the year.

During the school year, the downtown area is bustling with bakeries, taco shops and pizzerias trying to feed a hungry population of Beavers. You could easily spend a day just hanging out downtown and wandering the campus grounds. Athletics are big at OSU and cheering on the Beaver football team at **Reser Stadium** is a blast. The farmers market is held twice a week (on Wednesday and Saturday) from April to November.

About 7 miles north of Corvallis, Oregon State University maintains the 40-acre **Peavy Arboretum**, which is worth a visit to walk on shady trails. There are lots of interpretive signs to explain what is going on in the forest around you. It's dog-friendly and maps are available in the parking lot to help you get around. Around 25 miles west of Corvallis, **Mary's Peak** is the highest in the Coast Range and offers spectac-

PLACES TO EAT IN OREGON CITY

Mike's Drive-In
Old school American drive-in where you can grab a seat at one of their outdoor picnic tables. $

Don Pepe's Mexican Food
Sublime Mexican cuisine served with a variety of sauces and salsas and choices of flavorful meat. $

Nebbiolo Restaurant
Gourmet Northwest dishes with Italian and New Mexico influences. Steaks, seafood, chicken and chops. $$$

Reser Stadium

ular views. A slightly more than half-trail of moderate difficulty connects the parking lot and the peak.

Corvallis is home to several festivals that attract people from around the state. The **Fall Festival** (last weekend of September) features artists and musicians in Central Park. The **Shrewsbury Renaissance Faire** (Kings Valley, September) sees costumed performers wandering an Elizabethan marketplace. **Da Vinci Days** is an arts and science fair held in July at the Benton County Fairgrounds.

ALBANY CAROUSEL

A family-friendly stop along I-5 is the whimsical Albany **Historic Carousel & Museum** (open Wednesday to Sunday, 11am to 4pm), 10 miles east of Corvallis. The 1909 carousel was originally located in New Jersey and Pennsylvania before being shipped to Santa Barbara where it was left in a yard (the city rejected plans to allow its operation). It was then shipped to Oregon in pieces like a giant Lego set.

A 10-year restoration project brought the carousel back to pristine condition. All the animals on the carousel were carved by community volunteers in Albany and the on-site workshop continues to carve and repair animals – visitors can get a glimpse of the work through windows.

BEST PLACES TO EAT IN CORVALLIS

American Dream Pizza
Its claim to fame is that Barack Obama had a slice here in 2008. Tasty pies that cater to the college crowd. **$**

Castor
Marries European-style cuisine with Northwest ingredients. Gourmet cooking with a casual atmosphere. **$$**

del Alma Restaurant
Beautifully plated Latin American cuisine that could pass for works of art. Tuesday to Saturday dinner. **$$$**

Eugene

GETTING AROUND

Renting a bike (or using the local bike share program, PeaceHeath Rides) is the best way to get around as the city is well connected with paths and bike routes. Lane County Transit also offers bus routes around the city.

EVENTS IN EUGENE

Running is a big deal in Eugene and joining an afternoon jog with a running club is a great way to get to know the city. **Run Hub Northwest** and the **Eugene Running Company** both organize group runs around town.

By far the most popular event is the **Oregon Country Fair**, a three-day music and arts festival that feels like a cross between Burning Man and Renaissance faire. It's a great place to experience Eugene's counterculture movement.

Eugene wears many hats. It's well left of center on the political spectrum and is known for its environmental activism and counterculture vibe. It's also Tracktown USA thanks to a strong history of track and field support and Nike roots. Eugene is also home to the University of Oregon, known for its strong liberal arts program and popular Duck mascot. But at heart, Eugene is a working-class town with a history of logging and manufacturing. It's home to artists and has a thriving art and maker scene. Organic farming, backyard gardens and outdoor activities are also popular. Eating healthy and communing with nature are popular pastimes. Eugene is a good base to explore this corner of Oregon. The coast, the Willamette National Forest, excellent wineries and quaint rural towns are within a one-hour drive from the city.

Go Old School at the University of Oregon

World-class museums on the historic campus

The University of Oregon, founded in 1872, is deeply woven into Eugene's urban fabric and a hub of its intellectual and cultural community. A wander around its leafy grounds reveals some beautiful brick architecture and little courtyards shaded by more than 20 tree species. Students crisscross these grounds for nine months of the year but in summer you'll have it almost to yourself.

A campus highlight is the **Jordan Schnitzer Museum of Art**, which houses a world-class collection of 13,000 pieces of art from around the globe, with an emphasis on Asia. New exhibits are rotated regularly. Just south of the museum, you'll find a large, moss-covered **Eugene Pioneer Cemetery**. A wander among the headstones gives some insight into life (and death) in the town's early days.

A five-minute walk further east is the **Museum of Natural and Cultural History**, housed in a replica of a Native American longhouse. This highly educational science-focused

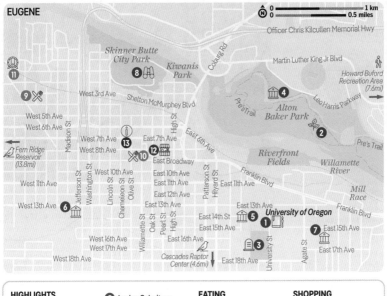

EUGENE

0 — 1 km
0 — 0.5 miles

Officer Chris Kilcullen Memorial Hwy

Skinner Butte City Park
Kiwanis Park
Coburg Rd
Martin Luther King Jr Blvd
Howard Buford Recreation Area (7.6mi)
Leo Harris Parkway

West 3rd Ave
Shelton McMurphey Blvd
Pre's Trail
Alton Baker Park
Pre's Trail

West 5th Ave
West 6th Ave
Madison St
West 7th Ave East 7th Ave
West 8th Ave
East Broadway
Riverfront Fields
Willamette River
Fern Ridge Reservoir (13.8mi)
High St
East 6th Ave

West 10th Ave East 10th Ave
East 11th Ave
East 12th Ave
Franklin Blvd
East 11th Ave
Mill Race
West 11th Ave
Jefferson St Washington St Lincoln St Chameleon St Olive St
Patterson St Hilyard St

West 13th Ave East 13th Ave
East 13th Ave
University of Oregon
Franklin Blvd

Willamette St Oak St Pearl St High St
East 14th St
East 15th Ave
East 15th Ave

West 16th Ave West 17th Ave
East 16th Ave
Agate St
East 17th Ave

West 18th Ave
Cascades Raptor Center (4.6mi)
East 18th Ave
University St

HIGHLIGHTS
1 University of Oregon

SIGHTS
2 Alton Baker Park
3 Eugene Pioneer Cemetery
4 Eugene Science Center

5 Jordan Schnitzer Museum of Art
6 Lane County Historical Museum
7 Museum of Natural & Cultural History
8 Skinner Butte

EATING
9 Red Barn
10 Voodoo Doughnut

DRINKING & NIGHTLIFE
11 Ninkasi Brewing Company

SHOPPING
12 Saturday Market

INFORMATION
13 Eugene Cascades and Coast Visitor Center

---

facility is kid-friendly with interactive exhibits. Look out for the (at least) 9000-year-old sandals found at Fort Rock (p238) in Central Oregon.

If you're hunting some U of O Ducks souvenirs or a quick meal, visit 13th St, just west of campus. It's packed with shops and eateries that cater to the college crowd.

Museums & Science Centers

Hands-on learning in Eugene

Off-campus, Eugene has enough museums and learning centers to fill up a day. Swing by the expansive **Alton Baker Park** complex for visit to the **Eugene Science Center** – a terrific place to let your little ones charge around and play with STEM-focused exhibits and marvel at the planetarium.

> ☑ **TOP TIP**
>
> The **Eugene Cascades and Coast Visitor Center** is located on Olive St and is open on weekdays. It's a good place to pick up bike maps and travel advice.

 BEST PLACES TO EAT IN EUGENE

Marché
French meals with a Northwest farm-to-table philosophy. The servers do a great job pairing wines to your meal. $$

Lion & Owl
Seasonal and local ingredients are used here to build a range of French-influenced dishes. $$

Izakaya Meiji Company
Japanese tavern serving small plates for snacking. Pick from spicy or mild curries, rice balls and meat dishes. $$

207

GETTING ACTIVE IN EUGENE

Gary Tepfer (@ garytepfer.com), a Eugene-based landscape photographer, shares his favorite ways to stay active in Eugene.

Eugene's city planners were insightful in preserving natural areas for all people to enjoy and access on foot or bike. To the east is the **Howard Buford Recreation Area**, an extensive complex of hiking and horseback-riding trails. In spring, its hillsides burst with wildflowers.

Northwest of the city is **Fern Ridge Reservoir**, a large lake and marshland with the richest bird habitat in the region, reachable from Eugene on a dedicated bike path.

There are also running trails through most city parks and along the river, a basalt climbing cliff (The Columns) on **Skinner Butte**, and a canoe path in the Willamette River. One hardly needs to travel far to enjoy the out-of-doors.

Saturday Market

Another favorite among kids and wildlife enthusiasts is the **Cascades Raptor Center**, a facility that specializes in treating injured birds of prey. Around 40 birds that are unable to return to the wild are resident here.

For a more general history of the region, check out the **Lane County Historical Museum**, which houses a collection of carriages and covered wagons (some of the oldest in Oregon).

Downtown & the Whit
Get to the heart of Eugene

To get the full Eugene experience, one must walk its streets. Downtown Eugene is densely packed and easily explored on foot.

A highlight is the **Saturday Market** (from 10am to 4pm) where folks arrive from all around the valley to sell their locally made products, from food to crafts. It's also the best place in town to experience Eugene's hippie past and present. Young and old, colorfully dressed (or not at all), strumming guitars, juggling or selling crafts, the hippie scene is alive and well here.

Downtown also has great nightlife; a cluster of bars is located near the corner of Olive and Broadway. This neighborhood is also home to an ever-popular **Voodoo Doughnut** shop, where you can sample doughnuts with all sorts of wacky toppings and designs.

A mile west of downtown, check out the Whiteaker neighborhood (aka The Whit), a residential area that is also a cultural hub, filled with diverse restaurants, hip shops, hostels, public art and activists. Stop by the **Red Barn**, a grocery store packed with healthy food and vegan specialties. Whiteaker is also home to **Ninkasi Brewing Company**, Eugene's most popular brewery.

 BEST PLACES TO STAY IN EUGENE

Eugene Lodge and International Hostel
A variety of rooms and dorms with laundry facilities and kitchen access. **$**

The Campbell House Inn
Upscale B&B inside an elegant 1892 Victorian home. Some rooms have fireplaces and the breakfast is superb. **$$**

Riverpath Inn
A comfortable inn in a leafy neighborhood close to the Whiteaker area. Tasteful and modern rooms. **$$**

Beyond
Eugene

Surrounding Eugene you can leave the crowds behind and discover a wealth of small towns, wineries and untouched wilderness.

Not far from Eugene the vehicle traffic on the valley's main roads starts to thin out as they head deeper into the hills and mountains. East of the city, on Hwy 126, white-water rafting and hiking are two popular activities near the town of McKenzie Bridge. In a southeast direction, Hwy 58 meanders toward Crater Lake, with Oakridge and Crescent Lake among the places to stop en route. Hot springs can be found in these areas and if you've got a tent there are several excellent campgrounds where you can get off the grid for a few days. For a bit of the high life, head southeast of Eugene where fertile valleys are dotted with distinctive vineyards.

GETTING AROUND

From Eugene, there are four daily buses to the McKenzie Ranger Station, a great way to get onto the McKenzie River Trail. Public transportation runs around the Willamette Valley but connections can be time-consuming. Getting out to hot springs, state parks and wineries is best done with your own vehicle.

☑ TOP TIP

You can extend your travels in the area by simply heading over the Cascades to meet up with Hwy 97, creating a loop that passes through Bend.

MICHAL BALADA/SHUTTERSTOCK ©

McKenzie River (p211)

The 139-mile drive from Eugene to Crater Lake along Hwy 58 takes you through some of Central Oregon's most beautiful high country. Before heading into the mountains take a slight detour into **1 Westfir** to see the Office Covered Bridge, the longest covered bridge in Oregon at 180ft. Built in 1940 to accommodate lumber trucks, this bridge also features a pedestrian walkway. Opposite the bridge is the Westfir Lodge, a cozy guesthouse and a market. Next up, **2 Oakridge** is a popular destination for mountain bikers and in summer the town is chockablock with cyclists from around the Northwest. Cog Wild offers mountain bike tours and shuttles. Willamette Mountain Mercantile rents bikes. Some 10 miles east of Oakridge you'll spot the turnoff for the **3 McCredie Hot Springs**, a sublime streamside set of hot pools that are definitely worth

a soak in. Travel 12 more miles to **4 Salt Creek Falls** (287ft), the second-highest waterfall in the state after Multnomah Falls. Parts are wheelchair-accessible and hikers can reach the bottom of the falls and a viewing area. Some 11 miles from the falls, **5 Waldo Lake** is the second-largest lake in Oregon and is incredibly clear, with visibility up to 120ft on a calm day. Miles of hiking and biking trails circle the lake. Close to the Willamette Pass Resort, Hwy 58 parallels **6 Odell Lake**, a perfect spot for both fishing and boating. A pleasant 3.1-mile out-and-back trail follows the shore from Odell Creek Campground to Sunset Cove Campground. Odell Lake Lodge & Resort is a relaxing place to put your feet up. From Odell Lake you can continue to Bend or Crater Lake, or explore the Diamond Peak Wilderness to the southwest.

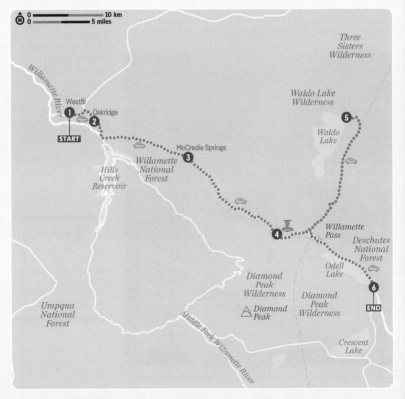

Brownsville

Step back to another era

Small towns east of Eugene have a certain magic to them and are great places to spend some time and get a feel for rural Oregon.

Brownsville, 31 miles north of Eugene, is one such town. In addition to being home to the **Linn County Museum**, Brownsville was also the primary filming location of the 1986 film *Stand by Me*. Fans of the film can poke around the main street and spot filming locations. As you drive into town on Green Bridge the buildings become eerily familiar. It's otherwise a sleepy, off-the-beaten-path destination that sees few visitors but gives a sense of life as it was in the 1950s. Since it's just off I-5 it makes an easy detour for north–south travelers.

East of Brownsville, if you are traveling along Hwy 20 toward Bend, there are several historic covered bridges to look out for, including the **Weddle Covered Bridge** (Sweet Home) and the **Short Covered Bridge** (Cascadia).

McKenzie Region

Hike, fish and raft along the stunning McKenzie River

Driving northeast of Eugene on Hwy 126 takes travelers out of the Willamette Valley farmlands and into a wild region of rushing rivers and dense forests dominated by Douglas fir trees. As you head up the highway, look out for a handful of historic covered bridges, including **Goodpasture Bridge** (Vida) and **Belknap Bridge** (Blue River).

This highway follows the **McKenzie River**, popular with rafters and kayakers wanting to tackle class I to III rapids. The fishing is also very good on this river. High Country Expeditions and Oregon Whitewater Adventures both run rafting day trips on the McKenzie.

The area also has a number of hiking trails, including the 26-mile-long McKenzie River National Recreation Trail from McKenzie Bridge. The **McKenzie River Ranger station**, 2.5 miles east of McKenzie Bridge, is a great resource for travel in the area and contains exhibits describing local flora and fauna.

The town of **McKenzie Bridge** is small but serves as a good place to pick up supplies, eat and perhaps stay the night. One of the best spots to get food is **Takoda's Restaurant** in the town of Rainbow. It serves sandwiches, burgers and a delicious marionberry pie.

BEST PLACES TO STAY ON HWY 128

Travelers heading east on Hwy 126 will find rustic accommodations in the McKenzie Bridge area.

Caddisfly Resort
Redwood cabins with kitchenette, fireplace and decks that overlook the McKenzie River. **$**

Belknap Hot Springs Lodge
Dated rooms but the tent sites have a scenic, wooded location. It's on the McKenzie River 6 miles from McKenzie Bridge **$**

Harbick's Country Inn
A friendly place in the town of Rainbow; rooms are updated and affordable. **$**

Eagle Rock Lodge
In the town of Vida; has eight clean rooms, some with a fireplace and Jacuzzi. Delicious breakfasts are served by friendly hosts. **$$**

Columbia River Gorge

AMERICA'S FIRST SCENIC ROUTE

From waterfalls and adventure sports to family farms and fascinating museums, the Columbia River Gorge has something to suit all tastes.

In 1805 William Clark – co-leader of the Lewis and Clark Expedition – lamented the difficulty of sleeping through the night in the Columbia River Gorge, writing of the extraordinary noise created by enormous flocks of squawking waterfowl. That wasn't the only challenge for expedition members. Fierce winds, inescapable fleas and dangerous rapids also made the gorge an exhausting and hellish stretch of travel on the expedition's final push toward the Pacific.

Today the Columbia River Gorge's I-84 and its country byways make travel an easier experience. Adventure tourism is big here, with world-class mountain biking and kiteboarding. Activities requiring less adrenaline include hikes to waterfalls and visits to small farms where kids (and adults) can pick berries. There's also a handful of excellent museums in the region. The gorge itself is a geologic marvel, formed over millions of years by volcanic and hydraulic forces. Take some time to simply absorb the alternating vistas, from snow-capped peaks to fields of wildflowers.

Interstate travel allows visitors to zip between the sites but the Historic Columbia River Hwy creates a slower pace of travel. Cyclists will also find miles of peaceful bike paths along most of the gorge. Hood River serves as the region's tourism hub but it's also worth exploring some of the smaller towns on either the Oregon or Washington side of the river.

JACOB BILLINGS/SHUTTERSTOCK ©

THE MAIN AREA

HOOD RIVER
Kiteboarding, beer
and fruit farms.
p216

Left: Wine barrels, Hood River (p216); Above: Vista House (p222) and Columbia River

214

Find Your Way

The Columbia River Gorge stretches for 80 miles east of the Portland metro area. You can base yourself almost anywhere and make day trips. Cyclists will enjoy an excellent network of trails and bike paths.

Hood River, p216

The gorge's main tourism hub and a center for kiteboarding. It's a good base to explore nearby fruit farms.

CAR

With your own vehicle, you can explore the sights in the gorge at your own pace and reach areas not easily accessible on public transportation. Wineries, farms and trailheads are accessible on a good road network.

BUS

Columbia Area Transit (CAT) operates the Columbia Gorge Express, a small-sized bus that has stops at the main visitor sites in the gorge, including Multnomah Falls, Cascades Locks and Hood River.

Goldendale

Little Klickitat River

Columbia River

Biggs

97

206

Deschutes River

Wishram

Fifteenmile Creek

The Dalles

84

30

The Dalles Dam

The Dalles

The Dalles Bridge

Klickitat River

Lyle

Mosier

Columbia River Gorge National Scenic Area

White Salmon Bingen

Hood River

Odell

Columbia River Gorge National Scenic Area

Dog Mountain

Dog Mountain

Hood River

Dee

Mt Hood

35

Parkdale

East Fork Hood River

Badger Creek Wilderness

Carson

14

84

30

Cascade Locks

Mark O. Hatfield Wilderness

Mt Hood National Forest

35

Mt Hood

Barlow Pass

Wind River

Stevenson

Bonneville Dam

Eagle Ck

Larch Mountain

Lost Lake

Mt Hood Wilderness

Government Camp

Columbia River Gorge National Scenic Area

Hamilton Mountain

Warrendale

Dodson

Multnomah Falls

Bull Run River

Cascade Range

Washougal River

Columbia River Gorge National Scenic Area

26

Salmon-Huckleberry Wilderness

Sandy River

Camas

Washougal

Vista House

14

Troutdale

Corbett

30

84

211

Sandy

Estacada

Gresham

26

212

224

0 ——— 20 km
0 ——— 10 miles

Cascade Locks (p223)

Plan Your Time

Take in the main sites along I-84 but book some time to get off the highway and into the region's hills and valleys that shelter hiking trails, vineyards and fruit farms.

Pressed for Time

If you have only a weekend, head for Hood River, making stops at **Vista House** (p222), **Multnomah Falls** (p222) and **Bonneville Dam** (p223). Explore **downtown** (p218) and visit nearby **farms along the Fruit Loop** (p219). Get active with a rental bike or a kiteboarding lesson and enjoy some locally made beer. Return to Portland on the Washington side of the gorge.

Five Days to Explore

Spend an extra day or two around the **western gorge** (p222), exploring waterfalls and hiking areas, with a night or two in **Cascade Locks** (p223). There's good hiking on the **Washington side of the gorge** (p224) too. East of Hood River, visit the **Columbia Gorge Discovery Center** (p225) in The Dalles. Continue to the **Maryhill Museum of Art** (p225) and the **Stonehenge Memorial** (p225).

Seasonal Highlights

SPRING	SUMMER	FALL	WINTER
Wildflowers start to bloom but you may also get some rain. See waterfalls in all their glory.	Optimal time for berry picking, hiking and cycling. Accommodations prices are at their peak.	Apples and pears are in season and fruit stands overflowing. Good weather for horseback riding and hiking.	Snowcapped mountains and wintery forests. Snowshoeing and cross-country skiing are available.

Hood River

GETTING AROUND

Using your own bike or vehicle is the best way to explore Hood River. CAT is the local bus service with a route around town and service through the Gorge.

Hood River grew up on agriculture and still produces a bounty of crops that overflow on farm tables throughout the summer and fall. But the hillside city overlooking the mighty Columbia River increasingly turns its attention to tourism for economic development. There's good reason for that – the town retains its historic charm but is also surrounded by a wealth of natural beauty that is perfect for hiking, biking, rafting and other activities. The strong local winds blasting through the gorge are also an important draw for some, as they create perfect conditions for kiteboarding and windsurfing – the city is considered one of the best places in the world for these two water sports.

☑ TOP TIP

If getting on a kiteboard sounds daunting, the next best thing is to hang out on the Hood River Waterfront Park and watch the experts blast their way across the river. Bring a blanket and some takeout food from one of the restaurants or brewpubs on nearby Portway Ave.

SAWAYA PHOTOGRAPHY/GETTY IMAGES ®

Cyclist, Columbia River

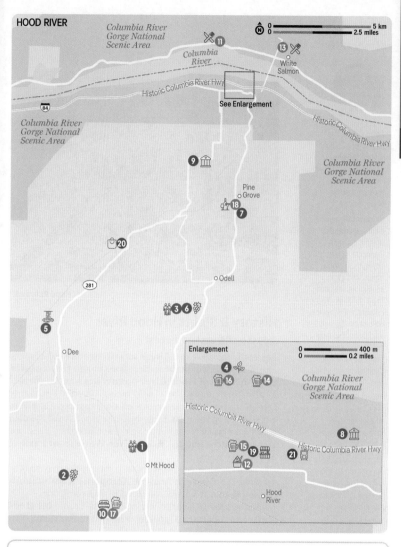

SIGHTS
1 Draper Girls Country Farm
2 Grateful Vineyard
3 Hood River Lavender Farms
4 Hood River Waterfront Park
5 Punchbowl Falls
6 Stave & Stone Winery
7 Fruit Company
8 History Museum of Hood River County
9 Western Antique Aeroplane & Automobile Museum

SLEEPING
10 Old Parkdale Inn

EATING
11 Manny's Lonchera
12 Mike's Ice Cream
13 White Salmon Bakery

DRINKING & NIGHTLIFE
14 Ferment Brewing Company
15 Full Sail Brew Pub
16 pFriem Family Brewers
17 Solera Brewery
18 Gorge White House

SHOPPING
19 Hood River Farmers Market
20 Old Trunk

TRANSPORTATION
21 Mt Hood Railroad

HOOD RIVER

217

COOL HANGOUTS IN HOOD RIVER

John Cody, the manager of Hood River Stationers, recommends these Hood River area food and drink experiences.

Grateful Vineyard
A family-friendly tasting room in Parkdale where they serve their own wines, beers and ciders as well as seasonal food pairings. You can also pick your own cherries, apples and pears from the orchard. The apple cider doughnuts from their produce stand are a must-try. **$$**

White Salmon Bakery
Head here on Monday nights for their once-a-week pizza night. **$**

Manny's Lonchera
Right next to the White Salmon River; always a must-stop for lunch. **$**

Punchbowl Falls
To get outdoors, hike to the confluence of the east and west forks of the Hood River.

PETER MARBACH, PUBLIC DOMAIN, VIA WIKIMEDIA COMMONS ©

Mt Hood Railroad

History & Sights in Hood River

Ride the rails, explore the past

Before diving into Hood River's action adventure scene, spend an afternoon learning about the region's unique past. The **History Museum of Hood River County** has some displays of local history, ranging from Indigenous artifacts to kiteboards. One exhibit and movie focuses on the Japanese Americans who settled in the area. Close by is the Hood River Sandbar where kiteboarders assemble their gear and depart the shore. You can watch from the **Hood River Waterfront Park**, or give it a try yourself.

Fans of classic airplanes, cars and motorcycles may want to seek out the **Western Antique Aeroplane & Automobile Museum** (aka WAAAM), on Hood River's southside.

Another family favorite is a ride on the scenic **Mt Hood Railroad** (operates Thursday, Friday and Saturday). The railroad once transported timber and fruit from the Upper Hood River Valley but now shuttles tourists past rivers and through orchards, with good views of Mt Hood. There's a stop en route at the **Fruit Company**, a gift store and orchard. Two-person, motorized railbikes are also available, giving visitors an open-air rail experience.

 WHERE TO EAT IN HOOD RIVER

Egg River Café
Breakfast spot serving big portions of American breakfast classics plus crepes, sandwiches and pastas. **$**

Solstice Wood Fire Pizza
Wood-fired pizzas served near the waterfront. It has a kids menu that's sure to please small diners. **$$**

Celilo Restaurant & Bar
Tender steaks, perfectly cooked fish, a good selection of wines and an attentive waitstaff. **$$$**

Tastes of Hood River
Unmissable gastronomic experiences

For a small town Hood River packs in a number of great eateries. Much of the local fare is grown nearby and you can sample some of the produce at the lively **Hood River Farmers Market** (Saturdays from May to November). The Hood River Waterfront Park is the place to take this bounty and enjoy a riverside picnic. Don't miss **Mike's Ice Cream** and its atmospheric outdoor seating area overlooking Oak St, Hood River's main drag. When it comes to breweries, Hood River rivals some of Oregon's best beer towns. **Full Sail Brew Pub**, **pFriem Family Brewers** and **Ferment Brewing Company** all offer excellent beers and filling pub grub.

The Hood River Fruit Loop
Berry picking, lavender fields and more

The 35-mile-long Hood River County Fruit Loop winds along country roads south of town, passing by family-run fruit stands, u-pick orchards, lavender fields, alpaca farms and various places to taste locally made wines and ciders.

There are nearly 30 local farms and businesses listed along the route, so you'll have to plan out what is most interesting for you. Availability changes with the seasons. Berries are in season in the early part of summer, while pears and apples are ready in the late summer and fall. A harvest calendar (and map) is available on the website hoodriverfruitloop.com.

If you're keen on doing u-pick (a kid favorite), the **Gorge White House** is one of the best and has a good onsite food cart. **Draper Girls Country Farm** is also popular and has a country store stocked with local products. **Hood River Lavender Farms** is set on pretty grounds: July to September is lavender-picking season. Anywhere you go, try to call ahead because fruit availability and timetables change often. Ask about costs as some places charge by the pound while others require a minimum payment made upfront.

For oenophiles, **Stave & Stone Winery** is worth a stop for its excellent Mt Hood views and tasting room. Don't miss the **Old Trunk**, a small shop with antiques, vintage clothing, a fruit stand and an old-fashioned soda fountain. The town of Parkdale marks the halfway point on the Fruit Loop and is a logical place to spend the night if you're cycle touring and it's late. The **Old Parkdale Inn** offers overnight accommodations and **Solera Brewery** is where locals gather for a drink and to enjoy great views of Mt Hood from the patio.

ACTIVE ADVENTURES AROUND HOOD RIVER

Hood River is a paradise for active travelers. For kiteboarding and windsurfing, **Hood River Waterplay** and **Big Winds Hood River** are water-sports companies offering lessons and rentals. **Zoller's Outdoor Odysseys** and **Wet Planet Rafting and Kayaking**, both based in White Salmon, organize rafting trips on class III to V rapids. Mountain bikers will want to make a beeline for the **Post Canyon Trail System**, a network of bike trails on Hood River's west side. **Sol Rides** rents e-bikes while **Fat Tire Farm** is the place to rent a mountain bike. For hiking, drive 20 minutes south of Hood River on Hwy 35 to the trailhead for Tamanawas Falls: an easy to moderate 3.4-mile out-and-back hike. You'll follow the creek most of the way to the 110ft-high waterfall.

 WHERE TO STAY AROUND HOOD RIVER

Columbia Gorge Hotel & Spa	The Society Hotel – Bingen	Hood River Hotel
Atmospheric and historic hotel set amid lush gardens with its own natural waterfall. **$$**	There's something for every budget here, from upscale rooms down to hostel-style bunk beds. **$$**	This historic hotel built in 1912 retains some of its early-20th-century character. **$$**

Beyond Hood River

Experience one of Oregon's most glorious mountains and all the lakes and mountain trails that lie hidden in its flanks.

GETTING AROUND

Before setting off in winter, pack chains, extra food and check road conditions on the Oregon Department of Transportation (ODOT) website, tripcheck.com. It's best to tackle the sites in the gorge with your own vehicle or by bike. If you are relying on public transportation, CAT is a handy bus service with stops at a handful of main sites.

Point your car, motorcycle or bike in any direction from Hood River and you'll soon be surrounded by glorious lakes, rivers, waterfalls and snowcapped peaks. South of town, travelers wind their way up alluvial valleys toward Mt Hood, the state's highest peak. East and west of Hood River, the Columbia Gorge offers a string of beautiful waterfalls, including the famed Multnomah Falls, the tallest in Oregon. Crossing the river brings you over to the more rural Washington side where small towns offer a low-key vibe. Throughout the region, museums and interpretive trails help tell the story of the gorge, from its time as a center for Native American culture through the era of pioneer settlement.

RYBARMAREKK/SHUTTERSTOCK ©

Benson Bridge and Multnomah Falls (p222)

Mt Hood

Adventuring around Oregon's highest peak

Mt Hood is less than an hour's drive from Hood River, accessible on Hwy 35. It's an ideal destination for a day trip or overnight stay for summertime hikes and winter sports. The views are great year-round.

The hiking trails around Mt Hood can keep you busy for weeks. One of the most popular is the 7-mile loop trail passing by **Ramona Falls** (120ft). A shorter hike (4.2 miles) goes to pretty **Mirror Lake** from a parking lot right off Hwy 26 near Mt Hood SkiBowl. The trail to the lake is well marked and good for small kids, but around the lake it's a bit overgrown. Another kid-friendly trail is the **Old Salmon River Trail** (4 miles, out and back). The trailhead is about 3 miles south of Zigzag.

For those up for a more rigorous challenge, the **Timberline Trail** is a 42-mile trail that circumnavigates Mt Hood, passing by waterfalls and alpine meadows. Check ranger stations on current conditions as parts of the trail get washed out. You can do day hikes on portions of it, including a section from Timberline Lodge to **Zigzag Canyon Overlook** (4.4 miles, out and back).

A Northwest Forest Pass is required at most Mt Hood area trailheads. Passes and permits are available at an information center in Government Camp and the Zigzag Ranger Station.

Mt Hood is also popular among climbers – it's the world's second-most-climbed peak over 10,000ft after Japan's Mt Fuji. Parts of the climb are technical and inexperienced climbers should go with a guide, such as **Timberline Mountain Guides**. The **Mazamas Club** offers training. For mountain-bike-specific areas, the **44 Trails** network, located on the east side of Mt Hood, has a good variety of terrain.

Travelers who just want to kick back and appreciate the mountain from a distance can do so from **Lost Lake** on the north side. **Trillium Lake** and **Timothy Lake** on the south side of Mt Hood offer equally superb views. Camping is available in all these areas.

Skiers have several options in the Mt Hood area for wintertime fun: **Mt Hood Meadows** and **Timberline Lodge Ski Area** are the largest. Timberline's legendary lodge is perfect for an après-ski drink. **Mt Hood SkiBowl** is smaller but has night skiing. **Cooper Spur Ski Area** has affordable skiing for families. Cross-country skiers and snowshoers can try **Trillium Sno-Park** or the **White River West Sno-Park**. **Teacup Nordic Sno-Park** has around 15 miles of groomed trails, just off Hwy 35.

TIMBERLINE LODGE

An Oregon icon, Timberline Lodge was built between 1936 and 1938 as a Depression-era project to create jobs. Construction costs were minimized by repurposing discarded local materials. The metal screens in front of the fireplaces were made from old tire chains and the carved wooden newel posts on the staircases used discarded cedar utility poles. Even if you are not staying it's worth visiting for the views and a browse around the lobby and grounds. Make your way to the back patio and check out the cozy **Ram's Head Bar** on the upper floor. If the exterior looks familiar it was the filming location for Stanley Kubrik's 1980 film *The Shining*. Terrific Northwest food and drink are available at its restaurant and two bars.

WHERE TO SLEEP NEAR MT HOOD

Timberline Lodge
A gorgeous lodge oozing with history and charm, Timberline offers a variety of cozy rooms, from dorms to deluxe. **$$$**

Lost Lake Resort & Campground
Rustic spot with simple cabins and lodge rooms. Campsites are spacious and private. **$**

Campsites
Excellent camping options include Tollgate, Trillium Lake or Camp Creek campgrounds. Book through recreation.gov. **$**

MT HOOD LOGISTICS

A Northwest Forest Pass is required at most Mt Hood area trailheads. A Sno-Park permit is needed for winter recreational areas. Passes and permits are available at Welches and Government Camp. With your own wheels (car or bicycle) you can easily reach the trailheads and lakes around Mt Hood. If you don't have either, the Mt Hood Express is a public bus running daily between Sandy and Timberline Lodge with stops at Zigzag and Government Camp. Timberline Lodge also runs its own shuttle throughout the day from Government Camp. The Sea to Summit Shuttle from Portland has stops at Mt Hood Meadows, Mt Hood SkiBowl and Timberline Lodge. The Gorge to Mountain Express operates from Hood River to Mt Hood Meadows in winter.

FREEBILLY PHOTOGRAPHY/SHUTTERSTOCK ©

Vista House

The Western Gorge TIME FROM HOOD GORGE: **30 MINS** 🚗

Exploring the waterfall corridor

The western edge of the Columbia River Gorge rises from the valley floor like an elongated natural wall, from which spouts a succession of stunning waterfalls. The waterfalls are best viewed by traveling along the **Historic Columbia River Highway** (completed in 1915), America's first scenic highway and the first paved road in the Pacific Northwest.

Coming from Portland, most people start their tour by driving (or cycling) to **Vista House** at **Crown Point**. The 1918 Vista House observatory is a domed rotunda, built in the art nouveau style, that now houses a visitor center and gift shop.

From Crown Point, you'll pass **Latourell Falls** (249ft), the multi-tiered **Shepherd's Dell Falls** (220ft), **Bridal Veil Falls** (140ft) and **Wahkeena Falls** (242ft). Good hikes to and around the falls are signposted.

Next comes **Multnomah Falls** (620ft), the tallest waterfall in Oregon. A 1-mile trail leads to the top with a stop at picturesque **Benson Bridge** along the way. From the top, it's possible to continue on Trail 420 on a loop route to Wahkeena Falls. At the bottom of Multnomah Falls is the historic 1925 **Multnomah Falls Lodge**, containing a small visitor center and restaurant. If you are traveling on I-84 and only have time for Multnomah Falls, take exit 31, where you can park and access the falls via a tunnel under the freeway. Multnomah

---

WHERE TO EAT NEAR MT HOOD

Barlow Trail Roadhouse
Century-old rustic restaurant and bar along the highway near Zigzag. Serves big-portioned diner-style meals. **$**

Ram's Head Bar
Located on the atmospheric 2nd floor of Timberline Lodge. Soups, salads, sandwiches and other light fare available. **$$**

The Glacier Haus
Right in Government Camp, the Eastern European–inspired menu includes very good Hungarian beef goulash. **$$**

Falls is a major attraction in the gorge and in summer you'll need a timed-use permit (from recreation.gov).

Continuing east from Multnomah Falls on Hwy 30, it's 2 miles to **Lower Oneonta Falls** (65ft): a particularly good adventure for those who don't mind getting wet. The 'trail' between sheer rock walls is the riverbed itself and you'll need to negotiate log jams and waist-deep (sometimes chest-deep) water before the falls. From the **Oneonta Trailhead**, it's just a half-mile east to **Horsetail Falls** (176ft), an easily accessible waterfall near the parking lot. There's a good 3.6-mile hike from here to **Ponytail Falls** (82ft) and **Triple Falls** (64ft). Ponytail Falls is one of the few in the area where you can walk behind the waterfall.

Just past Ainsworth State Park, **Elowah Falls** (230ft) and **Upper McCord Creek Falls** (64ft) are two final places to visit along the waterfall corridor (or the first if you are going in the opposite direction).

Sights of the Western Gorge
Engineering marvels on the Columbia River

The mighty Columbia River near Cascades Locks is dotted with unique sights that together are a testament to the power of 20th-century engineering.

The most impressive of these sights is the **Bonneville Dam complex**, a Depression-era public works project 6 miles southwest of Cascade Locks.

The dams back up the Columbia River for 15 miles and generate 1200 megawatts, enough to power 900,000 homes. Driving into the complex, you may feel small compared to the massive concrete barriers that appear around each bend. The thundering sound of the spillway and the mist that it generates adds to the imposing feel of the place.

The main place to stop is the **Bradford Island Visitor Center**, which houses a museum and a fish ladder where you can spot lamprey and salmon on their journey past the dam. The Washington side of the complex has its own visitor center and museum.

For a different kind of engineering feat, take a walk along the stately **Bridge of the Gods**, a steel truss cantilever bridge completed in 1926 in Cascade Locks. If the bridge looks familiar it's because it was featured in the final scene of the Reece Witherspoon film *Wild*.

While here, don't miss the Native American fishers gathered under the bridge to sell smoked and sometimes fresh salmon. The scaffolding where the fishers catch the salmon is located just downstream. The murals painted below the bridge give a visual history of the area.

CASCADE LOCKS LOCAL LORE

Tom Cramblett, captain of the stern-wheeler *Columbia Gorge*, shares some local knowledge connected to Cascade Locks.

Cascade Locks started as a portage community, moving freight and people around the rapids. Now what we are all about here is hiking – the Pacific Crest Trail crosses the Columbia right here at the Bridge of the Gods. One of my favorite pastimes is getting on the Pacific Crest Trail and hiking to Dry Creek Falls. It's an easy hike and not too crowded; spring and fall are my favorite times to visit. On the boat, we pass by kiteboarders and windsurfers, and kayakers jump in our swell. With the scenic beauty around us and the constant activity on the river, there is always something to see.

 BEST PLACES TO STAY NEAR THE WATERFALL CORRIDOR

McMenamins – Edgefield
Rustic hotel and hostel accommodations set on 78 acres, plus quirky amenities, such as a cinema and spa. **$$**

Ainsworth State Park
The campground at this state park caters mainly to the RV crowd but also has six walk-in tent sites. **$**

Bridal Veil Lodge B&B
This cozy lodge located close to Bridal Veil Falls is perfect for exploring the waterfall corridor. **$$**

HERMAN THE STURGEON

Close to the Oregon side of the Bonneville Dam, the **Bonneville Fish Hatchery** has shady walking areas and an underground viewing area for watching some massive sturgeon swim past. The most famous among them is 80-year-old 'Herman the Sturgeon.' He's the big fish in this little pond: an impressive 11ft long and weighing around 500 pounds. Herman is a survivor, having endured a kidnapping, a stabbing and a wildfire, but now appears to be living the good life. The site is open year-round but the best time to visit the hatchery is September and October when Chinook and coho salmon are spawning.

Complete the engineering tour with a visit to Thunder Island, the site of two locks and a 3000ft canal that allowed boats to navigate around rapids before the construction of Bonneville Dam. A portion of the lock and canal were flooded when Bonneville Dam was completed in the 1930s. Head downhill from the town of Cascade Locks to Thunder Island where you can make some parts of the lock and canal.

Good commentary on these engineering marvels is provided on a river trip aboard the *Columbia Gorge* stern-wheeler, which operates from May to October.

The Washington Side of the Gorge

TIME FROM HOOD RIVER: **30 MINS**

See the quieter side of the Columbia River

The Washington side of the Columbia River, which lacks a busy freeway, sees fewer visitors compared to sites along the waterfall corridor. Make your way here to experience good hiking trails and quaint towns while leaving the crowds behind.

Start your visit by crossing the Bridge of the Gods at Cascade Locks, from where it's 2 miles to the **Columbia Gorge Museum**, a gorge highlight that is full of surprises. Located below Skamania Lodge in Stevenson, the museum covers the gorge's complex history and includes an unusual collection of Catholic rosaries, said to be the largest in the world. If wandering the museum has left you hungry, the nearby **Skamania Lodge** has excellent pizzas and seafood meals.

The main natural landmark in the area is **Beacon Rock State Park**, where you can hike a dizzying mile-long switchback trail to the top of the towering Beacon Rock.

Around 10 miles east of Stevenson, **Dog Mountain** is one of the best hiking areas in the gorge, especially in spring when its upper slopes are covered in yellow balsamroot wildflowers. The 6.8-mile loop trail is a hard hike. Bring good boots and a lot of stamina. In addition to a Northwest Forest Pass, Dog Mountain hikers will also need a special permit on weekends between April 29 to June 19, available through recreation.gov.

The Dalles & the Eastern Gorge

TIME FROM HOOD RIVER: **25 MINS**

Immerse yourself in gorge culture

East of Hood River the gorge widens into rolling plains. You can get one of the best views of the gorge from the **Rowena Crest Overlook**. From the Overlook you can glimpse the Rowena Loops, an impressive horseshoe-shaped road. There's good hiking at the nearby **Tom McCall Preserve**.

 WHERE TO EAT IN CASCADE LOCKS

Thunder Island Brewing Co
Craft Brewery with a patio that overlooks the Bridge of the Gods. Rice bowls, salads and kid-friendly options. **$$**

Eastwind Drive-in
Shack on the main drag with a classic burger-and-fries menu. But it's best known for its towering ice-cream cones. **$**

Brigham Fish Market
A delightful array of fish offerings. The owners are members of the Confederated Tribes of the Umatilla. **$$**

Rowena Crest Overlook

A few miles east is the **Columbia Gorge Discovery Center & Museum**, an excellent museum and raptor center that tells the story of the gorge's natural and human history. At the eastern edge of the Gorge is The Dalles, home to the **National Neon Sign Museum**, a quirky place that tells the history of the light bulb to the development of neon lights. The Dalles is also home to Oregon's oldest museum, the **Fort Dalles Museum**, originally part of a fort constructed in the 1850s.

Across the river, the **Schreiner Farms** is home to around 20 exotic animals (including zebra, giraffe and antelope) that you spot from your car. Admission is free. Nearby **Columbia Hills Historical State Park** contains some of the best remaining petroglyphs (rock drawings) in the Columbia Gorge.

Stay on the Washington side of the river and continue east on Hwy 14 for around 15 miles to the **Maryhill Museum of Art**. This hilltop mansion was founded by businessman Sam Hill who dreamed of creating a Quaker farming community here in the early 1900s. A lack of irrigation water doomed the project and the mansion was converted to an art museum. Today the permanent collection contains European and American art, including works by Auguste Rodin. Push on five more miles to reach the **Stonehenge Memorial**, a replica of Stonehenge (an intact version), erected in 1918 to honor WWI soldiers from Klickitat County who died in battle.

RAFTING THE LOWER DESCHUTES

The lower Deschutes River winds through rocky escarpments and mesas in northern Oregon before converging with the Columbia River near The Dalles. The river offers excellent opportunities for rafting, with day- and multiday trips departing from the hamlet of Maupin. **Imperial River Company** is a popular outfitter that also offers riverside lodging on the Deschutes. **Deschutes River Adventures** also organizes trips. Day trips usually start from Harpham Flat and go for 10 miles to Sandy Beach. Just past Sandy Beach is **Sherars Falls** (15ft), a thundering waterfall that has a class VI white-water rating. Native Americans are sometimes seen at the falls catching fish with dip nets.

WHERE TO EAT & DRINK IN THE DALLES

Cousins' Restaurant & Saloon
Enjoy some homestyle comfort food like meatloaf, burgers and big ol' breakfasts. **$**

Clock Tower Ales
Inside the former 1883 county courthouse (home to public hangings), with more than 30 beers on tap. **$**

Freebridge Brewing
Local brewery serving up a dozen or so beers and tasty meals in a bright, downtown space. Good pizza. **$**

BOB POOL/SHUTTERSTOCK ©

Above: **South Sister (p237); Right: Deschutes Brewery beer (p233)**

Central Oregon & the Oregon Cascades

OREGON AT ITS HIGHEST

Glaciated peaks, high desert and volcanic lava fields form a spectacular backdrop to a region where craft beer flows freely and adventure is around every turn.

Nestled in the shadow of the Cascade Mountains, Central Oregon's dry climate and abundant natural resources have long lured those in search of economic opportunities and a break from the Pacific Northwest's notoriously wet weather.

Native Americans were the first to arrive, hunting and fishing along the Deschutes River. Settlers followed from the east, mainly from Minnesota, setting up timber mills and transforming the arid high desert into farmland by creating a vast network of canals. More recently, natural resource extraction has been supplanted by tourism based on active sports, camping and hiking.

At the heart of it all is Bend, a quintessential mountain town that has become a haven for small business start-ups ranging from light aircraft manufacturing to outdoor sports gear. Beer is big here but there's also cider, spirits and wine. Remote workers have recently set up shop in the town, working hard but taking time to ski, bike and hike when time allows.

Smaller cities in the area, each with local attractions and friendly vibes, also welcome visitors. In summer they come alive with festivals, fairs, concerts and the occasional rodeo. But arrive any time of year and you are likely to be greeted with something locally brewed and a smile by someone who knows how lucky they are to live in this magical place.

JOSHUA RAINEY PHOTOGRAPHY/SHUTTERSTOCK ©

THE MAIN AREAS

BEND
Beer culture and
adventure tourism.
p230

SISTERS
Thick forests and a
Wild West atmosphere.
p239

Find Your Way

The snowcapped Cascades form the spine of Oregon, reachable through high passes from the Willamette Valley. Bend is a natural base to explore the area.

Bend, p230

Straddling the Deschutes River, this former timber town is now known as a tourist destination and epicenter for craft beer.

Sisters, p239

An artsy little town of craft and antique shops; the nearby Deschutes National Forest offers stunning lakes, rivers and mountains.

CAR

Getting around by car will save time and give you the greatest freedom to stop and explore the area. It's also the most practical way to reach Central Oregon's iconic lakes and rivers.

BUS

Cascade East Transit operates buses around Bend and to nearby cities. A shuttle to Mt Bachelor runs in summer and winter. Central Oregon Breeze connects Bend with Portland, with several stops including Government Camp.

Deschutes River (p230), Bend

Plan Your Time

Central Oregon is a region to plan for extra days as it can take some time to get out to the highlights located deep in the Cascades.

If You Only Do One Thing

Head for **Bend** (p230) and float the **Deschutes River** (p230) from Old Mill to downtown. Spend the evening at a brewpub or go for an afternoon hike in the **Upper Deschutes area** (p232) or **Tumalo Falls** (p233). On a second day, head south of Hwy 97 to **Lava Butte** (p237) for excellent views of the Cascade Mountains and trails through lava fields.

Four Days to Travel Around

From Bend travel up the **Cascade Lakes Scenic Byway** (p235) and stop at one of a dozen lakes to fish, hike or camp. The next day head to **Sisters** (p239) to soak in some small-town atmosphere before spending time around quiet **Camp Sherman** (p241). With another day, travel to Terrebonne for a day of hiking or rock climbing at **Smith Rock** (p238).

Seasonal Highlights

SPRING	SUMMER	FALL	WINTER
Ski **Mt Bachelor** in the morning and then go mountain biking or rock climbing in the afternoon.	Peak travel season brings big crowds to **Bend** for river floating, concerts and festivals.	Crowds thin out and white-water rafting season winds down. A good time for alpine hikes and rock climbing.	Ski season at **Mt Bachelor** and **Hoodoo**. Cross-country skiing and snowshoeing are popular.

229

Bend

GETTING AROUND

Downtown Bend is easily walkable and Bird Bikeshare stations are available if you need to pedal your way to other parts of the city. The bus network, Cascades East Transit (CET), is free to use. CET offers a shuttle bus to Mt Bachelor for winter skiing. The service also runs in summer to stops on Century Drive and Mt Bachelor.

☑ **TOP TIP**

Midweek travel means lower prices and smaller crowds. July and August are peak times for travel and hotels can get booked out so plan your stay well in advance. For floaters, note that the Deschutes River 'turns off' in mid-October as the river level starts to decline.

In the early 1900s a small wave of Midwesterners arrived on a particularly crooked section of the Deschutes River and established a timber industry, and around it a settlement called 'Farewell Bend,' eventually shortened to simply 'Bend.' Two competing sawmills grew up on the banks of the river and at their peak, they were the largest in the world. The mills are now long gone and Bend has since diversified its economy with light industry and tourism. Arrive in summer and you'll find the place buzzing with visitors hauling around mountain bikes, kayaks and climbing equipment. In place of logs in the Deschutes, locals and tourists alike are seen floating down the river on inner tubes. Skiers and snowboarders take over in winter. All year-round, brewers are cranking out malts at one of around 30 craft breweries. New arrivals find it hard to escape and, increasingly, some never do.

Experiencing the Deschutes River

Explore the Deschutes by tube and on foot

Floating the Deschutes River through town is the quintessential Bend experience. Everyone who visits does it at least once, sunburn be damned.

From mid-June through Labor Day (the first Monday in September), **Tumalo Creek Kayak & Canoe** operates a tube-rental and shuttle service that is bookable online. The float (plan on 60 to 90 minutes) is gentle most of the way except for a short stretch of rapids. Alternatively, forgo the shuttle and enter the river with your own tube at **Riverbend Park**. Sunblock and a hat are essential.

Tumalo Creek also rents out various other watercraft for fun on the river, including stand-up paddleboards (SUPs), kayaks and rafts.

Sunbathers and river watchers can check out the **Bend Whitewater Park**, a fun place to splash and watch the floaters and surfers (one channel has a rideable surf wave).

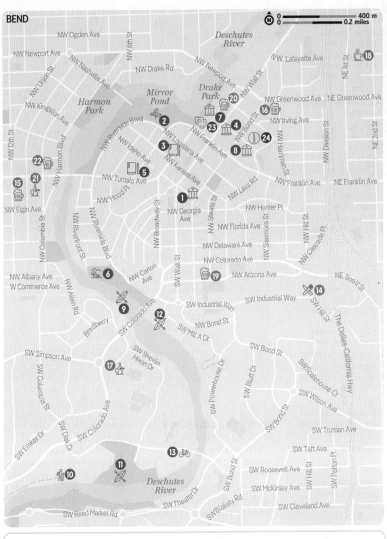

BEND

0 400 m
0 0.2 miles

SIGHTS
1 Deschutes Historical Museum
2 Drake Park
3 GP Putnam House
4 Jeffrey Murray Photography
5 McCann House
6 Miller's Landing Park
7 Mockingbird Gallery
8 Scalehouse Gallery

ACTIVITIES, COURSES & TOURS
9 Bend Whitewater Park
10 Deschutes River
11 Riverbend Park
12 Tumalo Creek Kayak & Canoe
13 Wheel Fun Rentals

EATING
14 Crux Fermentation Project

DRINKING & NIGHTLIFE
15 10 Barrel Brewing
16 Deschutes Brewery & Public House
17 Deschutes Brewery Tasting Room & Beer Garden
18 Humm Kombucha Taproom
19 Podski
20 Porter Brewing Company
21 Sunriver Brewing Company
22 The Lot

ENTERTAINMENT
23 Tower Theater

INFORMATION
24 Visit Bend

SIGHTS
1. Benham Falls
2. Blockbuster
3. Dillon Falls
4. High Desert Museum
5. Lava Island Falls
6. Pilot Butte

ACTIVITIES, COURSES & TOURS
7. Cog Wild
8. Riley Ranch Nature Reserve
9. Shevlin Park
10. Tumalo State Park
11. Wanderlust Tours

DRINKING & NIGHTLIFE
12. Crater Lake Spirits Distillery Tasting Room
13. Tumalo Cider Company

THE LAST BLOCKBUSTER

In Bend, you don't need a DeLorean to travel back in time 30 years. Just visit the corner of Revere and Third St where you'll find the world's last Blockbuster video store. Inside, the DVD racks, blue-shirted employees and packages of microwave popcorn will transport you back to the 1990s. Even if you haven't brought along a portable DVD player to watch a film, it's worth stopping by to browse some of their movie memorabilia or just relive some memories as you flip through the racks. For the backstory on how Bend's Blockbuster survived, watch the 2021 Netflix documentary *The Last Blockbuster*.

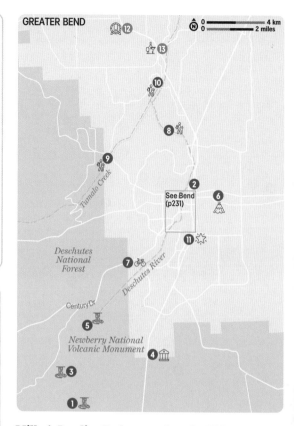

Miller's Landing Park, across from the Whitewater Park, is a good picnic spot.

Wheel Fun Rentals is a bike-rental kiosk near Old Mill where you can rent bikes and surreys (four-wheeled bikes) to peddle along the Deschutes. Walkers can check out the paths south of Bill Healy Bridge. For a thrilling half-day adventure, professional rafting trips in the upper Deschutes River include three rapids. Several outfitters in town run trips.

As the river winds through Bend most of it gets diverted for irrigation on the northern end of town, leaving little in the streambed. But some stretches are still scenic; walk the riverside 3.5-mile trail from **Riley Ranch Nature Reserve** to **Tumalo State Park**. Note that dogs are not allowed in Riley Ranch but you can start from Tumalo State Park.

Touring Historic Bend
Leisurely strolls and local history

Bend's historic downtown buzzes with activity, especially in summer. The **Visit Bend** office is a good place to pick up maps and get your bearings.

To capture some of Bend's logging and settler history, stop by the **Deschutes Historical Museum**, which covers the town's timber-producing past and its present as a hub for adventure tourism. Historic walking tours are held on Saturday mornings from May to August. The main landmark downtown is the 1940 **Tower Theater**, which regularly puts on movies and live shows.

You can get a feel for Bend's natural beauty by visiting a few of its downtown art galleries, including **Jeffrey Murray Photography** (features Central Oregon photography) and **Mockingbird Gallery** (Western art). **Scalehouse Gallery** has art focusing on contemporary matters impacting Oregonians.

Stretch your legs, catch an outdoor concert or watch slackliners in leafy **Drake Park**, just west of downtown. Then stroll through the nearby neighborhood of historic homes developed by Bend's timber barons. The 1915 **McCann House** at 440 Congress St is a particularly beautiful mansion. A couple of blocks north at 606 Congress St is the **GP Putnam House**, a simpler home built in 1911. Its former owner, George Putnam, was a well-known author, publisher, film producer and husband to Amelia Earhart. Richard Gere portrayed him in the 2009 film *Amelia*.

For a comprehensive telling of the region's history, both natural and cultural, don't miss the exceptional **High Desert Museum**, 7 miles south of Bend. It features animal exhibits, a replica homestead and a hall dedicated to the telling of Native American culture.

The best views of the city are from the top of **Pilot Butte**, one of just six volcanoes in the US to be located within city boundaries. On a clear day, you can see most of Central Oregon's peaks, from Mt Bachelor to Mt Hood. The summit can be reached by car or on foot.

Craft Beer, Cider & Spirits

Welcome to Beer Town, USA

Beer is to Bend as wine is to the Willamette Valley. At last count, there were around 30 breweries in the city and nearby towns.

A good way to start your beer grand tour is a visit to the granddaddy of all local breweries, the **Deschutes Brewery Tasting Room & Beer Garden** near the Old Mill District. Three types of tours are available. Fans of Deschutes will also want to make a pilgrimage to the original **Deschutes Brewery & Public House** downtown on Bond St.

If you are traveling with kids, the **Crux Fermentation Project** is a good spot for a meal and drink with outstanding views.

BEST TRAILS NEAR BEND

There's good hiking and biking just a short drive from Bend.

Phil's Trail
On Bend's west side, this is one of the best networks of mountain-biking trails in the state. Young riders will enjoy the skills course.

Tumalo Falls
Central Oregon's most photographed waterfall (97ft) has trails that lead to several smaller falls upstream.

Shevlin Park
A popular spot with locals for hikes along Tumalo Creek. There are trails of varying lengths (up to 6 miles) through old-growth ponderosa forest and mountain-bike trails.

Deschutes River
Great trails can also be found along the Deschutes River south of town. Start at **Lava Island Falls** from where it's a 2.5-mile hike to **Dillon Falls**, a good spot for a picnic. From Dillon Falls, continue another 2.8 miles to thundering **Benham Falls**.

 WHERE STAY IN BEND

Bunk + Brew Hostel	Mill Inn B&B	McMenamins Old St Francis School
This central and social hostel has mixed dorms and private rooms in a historic house near downtown. $	Boutique hotel close to downtown with 10 stylishly designed rooms, each with a different theme. $$	A historic school converted into a hotel. Movie theater and Turkish-style bath. $$

WHY I LOVE BEND

Michael Kohn, writer

During a chance visit to Bend a decade ago, I became instantly enchanted with this sunny mountain town on the east side of the Cascades. Sure enough, I was soon living there.

Bend is still home and I love its sense of community. Friends and neighbors are always spotted at the constant stream of events happening in town, from farmers markets to festivals and concerts. It's a small but dynamic city, with new food carts and restaurants opening up all the time and a creative spirit that is on display at its summertime night market and craft events. And when quiet time is called for, the mountains, lakes and gurgling streams are essentially our backyard, just waiting for a visit.

10 Barrel Brewing

A clutch of local breweries can be found on Galveston St including **10 Barrel Brewing** and **Sunriver Brewing Company**. For a cozy, UK pub-style experience, don't miss **Porter Brewing Company** downtown. It serves hand-pumped cask ales and sometimes has live Irish music. The Bend Ale Trail passport, available at Visit Bend (for $5), helps guide you to the various breweries or use the app (bendaletrail.app).

The beverage scene has been expanding in recent years. **Crater Lake Spirits Distillery Tasting Room** on the road to Sisters is the place to go for locally made vodka, gin and whiskey. For something non-alcoholic that (some) kids may enjoy, check out the delightful **Humm Kombucha Taproom** a few blocks northeast of downtown.

On top of its breweries, Bend has several food cart pods, each featuring local beers. Try **Podski** near the Box Factory or **The Lot** on Galveston St. **The Bite** in Tumalo has beer, food and occasional live music. **Tumalo Cider Company**, across the street from The Bite, pours delicious ciders straight from the tap.

 ## CASUAL EATING IN BEND

El Sancho Taco Shop
Flavorful tacos topped with a tasty cotija cheese and served on a sunny outdoor patio. Located on Galveston. **$**

Active Culture
Healthy and beautifully plated meals. Specializes in acai bowls (a Brazilian dessert made from the acai plant). **$**

Spork
Eclectic restaurant that embraces fusion recipes, taking influences from Latin America and Asia. **$**

Beyond Bend

The Painted Hills
Camp Sherman
Madras
Smith Rock State Park
Mitchell
Sisters
Redmond
Prineville
Post
Paulina
Belknap Springs
Bend
Alfalfa
Cascade Lakes Scenic Byway
Brothers
Hampton
Newberry National Volcanic Monument
Christmas Valley
Fort Rock

Mountains, lakes, extinct volcanoes and pine forests: days (or weeks) could be spent day-tripping around Bend.

Bend sits between the forested eastern flank of the Cascade Mountains and Central Oregon's high desert landscape of juniper trees and eerie rock formations. A 30-minute drive in any direction gets you off the grid and deep into these landscapes. Head south to get a feel for the area's volcanic landscape, with Newberry Crater as the focal point. To the north, there's Smith Rock, an epicenter for rock climbers and lovers of desert scenery. In the Cascades west of Bend, you can escape to one of dozens of spring-fed lakes and streams. Sisters and other small towns offer accommodations but you can also bring along a tent and spend time in the area's wealth of campgrounds.

Cascade Lakes Scenic Byway

TIME FROM BEND: **30–60 MINS**

Head for the hills

Right on Bend's western doorstep lies the 1.6 million-acre **Deschutes National Forest**, consisting mainly of ponderosa pine trees, which favor the dry climate of the eastern Cascades. Threading its way into the forest is the Cascade Lakes Scenic Byway (Hwy 46), a 66-mile road that begins in Bend and winds its way south through the volcanic highlands. Spring-fed lakes surrounded by snowcapped peaks make for photogenic stops along the way. A day trip is possible but campsites and resorts make overnights an easy option.

Setting off from Bend along Century Dr, it's about 20 miles to **Mt Bachelor** (elevation 9065ft), a world-class ski resort built on a dormant stratovolcano. Most visit in winter to experience its 3365ft vertical drop but the resort remains busy in summer, with mountain biking and the longest zipline in the Northwest. Hiking is also possible, with a walk to the peak from the main lodge taking around two hours. **Pine Marten Lodge**, halfway up the mountain, is open for lunch daily. Sunset dinners are four days a week. A shuttle connects Bend to Mt Bachelor five days a week (Wednesday to Sunday) in summer.

GETTING AROUND

Central Oregon is best explored by car, opening up areas that don't get regular public transportation. The region is also bike-friendly but distances are vast. East Transit does have some inter-city bus connections but times are infrequent. If you are planning a drive along the Cascades Lakes Hwy (past Mt Bachelor) or Paulina Lakes Hwy, bear in mind these are closed in October, opening sometime in May depending on snow levels.

HIKING PERMITS IN THE CASCADES

Central Cascades Wilderness Permits ($1 per person) are required on 19 of the 79 trailheads in the Mt Jefferson, Mt Washington and Three Sisters wilderness areas from June 15 to October 15. A Forest Service employee is usually at the trailhead to check permits and provide trail information. The permits are also needed for overnight stays ($6 per group) in all three wilderness areas.

In addition to the hiking permits it's also a good idea to have a Northwest Forest Pass, which allows parking in the national forest parking areas. Printable day passes ($5) are available online. Several retailers in Bend also sell the passes. Some (but not all) trailheads have parking ticket machines.

Todd Lake

Tumalo Mountain Trail is a good hike (4 miles, out-and-back) that starts across from Mt Bachelor from Dutchman Sno-Park. It's steep from the start and popular with trail runners. From the top, you'll get fine views of Mt Bachelor and the Three Sisters.

Past Mt Bachelor, the highway has a gate that is closed in winter, usually opening up again in May. From the gate, it's less than 4 miles to the Todd Lake Trailhead (permit required) – the easy 1.7-mile hike around **Todd Lake** is good for families. Adventurous hikers will want to tackle the hike to **No Name Lake** (elevation 8018ft), a spectacular glacier-fed lake that thaws out in late July revealing its turquoise-green color. Get there from one of three trailheads: Broken Top Crater, Crater Ditch or Todd Lake – all three require a permit.

Another 3 miles west along the highway is **Green Lakes Trailhead** for a 9-mile out-and-back hike (permit required) that is challenging but rewarding with great views of **South Sister**. Hikes around **Devils Lake** and to secluded **Sisters Mirror Lake** are also gorgeous.

Elk Lake, a popular family destination, has a beach and boat rentals. Nearby **Hosmer Lake** is shallow and popular with kayakers thanks to its narrow channels, islands and

BEST RESORTS ON THE CASCADES LAKES

Elk Lake Resort
A hive of activity with boat rentals, a restaurant and a resort with cabins for rent. **$$**

Cultus Lake Resort
One of the quieter resorts in the area, it offers excellent food and boat rental. **$$**

Twin Lakes Resort
A popular resort with a restaurant and cabins. Live music is played on Saturdays. **$$**

twisting shoreline. Atlantic salmon, rainbow trout and brook trout are easily spotted (fly-fishing only). Boaters should try for a weekday to avoid the crowds.

Next along the highway are **Lava Lake** and **Little Lava Lake**, the latter being the source of the Deschutes River. Both lakes have campsites and there's a shop selling basic supplies. Continuing south from Lava Lake, it's a 10-mile drive to **Cultus Lake**, a large and beautiful lake with a 3.7-mile out-and-back lakeside trail.

The road eventually reaches **Twin Lakes**, two almost circular lakes surrounded by forests, both with good fishing and easy walking trails. If you're coming from Bend, the shortest route is on Hwy 97.

Newberry National Volcanic Monument

TIME FROM BEND: **15–50 MINS** 🚗

Go crater-hopping

The **Newberry National Volcanic Monument**, south of Bend, is a sprawling landscape of lava flows, tubes and dormant craters. The gateway to the area, **Lava Lands Visitor Center**, features a small museum and pathways through the lava flow. A shuttle bus takes visitors to the top of nearby **Lava Butte**.

From the visitor center, it's a short drive to **Lava River Cave**, a mile-long lava tube under the forest. Tours are self-guided but permits from recreation.gov are required. Bring long sleeves because it's cold in the cave, even in summer. Flashlights can be rented for $5.

The **Newberry Caldera**, 28 miles south of the visitor center, is a massive crater 5 miles in diameter. This active shield volcano is the largest in the Cascade Volcanic Arc, which stretches 700 miles from Northern California to Canada.

Paulina Lake and **East Lake** are located inside the caldera. Most visitors start their exploration at **Paulina Falls** (80ft), where a short trail (150yd) leads from the parking lot to the top of a beautiful twin waterfall. Just uphill, by the lake, the **Paulina Visitor Center** (open Friday to Monday) has maps of the area.

The two lakes both offer good fishing, hiking trails, campgrounds and hot springs. The **Paulina Lakeshore Trail** (7.5 miles long, loop trail) takes about 2½ hours to complete. Mountain bikers can tackle the 21-mile-long **Crater Rim Trail**, encircling both lakes.

The **Big Obsidian Flow** between the lakes is just 1300 years old; the youngest lava flow in Oregon. A 1-mile interpretive trail into the flow is fascinating but take care because

CLIMBING SOUTH SISTER

For peak baggers, the hike to the top of South Sister is tough but not technical. At 10,358ft it's the third-highest mountain in Oregon and should only be attempted by those in good physical condition and with some high-elevation climbing experience. It's an 11.6-mile out-and-back trek with a grueling elevation gain of 4986ft from the Devil's Lake Trailhead. Bring lots of water and sunscreen (trekking poles are also handy). It's about four hours each way. Dispersed camping is available at **Moraine Lake**, just above the treeline.

If the full trek to the top looks too challenging, try the shorter 6.8-mile out-and-back hike to the lake. It's steep but offers awesome views of the mountain.

 ## WHERE TO STAY AT NEWBERRY CRATER

East Lake Resort
Charming and historic resort with a sandy beach nearby and rustic but comfortable cabins. $$

Paulina Lake Lodge
Quiet resort with 13 cabins, a restaurant, a small store, tackle shop and boat rentals. $$

Paulina Lake Campground
Clean and well-maintained campground with clean bathrooms and great views of the lake. $

VOLCANIC ERUPTIONS

Bob Jensen, USGS volunteer and retired USFS geologist

Within fifty miles of Bend, there are abundant volcanic features including the 30-million-year-old Crooked River caldera (which includes Smith Rock), the massive Newberry Volcano (nearly the size of Rhode Island), as well as the much smaller but iconic Three Sisters volcanoes. These exhibit the full range of volcanic features and rock types. Eruptions have ranged from relatively quiet basalt eruptions to gigantic rhyolitic caldera-forming blasts. The eruptions produced thin fluid basalt flows, basalt cinder cones, thick rhyolite flows (obsidian), thick rhyolite airfall pumice deposits, hot ash flows resulting in welded tuffs (Smith Rock) and everything in between. The most recent eruption occurred 1300 years ago (Big Obsidian Flow).

the shattered pieces of obsidian are sharp. Nearby **Paulina Peak** (7984 ft) is accessible by car or on foot.

Fort Rock
TIME FROM BEND: **70 MINS**
Unusual geology and ancient history

One of the more unusual volcanic formations in Central Oregon is Fort Rock, a tuff ring sitting on the bed of a dried-up lake, about 38 miles southwest of La Pine. The 66ft vertical walls of this unusual site appear like a fortress rising from the plains. It once formed a complete circle but waves from the former lake collapsed the south side of the ring. There are good short hikes in the tuff ring.

The area is also of archaeological importance. In 1938 an anthropologist from the University of Oregon recovered dozens of ancient **sagebrush sandals** from a cave near Fort Rock. They were dated to more than 9000 years old – the oldest footwear in the world – and discovered under a layer of ash from when Mt Mazama erupted around 7600 years ago.

In the nearby hamlet of Fort Rock, check out the **Fort Rock Homestead Village Museum** (open Thursday to Sunday), a collection of 19th-century buildings. The buildings contain vintage artifacts from the early 20th century that give a feel for homestead life. It's open from Memorial Day (last Monday in May) through the second weekend in September.

Smith Rock State Park
TIME FROM BEND: **35 MINS**
Go climb a rock

Soaring high above the Crooked River, the towering formations at Smith Rock State Park are a stunning sight amid the vast plains of the high desert. The volcanic welded tuff spires rise hundreds of feet off the valley floor, sometimes forming unusual shapes, 'monkey face' being the most famous.

Hikers can take relatively easy strolls along the cliffs opposite Smith Rock and along the river below, or more difficult hikes over **Misery Ridge** (3.6 miles). Look out for wildlife; Smith Rock is home to a menagerie of critters, including rattlesnakes, eagles, marmots and river otters.

Wherever you go you'll spot rock climbers precariously clinging to the cliffs. Smith Rock is considered the birthplace of American sport climbing, with the area taking off in popularity in the 1980s. Climbers from around the country descend on the place in late October for the **Smith Rock Craggin' Classic**.

The state park is 26 miles northwest of Bend near the small town of Terrebonne. There's a walk-in **bivouac campground** ($8 per night) for tent campers with bathrooms, showers and

 BEST SHORT HIKES NEAR NEWBERRY CRATER

East Benham Falls
From Benham Falls East Trailhead hike the 1-mile trail to the spectacular Benham Falls.

Paulina Water Slides
An easy 1.5-mile hike from McKay Crossing Campground to a kid-friendly natural waterslide.

Lava Cast Forest
A 1-mile loop trail goes around this unusual lava flow created 7000 years ago.

FRANCISCO BLANCO/SHUTTERSTOCK ©

Misery Ridge trail

charging stations. It's open from March 15 to November 15. A handful of climbing schools and guides bring beginners out for lessons, including **Smith Rock Climbing School**.

If you don't already have an Oregon State Parks parking pass, machines here sell day passes for $5. Congestion has been a problem but at the time of research, plans were underway for expanded parking and a new welcome center.

Sisters

TIME FROM BEND: **30 MINS** 🚗

Experience rodeos, folk music & quilting

Quaint Sisters is just a 30-minute drive from Bend but feels a world away. The Western-themed town is loaded with antique shops, boutiques, bookshops and art galleries. There's a convivial atmosphere with friendly locals and, in summer, plenty of out-of-towners. To avoid the crowds, veer a block or two south of the main road where you'll likely encounter mule deer in the pretty, pine-shaded streets.

To learn a little local history, visit the **Three Sisters Historical Society & Museum** (open Friday to Sunday), which

COWBOY DINNER TREE

A long way from anywhere, the Cowboy Dinner Tree seems an unlikely place to go for a meal. But the 90-minute drive from Bend is worth it for what some consider the meal of a lifetime.

This wooden shack in the countryside was once a stopping place for cowboys moving cattle across the plains. Food is served today as it was then: hot, simple and plenty of it. The menu includes 30oz steaks and whole chicken, with bottomless sides of beans, bread, soup and baked potato. Ice tea, lemonade and coffee wash it all down. Come with an appetite and be prepared for leftovers. Reservations are required (tables book out weeks in advance). Dinner here pairs well with a day trip to Fort Rock.

 MORE TO SEE NEAR SMITH ROCK

Crescent Moon Ranch
A local favorite in Terrebonne where kids (and adults) can feed alpacas and llamas.

Peter Skene Ogden State Scenic Viewpoint
Incredible views of the river 300ft below the canyon rim. Bungee jumping available.

Steelhead Falls
A 20ft-high waterfall reached after a moderate 2.5-mile out-and-back hike.

CLIMBING SMITH ROCK

Alan Watts
(wattsrocks.xyz) has a 50-year climbing history at Smith Rock and shares why the area is special.

Set like an oasis in the middle of Central Oregon's high desert, the volcanic walls of Smith Rock tower high above the winding Crooked River. Famous as the birthplace of US sport climbing, Smith Rock State Park holds just as much appeal for those who prefer flatter ground.

While climbers challenge themselves on the 2300 climbing routes, sightseers and bird-watchers enjoy spectacular views of the multicolored cliffs, with bald and golden eagles soaring above. Hikers enjoy miles of trails, including the popular Misery Ridge Trail, with spectacular views of the towering spire of Monkey Face, and the entire Central Oregon region. With over one million visitors per year, Smith Rock has something for everyone.

BOB POOL/SHUTTERSTOCK ©

Quilt displays, Sisters

houses some exhibits and puts on family-friendly and free walking tours.

The most popular time to arrive is the second week in June when the **Sisters Rodeo** kicks up some serious dirt. Take a seat in the stands and watch bull riding, barrel racing and calf lassoing. Even if you are not much into rodeos, the cowboy atmosphere and delicious barbecue make it worth a visit.

Sisters is also known for its quilts. On the second Saturday in July it hosts what is purportedly the world's largest quilt show. Music is big here too. Every year, sometime in the fall, the city hosts the three-day **Sisters Folk Festival** with music played in various spots around town.

If you're in Sisters on a Sunday, don't miss their weekly farmers market. It's held June to September in Fir Street Park.

Eat & Drink Your Way Through Sisters
Small town, great meals

In Sisters, good food and drink are usually just a few steps away. The town is on a main highway and has a history of feeding passers-by.

 BEST GUIDED TOURS IN CENTRAL OREGON

Cog Wild	**Wanderlust Tours**	**Sunriver Trail Rides**
Half-day and full-day guided mountain-bike tours around Central Oregon. It also rents bikes.	Tours include canoe and kayaking trips on the Cascades Lakes. Specializes in cave tours.	Operates at Sunriver Resort, 16 miles south of Bend; horseback riding from 45 to 75 minutes.

The **Barn**, a food cart pod one block north of the main street, is one local gathering spot. The local pub is **Three Creeks Brewing Company**, which serves up surprisingly good seafood (try the clam chowder). **Ski Inn Taphouse and Hotel** is a little of everything with plentiful pub food, great service and even six boutique hotel rooms upstairs. Handy if you're too stuffed to leave.

Seekers of gourmet food should visit the **Open Door**, a family-owned wine bar with some of the best Italian meals and seafood dishes this side of the Cascades. If Tibetan momos are more your thing, try **High Camp Taphouse**, a colorful slice of Kathmandu in Central Oregon.

A highlight in summer is ordering some ice cream from the window at the **Sno Cap Drive In**, in business since 1952, and watching the town go about its business. In the colder months, the **Sisters Coffee Company** is a cozy nook with a warm fireplace and wood furniture.

Camp Sherman

TIME FROM BEND: **50 MINS** 🚗

Bike or hike near a spring-red river

Camp Sherman is an idyllic little community of around 250 people living among ponderosa pine trees and the ice-cold, spring-fed Metolius River. A short trail leads to a spot where the Metolius emerges from the ground, gushing at a rate of around 50,000 gallons a minute from the base of Black Butte. The river that forms from the spring is spawning habitat for redband trout and bull trout, which are prized by both fishers and raptors.

As you drive north there are several campgrounds where you can access the river. Fly-fishing is permitted and there are good stretches for tubing. The **Camp Sherman Store & Fly Shop**, in business since 1918, is well stocked with everything from fishing tackle to premium wine. Grab a sandwich and a popsicle, and have lunch on the back deck by the gurgling river.

Travel 5 miles north of Camp Sherman on Forest Service Rd 20, and you'll reach the **Wizard Falls Fish Hatchery**, a fun place for all ages, but kids especially love the chance to feed the fish (bring quarters for the machine). The walk here along the river is a delight.

Campsites along the Metolius are simple but offer great river access and decent spacing between sites, with large ponderosas creating some privacy.

Back on Hwy 20, head a few more miles west to reach **Suttle Lake**, a large lake with good beach access for swimming and boating, as well as campsites and lakeside trails. The 3.5-mile

ALPINE SCENERY NEAR SISTERS

To get a taste of alpine scenery and cool off in summer, head 16 miles south from Sisters to **Three Creeks Lake** (the last few miles are gravel). A small general store here stocks basic supplies and rents boats. A campground at the south end of the lake has 11 tent sites and basic facilities. Besides the beautiful lake, one reason to come up here is to hike along the 5.3-mile out-and-back **Tam McArthur Rim Trail** (permit required) that can be walked in around three hours. For a bigger adventure, continue south from the 'end of trail' sign to No Name Lake, an 11.5-mile round-trip hike.

WHERE TO STAY NEAR CAMP SHERMAN

Metolius River Lodges
Riverside cabins with decks that peer over the water. A little dated and small but cozy. **$$**

Suttle Lodge & Boathouse
Updated cabins close to Suttle Lake. Lakeside activities and weekly events keep it busy. **$$**

Riverside Campground
A campground with walk-in tent sites and clean pit toilets. Book on recreation.gov. **$**

ADVENTURING IN CAMP SHERMAN

Mark Morical
(@mmorical), sports editor/outdoors writer for the *Bend Bulletin* (@thebulletin), gives his recommendations for hiking and biking around Camp Sherman.

While fly-fishing is a main attraction of Camp Sherman and the Metolius River, the area also has numerous hiking and biking trails. The Metolius River Trail, both the east and west sides, are well-trod by anglers but also make for an easy, mostly flat hike along the crystal-clear river. It's an ideal trek for kids and it can be as long or as short as you want it to be. The Metolius River Trail is closed to bikes, but cyclists can find enjoyable, family-friendly rides along the Camp Sherman and Lake Creek trails. For a longer outing, mountain bikers can ride all the way to Suttle Lake.

---

trail around the lake takes around two hours on foot. The lodge here is very active with summertime live music and cookouts.

The Painted Hills

TIME FROM BEND: **2 HRS**

Explore fossils and hikes

The Painted Hills are a mystical landscape on the bucket list of many Oregon travelers. Short hikes are one of the main activities but most people come to marvel at this 30-million-year-old geological wonder.

Reached in under two hours from Bend, the Painted Hills are a good day trip or a stopover en route to points east. They make up one of three units in the **John Day Fossil Beds National Monument**, the other two (**Sheep Rock Unit** and **Clarno Unit**) being well-known sites for fossils and paleontology. The units are separated by around 100 miles of winding roads and visiting all three would require staying overnight in the area.

If you just want to visit the Painted Hills, the turnoff is a few miles before **Mitchell**. There are several spots to park and walk the interpretive trails, the **Painted Hills Overlook Trail** being the most famous, if your time is limited. Mitchell is the nearest place to get food and lodging. The solitary main street has a rustic, friendly atmosphere and is a good place for lunch before heading back to the hills for a sunset walk.

The **Thomas Condon Paleontology Center** is another 44 miles' drive east of the Painted Hills. It's a long detour but a must-visit for paleontology buffs. The exhibits contain fossils of creatures that lived here 50 million years ago when it was a swampy wetland home to saber-toothed tigers, camels, rhinos and other animals not usually associated with North America.

Rafting on the John Day River

Paddling a scenic river

Travelers wanting to unplug from cell service and crowds should consider a leisurely rafting trip on the John Day River. The John Day is unique in that it is undammed for its entire length, 284 miles from Central Oregon to the Columbia River, making it the fourth-longest free-flowing river in the lower 48 states (excluding Alaska and Hawaii). It's a mellow river with Class I to II rapids but can only be run in spring or early summer (in late summer the river is too low).

What it lacks in rapids it makes up for in stark, scenic beauty. Ouzel Outfitters runs rafting trips lasting trips from three to five days. Maha Outfitters also organizes rafting and fishing expeditions. Service Creek Stage Stop Lodge rents rafts for DIY adventures.

 BEST PLACES TO STAY & EAT IN MITCHELL

Tiger Town Brewing Co
Named after the old business district, this local brewery produces fine ales and serves excellent pub food. **$**

Spoke'n Hostel
This fun hostel is located inside a functioning church in Mitchell and caters to cyclists passing through town. **$**

The Oregon Hotel
An old-fashioned hotel in the center of Mitchell with rooms that have private baths and some with shared facilities. **$**

Oregon's Hwy 242, aka the McKenzie Pass Hwy, is a gorgeous scenic byway open in summer (July to October) with lots of volcanic and alpine scenery. The 84-mile route starts and ends in **1 Sisters**, a small but bustling town packed with galleries, restaurants and antique shops. Some 15 miles from Sisters you'll reach **2 Dee Wright Observatory** (elevation 5325ft), a castle-like structure built in 1935 at the McKenzie Pass. A half-mile interpretive trail describes the area's volcanic history. Six miles past the observatory, **3 Scott Lake** offers fine camping spots and views of the Three Sisters range reflecting in the lake. Nearby **4 Obsidian Trail** (12 miles, permit required) is a beautiful lollipop route that cuts deep into the Three Sisters Wilderness, a rugged region of ancient lava flows and snowcapped peaks. From here Hwy 242 winds downhill to the **5 Proxy Falls** (226ft) trailhead. This veil waterfall is one of the most photographed in Oregon due to its beautiful dome shape.

Hwy 242 connects with Hwy 126 where you'll head north, following the gorgeous McKenzie River. Next up is **6 Tamolitch Falls (Blue Pool)**, a remarkably clear pool of water in the forest. The path to the pool (less than two miles) is rocky so sturdy footwear is essential. Six miles north of the Tamolitch Falls Trailhead are **7 Koosah Falls** and **8 Sahalie Falls**. A mile-long trail connects these two picture-perfect waterfalls. Nearby **9 Clear Lake** has a campground, cabins and a small store that rents out canoes and boats. An easy hiking trail encircles this shimmering alpine lake. From Clear Lake drive back to Sisters (via Santiam Pass). Alternatively, head to Eugene via the town of McKenzie Bridge.

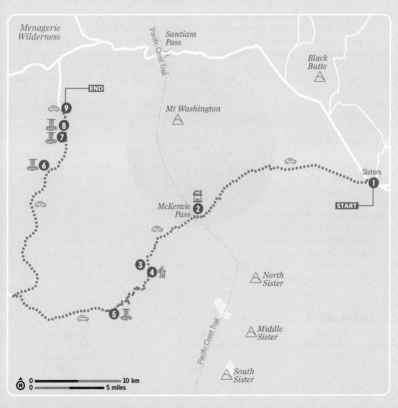

The Oregon Coast

FOREST-FRINGED BEACHES AND ARTSY COMMUNITIES

Welcome to a region where you're never far from the sand – or the forest – and where marine wonders and a thriving arts scene exist side by side.

The Oregon Coast may challenge your notions of what beach life should look like. While there are surprises at seemingly every hairpin turn along this 373-mile stretch of shoreline, most are of the pleasant variety. Sure, you'll find all the trappings of coastal communities, from sandy beaches where kids – and dogs – have plenty of room to frolic, to seafood shacks so popular that they inspire lines around the block. You'll also find rows of cozy vacation cabins decked out in wood-shake siding, candy shops stocked to the ceiling with saltwater taffy, and compact boutiques selling everything from whale sculptures to tie-dye T-shirts (you are in Oregon, after all). What you won't find is beachfront mega-resorts,

bass-pounding nightclubs, or row upon row of lounge chairs blocking the views of the powerful Pacific. And while summertime sunshine is always a possibility, especially as you make your way south toward the border with California, the Oregon Coast is not exactly known for warm weather – you'll probably be fine leaving your swimsuit behind. What you will find instead are gargantuan sea stacks that formed 17 million years ago, magnificent pines that have taken on otherworldly forms after a lifetime of wind-sweeping, and miles of impeccably preserved state parks and trail systems that will remind you there is no greater beauty than what's found in nature. We think you'll be pleasantly surprised.

THE MAIN AREAS

ASTORIA	**NEWPORT**	**COOS BAY**
Film fandom and westward-expansion history.	Marine wildlife and family fun.	Scenic drives and quiet coves.
p250	**p258**	**p262**

Left: Bandon (p265); Above: Cannon Beach (p255)

245

DANITA DELIMONT/SHUTTERSTOCK ©

Sea Lion Caves (p2

Find Your Way

The Oregon Coast is massive, stretching for over 360 miles. While there are loads of quiet beach towns along the coast that make for great getaways, we've selected three larger hubs from which to start your adventures.

CAR

The most convenient way to visit the Oregon Coast is by car, and having your own vehicle makes it easy to stop at scenic pullouts, state parks and small towns at your leisure. If you don't drive, consider booking a tour from Portland instead.

BUS

Bus service on the coast is limited. Transit companies NW Connector and POINT offer service between Portland and a few North Coast destinations. NW Connector also has a route between Salem and Lincoln City. Coos County Area Transit and Curry Public Transit serve the South Coast.

Astoria, p250

Where the Columbia River meets the Pacific Ocean, Astoria – the biggest city on the North Coast – is replete with gorgeous old Victorian homes and historic sites.

Newport, p258

Two marine science centers and easy access to caves full of sea lions make this Central Coast hub a hit among families.

Coos Bay, p262

The gateway to Oregon's ridiculously scenic South Coast is home to some of the state's most gloriously gorgeous state parks.

0   50 km
0   25 miles

Plan Your Days

It takes at least eight hours to drive the entire coast without stopping, so you're better off just tackling a little bit at a time.

Haystack Rock (p256), Cannon Beach

A Day at the Beach

● It's easy to get a taste of the Oregon Coast in just a day. If you're coming from Portland, take Hwy 26 west until you hit Hwy 101. Take the 101 south for 5 miles to visit the art galleries and boutiques at **Cannon Beach** (p255) before making your way over to the town's monolithic **Haystack Rock** (p256), an oft-photographed sea stack that's frequented by tufted puffins (bring binoculars!).

● On your way out of town, make a stop at **Ecola State Park** (p255) to take in Pacific Ocean views or hike through Sitka spruce forest.

Seasonal Highlights

Temperatures rarely get too hot on the Oregon Coast. Summers are generally dry, with cool, rainy weather the rest of the year.

JANUARY

Observe the highest tides of the year, known as **King Tides**, which occur around winter full moons.

FEBRUARY

Dark nights call for dark beer at Astoria's **Fort George Brewery** (p253), which celebrates stout at its Festival of Dark Arts.

MARCH

Learn about – and maybe spot – gray whales as they make their way up to Alaska during the **Oregon Spring Whale Watching Week**.

DAVIDKRUG/SHUTTERSTOCK ©, JASONRENFROW/SHUTTERSTOCK ©, KELLY VANDELLEN/SHUTTERSTOCK ©

A Coastal Weekend

● From Portland, take Hwy 30 to **Astoria** (p250), to visit the Fort Clatsop replica at **Lewis and Clark National and State Historical Park** (p250). Then head south to **Cannon Beach** (p255) to see Haystack Rock before turning in for the night.

● On your second day, drive south to **Tillamook** (p256) to visit Oregon's most famous cheese factory and then onward to **Lincoln City** (p257) to learn about glass-blowing (and, if you're lucky, find a colorful hand-blown float). Wrap your weekend up with a whale-watching cruise in **Depoe Bay** (p257) before returning to Portland or onward to your next destination.

A Week by the Seashore

● With a full week, you'll be able to drive the entire Oregon Coast Hwy 101, from **Astoria** (p250), clear down to the California border (or vice versa). Spend your first few days checking out the North Coast, making sure to stop at Haystack Rock in **Cannon Beach** (p255) and in **Tillamook** (p256) for a bit of cheese tasting.

● Continue south to **Lincoln City** (p257) to search for hidden glass floats on the beach and onward to **Depoe Bay** (p257) to see whales in the wild. Wrap your trip up with a drive along the South Coast's **Samuel H Boardman State Scenic Corridor** (p266).

JUNE
The sky over the D River State Recreation Site fills with colorful kites during the **Lincoln City Summer Kite Festival**.

JULY
Classical and jazz music fills the parks and concert halls of Coos Bay during the annual **Oregon Coast Music Festival**.

SEPTEMBER
The Bandon area's huge cranberry industry is feted with parades and fanfare at the **Bandon Cranberry Festival** (p265).

DECEMBER
More than 325,000 LED lights illuminate the botanical gardens at Shore Acres State Park during the annual **Holiday Lights** display.

Astoria

GETTING AROUND

While Astoria has lots of free parking around town, there are a few options for those who want to leave their cars behind. You can walk or cycle across town via the 5-mile-long Astoria Riverwalk, take a ride along the river aboard the seasonal Astoria Riverfront Trolley, or hop aboard the Sunset Empire Transportation District's bus #10, which passes through downtown.

☑ TOP TIP

With an extensive hot food and salad bar, a deli with a build-your-own burrito station, and lots of fresh local produce, the Astoria Co+op is a terrific place to pick up convenient picnic supplies before heading out on your coastal adventures.

Situated where the Columbia River merges into the Pacific Ocean, on the northwesternmost tip of Oregon, Astoria is not only the oldest city in Oregon, but also the first European-American settlement west of the Rockies to get its own post office. Founded at the turn of the 19th century as a fur-trading town, Astoria grew into a thriving, multicultural community by the late 1800s, with large populations of Nordic, Chinese and Punjabi immigrants moving to the city to work in the fishing and lumber industries.

These days, Astoria is better known for its tourism industry, bolstered by its state parks, its beaches and even its film industry. Many of the city's old commercial and municipal buildings have been converted into hotels or museums. And while this coastal community feels very different than it did a century ago, Astoria's well-preserved architecture adds a certain Victorian elegance to its hilly cityscape.

In the Footsteps of Lewis & Clark

The final frontier

Although the land now known as Astoria has been inhabited for millennia, its current incarnation started back at the turn of the 19th century, when explorers and fur traders began taking an interest in the region. Among them were Captain Meriwether Lewis and Second Lieutenant William Clark who, under the auspices of the US Army's Corps of Discovery, journeyed to the west, ultimately ending their journey in a forested area around 6 miles south of downtown Astoria. It was here that the Corps built **Fort Clatsop**, where they lived from December 1805 until March 1806 before beginning their journey home. Today, the Fort Clatsop area is protected as part of the **Lewis and Clark National State and Historical Park**, which has a collection of 12 different spots across Oregon and Washington related to the Lewis and Clark expedition. Although the original fort is no longer standing, there's a replica in its place that's furnished to give

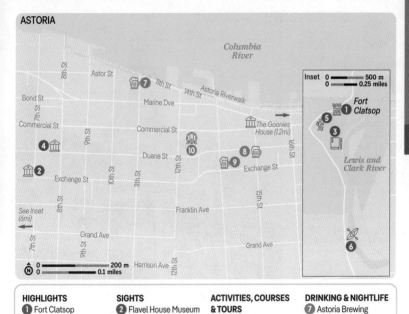

ASTORIA

HIGHLIGHTS
1. Fort Clatsop

SIGHTS
2. Flavel House Museum
3. Lewis and Clark National State and Historical Park
4. Oregon Film Museum

ACTIVITIES, COURSES & TOURS
5. Fort Clatsop Visitor Centre
6. Netul Landing

DRINKING & NIGHTLIFE
7. Astoria Brewing Company
8. Fort George Brewery
9. Fortune & Glory Cider Company
10. Pilot House Distilling

you an idea of what life in the fort was like over 200 years ago, complete with replica bunk beds with fur pelts for bedding. To add to the historic ambience, costumed interpreters are often on hand to provide talks and answer questions. When you're done exploring the compact fort, you can take a short walk through the woods over to the visitor center's exhibit hall to check out displays featuring everything from old weapons to a model canoe.

The **Fort Clatsop Visitor Center** is also the starting point for the Fort to Sea Trail, a 6.5-mile-long hiking trail that will take you from the fort, through the woods, and out to Sunset Beach on the Pacific Ocean. For a shorter hike, head south from the visitor center along the Netul River Trail, which runs south along what is now called the Lewis and Clark River to **Netul Landing**, a popular kayak launch spot. Come in the summer and you can even sign up for a ranger-guided paddle tour along the river.

 ## WHERE TO STAY IN ASTORIA

Norblad
Hip, century-old hotel offering budget-friendly rooms in the center of the city. $

Bowline Hotel
Cozy, contemporary hotel with 40 rooms, many with views out over the Columbia River. $$

Cannery Pier
Upscale spa hotel at the end of a pier that juts into the Columbia River. $$$

THE GOONIES HOUSE ETIQUETTE

A film fan from out of state bought the big white Goonies House in 2023 and plans to keep it accessible for fans to see for the foreseeable future. For now, visitors are welcome to stop by and view the exterior of the house, provided they come during the day or early evening. Out of respect for the neighbors, you should not attempt to drive up the steep gravel drive that leads to the house. Instead, park your car near John Jacob Astor Elementary School, a couple of blocks away, and walk. Remember to stay on sidewalks, keep your visit brief and try not to make too much noise.

MARIUSZ S. JURGIELEWICZ/SHUTTERSTOCK ©

Flavel House Museum

FOR FREE WILLY FANS

Keiko, the baleen star of 1993 film *Free Willy*, was the first captive orca to be released into the ocean. He was rehabilitated at **Oregon Coast Aquarium** (p258) before regaining his freedom in 1998.

Goonies Never Say Die!

The Hollywood of Oregon

If you've ever watched the 1985 kids' film *The Goonies*, then you've seen Astoria, at least on a screen. The continued popularity of this cult classic has been summoning film fans to Astoria for decades. You can start your Goonies-themed adventure with a visit to Mikey's house, known locally simply as **The Goonies House**, located at 368 38th St – just note that you can only see it from the outside. From here, it's a 2-mile drive to the **Flavel House Museum**, where Mr Walsh (aka Mikey's dad) worked in the movie.

While *The Goonies* is undoubtedly the most famous film to have been shot in Astoria, it's certainly not the only one. The city provided a set for flicks such as *Short Circuit*, *Kindergarten Cop* and *Free Willy* – not to mention *Teenage Mutant Ninja Turtles III*. You can learn all about the films shot in Astoria, see movie ephemera (including plenty of Goonies stuff) and even hop in front of a green screen to DIY your own mini film at the **Oregon Film Museum**, just around the corner from the Flavel House in the old Clatsop County jailhouse.

Hiking the Oregon Coast Trail
The ultimate slow travel experience

One way to experience the entirety of the Oregon Coast is by hiking the Oregon Coast Trail (OCT), which leads from the mouth of the Columbia River to the California border. The trail is divided into 10 segments, which pass through woodlands, beaches and coastal towns. Each segment is around 40 miles in length and can take a few days to complete, depending on the tides – note that some areas of the trail are only accessible when the tide is low.

Most hikers camp at numerous state park hiker/biker campsites found along the way. Beach camping is also an option in some areas, but make sure to set your tent up well above the high-tide line. You'll also need to be careful not to set up your tent on signposted western-snowy-plover nesting areas between March 15 and September 15 – if you encounter such an area, you'll need to only walk on wet sands to protect these tiny threatened shorebirds.

The first segment of the hike is a solid option if you want to see a bit of the North Coast but don't have the time or interest in covering the entire coastline. It starts at Fort Stevens State Park and ends at Oswald West State Park, with the option to stop for the night at one of three Adirondack shelters at Tillamook Head along the way.

The OCT is managed by the Oregon Parks and Recreation Department, which provides maps and updated information about route closures and detours on its website.

Fort Stevens State Park
Military history in a state park

A 20-minute drive west of Astoria, the 4300-acre Fort Stevens State Park protects a historic military installation that was active until WWII. Today, this massive expanse is a popular spot for outdoor adventure, with miles of biking and walking paths, a freshwater lake and one of the largest public campgrounds in the US.

If you're a fan of military history, be sure to check out the park's old batteries and the military museum. Don't bid adieu to the park before checking out the wreck of the *Peter Iredale*, the remains of a 1906 shipwreck on the southern end of the park's Columbia Beach.

ASTORIA'S BEST PLACES TO TRY CRAFT BEVERAGES

Pilot House Distilling
Sample everything from agave spirits to absinth at Astoria's very own artisanal distillery.

Astoria Brewing Company
Sip on locally crafted ales and porters while taking in views of the Columbia River at this unfussy spot.

Fortune & Glory Cider Company
Belgian- and English-style hard ciders dominate the offerings at this small-batch cidery, which brews its beverages using apples and other fruits grown right in the Pacific Northwest.

Fort George Brewery
Occupying a full city block in the heart of downtown Astoria, this popular craft brewery serves up a mix of house-brewed seasonal specialties and year-round mainstays.

 WHERE TO GET COFFEE IN ASTORIA

Blue Scorcher Bakery & Café
Spacious spot serving delicious coffee, drinks and sandwiches made with house-baked organic artisan bread. **$**

Astoria Coffee Company
Cozy roaster close to the Goonies House that hawks bags of beans from an on-site vending machine. **$**

Coffee at Cambium
Compact gallery and coffee shop serving espresso drinks with a dash of fine art. **$**

Beyond Astoria

Head south from Astoria to experience the best of coastal Oregon's orthern reaches, from epic natural attractions to cozy, artsy towns.

☑ **TOP TIP**

You can score deals on brand-name clothes while taking advantage of Oregon's lack of sales tax at the Seaside Outlet Mall.

Although Astoria's northern location makes it perfect for exploring Oregon's North Coast, there are plenty of equally fantastic spots in this popular region to consider making your base, from the budget-friendly city of Seaside to the slightly sleeker (and smaller) towns of Cannon Beach and Manzanita, both darlings among day-tripping Portlanders. While the North Coast has plenty of developed communities, it's an equally attractive option if you want to converge with nature, whether taking in ocean views from conifer-lined hiking trails or dipping your toes in the Pacific Ocean as you walk along some of the area's many sandy beaches.

ZSCHNEPF/SHUTTERSTOCK ©

Cannon Beach

SIMONKADZ/SHUTTERSTOCK ©

Ecola State Park

Ecola State Park

TIME FROM ASTORIA: **40 MINS**

Oregon beaches need no filters

Drive south from Astoria for about 25 miles and you'll find yourself at Ecola State Park, which protects roughly 9 miles of shoreline and some of the most photo-worthy views on this part of the coast. While there are a few parking areas throughout the park, your best bet is to park at **Ecola Point** on the park's southern end, where you can take in views of sea stacks, sand and crashing waves from a bluff-top perch. There are a few small trails that weave around the bluff. For a more challenging hike, there's a 2.1-mile-long trail north through windswept forests to **Indian Beach**, a small sandy spot that surfers adore.

Cannon Beach

TIME FROM ASTORIA: **45 MINS**

Postcard perfection

A few minutes' drive south of Ecola State Park sits Cannon Beach. Start at the main thoroughfare, **Hemlock Street**, a boutique-dotted drag that is among the best places in the region to pick up fine art and higher-end souvenirs. Book lovers can easily spend hours poring over the tomes in the **Cannon**

OSWALD WEST STATE PARK

Despite being only a 10-minute drive from Cannon Beach, Oswald West State Park feels like it's worlds away from town life. Covering an expanse of nearly 2500 acres of temperate rainforest filled with western hemlock and Sitka spruce, this day-use area is perfect for quick hikes, with over a dozen trails, the vast majority of which are under a mile. For something a bit more challenging, you can brave a 13-mile stretch of the Oregon Coast Trail that extends from Arch Cape to the town of Manzanita, or take a hike along the Arch Cape to Cape Falcon Trail, which clocks in at 6.5 miles.

 WHERE TO STAY IN CANNON BEACH

Surfsand Resort
Family-friendly beach hotel with direct beach access and views out to Haystack Rock. **$$$**

Stephanie Inn
Romantic, upscale inn where the dining is fine and the wine flows freely. **$$$**

Hallmark Resort
Beachfront property with everything from budget-friendly rooms to expansive suites, some with kitchens. **$**

THE IMAGE PARTY/SHUTTERSTOCK ©

Tillamook Creamery

NESKOWIN GHOST FOREST

In 1998 something mysterious occurred off the Oregon Coast town of Neskowin, about a 30-mile drive south of Tillamook: Sitka spruce stumps suddenly appeared on the shore, as if they were growing out of the sand. What actually happened was that heavy storms that winter had unearthed a 'ghost forest,' the remnants of an old forest that once stood here before a seismic event altered the face of the coastline. The millennia-old stumps are still visible in Neskowin to this day, but only when the tide is particularly low. To see the phenomenon for yourself, come during the summertime low tides when the Pacific Ocean is in its most receded state.

Beach Book Company. Once you've had your retail fix, head to the beach to see **Haystack Rock**, a 17-million-year-old Oregon icon. If you've got binoculars, bring them: this frequent star of Oregon Coast postcards is around 235ft tall and provides refuge to all sorts of seabirds, including fluffy tufted puffins. The area around the monolith is particularly fun during low tide, when the waves recede to reveal lots of little tide pools.

Tillamook

TIME FROM ASTORIA: 1½ HRS 🚗

A different type of tasting room

Sandwiched between large expanses of fertile farmland and the roar of the Pacific Ocean, 40 miles south of Cannon Beach, the city of Tillamook is a very cheesy place – literally. The city's biggest draw is the **Tillamook Creamery**, where you can take a self-guided walk through Oregon's best-known cheese and dairy product factory or get a closer look at what goes into making Tillamook products with a guided cheese or ice-cream tour. No matter what option you go for, you can expect plenty of free samples. After your visit, continue your adventures in dairy land at **Blue Heron French Cheese Company**, about a mile south of the creamery, where you'll find a large gourmet shop selling Blue Heron's signature brie

WHERE TO EAT IN LINCOLN CITY

Cheeky Cauldron
Harry Potter–inspired cafe serving whimsical coffee and tea elixirs accompanied by light nibbles. $

M & P Thai Noodle
Popular among residents, this Thai spot's portions are as massive as its menu. $

Zest Garden Cafe
Ecologically minded cafe with living room vibes and a plant-forward menu of crepes and pizzas. $$

and global goodies, plus a wine bar and a candy shop. There's even a petting zoo that's home to a whole host of friendly barnyard critters, from pigs and ponies to goats and llamas.

Lincoln City

TIME FROM ASTORIA: 2½ HRS 🚗

Search for hidden treasure

Drive south from Tillamook for another 45 miles and you'll end up in Lincoln City, the coast's de facto capital of glass art. The city runs a program known as Finders Keepers in which around 3000 blown glass floats per year are hidden on the beach for lucky visitors to find. If you find one of the colorful baubles, it's yours to keep – you can even register it online for a certificate of authenticity. If you don't find any treasure, don't despair – just head over to the Lincoln City Glass Center, where you can buy glass-art creations made by Oregon artists, watch glassblowing demonstrations or learn how to blow your own float.

Depoe Bay

TIME FROM ASTORIA: 3 HRS 🚗

Discover the world's largest animals

A 20-minute drive south of Lincoln City, Depoe Bay is the state's capital of whale-watching – and for good reason. While you can see migrating whales all along the coast, Depoe Bay has its own group of whales who spend their summers in Oregon and their winters in the waters of Baja California. Learn all about them at the **Whale, Sea Life & Shark Museum**, a compact but jam-packed museum founded by marine biologist Carrie Newell, who was responsible for discovering that the whales of Depoe Bay dine on mysid shrimp. Newell also takes visitors out to see whales in the flesh through her eco-tourism venture, **Whale Research EcoExcursions**. Newell's whale-watching dog, Koda, usually comes along for the ride to help sniff out whales. If you're short on time, you still may be able to spot a whale from the **Oregon State Parks Whale Watching Center**, about a two-minute walk from Newell's museum. This two-story bay-facing complex has giant picture windows and an outdoor observation deck, and there are always rangers on hand to provide talks and answer questions.

DEPOE BAY'S SUMMER RESIDENT WHALES

Marine biologist **Carrie Newell** (@ carriesoregonwhales) – who has been studying gray whales in Depoe Bay since 1992 – explains what sets the area's whales apart from migrating gray whales.

There's a total population of 232 summer resident gray whales that extend from Northern California to Vancouver Island. Depoe Bay has the greatest concentration of these whales, with up to 30 being seen at one point in time. They come at the end of May and stay until the end of October. They're individuals – I've named them – and the same ones come back every summer. They're here to feed on mysid shrimp that are found in huge swarms near the shore. The whales are not rubbing barnacles and whale lice off when they're near the shore: they're eating.

 WHERE TO SLEEP IN DEPOE BAY

Channel House
You might be able to spot a whale from your room at this central, bay-facing inn. $$

Inn at Arch Rock
Quiet bluff-top property with home-like rooms, some with fireplaces, balconies and fridges. $$

SCP
Cozy eco-hotel with minimalist but sleek rooms, including family-friendly options with two sets of bunk beds. $$

Newport

GETTING AROUND

You're best off driving in Newport, as many of the attractions are a bit spread out. Lincoln County Transit's Newport City Loop Bus connects key areas and attractions in and around town and operates every day of the week.

Straddling both sides of Yaquina Bay, Newport is a popular gateway to the Central Coast. A major hub for Oregon's commercial fishing industry, this city is famous for its educational attractions, as well as its pretty beaches and historic lighthouses.

Most of Newport's attractions are spread across three neighborhoods. The northernmost is Nye Beach, a compact, walkable area on the Pacific Ocean where many of the city's artsiest boutiques and restaurants are located. A few minutes' drive south, the historic Bayfront on Yaquina Bay offers great views out over the 3223ft-long Yaquina Bay Bridge. Stay here and you may even see commercial fishing boats bringing their catches to shore. Across the Yaquina Bay Bridge, on the south side of town, South Beach is where the city's marine science centers are located. It's also the site of South Beach State Park, a massive expanse of sand with its own forested year-round campground.

☑ TOP TIP

Cycling is a great way to get around Newport, but if you bring your own bike, you may struggle when you hit the sand. For a beach-friendly pair of wheels, head to Bike Newport, where you can rent a fat bike, a type of thick-tired bicycle that's perfect for sand and concrete alike.

Channel Your Inner Marine Biologist

Newport's marine science hubs

The **Oregon Coast Aquarium** is Newport's star attraction and is a good place to immerse yourself in all things marine. This aquarium gained fame in the late 1990s, when it provided a temporary home for Keiko, the orca star of the film *Free Willy*, while he was prepared for his release into the wild. These days, the aquarium draws in the masses with its mix of indoor and outdoor exhibits that focus primarily on the flora and fauna native to the region – including a seabird aviary. Don't miss the Passages of the Deep exhibit, housed in Keiko's former tank, which features underwater passageways that take you through replicas of three different Oregon Coast ecosystems.

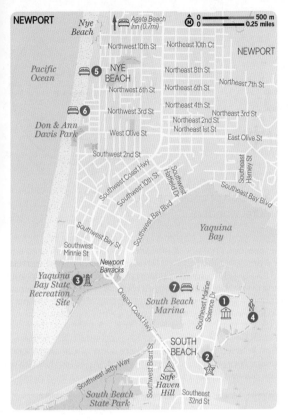

NEWPORT

SIGHTS
① Hatfield Marine Visitor Center
② Oregon Coast Aquarium
③ Yaquina Bay Lighthouse

ACTIVITIES, COURSES & TOURS
④ Yaquina Bay Estuary

SLEEPING
⑤ Inn at Nye Beach
⑥ Sylvia Beach Hotel
⑦ Newport Belle, Riverboat Bed and Breakfast

BEST PLACES TO STAY IN NEWPORT

Sylvia Beach Hotel
Grab a novel and unplug at this screen- and internet-free literary-themed hotel, where the decor of each room is inspired by a celebrated author. **$$**

Inn at Nye Beach
Cozy up to oceanfront views from the infinity-edge whirlpool hot tub at this eco-chic boutique hotel in the adorable Nye Beach neighborhood. **$$$**

The Newport Belle, Riverboat Bed and Breakfast
All aboard this 97ft-long paddlewheel boat moored in the South Beach Marina that's been converted into an adults-only bed and breakfast. **$$$**

Agate Beach Inn
Fall asleep to the sounds of the ocean at this budget-friendly spot abutting the Agate Beach State Recreation Site. **$**

A 10-minute walk north of the aquarium, the **Hatfield Marine Visitor Center** is an excellent spot to continue your on-land explorations of the deep blue, particularly if you're a parent with budding marine biologists in tow. This working research center has all sorts of hands-on activities, from an augmented reality sandbox to tide-pool touch tanks. Come on a Tuesday or Thursday morning for a free guided walking tour of the adjacent **Yaquina Bay Estuary**.

Before leaving the area, make a stop at the **Yaquina Bay Lighthouse**, the only lighthouse in the state with attached living quarters. There's a small interpretive display in the basement where you can learn about the history of this working lighthouse.

Beyond Newport

From gargantuan sand dunes to bogs full of carnivorous plants, the stretch of coastline south of Newport is full of natural wonders.

☑ **TOP TIP**

Don't let the spelling fool you: the town of Yachats is pronounced 'yah-hots.'

The area south of Newport is characterized by a mix of sandy beaches, pretty overlooks and wooded state parks and forest areas, not to mention a few smaller communities, starting with the small city of Waldport, a popular fishing and birding destination a 20-minute drive from Newport. Another 10 minutes down the coast, Yachats is a tiny vacation town that's loaded with fantastic places to eat, while the wooded headlands at Cape Perpetua Scenic Area offer some of the most dramatic views on the coast. Keep driving and you'll soon find yourself near Florence, where some of the area's most magnificent natural sights are located, including the start of the colossal Oregon Dunes.

WOLLERTZ/SHUTTERSTOCK ©

Sea Lion Caves

Florence

See Steller sea lions

Right on Hwy 101, just over an hour south of Newport and 15 minutes north of Florence, the privately owned **Sea Lion Caves** is *the* place to go if you want to see Steller sea lions in the wild. This roadside attraction touts itself as the largest sea cave on earth, but it's its residents – not its geological grandeur – that draw in throngs of visitors. Hop aboard an elevator in the gift shop and descend into a 12-story basalt sea cave to spot these massive creatures hanging out in large groups. They tend to congregate inside the caves themselves in the fall and winter, while they spend the spring and summer months breeding and birthing on the rocks just outside the grotto. Note that this attraction is not a zoo but a natural feature of the larger **Cape Perpetua Marine Reserve** and the sea lions are free to come and go as they please.

Darlingtonia State Natural Site

Tiptoe through the bug-eating plants

About a 5-minute drive north of downtown Florence sits yet another natural attraction – the 18-acre Darlingtonia State Natural Site. This little park protects the carnivorous *Darlingtonia californica,* a type of pitcher plant also known as the cobra lily. A wooden walkway leads from the parking lot and over a large bog full of these coastal plants, allowing you to get a closer look without trampling on the delicate ecosystem.

OREGON DUNES NATIONAL RECREATION AREA

Extending for around 40 miles from just south of Florence all the way to Coos Bay, the Oregon Dunes National Recreation Area is the largest expanse of coastal sand dunes on the continent. It was these very dunes that provided the inspiration for Pacific Northwest author Frank Herbert's eco-sci-fi novel *Dune,* which was later adapted into film versions.

The dunes are popular for off-highway vehicle (OHV) adventures, though if you'd rather approach the sands with a little less adrenaline, you can take a hike along the **Oregon Dunes Loop Trail** (the first half-mile is paved and wheelchair-friendly).

 BEST PLACES TO EAT IN YACHATS

The Green Salmon
Wood-clad cafe with an extensive menu of coffee and tea plus hearty breakfast plates and sandwiches. $

Beach Street Kitchen
This cozy spot serves hearty soups and paninis, plus burritos and tacos with a gourmet spin. $$

Yachats Brewing
Casual brewpub with a rotating tap and a small menu of gastropub fare. $$

Coos Bay

GETTING AROUND

Although bus service is available through Coos County Area Transit, you'll need a car (or bicycle) to get around the Coos Bay area, particularly if you want to spend time exploring nearby state parks. Some hotels, such as the Itty Bitty Inn, also have loaner bikes.

☑ **TOP TIP**

Most people base themselves in Coos Bay or North Bend, where the majority of restaurants and shops are located, though you'll find plenty of lovely options just south of town, along Hwy 540. If you choose this option, you'll be close to three of the Coos Bay area's prettiest state parks.

Coos Bay is the largest city on the Oregon Coast and the site of the only international harbor in the state – in fact, you can still see massive piles of timber and sawdust being prepared for shipment overseas if you take Hwy 101 through town. Coos Bay is the largest of three adjacent communities – the other two are Charleston, across the Cape Arago Hwy Bridge to the south, and North Bend, on the northern side of town. Collectively dubbed 'Oregon's Bay Area,' this trio of cities has lots of creature comforts – including terrific restaurants and hotels plus a couple of casinos. The Bay Area is also a good base for travelers wanting easy access to both hotels and restaurants and to outdoor activities, including sea kayaking, off-roading on the Oregon Dunes to the north of town, and hiking along the area's forested cliffs that flank the Pacific Ocean.

A Trifecta of State Parks

A trail runs through them

On the south side of Coos Bay sit three contiguous state parks that are connected by one long trail. The northernmost of the trio is **Sunset Bay State Park**, which sits on a small bay that's protected by soaring cliffs. The Cape Arago Trail leads from the beach to **Shore Acres State Park**, about a mile to the south, and while hiking will give you the chance to stop at the Cape Arago Lighthouse viewpoint to take in the views along the way, people usually just drive.

Shore Acres is the most popular of the three parks, owing to its incredible views of waves crashing against rocky headlands and its elegant botanical garden, replete with roses and rhododendrons. From here, you can hike down to Simpson Beach, where seal pups are not an uncommon site, or continue south to **Cape Arago State Park**. There are a couple of

COOS BAY

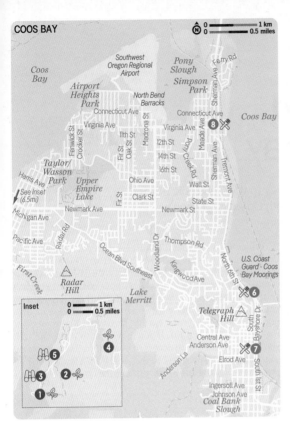

SIGHTS
1 Cape Arago State Park
2 Shore Acres State Park
3 Simpson Reef Overlook
4 Sunset Bay State Park
5 Two Guardians

EATING
6 7 Devils Waterfront Alehouse
7 E Z Thai Restaurant
8 Tin Thistle Garden Café

BEST PLACES TO EAT IN COOS BAY

The Tin Thistle Garden Café
Nourish your body with tasty, plant-based tacos and sandwiches at this North Bend spot with British pub vibes, a sunny patio and loads of live-edge furniture. **$$**

E Z Thai Restaurant
Satiate your appetite at this downtown Thai spot, which serves large portions of rich curry dishes, stir-fries and comforting soups. **$$**

7 Devils Waterfront Alehouse
Sample everything from freshly caught seafood dishes to hearty bean burgers while you take in views of the water from this contemporary pub. **$$**

overlooks worth stopping for whether you're traveling on foot or by car. The first is the **Two Guardians**, a duo of towering trees on a small cliff that juts out over the sea. The second is the **Simpson Reef Overlook**, which looks out onto Shell Island. Bring your binoculars to get a better view of the island's regular visitors, which include seals, sea lions and all sorts of seabirds. Wrap your tour up at Cape Arago State Park, at the end of the road. From here, you can take the South Cove Trail to a sandy beach with great tide pooling or simply enjoy the views from above.

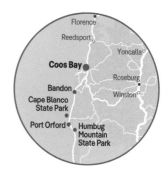

Beyond Coos Bay

From beyond Coos Bay to the California border at Brookings, the South Coast is Oregon's quietest – and wildest.

☑ **TOP TIP**

Travelers crossing into California from Oregon must pass an agricultural inspection and may be required to surrender any produce in their possession.

It's difficult to deny that the southernmost part of the Oregon Coast is the state's most serene. Part of this is because it's not that easy to get to – while there are lots of east–west highways connecting Oregon's I-5 corridor with the coast further north, getting to this part of the coast from Southern Oregon's urban hubs means either cutting across near Bandon or driving down into California, cutting across the Redwoods, and then heading up the 101. If you're willing to make the trek, you'll be rewarded with access to miles of stellar views of the coast, quiet and spacious beaches, and even a few beautifully preserved historic sites – all without the crowds.

ARTAZUM/SHUTTERSTOCK ©

Bandon

Flooded cranberry field, Bandon

Bandon

TIME FROM COOS BAY: **30 MINS** 🚗

Oregon's cranberry country

Oregon is one of the largest cranberry producers in the nation, producing around 50 million pounds of the tart fruit per year. Cranberries are celebrated with aplomb in **Bandon** – a half-hour drive south of Coos Bay – and not just during the annual **Bandon Cranberry Festival**. You can fill up on free samples of cranberry jelly candies at downtown's Cranberry Sweets & More, imbibe cranberry cider at the Bandon Rain taproom, or cranberry rum at Stillwagon Distillery, or even sample cranberry-infused cheese at Face Rock Creamery. If you visit around the late-autumn harvest season, you can see ripe cranberries in the bog – and pick up some fresh fruit to take home – at Bowman Bogs, a 6-mile drive south of Bandon.

Cape Blanco State Park

TIME FROM COOS BAY: **1¼ HRS** 🚗

See the South Coast of yesteryear

A 25-mile drive south from Bandon will take you to Cape Blanco State Park on the westernmost tip of Oregon. This natural expanse has all the trappings of a typical Oregon

THE WASHED ASHORE PROJECT

Walk along Bandon's waterfront and you'll soon find yourself face-to-face with *Finnian*, a massive tiger rockfish made entirely of old garbage, most of which is plastic. This big orange sea creature is just one of many sculptures created by the Washed Ashore Project, an ocean conservation awareness program designed to educate the public about the perils of plastic pollution by creating sculptures of sea creatures using garbage collected from the beach. You'll find more sculptures on display inside the nearby Old Town Marketplace, including *Steve the Weedy Sea Dragon* (a not-so-distant relative of the seahorse) and a fluffy penguin. Don't forget to look up to see jellyfish made from trash suspended from the ceiling.

BEST BEACHES ON THE SOUTH COAST

Face Rock State Scenic Viewpoint
Bandon beach with labyrinths drawn in the sand by the Circles in the Sand art team.

Tseriadun State Recreation Site
Called Agate Beach by Port Orford residents due to ample rockhounding.

Harris Beach
Brookings beach with year-round camping, pretty sea stacks and excellent bird-watching and tide pooling.

The South Coast's 12-mile-long Samuel H Boardman State Scenic Corridor might just be the prettiest stretch of an already gorgeous coastline. Just give yourself plenty of time to stop at scenic spots along the way. Start at 1 **Arch Rock** (Mile 344.8), where a small path leads to a couple of benches that look out over gorgeous sea stacks, including the aptly named Arch Rock itself. The sunsets here are particularly moving. From here, continue south to the not-so-secret 2 **Secret Beach and Thunder Rock Cove** (Mile 345.8). You can take in views from the parking lot or make your way down a ¾-mile trail to the beach – just don't attempt this during high tide when most of the beach is submerged. Make 3 **Natural Bridges** (Mile 346) your next stop to see bridge-like rock formations as they're lapped by frothy sea spray. By now, you've probably spent enough time looking at the beach that you'll actually want to head down to the sand. Continue south over the 4 **Thomas Creek Bridge** (Mile 347.8), which, at 345ft tall, is the highest bridge in the state, until you reach 5 **Whaleshead Beach** (Mile 349.1). This popular beach is named for its offshore sea stack that resembles the head of a giant whale – when the waves hit it, the rock sometimes looks like it's spouting water. You can drive right down to the beach or park at the 6 **Whaleshead Viewpoint** (Mile 349.3) and follow a steep trail down to the shore. Wrap your drive up at 7 **Cape Ferrelo Viewpoint** (Mile 351.9), where you can take a mile-long loop hike up to the precipice of a grassy, ocean-facing hill. If you're lucky, you may even spot a migrating whale.

state park, including gorgeous views, hiking trails and year-round camping.

Much of what is now the state park was originally owned by a dairy-farming family, who built their home here – the **Historic Hughes House** – in 1898. You can get a glimpse of what life was like for the family by paying a visit to their two-story historic home, which has been refurbished in an 1890s style. Volunteer docents are on hand to give brief lectures and answer questions when the house is open, from May through September (except on Tuesdays).

A couple of minutes' drive from the Hughes House, the **Cape Blanco Lighthouse** is both the oldest continually operating lighthouse on the Oregon Coast and the tallest. It was the first lighthouse in the state to have a woman keeper, back in 1903. There's a gift shop and an interpretative center on-site and docents are sometimes available to lead tours.

Port Orford

TIME FROM COOS BAY: 1 HR

A summit above the sea

Easily one of the most rewarding, if challenging, hikes on the South Coast is the Humbug Mountain summit hike in **Humbug Mountain State Park**, a half-hour drive from Cape Blanco on the outskirts of Port Orford. This 5.5-mile adventure will take you through groves of old-growth Douglas fir – Oregon's state tree – and up to the 1765ft summit of the mountain. Here you can take in south-facing views of ocean, forest and rocky headlands before beginning your descent.

Dinosaur Rainforest

A prehistoric roadside attraction

Drive south from Humbug Mountain for 10 minutes and you'll spot a colossal T. rex statue on the side of the road, beckoning you to visit the **Prehistoric Gardens**. Built in the 1950s, this roadside attraction houses a collection of 23 true-to-scale model dinosaurs, including lesser-known species, all tucked among a temperate rainforest full of giant ferns, skunk cabbage and fir trees. Interpretive panels tell the story of the earth's flora and fauna hundreds of millions of years ago. While the attraction does seem a bit kitschy at first, it's actually wildly informative.

WHERE TO READ ON THE SOUTH COAST

Charlie J Stephens, owner of Port Orford's Sea Wolf Books & Community Writing Center – the westernmost bookstore in the contiguous US – recommends these South Coast spots for retreating into a good book.

Cafe 2.0, Port Orford
Sit in a chair right next to a cozy wood stove, spread out on their blue velvet couch or sit in a light-filled window to soak up every possible scrap of vitamin D.

Floras Creek Coffee, Langlois
Stay warm right next to the coffee roaster. For a heightened reading experience, their espressos are potent and excellent.

Redfish, Port Orford
Channel your inner Hemingway and imbibe. Their floor-to-ceiling windows give a long view of forest and beach. They make a sublime Old Fashioned.

 BEST PLACES TO STAY ON THE SOUTH COAST

Pacific Reef Hotel
Well-maintained value hotel in Gold Beach with simple rooms, suites and cottages, some with full kitchens. $

Wildflower Inn
Four-room boutique hotel with bright, contemporary furnished rooms on the main drag in Gold Beach. $$

WildSpring Guest Habitat
Eco-luxe bed-and-breakfast resort in Port Orford with ocean views and elegant cabins among the trees. $$$

Above: Wizard Island (p280), Crater Lake National Park; Right: Ashland (p272)

Ashland & Southern Oregon

BLUE SKIES OVER VOLCANOES AND VINEYARDS

Home to the state's sunniest city and bluest lake, Southern Oregon is a land of superlatives, both profound and inviting.

The discovery of gold near Jacksonville, Oregon, in 1851 ushered in a wave of new arrivals, determined to lay claim to the land and riches of the Rogue River Valley. That arrival – easily associated with the 'thrill of discovery,' along with the trials and tribulations of the long roads taken to get there – led to much violence against Native American people, and the places they'd called home for time beyond memory.

Southern Oregon is a place where one can sense gold rush nostalgia. There are model wagons at highway rest stops and murals depicting the gold rush boom. However, there's also ample opportunity to consider the painful legacy of colonialism, and the ongoing impact of humans on the natural landscape, especially as climate change has intensified the

ALESSANDRARC/SHUTTERSTOCK ©

risks and devastation of drought and wildfires. Today, driving south past sprawling vineyards and east through forests where snowcapped mountains and volcanoes rise in the distance, the striking landscape displays the power of both human and natural forces.

Millennia before settlers arrived, a period of intense volcanic activity left calderas, lava flows, and caves. Amid that landscape, towns first settled by homesteaders maintain agricultural traditions passed down from generations, alongside bustling breweries and restaurants, theaters and outfitters for outdoors tourism. Southern Oregon is a confluence of intense natural and human forces, the consequences and beauty of both.

THE MAIN AREAS

ASHLAND
A busy downtown revolves around showtime.
p272

CRATER LAKE NATIONAL PARK
The deepest, bluest wonder of Oregon.
p279

Find Your Way

Medford is the only commercial airport in Southern Oregon, but most people drive to reach this region that's ripe for road trips. East of I-5, winding roads run along rivers and through multiple national forests.

CAMPERVAN

A vehicle that doubles as accommodationw is an excellent way to experience Southern Oregon, where established campgrounds and dispersed camping are plentiful. For the campervan-curious, rent a camper equipped with all the camping essentials.

Crater Lake National Park, p279

Oregon's only national park can be tricky to visit, thanks to crowds and variable windows of accessibility. But this stunning lake is worth the effort.

Ashland, p272

Golden foothills drop into a dense downtown. Shops, restaurants and bars are busy with theater-goers and those who come for access to outdoorsier adventures.

CAR

Unless you're a thru-hiker spending weeks on the Pacific Crest Trail, you'll want a car to thoroughly experience Southern Oregon, where pull-offs for mountain views and river dips can be as fun as the destination. Carry chains in the winter months to cross mountain passes.

PACIFIC OCEAN

Christmas Valley

Summer Lake

Silver Lake

Fort Rock

Silver Lake

Gearhart Mtn

Quartz Pass

Dreus Reservoir

Fremont National Forest

Bly

Beaty

Gerber Reservoir

Dairy

Deschutes National Forest

Chemult

Winema National Forest

Crater Lake National Park

Crater Lake

Mt Thielsen

Mazama Village

Fort Klamath

Chiloquin

Klamath Falls

Keno

Worden

Odell Lake

Davis Lake

Crescent Lake

Willamette Pass

Diamond Lake

Upper Klamath Lake

Mt McLoughlin

Aspen Lake

Klamath River

Hills Creek Reservoir

Lookout Point Reservoir

Steamboat

Umpqua National Forest

Union Creek

Prospect

OREGON

Howard Prairie Lake

Shady Cove

Eagle Point

Medford

Phoenix

Ashland

Ideleyd Park

Glide

Tiller

Cascade Range

Roseburg

Winston

Canyonville

Grants Pass

Jacksonville

Applegate

Siskiyou Mountains

Coast Range

Wolf Creek

Merlin

Galice

Kerbyville

Cave Junction

Takilma

Klamath Mountains

Siskiyou National Forest

Powers

Illahe

Agness

Coquille

50 km

25 miles

N

RF CLARK/SHUTTERSTOCK ©

Wolf Creek Inn (p278)

Plan Your Time

Travel between destinations is slow, not because of traffic, but because there are so many reasons to stop, from stunning vistas and picnic opportunities to wine tasting and little drive-through coffee stands.

A Whirlwind Three Days

Spend a night at **Steamboat Inn** (p283) where the Umpqua flows outside your cabin. Depart early and beat the crowds at **Crater Lake National Park** (p279). Hike down to the water on the **Cleetwood Cove Trail** (p280), and up to the best views at **Crater Lake Lodge** (p280). Head to **Ashland** (p272) for a a show at **Allen Elizabethan Theater** (p274).

Relax for a Week

After Crater Lake, head to **Crater Lake ZipLine** (p282), where you can fly through the trees, or rent kayaks along **Spring Creek** (p282). Travel south to **Klamath Falls** (p282), home to over 350 species of birds. Bookend a night in **Ashland** (p272) with a trip to **Oregon Caves National Monument** (p276) and **Applegate Valley vineyards** (p277). Brave a night with ghosts at **Wolf Creek Inn** (p278).

Seasonal Highlights

SPRING	SUMMER	FALL	WINTER
Snow lingers in higher elevations and opening weekend of the **Shakespeare Festival** lights up Ashland.	Campgrounds and lakeshores are busy. Keep an eye on fire restrictions and the AIR Quality Index.	Arguably the best time to visit **Crater Lake**, after the most crowded season and before the snow arrives.	Winter Wings Festival brings birders to **Klamath Falls**. Crater Lake has cross-country skiing and snowshoeing.

Ashland

GETTING AROUND

Main St in Ashland is flat and very walkable, but a detour on side streets can be a bit of a climb. Many accommodations are centrally located, so you can walk to most of what you need. But if you're staying on the outskirts and need to drive in, there's plenty of parking along Lithia Park. Rogue Valley Transportation District is the local bus service with routes running Monday through Saturday, within Ashland and to neighboring towns.

✅ **TOP TIP**

You don't need a ticket to experience the showmanship of Ashland. Green Shows take place Wednesdays through Saturdays at 6:45pm on The Bricks courtyard, outside of the main OSF theaters. The free events feature a wide variety of performance art, from Afro-jazz and folk music to storytelling and comedy.

This town of approximately 20,000, tucked into the foothills of the Siskiyou and Cascade ranges, welcomes over 10 times its population in theater-goers each year. The Oregon Shakespeare Festival (OSF), founded in 1935, produces classical and contemporary plays, performed daily from April to October, but there is much to love about Ashland offstage, too. The center of town is a lively conglomerate of shopping (think New Age meets artsy chic), locally sourced food, and perfect places to sit and sip something while people-watching. It's a town infused with off-kilter, creative energy – and local wine! Small businesses reinforce the quirky town persona, like the vintage dress shop where you can have your tarot cards read in the oracle room downstairs.

Ashland offers outdoor adventures, too: stroll through Lithia Park, hit up a nearby hiking trail, or depart for river rafting from one of several outfitters in town.

VICTORIA DITKOVSKY/SHUTTERSTOCK ®

Lithia Park

When you're not sitting at a show, there's so much to see in Ashland by foot. Start at the south end of **1 Lithia Park** to enjoy the length of its peaceful greenery, and follow trails along **2 Ashland Creek**. Listen for the thwack of pickleball on the north end; just past the courts you'll spot the marble **3 Butler-Perozzi Fountain**. Sculpted in Italy, the fountain was a gift to the city after it appeared at the 1915 San Francisco Panama–Pacific International Exposition. The trail and park terminate at the **4 Downtown Plaza** where you'll find an information booth and the **5 Lithia Fountains**, surrounded by shopping and restaurants. Mineral water with high levels of barium, thought to be healing, once flowed through the fountains to be sipped. But the town shut them down due to health concerns in 2016.

If you're trying to catch a show, stop by the **6 OSF box office**, just southeast of the plaza. Or continue southeast on Main St. **7 The Street Scene** by Marion L Young is like a mural come to life – a sculpture, really – in which a collage of hypothetical Ashland characters (including Shakespearean ones) look out at the town.

The **8 Ashland Springs Hotel**, built in 1925, is the tallest building in town. Pop into the ornate, two-story lobby. If you're thirsty, **9 Larks** is the French-influenced restaurant inside the hotel where you'll want a reservation for dinner. But you can also saddle up to the original 1920s bar, shipped to Ashland in one piece from San Francisco, where your cocktail will come with an air of Prohibition. Further along on Main St, **10 Bloomsbury Books** does an excellent job at curating staff favorites and local authors; you might feel compelled to crack one open in the cafe upstairs. Cross Main St and head back northwest, window shopping on your way.

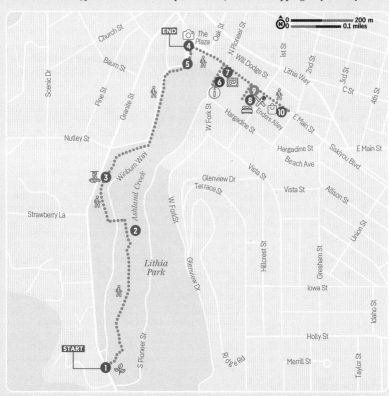

WHY I LOVE ASHLAND

Britany Robinson, Writer

My first time in Ashland, I scored rush tickets to *The Tempest* and watched through the sparkle of rain. The second, I experienced the full range of classic and contemporary, tragedy and comedy, at opening weekend. Most recently, I skipped theater; my husband and one-year-old came with me and she's too young for a play.

I've loved Ashland on every visit, but this time felt extra special. We caught Afro-jazz on The Bricks, and we watched her dance and clap with the audience. So many people smiled and waved at her, like she was the actual star. Performance is the lifeblood of Ashland, but what I really love is the community that forms around it.

Allen Elizabethan Theater

Get Shakespearean

The Many Stages of Ashland

The paint was still wet when audience members filed into the third iteration of **Oregon Shakespeare Festival**'s Elizabethan theater in 1959. (The first, built in 1935, was largely destroyed in a fire. The second was deemed a fire hazard and demolished.) But the show must go on, and on it did. It was remodeled again in 1991, to reduce ambient noise and amplify actors' voices. That's all to say, great effort has gone into maintaining an Elizabethan theater in Ashland. To sit in the audience of the **Allen Elizabethan Theater** today is to witness historic, world-class theater beneath a canopy of sky, which might feature the melting light of a summer night or the twinkly stars of springtime (or it might feature rain). The show doesn't stop for rain, unless unsafe, so you'll want to bring a poncho if the forecast looks wet. The other two theaters on the OSF campus are indoors.

There is a casual, social atmosphere to theater at OSF. You can dress up and plan a classy night on the town around a show, or you can grab rush tickets after a packed day of adventures; you won't feel out of place if you don't have time to change after your hike.

The tenacity of OSF, first displayed by the building and rebuilding of the flagship theater, continues to propel the company. Despite the popularity of OSF, financial troubles have plagued it ever since COVID-19 and wildfire smoke forced them to cancel so many shows. Right now the future of OSF is unclear, but the town has molded itself around theater for so long, it's hard to imagine that ever going away.

Beyond Ashland

Merlin
Gold Hill
Wilderville
Red Lily Winery · Jacksonville
Illinois Valley Visitor Center · Ruch · **Ashland**
Cave Junction · Oregon Cave National Monument
Happy Camp · Horse Creek
Hamburg

The landscape surrounding Ashland contains so much variety, from sprawling vineyards to moss-draped forests hiding deep caves and ancient tunnels.

To the north of Ashland, Applegate Valley is alive with vineyards, produce and history. The first settlers to arrive in the region were looking for an alternative to the treacherous final leg of the Oregon Trail. Wine grapes were planted not long after those first wagon wheels pressed paths into the dirt. The Wild and Scenic Rogue River runs west, with 40 miles of hiking on the Rogue River Trail alongside it. Head northeast to Grants Pass, then south to reach Oregon Caves National Monument, where suddenly the most stunning formations are underground, rather than stretching skyward like the many mountain peaks you can spot in the region.

GETTING AROUND

The road from Cave Junction to Oregon Caves National Monument is not accessible to large RVs. If you're prone to car sickness, give yourself some time to recover after that drive. Elsewhere in the region, driving is pretty straightforward.

EUGENE KALENKOVICH/SHUTTERSTOCK ©

☑ TOP TIP

You'll pass through Grants Pass at least once, where Babe's Bakery is a great local spot for sweets and breakfast sandwiches.

Oregon Caves National Monument (p276)

Caves and Tunnels

Follow the Path Down Deep

A towering tree can mark the passage of centuries. But below the trees and the soft pine floor of the Northern Siskiyou Mountains, one can witness millions of years of natural forces at work.

Oregon Caves National Monument is tucked into a largely inaccessible swath of wilderness. Tickets for cave tours are sold at the Illinois Valley Visitor Center in **Cave Junction**, at the start of 15 miles of hairpin turns, the only paved road in and out of the park.

This underground wonder consists of 15,000ft of passages and otherworldly rooms, all carved into the marble by the slow and gentle (and at times sudden and explosive) passage of water. Stalagmites cluster on the floor in lumpy pyramids and stalactites hang from the ceiling like alien icicles; it takes about 1000 years for these features to grow an inch, as water drips from the ceiling depositing calcium carbonate along the way. Cave tours guide visitors through winding tunnels, some barely wide enough to stoop and squeeze through.

The caves were likely known by local tribes first, but a young boy stumbled upon them while searching for his dog that ran off during a hunting trip in 1874. The earliest white explorers braved pitch-black passages. Today, the only way to access the caves is by guided tour, during which guides take you back in time with harrowing stories of those early expeditions, on paths that are now well lit. The lights are then flipped off to demonstrate the unnerving darkness to be found below ground.

The caves are a constant 41°F (5°C) – a lovely respite on hot days. Dress for the cold, year-round.

White Water on the Rogue

Rafting the Wild and Scenic

Ashland-based companies will take you on a 30-minute drive to a bank of the Rogue River where you'll get to know the power and beauty of this waterway's rapids. Rafting on the Rogue can be relaxing or a thrill, depending on the style of tour you choose. Either way, it's an entry point to the complexity of water management in a region facing drought. The level of water, and number of rapids, is impacted by how much of the river water is being diverted to farmers or being used to maintain healthy populations of salmon. While a class III rapid will leave you charged with the natural power of waterways, it's also tells a resource management story as the region's conflicting water needs are balanced.

 WHERE TO EAT IN CAVE JUNCTION

Wild River Pizza Company
The longest-running brewpub in Southern Oregon serving wood-fired pizzas and microbrews. **$$**

Carlos Mexican Cuisine
Hearty Mexican dishes with vegetarian options and an outdoor patio (and you might leave with leftovers). **$**

Trillium Bakery
This family-owned bakery specializes in doughnuts and savory lunch specials like a tri-tip Philly. **$**

Rafting, Rogue River

Noah's River Adventures leaves directly from downtown Ashland; it's been leading white-water tours since 1974. The 'half-day' and 'express' introductions to white-water rafting are convenient trips when you're trying to fit other activities into your day. Even on these short excursions, you'll get to experience an exciting stretch of water and view the Lower and Upper Table Rocks plateaus.

For those looking to spend extended time on the water, you can choose between camping, or lodge-to-lodge, multiday tours that include meals and a range of thrill levels, depending on your experience and desire.

Applegate Wine Tasting

The quieter wine region

On a bank of the Applegate River in Southern Oregon, you can taste vintages from Spain. **Red Lily Winery**, one of 18 wineries that make up the Applegate Valley wine country, welcomes visitors to their high-ceilinged tasting room. Order a tasting flight and some food, like the bruschetta that comes piled on a blob of fresh mozzarella, and head down to the picnic tables on the water. There is something extra satisfying about sipping a glass of tempranillo on a sunny day with your feet

BEST HIKES OUTSIDE OF ASHLAND

Grizzly Peak
This lollipop-shaped trail is a moderate 5 miles, featuring wildflowers, burn areas, and rocky overlooks with sweeping views of the Rogue Valley.

Pilot Rock
A thrilling scramble that doesn't require ropes, this one's only for experienced hikers. Gaze all the way to Mt Shasta from the top.

Hobart Bluff
Despite only a 413ft elevation gain, you get impressive views of Ashland and Mt McLoughlin on this 2.5-mile hike.

WATER-SPORT OUTFITTERS ON THE ROGUE

Momentum River Expeditions	**ROW Adventures**	**Rogue River Outfitters**
Stand-up paddleboarding is beginner-friendly but also uniquely challenging. It also offers rafting and fishing trips.	Hike the 40 miles of the Rogue River Trail with ROW. Ten to 15 miles each day takes you from lodge to lodge.	This second-generation outfitter offers rafting and fishing trips. Rogue drift fishing trips run September through November.

CULTURA RM EXCLUSIVE/JARED CRUCE/GETTY IMAGES ©

Applegate Valley (p277)

THE GHOSTS OF WOLF CREEK

A sharp exit off I-5 curves down into the green folds of the Rogue Valley where one white structure stands out in what feels like a mostly deserted town. **Wolf Creek Inn** first welcomed guests in 1883, most of whom were seeking refuge from an arduous wagon journey. Applegate Trail was established in the mid-1800s as a safer alternative to crossing the Columbia River on the final leg of the Oregon Trail, but it was still treacherous travel.

Rooms originally cost 75¢ a night. Today the doors and floorboards creak with that history, and the inn is said to be haunted with those early guests – but the rooms are comfortable and the service is friendly.

in the cold river. Bring the dog and the kids, too. While Oregon is best known for its pinot noir, tempranillo is perfectly suited to the Southern Oregon climate.

The *New York Times* called this region 'a quiet place to experiment,' and much of that experimentation has involved stewardship of the land on which the grapes grow. **Troon** winery, under its current ownership since 2016, has made a name for itself with biodynamic and regenerative farming that focuses on soil health and building up a self-regulating ecosystem in which different plants support each other, eliminating the need for fertilizers and herbicides. Troon is also considering climate change in its long-term plans for a healthy vineyard, planting grapes that will do well even as temperatures continue to increase.

You can start your tour of Applegate Valley wine in historic **Jacksonville** with its well-preserved, gold-rush-era downtown. Jacksonville was established around the same time as the first grapes were planted in the area, and is now home to nine wineries within a mile of the main drag.

Crater Lake National Park

When Mt St Helen's erupted, a column of super-heated ash and rock shot 8000ft into the sky. Now multiply that power by 40. That's how Mt Mazama's eruption, 7700 years ago, formed Crater Lake and shaped the surrounding landscape, with the most cataclysmic Cascadian eruption in one million years. The collapsed caldera of Mt Mazama filled with glacial melt and rainwater to form the deepest, bluest lake in the United States. Crater Lake National Park was established in 1902 – the only national park in Oregon – and it continues to be a place of extremes with snow piling up to 16ft through winter months. These mind-bending superlatives are wondrous to behold, whether you visit to view the cobalt expanse from paved paths at the rim, or venture deeper for hikes, camping, or even a swim at the surface of water that continues down 2000ft.

GETTING AROUND

Rim Dr stretches 33 miles around the lake, providing car access to a variety of vistas and trailheads. During the winter, which typically stretches from November to June, the drive is closed to cars and it's possible to cross-country ski the lake's perimeter.

In the summer, there is no hiking trail that goes all the way around, but there are over 100 miles of trails, branching out from the rim. In the summer, visitors can also hop a trolley for a five- to seven-stop tour of the rim with a knowledgeable ranger who shares history and fun facts about this park.

☑ TOP TIP

Rim Dr is getting some upgrades. The five-year construction project kicked off in 2023. Most of the road will remain drivable, but check for closed sections before you depart.

WOLLERTZ/SHUTTERSTOCK ©

Crater Lake

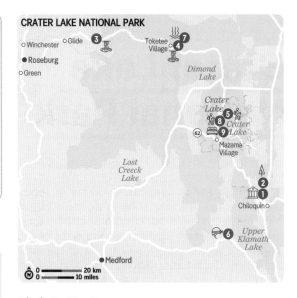

CRATER LAKE NATIONAL PARK

CRATER CAMPING

As with everything at Crater Lake, camping is dictated by two things: snow and crowds. **Mazama Campground**, currently the only campground in the park, typically opens in late June. Sites are first-come, first-served in June. July through September you'll need a reservation, and they're claimed quickly when reservations open through Crater Lake Hospitality. Come prepared for cold nighttime temps through the summer.

Backcountry camping is another option, for the more adventurous. Campsites can be found along the Pacific Crest Trail. These spots require a backcountry permit, which can be obtained at a ranger's station.

Dip into the Deep

A steep hike to swim

Gazing at the deep blue of Crater Lake from one of many viewpoints along its rim, it's natural to ask yourself: can I get closer? The answer is yes, but only at one location. **Cleetwood Cove Trail** on East Rim Dr is the only trail that brings visitors down to the water. Steep switchbacks about 1 mile each way lead to a rocky lakeshore where you can jump into the lake – an experience that reveals the incredible clarity of the water. The end of Cleetwood Cove Trail is also the departure point for boat tours to **Wizard Island**.

A Hard-Won Beverage

Order drinks with a view

The idea to build a lodge on the edge of a caldera in the first decade of the 20th century – surrounded by deep wilderness, only accessible by unpaved roads – was a lofty one (not to mention the structure would need to withstand long, harsh winters). When the first iteration of the **Crater Lake Lodge** was completed in 1915, the difficulty of construction was reflected in the lodge's meager, rustic amenities. Eventually, the shoddy structure was deemed unsafe and the lodge was closed to visitors from 1989 to 1995 while extensive reconstruction took place. Today the lodge is a mix of cozy and rustic, with a stately exterior and some preserved remnants of its past. Rooms must be reserved weeks (sometimes months) in advance; they offer basic comfort and thrilling access to the edge of the lake. But even better than sleeping here might be the simple joy of grabbing a beverage at the lodge bar and sitting on the patio to gaze out at the stunning cobalt.

Beyond Crater Lake

Scenic byways, the Pacific Flyway and lava flows meander through a variety of ecosystems. Birders: bring binoculars!

Tens and hundreds of thousands of years ago, volcanoes shaped this landscape. Today the volcanoes are quiet, but fire has a dramatic impact. Wildfires have devastated Oregon communities in recent years, as climate change makes them more frequent and intense. You'll notice swaths of blackened trees while driving in most directions. But you'll also witness the resiliency of living things that call this region home, like the fuchsia fireweed that blossoms in burn zones, midsummer.

Despite the fire risk, outdoor activities like hiking and fishing are the main attraction.

GETTING AROUND

Crater Lake is surrounded by national forests and has very limited cell-phone coverage. To navigate between destinations, it's helpful to carry an old-fashioned road atlas or plenty of detailed maps. Not only will this help you find your way to your campground or trailhead; it will provide a helpful overview of all there is to see as so many of the sights are geographic landmarks, like Diamond Lake's busy beaches and Mt Thielsen with its lightening-bolt peak.

Ranger stations are also helpful in deciding where to go next (and which way).

☑ TOP TIP

You'll find long stretches of road without facilities in this part of Oregon. Fill the gas tank and stock up on snacks when you have the chance.

Geese, Klamath Falls (p282)

WOLLERTZ/SHUTTERSTOCK ©

Kayaking, Spring Creek

THE BIRDS OF KLAMATH FALLS

About 30 miles south of your Spring Creek paddle, you'll find the landscape flattens into wide-open fields with mountains suddenly more distinct in the distance. **Klamath Basin** is home to woodlands, grasslands, and wetlands and an incredible variety of bird species. In the winter, the basin welcomes the largest concentration of bald eagles in the lower 48. **Link Trail** in sunny Klamath Falls is a favorite place to walk and listen for the Barrow's goldeneye and hooded merganser in the wintertime and hundreds of migrating species in the spring. **Running Y Resort** hosts a crowd of birders each winter for the **Winter Wings Festival**, the longest running birding festival in the nation.

Clear Boats on Clear Water

A relaxing, stunning paddle

Spring Creek, accessed by Spring Creek Day Use Area in **Collier Memorial Park**, looks great for swimming. It's not (unless you enjoy being very, very cold). The water is about 40°F (4.4°C) year-round. A kayak is a great way to experience this unique body of water. A clear kayak is even better – and you can rent them through **Crater Lake ZipLine**, just 30 miles south of Crater Lake National Park.

Paddling a clear kayak up Spring Creek, you'll see clear water turn azure and aquamarine. If it weren't for all the ever-

WHERE TO STAY IN KLAMATH FALLS

Cimarron Inn
Basic motel lodging with an outdoor pool and a Starbucks next door. **$**

Running Y Resort
This golf and spa resort has a beautiful indoor pool and a cozy communal fire pit on the patio. **$$**

Crater Lake Resort
Between Crater Lake and Klamath Falls, Crater Lake Resort features cabins, and tent sites with a games area. **$$**

greens, you might think you were in the tropics. It's about 2 miles from launch to headwaters, where you'll want to look for movement in the bottom of the creek: the ground bubbles with water coming up from the earth. You might also spot mare eggs, a rare type of freshwater algae, found here and few other places on earth. The **Collier Logging Museum** is just down the road from the boat launch, so bring dry clothes and stop by before or after a historic tour of logging in the area.

On the Rogue-Umpqua Scenic Byway
So many waterfalls

Fill the tank in **Roseburg** before heading east on Hwy 138 where the landscape quickly morphs from small city to boundless forest on either side of the winding **North Umpqua River**. The second half of the Rogue-Umpqua Scenic Byway heads south, past Crater Lake, to follow the Rogue River. You can do the first 86-mile segment from Roseburg to Crater Lake, in just a few hours, or spend a whole day hitting every waterfall hike and riverside picnic spot off Hwy 138.

The Susan Creek Trailhead to **Susan Creek Falls** is a good place to start; it offers informational placards to get you acquainted with the local flora, including vines, maples, Pacific dogwoods and grand firs. The trail is an easy 1.5 miles return and there's a picnic table at the falls where you might enjoy a snack or stick your feet in the water.

Fall Creek Falls, a little further down Hwy 138, is a sparkling cascade over a rock wall into a shallow pool that's great for swimming on hot days. **Toketee Falls** is a very popular stop where the parking lot is often full. But people move in and out quickly as the trail is only 0.8 miles long. Keep driving past Toketee Falls on NF 34 where signs will guide you to **Umpqua Hot Springs**, an iconic Oregon spot to soak where cascading pools invite you to soak and relax in the mossy forest. Unfortunately, it's also well known for being overused and attracting litterbugs. Hopefully, the people before you will leave it better than they found it, and you can do the same.

STEAMBOAT INN

Cozy up to the North Umpqua River at Steamboat Inn, a charming motel that feels part summer camp, part bed and breakfast. Guests can stay in a variety of modern cabins, cottages and suites.

Enjoy your morning coffee or a meal outside and watch rafters riding the rapids – their 'yips' and 'hoots' breaking through the otherwise serene river sounds. The library lounge is a rainy-day dream, stocked with books, games, and a bar serving local wine, beer and cocktails.

Eastern Oregon

RUGGED COUNTRY AND FRONTIER TOWNS

Eastern Oregon's stunning landscapes range from deserts to snowcapped peaks, with rushing rivers and alpine lakes in between.

Eastern Oregon is vast and ecologically diverse. You could spend weeks crisscrossing its mountain ranges, deserts and rolling hills, always finding new places to explore. And exploration is what this region is all about – the long drives across unfamiliar territory, the multiday treks deep into the Eagle Cap wilderness, and the small towns that dot lonely highways.

Archaeological evidence of human habitation in Eastern Oregon dates back some 18,000 years, the end of the Pleistocene era. The Confederated Tribes of the Umatilla (pronounced you-matila) and the Burns Paiute tribes carry on the traditions of their ancestors in the region. The arrival of white settlers in covered wagons brought slow change to the area, then gold was discovered and railways were built, speeding up development. In the early 1900s, Eastern Oregon cities were on the move with places like Pendleton and Baker becoming major centers of business.

Logging and mining once held up Eastern Oregon's economy but in recent years tourism has taken over as a major employer, especially along Hwy 84. Travelers come to hike in glacier-carved valleys, take rural train rides and shop for locally made products like wool blankets and leather goods. Beyond the main arteries connecting Oregon and Idaho in the region's northeast corner, small towns still carry on rural traditions. While they don't see a lot of traffic, visitors who make it there are sure to receive a warm welcome.

CATHERINE MOOERS/SHUTTERSTOCK ©

THE MAIN AREAS

PENDLETON
Western garb
and famed rodeo.
p288

BAKER CITY
Cool vibes and
nearby nature.
p291

JORDAN SIEMENS/GETTY IMAGES ©

Left: Rodeo horses; Above: Eagle Cap Wilderness (p297)

Find Your Way

Eastern Oregon covers a massive area, around 360 miles from top to bottom and 200 miles across. The northeast is well connected to Portland via I-84. Other areas require long drives on twisting, windy roads.

CAR & MOTORCYCLE
Traveling independently by car or motorcycle is the best way to explore the region and gets you to some hard-to-reach areas not serviced by public transportation.

BUS
Greyhound buses depart Portland daily to Pendleton and Baker City. Community Connections of Northeast Oregon (ccno.org) has routes around the region once you arrive.

Pendleton, p288
Eastern Oregon's biggest city is known for its rodeo, wool products and cowboy culture. Explore and learn its quirky history.

Baker City, p291
A hub for history and culture, this former boomtown has lots to explore with the bonus of gorgeous nature on its doorstep.

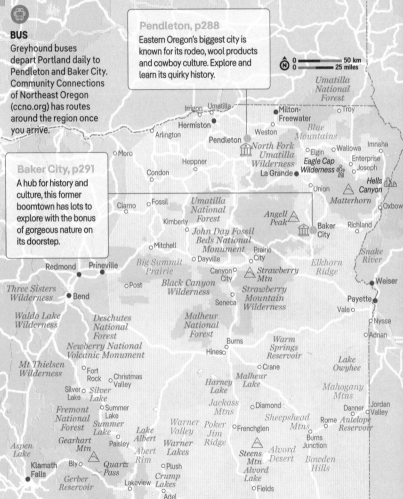

VICTORIA DITKOVSKY/SHUTTERSTOCK ©

Baker Heritage Museum (p291), Baker City

Plan Your Time

Plan for as much time as possible and go slow in this remote slice of the Pacific Northwest. Some of the side trips off I-84 could last weeks.

For a Weekend

Head to **Pendleton** (p288) for the underground tour and to shop for wool products. Continue along I-84 and stop in **La Grande** (p295) and **Baker City** (p291) to hike and explore these bustling towns. **Anthony Lakes** (p294) and the **Elkhorn Mountains** (p294) can be visited on a short trip. Loop back toward Central Oregon, making a stop at **John Day** (p297).

If You Have a Week

With one week you can follow the weekend route but extend your journey to the charming, artsy town of **Joseph** (p296) and the nearby **Hells Canyon** (p299). You could easily spend three days in this quiet corner of Oregon. If you are able to swing a long detour back west, remote **Steens Mountain** (p298) and the **Alvord Desert** (p298) beckon the adventurous traveler.

Seasonal Highlights

SPRING	SUMMER	FALL	WINTER
Visit **Hells Canyon** before it gets too busy. Wildflower blooms make for dramatic scenery.	Long days and warm evenings make this a great time to explore the outdoors and swim in lakes and rivers.	Enjoy sights and trails without peak-season pricing. A good time to visit desert areas and avoid the heat.	Awesome landscapes with snowcapped peaks and frosty towns. Skiing is possible near **La Grande**.

Pendleton

Pendleton is a city that embraces its cowboy history and rough-and-ready lifestyle. It grew up near the Umatilla Indian Reservation and by 1900 was Oregon's fourth-biggest city, known as a center for wool production and a hub for the railways. The handsome downtown area retains plenty of historic brick buildings from Pendleton's early days. Some have been renovated into hotels, bars and cafes. The Pendleton Round-Up is a big deal, luring rodeo fans for more than a century. And its wool production hasn't slowed either – Pendleton's famed blankets and Western garb are known nationwide. It works well as a place to stop and rest on a long journey but is well worth a few days to get under the skin of its cow-poking past.

Explore Downtown Pendleton

Above- and below-ground adventures in the historic district

Pendleton has a handsome main street that from certain angles looks like a stage for a Hollywood film depicting a bygone era. To experience the town's beautiful brick architecture at its best, visit the 1908 **old City Hall** at 34 SE Dorion Ave. For a meal and historic ambience, don't miss the **Rainbow Cafe** (209 Main St), which was established in 1883 and claims to be the oldest tavern in the state (another bar in Paisley makes a similar claim).

For an off-beat experience in Pendleton, head underground. **Pendleton Underground Tours** (daily except Sunday and Tuesday, reservations required) runs a two-hour tour of the city's basements, offering up colorful stories of bootleg whiskey bars and opium dens used during Prohibition. Some of the rooms have been reconfigured in recent years to create a maze of tunnels for dramatic effect (stories of Chinese laborers building the tunnels for illicit activities should be taken with a grain of salt).

GETTING AROUND

Most of the places of interest in Pendleton are easily reached on foot or a short drive. The handy Let'er bus transit system has two routes around the city.

☑ TOP TIP

Plan well in advance if you want to visit during the Pendleton Round-Up (the second week of September). Tickets for the rodeo and hotel rooms in the city both sell out fast. If you haven't booked a room, consider making a day trip from nearby Hermiston.

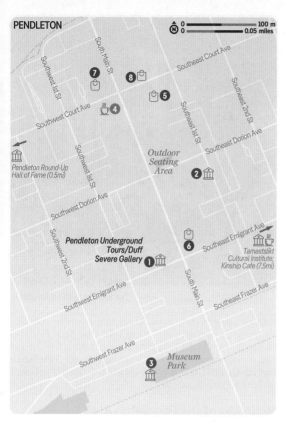

PENDLETON

N 0 ———————— 100 m
   0 ———————— 0.05 miles

*Pendleton Round-Up
Hall of Fame (0.5mi)*

*Outdoor
Seating
Area*

*Pendleton Underground
Tours/Duff
Severe Gallery* ❶

*Tamastslikt
Cultural Institute;
Kinship Cafe (7.5mi)*

*Museum
Park*

South Main St
Southwest 1st St
Southwest Court Ave
Southeast Court Ave
Southwest 1st St
Southeast 1st St
Southeast 2nd St
Southeast Dorion Ave
Southwest Dorion Ave
Southwest 2nd St
Southwest Emigrant Ave
Southeast Emigrant Ave
South Main St
Southeast Frazer Ave
Southwest Frazer Ave

HIGHLIGHTS
❶ Pendleton
Underground Tours/Duff
Severe Gallery

SIGHTS
❷ Old City Hall
❸ Umatilla County
History Museum

DRINKING & NIGHTLIFE
❹ Rainbow Cafe

SHOPPING
❺ Hamley Western
Store & Saddle Shop
❻ New York Clothier
❼ Pendleton Hat
Company
❽ Stapleman's Custom
Boot Shop

WOOLEN MILLS

**Pendleton Woolen
Mills** is famed for its
production of blankets
and wool clothing. It's
also one of the oldest
textile companies in
the Pacific Northwest.
The business was
started by one Thomas
Kay, an immigrant
from England, who
reopened the defunct
Pendleton Woolen Mill
in 1909. Kay and his
family started making
blankets and shawls
for Native Americans
living in the area. They
later expanded their
product line to include
men's and women's
apparel. Quality is high
with prices to match.

Today it's one of
four woolen mills still
operating in the US.
Book tours through
the website.

The tour office is also home to the **Duff Severe Gallery** featuring beautiful saddles and leather art. Lots of other shops downtown sell Western garb if want to leave town with a new belt buckle, pair of boots or Stetson hat.

Pendleton Round-Up

The biggest rodeo in the Pacific Northwest

The Pendleton Round-Up (second full week in September) is an Oregon classic that dates back to 1910. It draws around 80,000 visitors from around the world to enjoy bull riding, steer wrestling, Indian relay racing and other rodeo events. Native Americans are intimately involved in the event. In addition to the rodeo, you can expect a cowboy breakfast,

 BEST PLACES TO STAY IN PENDLETON

Working Girls Old Hotel
This former bordello has been converted into a historic hotel. Most rooms have a shared bath. **$**

Pendleton House Historic Inn
A pink 1917 mansion built in the Italian Renaissance style with beautiful vintage decor. **$$**

**Emigrant Springs
Campground**
Large campground 26 miles from Pendleton. Shady tent sites and clean bathrooms. **$**

PLACES TO BUY LOCAL

Pat Beard, rodeo contestant and Convention Center Manager in Pendleton, gives his advice on shopping for Western clothing in the city.

Bespoke culture thrives in Pendleton. Since the 1800s local residents have been making hats, boots, clothing, jewelry and accessories.

Hamley Western Store & Saddle Shop
Opened in 1905, they started as saddlemakers but evolved into high-end men's dress belts and accessories. They became the largest belt maker in the US.

Pendleton Hat Company
A custom hatter. They measure your head and can build you any kind of felt hat you can dream of.

Stapleman's Custom Boot Shop
Richard Stapleman is one of the finest bootmakers in the country – every boot is made to measure and you pick out the leather and design.

New York Clothier
A high-end classic shirtmaker, for made-to-fit collared shirts and jackets.

Tamastslikt Cultural Institute

outdoor concerts and an opening parade. Pendleton Whiskey also flows freely so expect a rowdy time after dark. Plan your stay well in advance to get a hotel room and stadium tickets.

At other times of the year you can visit the **Pendleton Round-Up Hall of Fame**, jam-packed with photos and memorabilia of past round-ups.

Museums of the Pendleton Area

Pioneer history and Indigenous culture

Get to know Pendleton's colorful past at the **Umatilla County History Museum**, located at the city's 1909 train depot. Look for the old schoolhouse and caboose. The museum prides itself on its exhibit of wheat and its importance in the local economy.

For a complete understanding of this region's history, a visit to the **Tamastslikt Cultural Institute** is essential. This beautifully constructed museum provides an honest history of the Indigenous peoples in the area through artifacts and learning resources. Items on display include incredible beadwork art, traditional headdresses and exhibits that show daily life of the Cayuse, Umatilla and Walla Walla tribes before and after contact with Europeans. It's an immersive experience with sights matched with sounds that cover more than 10,000 years of history.

Another reason to visit is the opportunity to sample Native American dishes at the on-site **Kinship Cafe**. The menu changes regularly but you may be able to try Indian tacos, huckleberry pie and salmon corn chowder. The museum is located on the Umatilla Indian Reservation, 8 miles east of downtown Pendleton.

Baker City

Wedged between the Wallowas and the Elkhorns, Baker City occupies a front-row seat to some of Eastern Oregon's most spectacular scenery.

The town itself reflects this natural beauty with rows of handsome structures, some dating back to the late 1800s. It was gold that helped bring wealth to the area, making Baker City the largest urban center between Salt Lake City and Portland. For a while, it was known as the Queen City of the Inland Empire and today there are more than 100 buildings on the National Register of Historic Places.

The gold is long gone but Baker City is undergoing a revitalization effort. Older buildings have been spruced up and new shops, restaurants and drinking establishments line the main drag. A couple of excellent museums explain the area's history and outdoor recreation is just a short drive away.

Relive History in Baker City

Gold rush and pioneer history

As you wander down Baker City's main street there are echoes of past wealth, from the 1889 Geiser Grand Hotel (once the finest between Portland and Salt Lake City) to the nine-story Baker Tower built in 1929 in the art deco style. The boom times are long gone but a handful of museums can help recreate the past for you.

Start at the **Baker Heritage Museum** located a few blocks from downtown in a 1920 natatorium (indoor swimming pool). It covers the area's frontier past and has one of the country's largest gem and mineral exhibits. Don't miss the famed Armstrong Nugget, an 80oz hunk of solid gold found in the area in 1913. The prospectors who found it kept the fist-size nugget in a local bank. After their deaths the bank took ownership and put it on display until it was moved to the museum in 2023.

Another museum, the **National Historic Oregon Trail Interpretive Center**, was closed for renovations when we passed. When it reopens you can expect to see exhibits showing

GETTING AROUND

Pendleton, La Grande and Baker City all sit on the I-84 corridor, which is covered by Greyhound buses from Portland. Pendleton's Kayak Public Transportation Company has three buses a day to La Grande. Union County (La Grande) has daily service to Baker City.

The public bus between La Grande and Joseph runs Monday, Tuesday and Thursday. Schedules change so check ccno. org/publictransit for updated information. Having a car is the most reliable way to get around.

☑ **TOP TIP**

Baker County comes alive in summer with festivals and events. One of the best to experience is the Miners' Jubilee, a three-day celebration held during the third weekend of July. In summer the city's farmers market appears every Thursday evening.

FOOD & DRINK OPTIONS IN BAKER CITY

Dan Sizer, guide and owner of Go Wild: American Adventures (@gowildusa), shares his favorite places to fuel up post-hike in NE Oregon.

A hike in Oregon's largest wilderness is not complete without a stop at one of our local eateries. For breakfast and caffeine, I take our guests to the **Liberty Theater Cafe** in La Grande. Pro-tip, go for a breakfast sammy.

Lunch usually finds me at the **Cheese Fairy** in downtown Baker City where owner Cody serves up charcuterie boards of imported meats and cheeses that pair perfectly with local Copperbelt Wines, owned by her brother and located in the same building.

For a post-hike beer, you can't go wrong with **Barley Brown's Brew Pub** in Baker City or **Side-A Brewing** in La Grande. Cheers!

BAKER CITY

Baker County Fairgrounds

National Historic Oregon Trail Interpretive Center (8mi)

Geiser Pollman Park

Central Park

Powder River

0   200 m
0   0.1 miles

SIGHTS	ACTIVITIES, COURSES & TOURS	DRINKING & NIGHTLIFE
① Baker Heritage Museum	**③** Go Wild	**⑤** Barley Brown's Brew Pub
② Leo Adler House Museum	**EATING**	
	④ Cheese Fairy	

life on the Oregon Trail some 200 years ago. More history is available on the 2.5-mile Oregon Trail Interpretive Center Loop, behind the Interpretive Center, which meanders past ruts created by passing wagons in the 1800s.

You can see some of the town's gold-rush-era opulence on display at the **Leo Alder House Museum**, an 1889 Italianate estate that was home to Leo Alder, a local philanthropist. Call ahead to reserve a tour. **Go Wild**, a local tour operator, takes visitors on an enthusiastic walking tour of downtown.

 BEST PLACES TO STAY IN BAKER CITY

Beaten Path B&B
Historic 1888 home converted to a B&B. Large bathrooms, excellent food and terrific hosts. $

Union Creek Campground
This quiet campground 18 miles southeast of Baker City is well kept and has clean, grassy tent sites. $

Geiser Grand Hotel
The best lodging in Baker City is this historic Italian Renaissance hotel right downtown. $$

Beyond Baker City

The fertile valleys between Baker City and La Grande rise to great heights in the Wallowa and Blue Mountains.

Oregon's northeast corner contains some of the state's most diverse scenery. The mountains, lakes and canyons are gorgeous but their distance from major urban areas is great enough to keep the crowds away. I-84 cuts through the region while smaller roads east of here encircle the Wallowas and wriggle toward Hells Canyon. Joseph is an isolated but beautiful town with surprising amenities. The region contains the Eagle Cap Wilderness, one of Oregon's most beautiful hiking areas. Travelers wanting a less-strenuous mode of travel can embark on a train trip through this rugged territory. Towns in the region are well equipped to fortify the weary traveler with good food and creature comforts.

GETTING AROUND

The corner of Oregon beyond Baker City is best explored by car to reach the lakes, mountains and small communities. Flixbus travels daily to Pendleton, La Grande and Baker City from Portland. Community Connections of Northeast Oregon has a bus to Joseph from Baker City.

☑ TOP TIP

A fun, multiday driving trip in the area circles the Wallowa Mountains, with Joseph as the halfway point.

Eagle Cap Wilderness (p297)

TRAIN WITH A VIEW

From the little town of Elgin, travelers can climb aboard the **Eagle Cap Excursion Train** for a scenic ride along the Joseph branch line built in 1884. In the early 1900s the train was mainly used to haul lumber to sawmills. The Joseph branch was abandoned in 1997 following the closure of the mill. Local governments purchased the line with plans to develop an excursion train and have been doing so since 2003.

The journey follows the pretty Grande Ronde River, most of which is along roadless terrain. Wildlife is sometimes spotted, including bald eagles. The train runs a couple of days a week and you'll need to book in advance through the website: eaglecaptrainrides.com.

Anthony Lakes

Elkhorn Mountains

TIME FROM BAKER CITY: **45 MINS**

Family-friendly hikes and camping

The Elkhorn Mountains sometimes get overlooked because most travelers to Eastern Oregon head for the more famous Wallowas. But those who do visit will experience some spectacular high-altitude scenery with craggy mountaintops and alpine lakes.

The area is also relatively accessible, being just 30 miles northwest of Baker City. Hiking, fishing, camping and wildlife spotting are a few of the activities here. Trails are well maintained and well marked.

Most visitors start by driving to **Anthony Lakes**. From the lakes, there is a beautiful 2.3-mile loop hike (steep in parts) to **Hoffer Lakes**. The Elkhorn Crest Trail to **Black Lake** (2.2 miles, out and back) is a moderate hike and there is a good campsite here for backpackers. You'll probably see more mountain goats than you'll see other hikers. The gentle hikes here are very good for families.

WHERE TO STAY IN LA GRANDE

Historic Union Hotel
Located 15 miles southeast of La Grande in the town of Union, this historic hotel has 15 themed rooms. $

Landing Hotel
This boutique hotel on La Grande's main street has loads of charm and excellent food. $$

Lodge at Hot Lake Springs
This historic hotel, 8 miles southeast of La Grande, has hot pools and rustic rooms. $$

For those who arrive in winter, the Elkhorns are home to **Anthony Lakes Mountain Resort**, a ski area with the highest base (7100ft) of any resort in Oregon. The resort has excellent downhill and cross-country skiing. Mountain biking is available in summer.

The **Anthony Lake Campground** is a great place to pitch a tent for those equipped with camping gear.

Trails Around La Grande

TIME FROM BAKER CITY: **45 MINS**

Hiking and biking local trails

La Grande, a mid-sized city halfway between Baker City and Pendleton, prides itself on its outdoor attractions and thrilling bike trails. Get yourself two wheels and drop into some of Eastern Oregon's best bike terrain.

The most well-known biking area is **Mt Emily Recreation Area** (MERA), a short ride north of town. The MERA trails are also used by hikers and equestrians. For bike rental, try **The Mountain Works** or **Eastern Wheelworks**, both in La Grande. The well-maintained network of forest trails offers a glimpse of the nearby Grande Ronde Valley, once home to multiple Native American tribes and settled by European farmers in the 1860s.

If you need to rest after a long ride there is no better place than the **Lodge at Hot Lake Springs**, a historic hotel that has outdoor hot pools with mineral water piped in for soaking.

Pushing West

Experience pioneer history near La Grande

For pioneers crossing the country in the 1800s, the Grande Ronde Valley was an important landmark, heralding the final push west. You can get a taste of the hardships and loneliness of their journey with a stop at the **Oregon Trail Interpretive Park**, 15 miles west of La Grande, just off I-84. It's a peaceful place with a few covered wagons and interpretive signs that show in pictures and words what life was like for pioneers crossing the wilderness in search of opportunities.

To get an idea of what life was like for those who settled in the region, stop by the **Union County Museum** in the small town of Union, 14 miles southeast of La Grande. The museum offers a quirky collection of well-preserved pioneer artifacts in a handsome brick building.

For those with kids in tow looking for an activity they will enjoy, visit La Grande's **Eastern Oregon Fire Museum**, which houses no less than six antique fire trucks.

BEST PLACES TO EAT IN & AROUND JOSEPH

Blythe Cricket
A good place to start your day with gluten-free and vegan meals served in a quirky, colorful space. Great for sandwiches and teas. **$**

Dog Spot
For lunch or dinner, don't miss this usual concept cafe. Serves healthy and beautifully plated food with Asian and Latin influences. The accompanying shop sells pet supplies. **$**

Terminal Gravity Brewing
When it comes to beer and pub grub, nothing beats this legendary craft beer maker in Enterprise. The menu has some surprises like coconut curry and steak pitas. **$**

Lostine Tavern
Barbecue lovers should look out for this tavern in the hamlet of Lostine. It contains Z's BBQ, a superb Texas-style menu of smoked meats. **$**

 BEST PLACES TO STAY IN JOSEPH

Barking Mad Farm B&B
Modern home located on a 42-acre farm around 8 miles northwest of Joseph. **$$**

Bronze Antler B&B
This charming inn has excellent rooms with Jacuzzi-style bathtubs and tasteful pieces of art. **$$**

Indian Lodge Motel
Built in the 1950s by the actor Walter Brennan, this motel has a convenient downtown location. **$**

WALLOWA LAKE TRAMWAY

If you want awesome views of the Wallowas without an arduous hike, don't miss the Wallowa Lake Tramway. This aerial gondola, built in 1970, whisks visitors to the top of 8150ft **Mt Howard** in 15 minutes – it's the steepest gondola in the US. Once at the top there are gentle trails to viewpoints, making this a great family outing. The views of Wallowa Lake and the Eagle Cap Wilderness are unparalleled and on clear days you can make out the Seven Devils Mountains in Idaho. You can refuel at the **Summit Grill** restaurant (but bring snacks and water too).

A tramway ticket is not cheap ($45 per adult) but for a one-off splurge, the incredible scenery is worth the price.

Joseph's Art Scene

TIME FROM BAKER CITY: 2¼ HRS

Art at the end of Oregon

Tucked behind the immense Wallowa Mountains on one side and the steep-sided Hells Canyon on the other, the Wallowa Valley may seem completely off the map. But despite its remoteness, the towns of Joseph and Enterprise are growing, with newcomers drawn by the incredible nature and art-loving community.

A good place to start a tour of the area's artistic side is the **Josephy Center for Arts and Culture**, which features beautiful works made by Wallowa County artists. You can also make your own art here; the center has classes for various mediums.

If you have been impressed with all the bronze statues in town, visit **Valley Bronze**, a foundry with a small shop and tours. Closer to the town center, stop by the **Maxvill Heritage Interpretive Center**, which preserves the history of Oregon's Black loggers and the challenges they faced, including segregation.

Native American History in Joseph

Walking the steps of the Nez Percé tribes

Joseph is one of the best places in Oregon to learn about Native American history and visit sites sacred to tribes. Start your tour at the Josephy Center for Arts and Culture, which has extensive resources on the Indigenous people who inhabited the area for thousands of years before European settlement. The center is dedicated to building relationships with Nez Percé artists and elders, and offers them space to share their tribal art.

Visitors are also welcome to stop by the **Old Chief Joseph Gravesite**, a sacred site dedicated to the Nez Percé leader who refused to sell the Wallowa lands. It's located 1.5 miles south of town. He is remembered during the annual **Chief Joseph Days Rodeo**, a four-day festival held in late July, featuring rodeo events, a parade and a stampede of horses down Joseph's main street. The area's history, including the culture of the Nez Percé, is also told at the **Wallowa County Museum** on Main St.

Kayaking Wallowa Lake

TIME FROM BAKER CITY: 2¼ HRS

Paddle on a natural wonder

Just beyond the town of Joseph lies Wallowa Lake, a stunningly blue body of water formed by Pleistocene glaciers and con-

WHERE TO STAY NEAR WALLOWA LAKE

Wallowa State Park Campground
Lakeside campground with plenty of trees and grass for pitching a tent, plus yurts. $

Wallowa Lake Lodge
A historic 1923 lodge with a rustic feel and pretty grounds where deer like to linger. $$

Flying Arrow Resort
Welcoming resort with cozy cabins. Some have decks overlooking the Wallowa River. $$

Joseph

tained by high moraines. For millennia, the shores of the lake were inhabited by the Wallowa band of the Nez Percé tribe.

Most of the action for travelers is at the southern end of the lake, where shops and rustic lodges offer travel services and rent boats. The shore has a busy beach and quiet picnic spots along the Wallowa River, which flows into the lake. **JO Paddle** runs glass-bottom kayak trips on Wallowa Lake. The guided tours along the shore come with historical commentary. Setting off on a peaceful paddle surrounded by high peaks of the Eagle Cap Wilderness is a sublime experience, especially when done under the light of the moon.

Eagle Cap Wilderness TIME FROM BAKER CITY: 2½ HRS 🚗

Hike in Oregon's Little Switzerland

The Eagle Cap Wilderness within the Wallowa Mountains is 565 sq miles of snowcapped peaks, dense forests and crystal-clear lakes. Good day hikes from Joseph start at the Wallowa Lake Trailhead. A challenging hike from here is the

KAM WAH CHUNG STATE HERITAGE SITE

A century ago the city of **John Day** was home to a thriving Chinese community, the legacy of which has largely disappeared, except for one notable building. The **Kam Wah Chung** (Golden Flower of Prosperity) business is located inside an 1865 building in the center of town. Its owner during the early 1900s, a doctor named Ing Hay (1862–1952), distributed herbs and medicine and became renowned across the West Coast for his skills as a healer. The building where he worked was boarded up in 1948 and preserved for more than two decades until it was reopened.

This time capsule is now part of a state park. Guided tours are available daily from May to October; book ahead if possible. It's open by appointment only the rest of the year.

🛏 BEST PLACES TO STAY IN SOUTHEAST OREGON

Historic Central Hotel
A 1929 hotel in Burns that had been boarded up for years was recently renovated. **$$**

Frenchglen Hotel
Cute hotel in Frenchglen built in 1917 with lots of historic charm and simple rooms. **$$**

Hotel Prairie
Located in Prairie City, this beautifully restored 1910 hotel has nine clean rooms. **$$**

THE GUIDE

EASTERN OREGON **BEYOND BAKER CITY**

BENEDEK/GETTY IMAGES ©

Southeast Oregon contains some of the state's most beautiful wilderness and travelers will find them mostly crowd-free. John Day makes a good starting point. From here explore the alpine peaks of 1 **Strawberry Mountain Wilderness** and hike to the beautiful Strawberry Lake.

Next head south on Hwy 395 to 2 **Burns** where you can fuel up before driving 32 miles to visit the 3 **Malheur National Wildlife Refuge**, an important habitat for birds traveling along the Pacific Flyway. More than 320 species are found here, including swans, loons, pelicans and herons. The visitor center has shaded areas and exhibits on the area's wildlife.

Continuing south it's 40 miles to 4 **Frenchglen** where you can turn off to the Steens Mountain Loop Rd, Oregon's highest road, reaching 9733ft. The Loop Rd is 59 miles and

takes around three to five hours to drive with stops to enjoy the mountain scenery and wildlife. From 5 **East Rim Overlook** you can see clear to Nevada, Idaho and California. Hiking trails and camping areas are found on the mountain. Keep your eyes peeled for herds of wild mustangs.

From Frenchglen, it's another 52 miles south to the hamlet of 6 **Fields**, the jumping-off point for the 7 **Alvord Desert**, a flat, dry lakebed with hot springs and miles of nothingness. At the Alvord Hot Springs Bath House & Campground the springs are cooled down and safe for dipping.

From Fields the possibilities are endless. Loop back to Burns or head northeast to the rugged but beautiful Owyhee Canyon area. Alternatively, travel west to the Hart Mountain National Antelope Refuge before reaching the city of Lakeview.

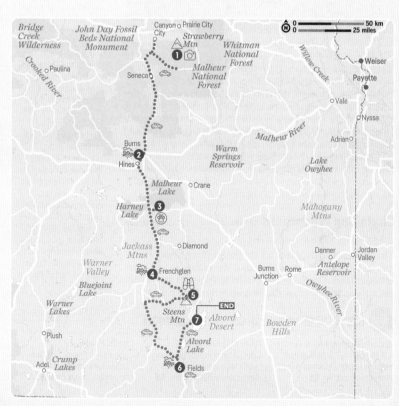

8.4-mile out-and-back **Chief Joseph Summit Trail**. The **BC Falls hike** is shorter (3 miles) and good for kids. The 15.6-mile trail to **Ice Lake** is tough but rewarding; on the way you'll get stunning views of waterfalls and the Matterhorn, the second-highest peak in the Wallowas.

Experienced hikers can summit **the Matterhorn** (elevation 9835ft) on a long day hike or overnight trip (after camping at Ice Lake). You may spot some mountain goats giving you curious looks as you hike.

Another challenging but rewarding hike starts at **Two Pan Trailhead** (accessed from the town of Lostine) and winds its way up the East Lostine River Valley for 7 miles to Mirror Lake where there are great views of **Eagle Cap** (elevation 9572ft). Summiting Eagle Cap from Two Pan Trailhead can be done in a single thigh-burning day but is best done in two.

Hells Canyon

TIME FROM BAKER CITY: **2 HRS** 🚗

Journey into America's deepest gorge

Travelers heading to the northeastern corner of Oregon are confronted with a formidable divide before they cross into Idaho. Hells Canyon, which marks the Oregon–Idaho state line, plunges 8000ft from peak to the Snake River, which winds through its bottom. This is the deepest canyon in North America, deeper than the Grand Canyon.

Stunning views of the 13-million-year-old canyon can be had from **Hells Canyon Overlook**, a 32-mile drive from the town of **Halfway**, the last place to stock up on supplies. From the overlook, you can peer deep into Idaho across the craggy landscape, portions of which are forested. Wildflowers carpet the hillsides in spring and into early summer. If the divide looks challenging to navigate today, spare a thought for the Native Americans and settlers who crossed this territory in past centuries.

From the overlook, most people continue another 45 miles to Joseph. Make sure to stop after 6 miles at the **Ollokot Campground** for a rest and picnic at the pretty Imnaha River. This is a perfect place to spend the night if you don't mind the primitive facilities.

For those wanting a more intimate experience in Hells Canyon, drive from Halfway for 17 miles to **Oxbow**, a small community in the gorge with a fish hatchery and basic services. From Oxbow it's another 23 miles along the Snake River to the **Hells Canyon Creek Visitor Center**, the end of the road. The drive to the center is dramatic and you may spot wildlife, including bighorn sheep and elk. **Hells Canyon Adventures** operates jet-boat tours along the river from the boat dock near the center, but you'll need to make reservations in advance.

GREATER IDAHO MOVEMENT

Oregon is suffering from an east–west divide. The deeply blue western half of the state means that most of its lawmakers are Democrats; a situation that is wearing on the mostly Republican areas in Eastern Oregon. In response residents in eastern areas have started a movement to break away from Oregon and join Idaho, creating a 'Greater Idaho' that would cut Oregon to about half its current size.

Proponents say Idaho would better represent conservative values. Opponents say Idaho is economically weaker than Oregon and wages would suffer. Even if there was strong local agreement, actually moving a state border is no easy task, requiring approval from both Oregon and Idaho state legislators and Congress.

AOLIN CHEN/GETTY IMAGES ©

Above: Downtown (p306); Right: Japanese food (p326)

Vancouver

GREEN CITY BY THE SEA

Stunning seascapes, majestic mountains and towering trees frame this coastal city, where you can cycle, shop, ski and swim all in one day.

Like a layered landscape painting, the skyline of Vancouver showcases a colorful foreground of sea and city, against a background of sierra and sky. The natural beauty is what draws people in, and the mild climate and friendly people are what make it hard to leave.

It's the combination of all of these qualities that lures long-term lodgers to the city, which is known as one of the world's most livable. And beyond its layered beauty is a layered cultural landscape that greatly contributes to how Vancouver has evolved, and what the city has become today.

First Nations have occupied the land since time immemorial, and Vancouver (originally called K'emk'emeláy, which means 'a place of many maple trees') was once a thriving village site before the land was taken from its original inhabitants, and turned into a city.

From the significant Indigenous sites found around scenic Stanley Park to the modern museums and galleries that showcase the stories and works of Indigenous artists, the rich history of Vancouver shines through the stories and experiences shared by those who first called the land home.

Vancouver's natural surroundings and diverse cultural offerings put the city on the world stage in 2010 when it played host to the Olympic Winter Games and Paralympic Winter Games, driving a huge boost in international tourism. Since then, Vancouver has been recognized as a top tourism destination and one of the most beautiful cities in the world.

THE MAIN AREAS

DOWNTOWN & CHINATOWN	**GRANVILLLE ISLAND & YALETOWN**	**MAIN STREET**	**FAIRVIEW & SOUTH GRANVILLE**
Gardens, galleries and green spaces. **p306**	Famed isle of the arts. **p314**	Vintage shopping and striking street art. **p320**	Stylish boutiques and casual cafes. **p324**

Find Your Way

Vancouver's core is compact, so attractions are easily accessible. It's a walkable city with paved pathways linking to most activities, and if you venture further afield, you can get anywhere by bike, bus or boat.

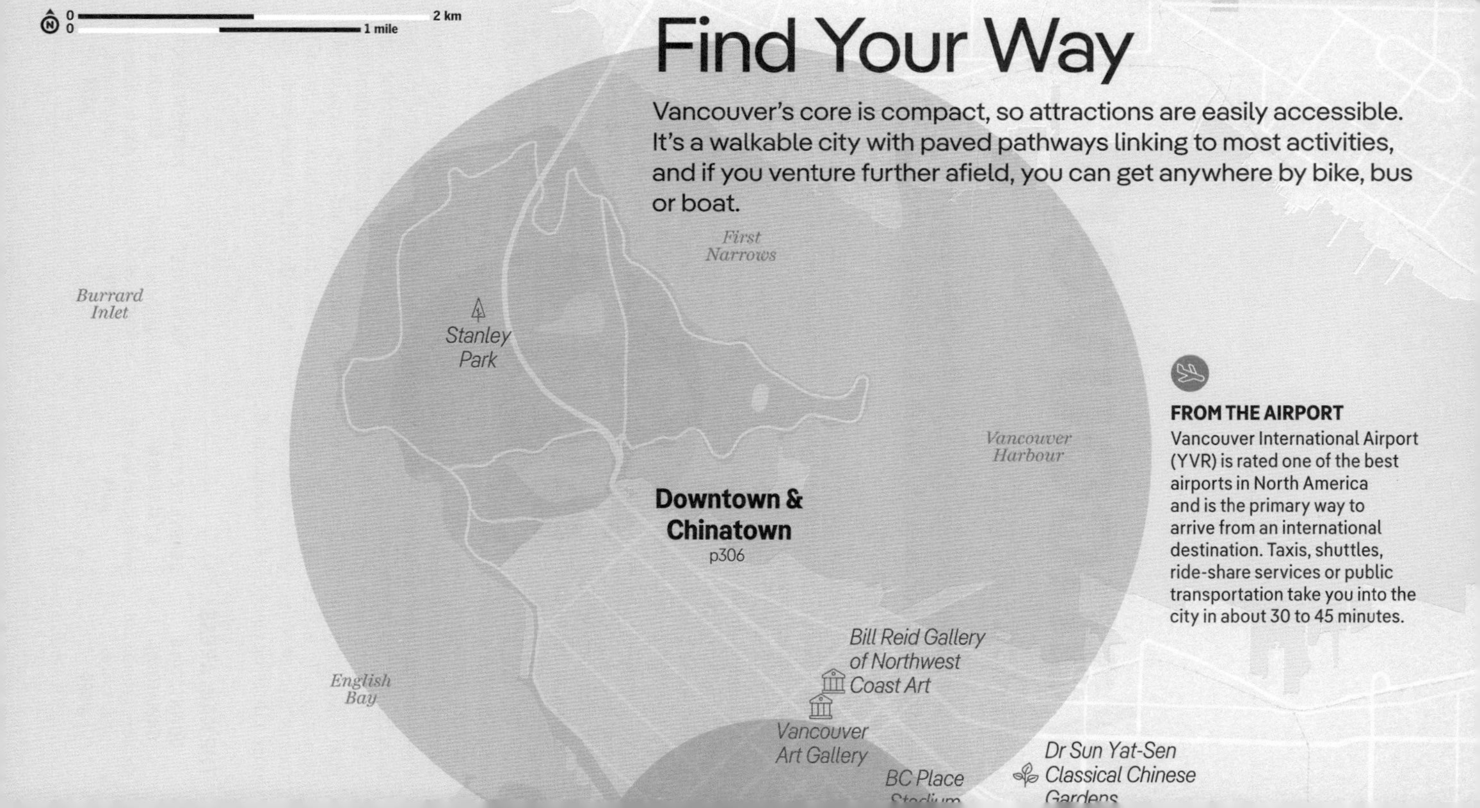

FROM THE AIRPORT

Vancouver International Airport (YVR) is rated one of the best airports in North America and is the primary way to arrive from an international destination. Taxis, shuttles, ride-share services or public transportation take you into the city in about 30 to 45 minutes.

0 1 mile

0 2 km

Burrard Inlet

English Bay

Stanley Park

First Narrows

Vancouver Harbour

Downtown & Chinatown
p306

Vancouver Art Gallery

Bill Reid Gallery of Northwest Coast Art

BC Place Stadium

Dr Sun Yat-Sen Classical Chinese Gardens

Public Market

Granville Island & Yaletown
p314

Kids Market

Stanley Theatre

Pavilion

Olympic Village

Science World

Main Street
p320

Fairview & South Granville
p324

Bloedel Conservatory

VanDusen Botanical Gardens

Richmond Night Market (6km)

BIKE

Vancouver's mild climate makes it easy to access attractions by bike, with rental shops on most streets, dedicated bike lanes, and trails weaving throughout the city. Mobi, a public bike-share system, offers an affordable way to get around.

BUS

The public-transportation system in Vancouver is a safe and an easy way to get around the city, with regular bus and SkyTrain services to get you anywhere you want to go.

BOAT

Vancouver's waterways make for easy transportation between neighborhoods like Yaletown and Granville Island, which are just across the water from each other and are accessible by Aquabus – a rainbow-colored mini ferry (you can even bring a bike!).

Plan Your Days

Not sure if you want to play outside, or peruse the city's museums and shops? With some planning, you can do it all in one day.

Stanley Park Seawall (p311)

Day 1

Morning
● Start with a morning stroll or cycle along the **Stanley Park Seawall** (p311). Keep an eye out for Siwash Rock and the *Girl in a Wetsuit* statue – seawall landmarks that you'll spot along the way.

Afternoon
● Visit the **Vancouver Aquarium** (p312), a must-visit site in the center of Stanley Park, and then head to **Totem Park** (p310) for an Indigenous-led Talking Trees tour with **Talaysay Tours** (p311).

Evening
● Finish your day with a visit to **Canada Place** (p312), where you can take a virtual flight with **FlyOver Canada** (p313), and then dine at one of the waterfront restaurants found nearby.

You'll Also Want to...

Venture beyond Vancouver's city center for a pint, a hike or just to smell the flowers and enjoy the views.

CELEBRATE SCIENCE
Get hands-on with engaging exhibits found at the family-friendly **Science World** (p322), housed in the city's famous dome.

GRAB A PINT
Check out the craft beer scene with a visit to **Brewery Creek** (p323), Vancouver's urban brewery district.

SEE A SHOW
For thespian pursuits, head to the **Stanley Theatre** (p328), Vancouver's famed art deco heritage theater.

JEFF WHYTE/SHUTTERSTOCK ©, WIRESTOCK CREATORS/SHUTTERSTOCK ©, JSMIMAGES/ALAMY STOCK PHOTO ©

MARC BRUXELLE/SHUTTERSTOCK ©

Day 2

Morning
● Begin with a browse through the **Vancouver Art Gallery** (p307), and then head to the **Bill Red Gallery of Northwest Coast Art** (p307), found just down the street.

Afternoon
● Make your way to the **Chinatown Storytelling Centre** (p313) to learn about Vancouver's Chinese Canadian roots. Then visit the **Dr Sun Yat-Sen Classical Chinese Gardens** (p307) for a tranquil walk and a complimentary cup of Chinese tea. Hungry for lunch? Pop into **Torafuku** (p313) for a 'Kickass Rice Bowl.'

Evening
● Gallivant through **Granville Island** (p314), a foodie's paradise. Then pick a patio, such as **Tap & Barrel Bridges** (p319), and settle in for dinner with sunset views.

Day 3

Morning
● Grab a coffee and meander along **Main Street** (p320), spotting massive murals along the way as part of the **Vancouver Mural Festival** (p320).

Afternoon
● Head to the **Brewery Creek** district (p323) and pop into Main Street Brewing for po'boys and pints, and then check out the vintage boutiques along the Main St corridor (p320), such as Mintage Mall and Turnabout Luxury Resale.

Evening
● Catch a SkyTrain to Richmond for an evening at the **Richmond Night Market** (p326), where you can choose from over 600 food dishes from around the world and take in a show before heading back Downtown.

CATCH A GAME

Football fans flock to **BC Place** (p318) or hit **Nat Bailey Stadium** (p329) for a summer ballgame.

ENTERTAIN THE KIDS

Granville Island's **Kids Market** (p318) is a wonderland for youngsters, with shops, snack spots, arcades and play spaces.

SMELL THE FLOWERS

The **VanDusen Botanical Gardens** (p328) are a garden-lover's paradise, and the **Bloedel Conservatory** (p328) is a must-see.

HIT THE WATER

Hop on the **Aquabus** (p317), a mini pedestrian ferry, for scenic city views from a new perspective.

Downtown/ Chinatown

GARDENS, GALLERIES AND GREEN SPACES

☑ **TOP TIP**

It's easy to go car-free here, as most parks, beaches, galleries and shops can be found within walking distance of Vancouver's Downtown core. Don't feel like going by foot? Try Mobi, the city's public bike-share system. Buses also stop frequently throughout the area.

Vancouver's Downtown core is an ocean-fringed peninsula easily divided into three parts: the grid-patterned city-center with shops, restaurants and glass towers fanning out from the intersection of Granville and west Georgia Sts; the well-maintained 1950s apartment blocks and residential side streets of the West End (home to Vancouver's gay district); and Stanley Park, Canada's finest urban green space and home to some of the city's best attractions.

As the city's oldest Downtown neighborhood, Gastown combines cobblestone streets and heritage buildings with modern galleries and trendy bars. The historic 12-block stretch is a hub for shopping and entertainment – best enjoyed on foot. Almost as old, neighboring Chinatown is one of Canada's largest, a vibrant community dotted with dim sum restaurants, traditional bakeries and food shops, and hip cocktail spots.

CLAUDINE VAN MASSENHOVE/SHUTTERSTOCK ©

Chinatown

Vancouver Art Gallery

Urban visual-arts institution

Step into Western Canada's largest public art museum, where blockbuster international shows are combined with selections from its striking contemporary collection. The Vancouver Art Gallery (or VAG to locals) is a magnet for art fans. There are often three or four different exhibitions on its public levels, but save time for the top-floor Emily Carr paintings, showcasing swirling nature-themed works from BC's favorite historic artist. If you're on a budget, consider the by-donation entry after 5pm on Tuesdays, but arrive early and expect a queue.

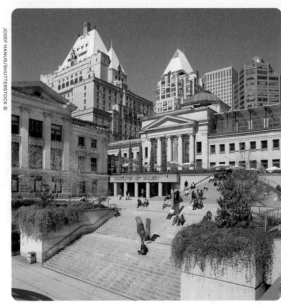

JOSEF HANUS/SHUTTERSTOCK ©

Vancouver Art Gallery

Bill Reid Gallery of Northwest Coast Art

Contemporary Indigenous art by hailed Haida artist

Opened in 2008, the Bill Reid Gallery of Northwest Coast Art is Canada's only public art gallery dedicated to the contemporary Indigenous art of the Northwest Coast. Hailed Haida artist Bill Reid (1920–98) was known for building bridges between Indigenous and settler people through his work as an artist, broadcaster and community activist. The gallery was named in his honor and showcases some of his artwork, as well as contemporary works by other Indigenous artists. Look for the full-scale totem pole carved by James Hart of Haida Gwaii, and a bronze masterpiece called *Mythic Messengers,* created by Reid himself.

Dr Sun Yat-Sen Classical Chinese Gardens

Tranquil Chinese garden in the city

Opened in time for Vancouver's Expo '86, this delightful oasis was the first Chinese 'scholars' garden' to be built outside Asia, and is one of the city's most-beloved ornamental green spaces. Wrapped with tile-topped walls and centered on a mirror-calm pond fringed by twisting trees, its covered walkways offer a tranquil respite from clamorous Chinatown.

The intimate 'garden of ease' reflects Taoist principles of balance and harmony. Entry includes an optional 45-minute guided tour, in which you'll learn about the symbolism behind the placement of the gnarled pine trees, winding covered pathways and ancient limestone formations. Look out for the colorful carp and lazy turtles in the water, and conclude your visit with a complimentary cup of traditional tea.

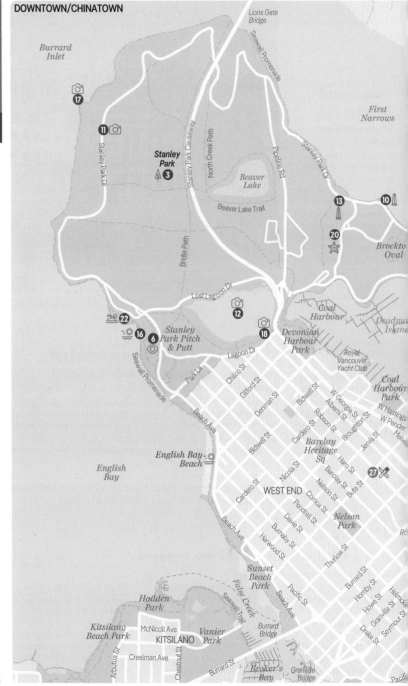

HIGHLIGHTS
1. Bill Reid Gallery of Northwest Coast Art
2. Dr Sun Yat-Sen Classical Chinese Gardens
3. Stanley Park
4. Vancouver Art Gallery

SIGHTS
5. Canada Place
6. Ceperley Meadows
7. Chinatown Millennium Gate
8. Chinatown Storytelling Centre
9. FlyOver Canada
10. Girl in a Wetsuit
11. Hollow Tree
12. Lost Lagoon
13. Lumberman's Arch
14. Marine Building
15. Nine O'Clock Gun
16. Second Beach
17. Siwash Rock
18. Stanley Park Nature House
19. Totem Poles
20. Vancouver Aquarium
21. Vancouver Police Museum & Archives

ACTIVITIES, COURSES & TOURS
22. Second Beach Pool

SLEEPING
23. Fairmont Waterfront
24. Rosewood Hotel Georgia
25. Skwachàys Lodge

EATING
26. Bao Bei
27. Breka Bakery & Cafe
28. Phnom Penh
29. Torafuku

Totem poles

PRACTICALITIES

Scan this QR code for a full digital map of Stanley Park.

TOP SIGHT

Stanley Park

One of North America's largest urban green spaces, Stanley Park is revered for its dramatic forest-and-mountain oceanfront views. But there's more to this 400-hectare woodland than looks. The park is studded with nature-hugging trails, family-friendly attractions, sunset-boasting beaches and tasty places to eat. There's also the occasional surprise sight to search for (besides the raccoons that call the place home).

DON'T MISS

Vancouver Aquarium

Totem Park

Nine O'Clock Gun

Lost Lagoon

Hollow Tree

Seawall Landmarks

Second Beach

Vancouver Aquarium

Over 65,000 animals and 30 galleries and exhibits can be found here, and the site is also home to a center for marine research and the country's only marine mammal rescue center. From swimming otters to jubilant jellies, the Vancouver Aquarium is a must-visit site to see aquatic animals. It's found in the center of Stanley Park

Totem Poles

Stanley Park showcases the history of the area through the totem poles that stand tall at the park's edge. Located on the traditional, unceded territories of the xʷməθkʷəy̓əm (Musqueam), Sḵwx̱wú7mesh (Squamish) and səlilwətaɬ (Tsleil-Waututh) peoples, the totem poles tell the story of the park's roots through the creative methods and people behind the works of art, which have stood erect just steps from the city since 1920.

Nine O'Clock Gun

Every night at 9pm, a cannon is fired from Brockton Point in Stanley Park, its blast heard from across the city. The Nine O'Clock Gun is a Vancouver tradition that has been seen and heard for over a century. Originally located at the Brockton Point Lighthouse and fired manually each night for people to set their timepieces, the tradition remains, now managed by the Parks Board. You can view the blast from its site, just be sure to wear earplugs for the big boom!

Lost Lagoon

Stanley Park's Lost Lagoon is loaded with local wildlife. On its perimeter pathway, keep your eyes peeled for blue herons, wrens, hummingbirds, chittering Douglas squirrels and wandering raccoons. You might also come across a coyote or two; treat them with respect and give them a wide berth. For an introduction to the area's flora and fauna, start at the **Stanley Park Nature House**. You'll find friendly volunteers and exhibits on wildlife, history and ecology – ask about their well-priced guided walks.

Hollow Tree

An old **Western Red Cedar** tree in Stanley Park has become one of the most visited sites in Vancouver, thanks to its huge hollow stump, which has become a desired photo spot for tourists. Known simply as the Hollow Tree, the remains of the nearly 1000-year-old tree features an interior opening with a circumference of about 18m.

Seawall Landmarks

As you make your way around the seawall, look out for the **Girl in Wetsuit statue** that sits on a rock in the water just off the north side of the park. The statue – which is often mistaken for a mermaid – was a gift from sculptor Elek Imredy in 1972 and represents Vancouver's dependence on the sea. **Siwash Rock** is another landmark to look out for, a famous rock with a tree on its tip. Over thousands of years, the water has separated the rock from the park, and it now sits on its own in the sea.

Second Beach

If it's sandy beaches you're after, the park has several alluring options. Second Beach is a family-friendly area on the park's western side, with a grassy playground, an ice-cream-serving concession and a huge **outdoor swimming pool**. It's also close to **Ceperley Meadows**, where popular free outdoor movie screenings are staged in summer.

TALKING TOTEMS TOUR

To gain a deeper understanding of Stanley Park and its significance, book a Talking Totems trek with Talaysay Tours, which takes you on an eye-opening journey through the towering totem poles that have stood erect in the park since 1920. Led by an Indigenous guide, you will be awed by the art of the gateways and totems that make the site a must-see stop.

TOP TIPS

- Save on paid parking by opting to walk, bike, bus, scoot, rollerblade or take a horse-drawn carriage to your desired park destination.
- Summer is best for beaches and pools, and during the fall you'll find colorful foliage and fewer crowds.
- Plan your route. The 8.8km (5.5mi) paved seawall leads to most sites. Spend a full day here to see it all.
- Sidestep the Vancouver Aquarium's summer queues by making it your first stop.
- Gather a picnic and snag a grassy spot near Lumberman's Arch.

RAINER PLENDL/SHUTTERSTOCK ©

Vancouver Aquarium

ART DECO ARCHITECTURE

Vancouver's most exquisitely ornate tower block, and also its best art-deco building, the elegant 22-story **Marine Building** is a tribute to the city's maritime past. Opened in 1930, the building was once recognized as the tallest building in the British Empire. Now its towering terra-cotta exterior is shaded by newer skyscrapers that dominate the skyline. Check out its elaborate shell of seahorses, lobsters and streamlined steamships, then nip into the lobby, which is like a walk-through artwork. Stained-glass panels and a polished floor inlaid with signs of the zodiac await, as does a working antique telephone (bring your coins).

MORE IN DOWNTOWN & CHINATOWN

Canada's Largest Aquarium

A collection of coastal aquatic creatures

As Canada's largest aquarium and Stanley Park's biggest draw, the **Vancouver Aquarium** is an obvious choice for connecting with coastal aquatic life. More than 65,000 animals can be found here, and while it's a great place to get up-close with ocean life, the site is also a center for marine research, ocean literacy and climate activism. The fluffy sea otters have unofficial celebrity status in the city, and the sea lions (one weighing in at more than 860kg) are a show-stopping sight. Other highlights include the 4D Experience, a multi-sensory film that allows you to see, smell and feel the special effects; the Wet Lab, an educational space where kids learn about live invertebrates; and Clownfish Cove, an interactive play space.

Fun under Five Sails

An iconic waterfront landmark

The area's original convention-center building, sail-shaped **Canada Place** is a top sight. Stroll its pier-like outer prome-

 BEST PLACES TO STAY

Skwachàys Lodge	Rosewood Hotel Georgia	Fairmont Waterfront
Canada's first Indigenous arts hotel with an on-site art gallery and immersive Indigenous experiences. **$$**	Historic Downtown hotel where a roaring 1920s vibe matches a more modern feel. **$$$**	Adjacent to Canada Place with amazing waterfront views and a rooftop garden and apiary. **$$$**

nade and watch the floatplanes taking off from and landing on the water here. Take flight with **FlyOver Canada**, a thrilling flight-simulation ride that takes you on a virtual trip through some of Canada's most beautiful natural sights. Strap in and let your legs dangle as you watch lifelike landscapes splash across a spherical screen. Stroll along the **Canadian Trail**, a pathway of colored glass found along the west promenade that represents Canada's 13 regions (10 provinces and three territories). This is also home to the city's cruise-ship port, and the city's largest convention centers.

Chinese Canadian History Uncovered
Vancouver's Asian community showcased

At the **Chinatown Storytelling Centre** you'll find a showcase of Vancouver's Chinese Canadian history, including a life-sized diorama of the first housing units built for the workers who arrived from China to work on the Canadian Pacific Railway in the 1880s, an interactive etiquette table, and the Robert HN Ho Living Legacy Project, which highlights the personal stories of Vancouver's most prominent Chinese Canadians from the 1880s to the present day. This is Canada's first permanent exhibit dedicated to the Chinese Canadian journey, and the individual stories shared create a truly unique perspective on the Asian community in Vancouver. Stroll through solo, or book a guided tour (only available for groups of 10 or more).

The City's Past Through a Blue Lens
North America's oldest police museum

Criminal cases, unsolved murder mysteries and forensic science are just some of the things you can discover at the **Vancouver Police Museum & Archives**, found on the edge of Chinatown. Housed in an authentic heritage building, the museum was first opened in 1986 by the Police Historical Society as a way to celebrate the centennial anniversary of the city's police department. Featured exhibits include True Crime, a deep-dive display of the city's most chilling criminal cases, highlighting real cases and real evidence; Behind the Lines: A Traffic Story, a behind-the-lens look at the history of Vancouver's evolving traffic scene – from carriages to riot control, to present-day road safety; and Morgue & Autopsy Suite, a peek into the morgue and autopsy suite where pathologists and coroners worked to uncover the city's most notable true crimes from 1932 until 1980.

CHINATOWN MILLENNIUM GATE

The triple archways that make up the grand entrance to Chinatown were only erected in 2002, but the Chinatown Millennium Gate is a fitting testament to the neighborhood's longevity. Crane your neck for the colorful upper-level decoration and don't miss the ground-level lion statues. Then stand well back, since the decoration is mostly on its lofty upper reaches, where you'll find an elaborately painted section topped with a terra-cotta-tiled roof. The characters inscribed on its eastern front implore you to 'Remember the past and look forward to the future.'

 BEST ASIAN CUISINE

Torafuku	Phnom Penh	Bao Bei
East meets West in exquisite Pan-Asian dishes and creative cocktails. Michelin recommended. $$$	Authentic Vietnamese-Cambodian haven where bold spices bring traditional recipes to life. Expect a wait. $$	Casual space serving modern Chinese sharing plates, where dishes like the sticky rice cakes satisfy. $$$

Granville Island/ Yaletown

CITY CHIC MEETS ARTISAN HUB

☑ **TOP TIP**

Both areas can be reached by transit or car, but cycling is your best bet. Yaletown is connected by a paved seawall; however, you may want to park your bike if you venture inland to browse shops. Granville Island is also suitable for cycling and offers free, secure bike valet service.

These coastal communities straddle tranquil False Creek. Yaletown, a revitalized warehouse district, has become one of the city's chicest, where cool boutiques and posh urban patios draw crowds. Yaletown's waterfront parks, including David Lam Park and George Wainborn Park, are connected by a seawall, and the expansive green spaces found only steps from the city streets invite grassy picnics with water views.

A short ride on a rainbow-colored mini pedestrian ferry will take you across the water to Granville Island, which combines industrial heritage with modern-day architecture. The area is lauded as Vancouver's artisan capital, home to Western Canada's biggest public market. The human-made peninsula (it's not actually an island) was once home to dozens of hard-toiling factories, and remnants from older times can be spotted throughout the area.

MFFOTO/SHUTTERSTOCK ©

Granville Island

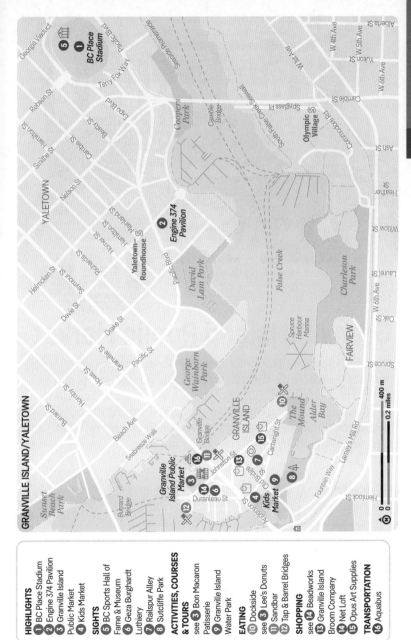

GRANVILLE ISLAND/YALETOWN

HIGHLIGHTS

1. BC Place Stadium
2. Engine 374 Pavilion
3. Granville Island Public Market
4. Kids Market

SIGHTS

5. BC Sports Hall of Fame & Museum
6. Geza Burghardt Luthiery
7. Railspur Alley
8. Sutcliffe Park

ACTIVITIES, COURSES & TOURS

see 3 Bon Macaron Patisserie
9. Granville Island Water Park

EATING

10. Dockside
see 3 Lee's Donuts
11. Sandbar
12. Tap & Barrel Bridges

SHOPPING

see 14 Beadworks
13. Granville Island Broom Company
14. Net Loft
15. Opus Art Supplies

TRANSPORTATION

16. Aquabus

JULIEN HAUTCOEUR/SHUTTERSTOCK ©

Granville Island Public Market

PRACTICALITIES

Scan this QR code for a full list of retail and restaurant offerings.

TOP SIGHT

Granville Island Public Market

Granville Island Public Market is one of North America's finest public markets – a foodie extravaganza specializing in deli treats and pyramids of shiny fruit and vegetables. It's ideal for whiling away an afternoon, snacking on goodies in the sun among the buskers outside or sheltering from the rain with a market tour. You'll also find side dishes of locally made arts and crafts here.

DON'T MISS

Foodie Tour

Lee's Donuts

Mini Ferries

The Net Loft

Boardwalk Buskers

Arts & Crafts

Food Court

Foodie Tour

If you're looking for a local take on the food found around the famed market, a guided walk organized by Vancouver Foodie Tours is the way to go. This leisurely stomach-stuffer weaves around the vendors and includes several tasting stops that will quickly fill you up. It also caters to vegetarians if you mention it when you book. The company runs friendly tasting tours in other parts of the city too, if you're keen to keep eating

Lee's Donuts

This mom-and-pop doughnut shop is legendary – just ask local celebrities like Seth Rogan who frequent the joint when they're in town. Serving handmade doughnuts since 1979, Lee's offers a large variety of classics that are made daily from scratch (the sugar-topped raspberry jelly doughnut tops the list). Be sure to arrive early and expect a line – don't worry, though, the doughnuts are worth the wait.

Mini Ferries

Found at the end of the boardwalk behind the market is a small dock where you can catch the **Aquabus** – a rainbow-colored mini pedestrian ferry. Take a short tour of the city by water, or use it as transportation to get to some of the city's best waterfront spots. The Aquabus connects Granville Island to several locations found between Downtown's Hornby St and Science World, with several scenic spots found along the way.

The Net Loft

Found across the street, the Net Loft is sort of an extension of the main market's artsy offerings. There you'll find a cluster of craft shops that offer a variety of handcrafted keepsakes. At **Beadworks**, shop through an expansive collection of beads, from Swarovski crystals to bone beads, and make your own jewelry.

Boardwalk Buskers

A park-bench picnic behind the market is a preferred pastime for Granville Island locals and tourists alike. Snack on treats collected during your stroll through the food stalls, and sit by the water, watching seagulls swoop (be sure to keep your food close or it might get snagged), while listening to talented buskers perform live music. In Granville Island, busking is done through a licensed program, allowing everyone from magicians to musicians to showcase their talents on-site. For updated schedules and locations check out granville islandbuskers.com.

Arts & Crafts

There's a cool arts-and-crafts focus here, especially among the collection of day vendors that dot the market and change every week. Hand-knitted hats, hand-painted ceramics, framed art photography and quirky carvings will make for excellent one-of-a-kind keepsakes. Further artisan stands are added to the roster in the run-up to Christmas, if you happen to be here at that time. For an updated list of day vendors that appear at the market, visit granvilleisland.com/public-market.

Food Court

In the unlikely event that you're still hungry after snacking your way through the market stalls, there's also a small international food court filled with varied offerings from around the world. Avoid off-peak dining if you want to snag a table and indulge in a good-value selection that runs from Mexican tacos to German sausages.

FORGOTTEN PAST

The Public Market is one of Canada's most impressive urban-regeneration projects. Originally built as a factory district, the abandoned sheds attracted artists and theater groups by the 1970s. New theaters and studios were built and the public market became a popular anchor tenant. Now, only independent businesses operate here.

TOP TIPS

- Arrive early to sidestep the summer crowds.
- If driving, weekdays are the easiest times to find on-island parking.
- Arrive by bike and enjoy the complimentary bike-valet service in summer.
- The food court is the island's best-value dining. But tables are scarce at peak times.
- Early-morning weekdays are best for shorter lines at the famous Lee's Donuts.
- Bird-watcher? Look for the cormorants nesting under the Granville Bridge.
- Venture to other neighborhoods via the mini ferry, which docks behind the market.

Engine 374 Pavilion
Vancouver's first transcontinental train

On May 23, 1887, CPR Engine 374 pulled the very first transcontinental passenger train into Vancouver, linking the country by train from coast to coast and kick-starting the eventual metropolis. Retired in 1945, the engine was, after many years of neglect, restored and placed in the splendid pavilion found at the Roundhouse Community Centre in the heart of the city. The friendly volunteers here will show you the best angle for snapping photos and at the same time share a few railroading stories from yesteryear.

CPR Engine 374

BC Place Stadium

BC Place Stadium
Sports-lovers' central

Vancouver's main sports arena is home to two professional teams: the BC Lions Canadian Football League team and the Vancouver Whitecaps soccer team. Also used for international rugby tournaments, rock concerts and consumer shows, the stadium – with its huge, crown-like retractable roof – hosted the opening and closing ceremonies for the 2010 Olympic and Paralympic Winter Games.

Inside you'll find the **BC Sports Hall of Fame & Museum**, a showcase of BC's top athletes, both amateur and professional, with an intriguing array of galleries crammed with fascinating memorabilia. There are medals, trophies and sports uniforms from yesteryear on display, plus tons of hands-on activities. Don't miss the Indigenous Sport Gallery, covering everything from hockey to lacrosse to traditional Indigenous games.

Kids Market
Massive kid-centric mall

Found adjacent to the entrance of Granville Island beside a picturesque pond, Kids Market is a three-story, warehouse-style shopping center aimed at kids. The yellow-hued building is topped with a rainbow sign, and invites youngsters to shop, eat and play, with over 25 shops and services on-site. There you'll find handcrafted toys, locally owned boutiques and bookstores, interactive arcades, multi-level play spaces, and sweet and savory snack spots to fuel up after a day of play. Be sure to check out the website (kidsmarket.ca) for family-friendly events, which happen year-round.

Isle of the Arts
Artists in action

Granville Island is packed with creative curiosities for art enthusiasts of all types. Stroll through **Railspur Alley** and watch artists create masterpieces before your eyes. See glassblowers, jewelers, potters, painters, blacksmiths and carvers craft beautiful pieces live in-studio and listen as they share the inspiration behind their work. Head to the **Granville Island Broom Company** and watch two sisters handcraft Shaker-style woven brooms in their whimsical storefront, and visit the **Geza Burghardt Luthiery**, where you can watch as a Hungarian luthier builds, repairs and restores guitars, violins, cellos and other string instruments.

Then, get hands-on at **Beadworks**, where you can shop through an expansive collection of beads, and then take a seat and create your own original piece of jewelry to take home. Satisfy your sweet tooth while mastering the art of macaron-making with a private class at **Bon Macaron Patisserie**, or sign up for an in-store painting class at **Opus Art Supplies**, a spacious store that has become a staple of the Vancouver art community.

Water Park Play
Spray, splash and slide

Granville Island is home to the largest free outdoor water park of its kind in North America, where fire hydrants, in-ground sprays, fountains and a twirly yellow slide make for the perfect summer cooldown for kids. Slather on the sunscreen and enjoy the splash pads, and then pick up some snacks from the Granville Island Public Market – a short walk from the park – and settle in on the expansive grassy green space of adjacent **Sutcliffe Park**.

WHY I LOVE GRANVILLE ISLAND

Bianca Bujan, Writer

I'm one of a rare group of local Vancouverites who grew up right in Granville Island. The area was my backyard, and even though it's been more than 30 years since I called it home, I visit regularly, witnessing first hand its slow transition from sleepy hideaway to major tourist hot spot. During Expo '86, I met Princess Diana and Prince Charles here, and I learned to ride a bike along the paved pathway that leads to Kids Market–my favorite childhood place to play. Today, the food here is the biggest draw – from the fresh meats and sweet treats found in the public market, to the warm raspberry jelly doughnuts at Lee's Donuts.

 WHERE TO DINE ALFRESCO

Tap & Barrel Bridges
Sprawling, sun-drenched patio with waterfront Vancouver views, housed in a historic yellow building. **$$**

Sandbar
Seafood shines at this restaurant perched over the water, and under the Granville St bridge. **$$**

Dockside
Luxury dining with majestic marina views, found in a quieter corner of bustling Granville Island. **$$**

Main Street

ALTERNATIVE AND MULTICULTURAL

☑ **TOP TIP**

The Main St neighborhood is easily accessible by bus – the number 3 runs the length of Main St in both directions. The SkyTrain connects to bus 3 services at the Main Street-Science World Station, and there's limited metered parking on Main St, with side-street parking the further south you drive.

Deemed one of North America's coolest streets, this formerly faded and gritty neighborhood is now a hub for hipsters and home to numerous independent shops, global restaurants and hip bars, all found within a 20-block stretch. Unlike some of Vancouver's other shopping districts, you won't find any big-box stores here.

The area is developing rapidly, including the lower Olympic Village area – a waterfront neighborhood that's always adding new drinking and dining options. Along the village, you'll also find a collection of massive murals that color the city streets, part of the Vancouver Mural Festival. Some of the city's best restaurants can be found here too, including a handful of newly Michelin-recognized spots. The restaurant scene is culturally diverse, offering a mix of laid-back and high-end restaurants serving up everything from Malaysian to South Indian to Caribbean classics.

GERRYROUSSEAU/ALAMY STOCK PHOTO ©

Main St shopping

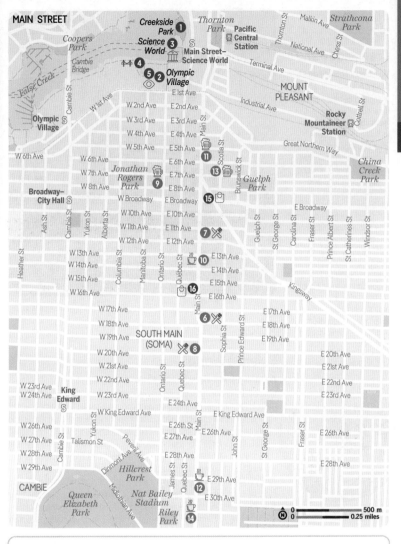

MAIN STREET

HIGHLIGHTS
1. Creekside Park
2. Olympic Village
3. Science World

SIGHTS
4. Canoe Bridge
5. Sparrow Sculptures

EATING
6. Anh & Chi
7. Burdock & Co
8. Published on Main

DRINKING & NIGHTLIFE
9. 33 Acres Brewing

10. 49th Parallel Coffee Roasters
11. Brassneck Brewery
12. Breka Bakery & Cafe
13. Main Street Brewing
14. Matchstick

SHOPPING
15. Mintage Mall
16. Turnabout Luxury Resale

Creekside Park

Vancouver's largest playground

A popular outdoor venue for summer events and festivals and the gateway to Science World, this accessible playground features a high-reaching wooden climbing tower, swings, giant tube and hill slides, musical instruments, water and sand play areas, and a play hut, all housed on a colorful rubberized surface. A zipline adds extra zest to the park's features. Surrounding shade trees provide cooler seating areas around the park's perimeter, perfect for picnics. And waterfront and skyline views attract park dwellers without kids too.

Science World

Creekside Park

Science World

A family-friendly science showcase

One of the city's most photographed structures, the dome isn't just a shiny shoreline bauble. Found inside is a multi-level mash-up of activities and exhibits that offer fun for all ages. There are two floors of educational play, from plasma balls to whisper dishes. Hands-on exhibits make learning fun, as do the live science demonstrations on the Centre Stage. Find live critters in the Sara Stern Gallery, behold the bodily functions exhibited in the BodyWorks area, then fly over a city on the virtual-reality Birdly ride ($8 extra). If the weather's fine, save time for the outdoor Ken Spencer Science Park. Focused on sustainable communities, it's a quirky collection of climbing frames, interactive games and stage demos, plus a coop full of beady-eyed chickens.

Olympic Village

Waterfront pubs, patios and parks

Originally built to house athletes for the 2010 Winter Olympic and Paralympic Games, Vancouver's Olympic Village has now evolved into a happening spot, packed with pubs, patios and parks on the waterfront. Look for a pair of giant **sparrow sculptures** created by local artist Myfanwy MacLeod – an artistic comment on the relationship between humans and birds, and the effects of urban development in a formerly natural space (standing at 5.5m tall in the center of the square, the birds are hard to miss). Be sure to cross **Canoe Bridge** (a popular photo spot), which is especially beautiful when illuminated at night.

Main Street's Michelin Meals

Savor the flavors

At the end of 2022, Vancouver's very first Michelin guide was released – a long-awaited status symbol collating the city's best restaurants, many of which are located along the Main St corridor. Eight spots in total received star recognition, and another 12 received bib gourmand designation. Several others were also added to the esteemed list of restaurants in the city. The dining options are definitely worth discovering, offering distinct dishes that showcase both the freshly plucked local ingredients found in the region (especially seafood) and the city's Asian influence, with many of the dishes found nowhere else outside Asia. Be sure to book your table well in advance.

Topping the list of must-try spots in the area is **Published on Main**, where executive chef Gus Stieffenhofer-Brandson and his team prepare picture-perfect dishes using ingredients foraged from local forests and farms. The food here is high-quality, and the presentation is equally impressive. The tender halibut with buttery broth is a crowd pleaser. **Anh & Chi** brings a modern, vibrant Vietnamese menu to life in Vancouver, backed by a brother-and-sister team who embrace their culinary roots, producing authentic Vietnamese dishes like Khay Bánh Hỏi Lụi Nướng, a DIY street-side platter served with a modern twist. **Burdock & Co** is another popular choice. With Andrea Carlson – the only female chef on Vancouver's Michelin list – at the helm, this spot is best known for its regional farm-to-table plates, which make up the ever-changing seasonal set-course menu here (open for dinner Mondays to Thursdays).

BREWERY CREEK

Beer lovers will want to pay a visit to Brewery Creek – a historic urban brewery district. The area was named after a fast-moving creek that once powered water wheels at several area breweries. But after decades of consolidation, the neighborhood's last brewery closed in the 1950s.

That wasn't the end of the story, though. In recent years, Vancouver's latter-day craft-brewing renaissance has seen several new producers open in the area, from **Main Street Brewing** to **33 Acres Brewing**. Wondering where to start? Quench your thirst at local favorite **Brassneck Brewery**. For a self-guided tour of the best of the rest, be sure to follow the BC Ale Trail (bcaletrail.ca).

BEST COFFEE SPOTS

49th Parallel Coffee Roasters
Sustainably sourced coffee roasted locally, with a selection of doughnuts.

Matchstick
Community coffee shop with five locations around the city, where pastries are baked fresh on-site.

Breka Bakery & Cafe
Latest location of the family-owned chain of cafes, offering an array of sweet and savory treats.

Fairview & South Granville

UPSCALE URBAN SHOPPING DISTRICT

☑ **TOP TIP**

For art galleries, start from the Granville St bridge and work your way up to W 8th Ave. If you're looking to browse boutiques, the best are clustered between Broadway and W 16th Ave. You'll need to hop on a bus or drive to explore the expansive gardens in the area.

Combining the boutiques and restaurants of well-to-do South Granville with Fairview's busy Broadway thoroughfare and cozy Cambie Village, there's something for everyone in this area. South Granville is home to tree-lined residential streets, heritage buildings and casual cafes intermixed with modern boutiques and high-end eateries. A stretch of stylish shops and independent galleries make this vibrant, upscale shopping district worth the trek.

Massive murals add charm, and colorful open-air plazas invite a rest stop after an afternoon spent shopping and snacking. Art lovers will want to walk along 'Gallery Row' – a stretch of art galleries that line the lower South Granville corridor. Green-thumbed visitors should also save time for some top-notch park and garden attractions here.

JOHN MITCHELL/ALAMY STOCK PHOTO ©

Eateries, South Granville

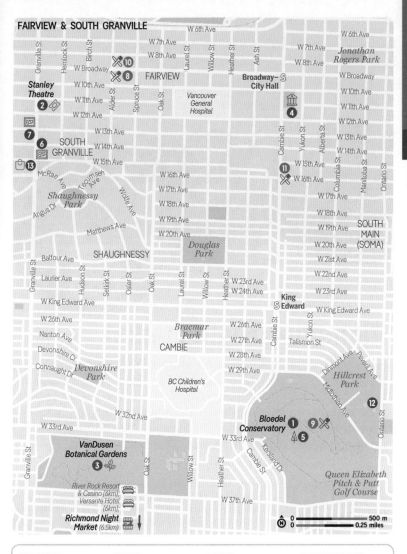

FAIRVIEW & SOUTH GRANVILLE

W 6th Ave
W 7th Ave
W 8th Ave

Stanley Theatre ❷

SOUTH GRANVILLE ❻

W 10th Ave
W 11th Ave
W 12th Ave
W 13th Ave
W 14th Ave
W 15th Ave

FAIRVIEW

Vancouver General Hospital

Broadway– City Hall ⓢ ❹

Jonathan Rogers Park

W Broadway
W 10th Ave
W 11th Ave
W 12th Ave
W 13th Ave
W 14th Ave

❼
❻ ❶³

McRae Ave
Tecumseh Ave

Shaughnessy Park

Angus Dr

Wolfe Ave

Matthews Ave

SHAUGHNESSY

Balfour Ave
Laurier Ave
W King Edward Ave

W 16th Ave
W 17th Ave
W 18th Ave
W 19th Ave
W 20th Ave

Douglas Park

W 16th Ave ❶¹
W 17th Ave
W 18th Ave
W 19th Ave
W 20th Ave
W 21st Ave
W 22nd Ave
W 23rd Ave

SOUTH MAIN (SOMA)

W 23rd Ave
W 24th Ave

King Edward ⓢ

W King Edward Ave

W 26th Ave
Nanton Ave
Devonshire Cr
Connaught Dr

Devonshire Park

Braemar Park

CAMBIE

W 26th Ave
W 27th Ave
W 28th Ave
W 29th Ave

Talisman St

Hillcrest Park ❶²

BC Children's Hospital

W 32nd Ave
W 33rd Ave

VanDusen Botanical Gardens ❸

River Rock Resort & Casino (6km); Versante Hotel (6km); **Richmond Night Market** (6.5km)

Bloedel Conservatory ❶ ❾ ⚠ ❺

W 33rd Ave

W 37th Ave

Queen Elizabeth Pitch & Putt Golf Course

Ⓝ 0 ————— 500 m
  0 ————— 0.25 miles

HIGHLIGHTS
❶ Bloedel Conservatory
❷ Stanley Theatre
❸ VanDusen Botanical Gardens

SIGHTS
❹ City Hall
❺ Queen Elizabeth Park
❻ South Granville Plaza East
❼ South Granville Plaza West

EATING
❽ Salmon n' Bannock
❾ Seasons in the Park
❿ Tojo's
⓫ Vij's

ENTERTAINMENT
⓬ Nat Bailey Stadium

SHOPPING
⓭ Turnabout Luxury Resale

325

DARRYL BROOKS/SHUTTERSTOCK ©

Richmond Night Market

TOP SIGHT

Richmond Night Market

Home to the Vancouver International Airport (YVR), Richmond is best known for its hyper-diverse population. The city has the largest number of Chinese residents found outside Asia, and the night market – the largest of its kind in North America – reflects Richmond's roots through its cultural and culinary offerings, with over 110 food stalls serving up over 600 different dishes from around the world.

DID YOU KNOW?

Richmond Night Market began in 2000 as a tented pop-up in a parking lot. Entrepreneur Raymond Cheung foresaw an event that nodded to the Asian night markets found in Hong Kong. Now, the market spans 7 hectares and draws over a million visitors a year.

Live Entertainment

Each year the decor reveals a special theme (previous years have included 'Summer Chill Party' and 'Magic Rainbow') with on-theme attractions to suit the mood. A 15m live performance stage brings nightly entertainment such as musical acts, martial arts displays, dance showcases and more.

Global Food Stalls

The night market isn't just a showcase for Asian cuisine – you can dine around the world here. Churros and butter beer are new additions to the tasty roster, along with foods from Indonesia and Turkey. Tornado potatoes, or 'rotatoes,' are a classic hit, and *takoyaki* (Japanese octopus balls), Bajan jambalaya and deep-fried bao buns add to the list of savory options. For sweet-toothed snackers, there are plenty of treats too! Mochido doughnuts, handcrafted rolled gelato and the quintessentially Canadian beaver tails top the list. There are always new offerings, so be sure to check the posted list of the

Asian food

> ### RICHMOND DUMPLING TRAIL
> Take your love for Asian eats beyond the market with a tasting tour through town. On the self-guided Dumpling Trail tour (dumplingtrail.ca) through Richmond, foodies can slurp on steaming hot wonton soup, nibble on crunchy, deep-fried dumplings, or gobble up a mouthful of pork-stuffed pouches at the over 20 eateries on the pre-planned route.

10 most popular vendors of the month on a supersized sign that you'll pass upon entry.

Colorful Keepsakes

Pack your wallet because you'll also want to browse the vendor stalls found throughout the site, where you can shop for toys, handmade goods, clothing and accessories, phone gadgets and quirky keepsakes. From samurai swords to cute Korean socks, you're sure to find something for everyone on your vacation gift list.

For the Kids

New in 2023, a larger-than-life, 18m-tall bouncy castle provides a fun place for kids to jump the night away after stuffing their faces with sweet treats. A games area, a candy-colored forest and oversized prop chairs will also lure the little ones. Marvel at the moving velociraptors, triceratops and T. Rex in the Magical Dino Park, and take a peek at the pooches in the dog play area, where four-legged friends can join in on the fun – as long as they stay away from the food.

Nearby Stays

Make a night of your visit to Richmond with a stay at one of the nearby hotels, where you can enjoy post-event drinks before drifting off to sleep. The **River Rock Resort & Casino** is only minutes away by foot, where you'll find an on-site casino (one of the largest in the province), a heated indoor pool with a waterslide, and a soothing spa. **Versante Hotel**, about a seven-minute walk from the market, is Richmond's only boutique hotel. There you'll find Bruno – likely the best brunch spot in the area.

TOP TIPS

- Parking is limited, so consider public transit. The market is only one block from the Bridgeport Station of the Canada Line SkyTrain that takes you directly to the site from several locations between Downtown Vancouver and the YVR airport.
- Browse the top 10 vendors of the month posted near the entry gates to help you decide where to start in a sea of food stalls.
- Skip the lines with a Zoom Pass, which gives you priority entry, access to shorter lines, and cost savings once you're inside.

Stanley Theatre

Stanley Theatre
Landmark heritage theater

Officially called the Stanley Industrial Alliance Stage, but better known as 'The Stanley' to locals, this art deco–style heritage theater is part of the Arts Club Theatre Company, Vancouver's biggest. The site originally opened in the 1930s as a movie cinema and vaudeville house, and has since become the flagship stage of Western Canada's largest theater company, showing everything from off-Broadway musicals to comedy shows to classic plays by up-and-coming actors. Unable to catch a show? The stunning exterior is worth a walk-by.

VanDusen Botanical Gardens
Outdoor oasis for garden lovers

Opened in 1975, this 22-hectare (55-acre) green-thumbed wonderland is home to more than 250,000 plants representing some of the world's most distinct growing regions. You'll find trees, shrubs, flowers, succulents and more from across Canada, the Mediterranean, South Africa and the Himalayas, many of them identified with little plaques near their roots. It's not just humans that are hooked by this sparkling nature spot; this is also a wildlife haven. Look out for turtles, herons and a variety of ducks in and around the main lake. A stroll through the Elizabethan Maze is also a must. Grown from more than 3000 pyramidal cedars, VanDusen's giggle-triggering garden maze is the perfect spot to tire out your kids.

VanDusen Botanical Gardens

Bloedel Conservatory
Tropical birds and plants in a domed paradise

Housed at the highest point of picturesque Queen Elizabeth Park, this domed conservatory is a delightful destination on a rainy day. Here you'll find tropical trees and plants bristling with hundreds of free-flying, bright-plumaged birds.

Listen for the noisy resident parrots, but also keep your eyes peeled for rainbow-hued Gouldian finches, shimmering African superb starlings and maybe even a dramatic Lady Amherst pheasant snaking through the undergrowth. Ask

nicely and the attendants might even let you feed the smaller birds from a bowl. If the kids get antsy, ask for a free scavenger hunt sheet so they can track what they spot.

Queen Elizabeth Park

Picturesque park at the city's highest point

At 125m above sea level, Queen Elizabeth Park offers panoramic views of the mountain-framed downtown skyscrapers. A tree-lover's dream, this 130-acre park claims to house specimens of every tree native to Canada. Sports fields, manicured lawns and formal gardens keep the locals happy, and you'll probably also see wide-eyed couples posing for their wedding photos in particularly picturesque spots. This is a good place to view local birdlife: keep your eyes peeled for chickadees, hummingbirds and huge bald eagles whirling high overhead. This park is home to the domed Bloedel Conservatory and has a great fine-dining restaurant, **Seasons in the Park**, which is perched at the park's top. Picnics and pitch-and-putt are popular pastimes for locals here.

Nat Bailey Stadium

Take me out to the ballgame

Catching a Vancouver Canadians minor-league baseball game at old-school Nat Bailey Stadium (known as 'The Nat' by locals) is a summer tradition for many Vancouverites. But for some, the experience isn't complete unless you also add a hot dog, peanuts and some ice-cold beers to the ball game. Non-traditional options are available too, like sushi. Be sure to check out the Wall of Fame exhibit while you're there, which highlights former Canadians players who have gone on to the majors. Enhancing the festivities are the non-baseball shenanigans, ranging from kiss cams to mascot races. Arguably the most fun you can have at a Vancouver spectator sport, it's also one of the most budget-friendly options (depending on how many hot dogs you down).

City Hall

Art-deco architecture

Despite the economic malaise of the 1930s, mayor Gerry McGeer spared no expense to build a new City Hall in 1936. Defended as a make-work project for the idled construction industry, the $1 million project (a huge sum for the time) was completed in just 12 months. Despite the controversy, the building is now one of Vancouver's most revered art-deco edifices, complete with a soaring, Gotham-style exterior and an interior of streamlined signs, cylindrical lanterns and embossed elevator doors.

PUBLIC ART

South Granville showcases an array of massive **wall murals** found on side streets lined with heritage homes, just steps from the main strip. The collection of colorful murals is always growing, and many provide a backdrop for open-air seating spaces that are perfect for picnicking during the warmer months. Look for the two main public plaza areas found at the center of the neighborhood: **South Granville Plaza West**, located at Granville St and W 13th Ave, and **South Granville Plaza East**, located at Granville St and W 14th Ave. These two community hubs combine creative seating structures with colorful murals to create inviting outdoor gathering areas, the perfect place to relax, connect and dine outdoors.

BEST GLOBAL CUISINE

Salmon n' Bannock
The only Indigenous-owned restaurant in Vancouver, serving modern dishes made using traditional ingredients.

Vij's
Famed Indian fusion restaurant with celebrity chef Vikram Vij at the helm.

Tojo's
First-class Japanese cuisine lauded by the world's top CEOs, celebrities and chefs.

Vancouver Island

CHARMING COMMUNITIES AND WILDERNESS WONDERS

Outdoor adventure meets laid-back lifestyle on this archipelago on the Pacific Coast, where sprawling beaches, snug inlets and rugged wilderness are speckled with cosmopolitan centers.

Vancouver Island is a vast archipelago with varied landscapes, spanning nearly 500km long and 100km wide. It's the largest populated landmass between western North America and New Zealand, and is packed with attractions and activities that distinctly differ from those offered on the more bustling mainland of Vancouver.

The region that we now know as Vancouver Island sits on the traditional ancestral and unceded territories of the Kwakwaka'wakw, Nuu-chah-nulth and Coast Salish. Many are familiar with its crown jewel on the coast – BC's capital city of Victoria – which is the island's main entry point and a hub for historic sites, but there's so much more to see and do beyond 'Canada's garden city.'

From the Swartz Bay ferry terminal (the primary arrival point), up through the Saanich Peninsula, the South Island region features clusters of charming communities, pretty parks, and scenic sights and attractions. Nanaimo (the secondary arrival point by ferry) introduces you to the Central Island region, where sandy beaches, underground caves and treed trails invite adventure outdoors. Things slow down and the wilderness opens up as you head toward North Island, where remote stretches of wilderness allow you to witness wildlife and explore Indigenous cultures in the unspoilt, raw beauty of Western Canada's last stop. Ecoadventures await those who are looking for truly off-the-beaten-path experiences here.

ELENA_ALEX_FERNS/SHUTTERSTOCK ©

THE MAIN AREAS

GREATER VICTORIA & INNER HARBOUR
Garden city and brunch capital.
p334

CENTRAL ISLAND
Relaxed coastal communities.
p343

PACIFIC RIM
Surfers' paradise.
p348

NORTH ISLAND
Rugged wilderness.
p354

RUSS HEINL/SHUTTERSTOCK ©

Left: Totem pole, Cowichan Valley (p337); Above: Pacific Rim (p348)

Find Your Way

If you're looking to enjoy a shorter stay in BC's capital city, it's possible to go car-free, but you'll need a vehicle if you plan on exploring beyond Victoria, as the island is vast.

Central Island, p343

Home to Horne Lake Caves, a significant spelunking site and home to Canada's first and only cave interpretive center.

Greater Victoria & Inner Harbour, p334

Location of the Malahat Skywalk, a striking spiral tower with sweeping views, and Butchart Gardens, one of Canada's National Historic Sites.

North Island, p354

Telegraph Cove is a tiny former fishing village that has become the launch point for eco-tourism experiences in the North Island region.

Pacific Rim, p348

Cox Bay is a surfers' paradise, named Canada's top surfing destination, and the largest surf beach in the area.

FERRY

From Vancouver (Tsawwassen), a car/passenger ferry will take you across the water to Victoria (Swartz Bay) or Nanaimo (Duke Point) via BC Ferries.

SEAPLANE

If you're planning on going car-free, seaplane service from Vancouver (downtown) or Richmond (YVR) will take you directly to downtown Victoria, Nanaimo and Tofino via Harbour Air.

Inner Harbour, Victoria (p334)

Plan Your Time

Vancouver Island is vast, so be sure to save enough time to either dive deeper into a single region or drive further and see a bit of it all.

Weekend by the Water

Take a day to discover downtown **Victoria** (p334), starting with brunch by the water (p338), then cruise by foot through historic **Chinatown** (p334). Head to Inner Harbour for a stroll, shop and snack along **Fisherman's Wharf** (p338). Sneak away to **Sooke** (p342) for a scenic hike along the Sooke River at **Potholes Provincial Park** (p342) and cool off with a dip at Crescent Beach.

Seven Days to Explore

Start with a night in **Nanaimo** (p343) and pick up some treats along the **Nanaimo Bar Trail** (p345), then take a few days to play in **Parksville** (p346), where you can spelunk through **Horne Lake Caves** (p346) before grabbing ice cream at **Goats on a Roof** (p347). Drive cross-island to **Ucluelet** (p351), and wrap up your stay with a few nights in **Tofino** (p349).

Seasonal Highlights

SPRING
Rising temps see the flora flourish. For the best blooms, check out **Butchart Gardens** (p338).

SUMMER
The warmer weather lures locals and visitors to the beaches and trails for hiking, biking, boating and swimming.

FALL
The changing leaves add a colorful backdrop to outdoor adventures, and you'll mostly have the trails to yourself.

WINTER
Storm-watching season, best enjoyed in **Tofino** (p349), and snowy **Mt Washington** (p346) welcomes skiing.

Greater Victoria & Inner Harbour

☑ TOP TIP
Victoria has a vibrant scene with 100+ festivals. Check out the Indigenous Cultural Festival (Jul) to learn about First Nations heritage, or sniff, swirl, and sip your way through the Victoria International Wine Fest (Sep). Foodies favor Dine Around and Stay in Town, the city's top culinary fest (Jan-Feb).

Greater Victoria is a coastal city rich in natural beauty and cultural gems. When it comes to achieving accolades, BC's capital city takes the top spot. Founded in 1858, Victoria's Chinatown was the first in Canada. One of its most notable streets, Fan Tan Alley, is recognized as the narrowest street in Canada, and in Beacon Hill Park, you'll find the world's tallest free-standing totem pole, which reaches a height of 38m (127ft) tall.

Victoria has the mildest climate in the country (it's located in a sub-Mediterranean zone) providing the perfect garden growing conditions, which is why the city is known as 'Canada's Garden City,' with Butchart Gardens, a designated Natural Historic Site of Canada, garnering international recognition. Victoria is also known as the 'brunch capital of Canada' with a wide roster of restaurants worthy of a stop, and a visit wouldn't be complete without partaking in a traditional afternoon tea.

Explore Chinese Canadian Culture
Canada's oldest Chinatown

In 1858 BC's port cities saw an influx of Asian immigrants arriving to work on the Canadian Pacific Railway. Since then, Victoria's Chinatown (Canada's oldest) has remained a historical gateway to the country's Chinese Canadian past and present.

Located right in the heart of downtown and only blocks away from the waterfront, Chinatown is easily walkable. As you enter the three-block stretch that makes up Chinatown, be sure to stop and admire the **Gate of Harmonious Interest**. The *paifang* (traditional Chinese archway) was built in 1981 to commemorate Chinatown's revitalization, and is adorned in ornate red and gold symbols.

Continue toward the center of Chinatown and take a turn down **Fan Tan Alley**, Canada's narrowest street (less than a meter wide at its narrowest point). The alley entrance can be found halfway down Fisgard St and the street stretches toward Pandora Ave. Browse the locally owned shops and then

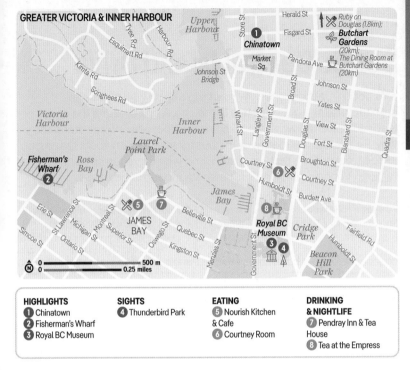

HIGHLIGHTS
- 1 Chinatown
- 2 Fisherman's Wharf
- 3 Royal BC Museum

SIGHTS
- 4 Thunderbird Park

EATING
- 5 Nourish Kitchen & Cafe
- 6 Courtney Room

DRINKING & NIGHTLIFE
- 7 Pendray Inn & Tea House
- 8 Tea at the Empress

be sure to duck in for dumplings at one of the many traditional Chinese dining spots found along the way.

High Tea History

Tea at the Empress Hotel

Inherited from the city's early tea-swigging British settlers, a devout love for afternoon tea still remains in Victoria, with nearly as many refined tea rooms as cafes found here. The cathedral of afternoon tea in Victoria (and possibly all of Canada) is at the castle-like **Empress Hotel**, where you can sip daintily from fragile china teacups and nosh on freshly baked scones with preserves and clotted cream while listening to the soft tinkling sounds of piano music.

An elegant spread of mini sandwiches and sweets paired with a pot of tea will cost you a weighty $95 per person, or you can go full royal with a Royal Champagne Tea featuring a glass of high-end champs for $142.

 BEST TEA ROOMS

Tea at the Empress
World-famous high tea in a château-style site where famed royals and celebrities have supped. $$$

Butchart Gardens
Traditional tea with gorgeous garden views at the Butchart family's former residence. $$

Pendray Inn & Tea House
Afternoon tea served in the decorative dining room of a historic home near Victoria's waterfront. $$

South-Central Island Drive

This action-packed, one-way road trip begins with must-see architectural and cultural sites in the city. A cruise along the coast leads to colorful towns with exciting outdoor adventures along the way. Further up the road, a cute country market with goats grazing on its roof makes for a tasty rest stop. End with a riveting spelunking tour through Vancouver Island's renowned underground caves.

1 Beacon Hill Park

Start at Beacon Hill Park, just minutes from Downtown Victoria. This 81-hectare parkland was once home to the Lekwungen People, now known as Esquimalt Nation and Songhees Nation. The park houses the world's tallest free-standing totem pole, the Story Pole, which was erected in 1956 and reaches 39m high. Meander along manicured pathways and look for *The Moss Lady,* a moss-covered statue that appears to be sleeping on the soil.

The Drive: A 50-minute cruise along the southern coast of Vancouver Island will take you to the town of Sooke, where outdoor adventures await.

2 Sooke Potholes Provincial Park

See Sooke River, where clear pools of water puddle in the crevices of naturally carved bedrock, creating splash-worthy swimming holes (potholes). Walk along weaving tree-lined trails and discover a waterfall, or creep up steeper slopes and stand above the rock pools for a different perspective. There are several spots around the park that are perfect for a picnic, so be sure to bring some snacks to enjoy while you're there.

The Drive: It will take 45 minutes to drive from Sooke up to Malahat, where a sky-high adventure reveals far-off views.

LUCA CAMAIANI/SHUTTERSTOCK ©

Coombs Old Country Market

3 Malahat Skywalk

Found just off the Malahat Hwy among the lush landscape of the Cowichan Valley, the Malahat Skywalk takes you 250m above sea level for a truly unique bird's-eye view of the surrounding area. Start with a short trek along the elevated Tree-Walk. Then wind your way to the top of the tower and take in breathtaking views from above. Brave the winding slide back down, and enjoy some snacks before heading back to your car.

The Drive: A smooth highway drive will get you to Coombs in about an hour and a half, where you'll want to leave plenty of time to shop and dine at the country market.

4 Coombs Old Country Market

Known famously as Goats on a Roof due to the goats grazing on the sod roof (May to October), this charming country market is more than a grocery store. Cool trinkets and keepsakes crowd the shelves of the shop, and on the grounds a delicious doughnut shop, an Italian eatery, an ice-cream stand and a Taqueria Cantina offer a range of snacks and treats. Stock up before you hit the road for your last stop.

The Drive: A mere 30-minute drive down the highway and along a forested road that wraps around Horne Lake will take you to an underground adventure like no other.

5 Horne Lake Caves

Often referred to as the best caves in Canada, the collection of caves found at Horne Lake Caves Provincial Park offers subterranean spelunking adventures for visitors of all ages and skills. Explore the untouched underworld on the more spacious Riverbend Cave Tour (best for beginners) or, for serious spelunkers, the five-hour Max Depth Adventure Tour involves rappels, crawlways and climbs into the deepest chambers of the cave.

Wander the Wharf
Fish and chips and floating homes

Around the corner from Victoria's Inner Harbour is **Fisherman's Wharf,** a quaint community of colorful floating houses, where you can stroll, shop, eat and play by the water. This is an ideal destination to pick up fresh fish (which you can buy right off the boat). The docks are also home to a selection of takeaway food stalls, where you can dine on pizza, tacos, fish n' chips, ice cream and sweet treats while taking in the bustling boatside surroundings. Pick up some locally made crafts at one of the shops, and watch quietly for aquatic wildlife to swim by.

Discover BC's Natural & Human History
Prominent cultural institution

Carrying the Queen-approved 'royal' prefix since 1987, the **Royal BC Museum** features the province's shared stories, nature, history and culture through engaging permanent exhibits and revolving world-class temporary exhibits. Start with a stroll through the adjacent **Thunderbird Park**, where you can admire towering totem poles by Kwakwaka'wakw master carver Mungo Martin and other Indigenous carvers, and the Northwest Coast–style **Wawaditła** (Mungo Martin House) where earlier totem carvings took place. Guests can visit the house to learn about past and present First Nations traditions. Add value to your visit with a show at the **IMAX Theatre**, located in the museum, where you can watch both modern and educational 3D films on BC's largest film screen.

Smell the Flowers
Garden City's best blooms

Home to over a million blooms, the **Butchart Gardens** became a designated National Historic Site of Canada in 2004 to mark the site's 100th birthday. Jennie Butchart transformed her former limestone quarry backyard into a grand garden that would eventually grow into a 22-hectare, 5-garden site, attracting visitors from around the world for generations.

See the original Sunken Garden, including the green-covered walls of the quarry. A torii (traditional Japanese gate) leads into the Japanese Garden, a serene space surrounded by maple and beech trees, where bridges and stepping stones showcase flowing streams and lush landscapes. Enjoy a gelato as you step through the Italian Garden, which was once the family's tennis court. Exotic international plants are showcased in the Mediterranean Garden, and 280 varieties of roses are revealed in the Rose Garden. Kids love taking a spin on the Rose Carousel.

BRUNCH CULTURE

Declared the 'brunch capital of Canada' by *You Gotta Eat Here!* host John Catucci back in 2016 due the high volume of restaurants in the area, Victoria still lives up to its name – the city is brimming with brunch spots that serve up bennies and bacon and eggs during that sweet spot between breakfast and lunch. Fuelled by fare sourced from the over 1000 local farms in the area, the food is fresh, delivering high-quality eggs, fruit and produce. Because brunch is so popular here, you can expect long lines – and not just on weekends. With so many options, the biggest challenge is deciding where to eat.

BEST BRUNCH SPOTS

Courtney Room
Centrally located in a boutique hotel downtown, serving fancy (and hearty) brunch feasts. $$

Nourish Kitchen & Cafe
Charming eatery serving farm-fresh, veggie-forward food in the cozy dining room of a heritage home. $$

Ruby on Douglas
Rainbow-hued retro-style eatery serving up everything from savory waffles to quinoa porridge. $$

Beyond
Greater Victoria
& Inner Harbour

Venture beyond Victoria's downtown core and discover scenic seascapes and forested frolics.

Spread along the southwestern coast of Vancouver Island, the town of Sooke is the gateway to outdoor adventure, where you can paddle, hike or bike through some of the area's most beautiful landscapes. Head to the harbor and kayak along the coast, or dip in the cool waters of the potholes that pool in the river's bedrocks. Take a trek along the world-famous 75km trail, and look for wildlife while you work your way through the woods. And if you'd rather wander through nature while staying closer to the crowds, climb the winding tower that gives you a beautiful bird's-eye view of the forest floor below. Beyond the city, there's so much more to discover.

 TOP TIP

Rent a car and cruise along the coast, where windswept beaches, bird-watching spots and hiking trails invite adventure beyond the city.

WIRESTOCK CREATORS/SHUTTERSTOCK ©

Sooke Potholes Provincial Park (p342)

MR NIKON/SHUTTERSTOCK ©

Spiral Tower

PRACTICALITIES

Scan this QR code for prices, hours and special events.

TOP SIGHT

Malahat Skywalk

Take a casual corkscrew climb to a platform perched above the trees. Reaching 250m above sea level, this stunning 10-story spiral structure is the first of its kind in BC. Situated on the traditional territory of the Malahat Nation, the Skywalk offers panoramic views of Finlayson Arm, Saanich Inlet, Saanich Peninsula, Gulf Islands, San Juan Islands, Mt Baker and the Coast Mountain range.

DON'T MISS

TreeWalk

Spiral Tower

Spiral Slide

Adventure Net

Art in Nature

Tower Plaza

Retro Food Carts

TreeWalk

Stroll along a long wooden boardwalk that sits on stilts, and smell the arbutus trees (or Pacific madrones) as you admire the red-colored, paper-like bark of their trunks. Weave through a forest of Douglas firs and keep your eye out for wildlife that call the trees home, including squirrels, birds and bears. You may even spot some striking animal sculptures too. Artist Tanya Bub has created life-sized creatures out of driftwood that can be spotted nestled in the trees throughout the walk, and Coast Salish master carver John Marston has created custom works of art, including a thunderbird and a cedar canoe.

Spiral Tower

It takes about 10 minutes before you approach the soaring Spiral Tower, which reveals itself as you emerge from the trees. As you ascend the 10-story sloped walkway, various views appear before you – from the woods that sit below to the waters that reach far along the horizon. At the top, 360-degree panoramic views are revealed. And once you've explored from above, an adventurous exit route provides a fun way down.

Spiral Slide
Instead of strolling back down, take a zip down the speedy spiral tube slide that runs 20m (65ft) down to the base (sliders must be at least five years of age and 106cm (42") tall, and everyone must slide solo).

Adventure Net
At the top of the tower, thrill-seekers can take a walk/bounce along a suspended cargo net, which provides an above-ground view of the forest floor below. Those afraid of heights may want to avoid this one though.

Tower Top Yoga
Wellness enthusiasts can partake in yoga sessions, hosted at the top of the tower on Sundays and Wednesdays between June and September – a great way to find your 'Om' outdoors.

Art in Nature
Wooden sculptures by Indigenous artists can be spotted throughout your journey, as well as a new addition to the art offerings: a series of one-of-a-kind, large-scale AI art installations created by two local Vancouver Island artists have been erected along the TreeWalk, in collaboration with the Riopelle Foundation and the Department of Canadian Heritage and Culture Pour Tous. The art pieces showcase reimagined, modern works of famed Canadian painter Jean Paul Riopelle. While this is a temporary exhibit, more works of art will be showcased among the natural surroundings throughout summer seasons.

Tower Plaza
A newly updated plaza can be found adjacent to the base of the tower, where a nature-inspired climbing structure provides a place for kids to play, and colorful chairs offer a welcome resting place to sit and enjoy the views while sipping on drinks and noshing on snacks.

Retro Food Carts
Grab a slice from Bicycle Pizza, where hand-stretched, oven-baked pizzas are made with local ingredients and served out of a vintage Airstream trailer. Then cool off with a cone from Softys, made fresh on Vancouver Island.

Summer SkyWalk Music Series
During the summer months, live music creates a fun atmosphere on the plaza, where local bands and artists hit the outdoor stage during the afternoon/evenings from July until September.

MALAHAT NATION

The Malahat SkyWalk is located on the traditional territory of the Malahat Nation of the W̱SÁNEĆ peoples, part of the greater Coast Salish First Nations community, and their Indigenous stories are embedded throughout the experience. The site was developed as part of a partnership between Malahat Nation and the Malahat Skywalk Corp.

TOP TIPS

- Avoid long lines and crowds by visiting during off-season (summer is busiest) and, if possible, plan for a weekday visit.
- Keep your eye on the weather (clear days are best) and book well in advance.
- Wear comfortable walking shoes as the area is explored by foot.
- The SkyWalk is fully accessible, so wheelchairs and strollers can enjoy the experience too.
- The top of the tower can be breezy, so bring an extra layer.
- Parking is free and there's plenty of space for RVs and motorhomes.

341

WEST COAST TRAIL

Sooke is the starting point for the world-famous West Coast Trail – a challenging 75km, multiday hike that takes experienced hikers through muddy landscapes and fast-flowing river waters, and up more than 100 steep ladders. This is no stroll through the woods – the West Coast Trail is rigorous, known to bring even the most advanced adventurers to their knees. Reservations must be made in advance, as camping spots should be secured for overnight stays.

The backcountry trek takes approximately six to eight days to complete, or for those looking for a shorter (but equally difficult) version, there's a midway entry point at Nitinaht Village. The trail was once used by First Nations for travel and trade routes through the West Coast.

Sooke

TIME FROM GREATER VICTORIA: **40 MINS**

See Sooke's river potholes

Running adjacent to the Sooke River, **Sooke Potholes Provincial Park** is a forested find favored by hikers, especially during the summer months. Located 40 minutes by car from downtown Victoria, this expansive park features a unique collection of naturally formed rock pools and potholes that brim the river's bedrock. The crystal-clear waters of these pools invite a refreshing dip after a day spent strolling the scenic park trails where waterfalls delight, and the remaining ruins of an abandoned resort invite curious questions from passersby.

For hikers, several shorter trails run along the river and into the forest, while more-advanced adventurers use this site as the start or end point of a longer hike or bike along the **Galloping Goose Trail**, a rail trail that runs 55km between Victoria and northern Sooke. Many choose to make it a multiday trip, camping or stopping for a stay in smaller communities found along the way.

Sooke Harbour By Water

Boating and wildlife

Water adventures await at **Sooke Marina**, where you can rent (and buy) Vancouver Island's only Hobie kayaks (pedal-powered kayaks) and Hobie Eclipse pedalboards (a souped-up version of the stand-up paddleboard) through West Coast Outdoor Adventure (westcoastoutdoor.com). Guided tours will take you along the coast of Sooke Harbour, where you can weave through the beams of the wooden boardwalk, glide through the crystal-clear waters of the Sooke Basin and, if you're lucky, spot wildlife along the way, such as seals, otters, jellyfish and orcas. For a more extensive wildlife-viewing experience, consider taking a whale-watching tour (there are several on offer in the area).

BEST BEGINNER HIKES IN SOOKE

Ed MacGregor Park
A Sooke boardwalk stroll shifts into a switchback wooden walkway through the woods.

Whiffen Spit Trail
Gravel pathway along a skinny slice of land with views of the Juan de Fuca Strait.

Ross Cove Regional Park Loop
Ocean views and old-growth cedar trees delight on this wander through the rainforest.

Central Island

Calm coastal communities speckle this stretch of the island, where sprawling sandy beaches and meandering mountain trails invite outdoor adventures for all ages and skill levels. Find natural feats and sweet treats in Nanaimo, Vancouver Island's 'second city' and home to the island's legendary Nanaimo Bar dessert. Comb the expansive beaches at low tide and creep through the underground caves that lure thrill-seekers to Parksville: nature's playground. Add country markets fueled by local farms and up-close encounters with local wildlife drawing visitors to Qualicum Beach for a laid-back stay by the water. Veer inland for a peek at the world's tallest waterfall, near Port Alberni. And just west of Courtenay, you'll find a surprising spot for snow lovers: the island's best (and only) ski hill.

Forested Fun in Nanaimo

Teeter above the trees

Found just south of the city of Nanaimo, **WildPlay Nanaimo** takes tree climbing to the next level with aerial adventure courses that challenge climbers of all ages. Cross wobbly bridges, crawl over cargo nets, grip rope swings and zoom across ziplines as you traverse along multi-level platforms set in the trees. Take your treetop thrills to the next level with a bungee jump off a sky-high steel bridge, or make like Tarzan and tackle the Primal Swing, where you drop to the river at speeds of up to 140km/h. Not gung-ho about heights? The scenic walkways are pleasant here too.

Nanaimo Culture

History and heritage

Located downtown, the **Nanaimo Museum** showcases the city's Indigenous origins and architectural highlights. Start with the Snunéymuxw exhibit and learn about the rich living

CANADA'S TALLEST WATERFALL

Della Falls, located in Strathcona Provincial Park in the Central Vancouver Island region, is Canada's tallest waterfall and the 16th highest in the world. Plunging 440m into Great Central Lake, these raging rapids are a sight to behold – if you can get to them. It takes a challenging multiday, high-elevation hike along the 29km (out and back) Della Falls Trail to see them. But first, you'll have to cross Great Central Lake to get to the trailhead, as it's only accessible by water.

A 55-minute water taxi is available during the summer months for $200 per person round trip. Be sure to do your research before you go.

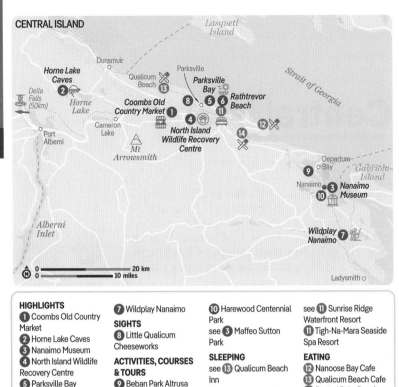

CENTRAL ISLAND

Lasqueti Island

Dunsmuir

Horne Lake Caves

Qualicum Beach **13**

Parksville

Parksville Bay **8** **5** **6** *Rathtrevor Beach* **11**

Della Falls (50km)

Horne Lake

Coombs Old Country Market **1**

Cameron Lake

Mt Arrowsmith

North Island Wildlife Recovery Centre **4**

14

Strait of Georgia

12

Port Alberni

Alberni Inlet

Departure Bay

9

Gabriola Island

Nanaimo

3 *Nanaimo Museum*

10

Wildplay Nanaimo **7**

0   20 km
0   10 miles

Ladysmith

HIGHLIGHTS

1 Coombs Old Country Market
2 Horne Lake Caves
3 Nanaimo Museum
4 North Island Wildlife Recovery Centre
5 Parksville Bay
6 Rathtrevor Beach

7 Wildplay Nanaimo

SIGHTS

8 Little Qualicum Cheeseworks

ACTIVITIES, COURSES & TOURS

9 Beban Park Altrusa Playground

10 Harewood Centennial Park
see **3** Maffeo Sutton Park

SLEEPING

see **13** Qualicum Beach Inn

see **11** Sunrise Ridge Waterfront Resort
11 Tigh-Na-Mara Seaside Spa Resort

EATING

12 Nanoose Bay Cafe
13 Qualicum Beach Cafe
14 Rusted Rake Brewing

☑ TOP TIP

If you're visiting the area from Vancouver, consider taking the car ferry from Horseshoe Bay in West Vancouver to Departure Bay in Nanaimo instead of the more popular Tsawwassen to Victoria route. This will cut down on driving time once you reach the other side.

culture of the Snunéymuxw First Nation. Other highlights include the heritage miner's cottage; the restored steam locomotive, originally built in 1889; the Bastion, the last remaining wooden Hudson's Bay Company bastion built in 1853; and the Sports Hall of Fame.

Nanaimo's Popular Pathway

Hiking and biking

Park the car and take the **E&N Trail** (named after its origins as the Esquimalt to Nanaimo Railway back in the day) through the city instead. This multi-purpose paved pathway connects Nanaimo's waterfront with the Parkway Trail, offering over 8km for walking, biking or blading through the

---

BEST PLAYGROUND IN NANAIMO

Maffeo Sutton Park
Expansive playground with harbor views featuring climbing structures, slides, a zipline and a canoe.

Harewood Centennial Park
Community park with accessible swings, a merry-go-round, a water park and a mountain-bike park.

Beban Park Altrusa Playground
Playground with slides, swings, and a racing track for tikes on trikes.

Sweet-toothed travelers haven't completed a visit to Nanaimo without a taste-testing tour of the tasty tri-layered, no-bake bars that were born here. A wafer crumb base with a creamy custard center, topped with a layer of chocolate ganache – locals may roll their eyes (they've likely had one too many), but these treats are definitely worth a try.

Start your tour at 1 **La Isla Cafe**, where a selection of baked goods (including Nanaimo Bars) are made fresh on-site. A mere three-minute walk away, 2 **A Wee Cupcakery** serves up the classic bars too, as well as a cupcake take that is equally as tasty. Walk it off and stretch your legs on a five-minute stroll to 3 **Red's Bakery**, which offers a variety, including a peanut butter version of the classic bar, and even a Nanaimo Bar cheesecake. Don't eat too much though, as there are plenty more places to try. 4 **Serious Coffee** is only steps away. It has several locations around Vancouver Island (and on the mainland too), and for good reason. Serious Coffee may be best known for its high-quality coffee beans, but its baked goods are tasty too. 5 **Vault Cafe** is close by, and housed in a pretty pink building – it's easy to spot. There you'll find eclectic decor, green-hued walls and a packed pastry case with the classic bars on display. Round out your tasting tour with a final stop at 6 **BOCCA Cafe**, found in the Old City Quarter, serving up a gluten-free, dairy-free version of Nanaimo Bars for those with dietary restrictions. These are only a few stops on the extensive Nanaimo Bar Trail, which includes over 30 spots around the region. See the full list at nanaimo.ca.

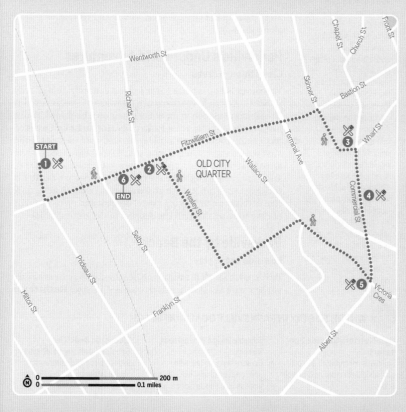

Horne Lake Caves

CENTRAL ISLAND SKIING

Visitors to Vancouver are very familiar with the trifecta of ski hills found on the North Shore mountains, but many don't realize that Vancouver Island offers slopeside fun too. **Mt Washington**, located 30 minutes north of the Comox Valley, has over 680 hectares of alpine terrain, where skiing, snowshoeing trails and a tube park offer snow play (with smaller crowds than the more popular mainland slopes).

During the warmer seasons, mountain biking, hiking and wildlife viewing are big here too. Music lovers: be sure to check out the **Music in the Mountains** concert series during the summer months, where musical acts are paired with samplings of local beer, wine and ciders on Sundays.

area, passing the city's schools, shops and recreational sites along the way.

Parksville's Underworld Adventures
Creep through caves

Vancouver Island is home to the highest concentration of caves in North America, yet many are unaware of the spelunking sites that are hidden in (or under) their own backyard. Found just over 30 minutes from Parksville, **Horne Lake Caves** offers caving tours for all skill levels. Get your toes wet (literally) with a shorter, multi-cave tour fit for beginners. Choose a more action-packed option where you crawl, climb, slide and squeeze through the crevices of the deeper depths of the caves, or go all in with an extreme, max-depth adventure that involves a challenging rappel descent and up to six hours of cave touring through the deepest underground tunnels.

Parksville by the Beach
Low-tide beach play

Best known for its breathtaking beaches, Parksville is a place packed with seaside fun. Unsurpassed in size, **Rathtrevor**

WHERE TO STAY IN PARKSVILLE QUALICUM BEACH

Tigh-Na-Mara Seaside Spa Resort
Spacious rooms with a grotto spa, an indoor pool and beach access.

Sunrise Ridge Waterfront Resort
Condo-style suites with seasonal pool and hot tub, and access to a sandy beach.

Qualicum Beach Inn
Seaside boutique hotel with indoor pool and stunning sunset views.

Beach has 2km of shoreline, with far-reaching low tides that invite treks along the sandy shores in search of seashells and sand dollars. The beach at **Parksville Bay** has a beach party atmosphere, where rounds of beach volleyball create a buzzing vibe. Paddleboarding and swimming are also popular here. The Waterfront Walkway is also a favorite place for locals to get moving outdoors. In July, be sure to check out the Parksville Beach Festival, a five-week festival best known for the sand-sculpting competition where master sculptors from around the world compete for the top title.

Goats on a Roof in Coombs

More than a market

Since 1973 the **Coombs Old Country Market**, found about 10 minutes by car from Parksville, has drawn crowds for its unique feature: a sod roof topped with grazing goats. Inspired by their Norwegian heritage, the original owners built the market with a grass roof, later deciding to add goats to keep the grass mowed, and to add entertainment for passing cars. Today, the roof-roaming goats are a top attraction on likely the most famous sod roof in the world. Not just a spot to gaze at goats, the massive indoor market houses some great gifts and international foods. The site is also home to a delicious doughnut shop, an ice-cream stand, an authentic Italian restaurant and a Taqueria Cantina food truck.

Wildlife Encounters

Eagles, owls and bears

Sitting on 8 acres of meticulously manicured land, **North Island Wildlife Recovery Centre**, only five minutes from Parksville, is a haven for rescued wildlife. The nonprofit association cares for and rehabilitates local wildlife in need. See a rescued eaglet that was found with a broken wing, or a great gray owl (the tallest owl breed in BC). A large outdoor bear den houses a trio of motherless black bear cubs, and there's a super-rare white raven that's unable to survive in the wild. A glistening pond is encircled by a gravel pathway, where you can stroll and spot tons of turtles and ducks, and if you time it just right, a public animal release ceremony is a must.

FAMOUS FARMSTEAD

Cheese lovers will want to make time for a stop at **Little Qualicum Cheeseworks**, a family-run farm that produces Swiss-style, handcrafted artisan cheeses found in shops throughout BC. The farm is home to Canada's first-ever milk on tap dispenser, where locals can bring in their own reusable bottles and fill them with fresh milk for a small fee. Pet calves, sheep and goats as you roam the farmstead, learn about milking and even take a peek at the cheese production plant.

Guided tours are also available if you want to learn more about the farm life and get a behind-the-scenes tour of how it all works.

 BEST BITES IN QUALICUM BEACH

Qualicum Beach Cafe
West Coast–inspired fare with Italian influences, enjoyed from a spacious dining room or patio with sweeping sea views.

Nanoose Bay Cafe
Modern dining room with marina views serving fresh, seafood-forward food with Asian influences.

Rusted Rake Brewing
Gourmet eatery and farm-to-tap craft brewery set on a scenic farmstead in Nanoose Bay.

Pacific Rim

☑ TOP TIP

Fuel up and get an early start to your day, as the drive from Victoria to the Pacific Rim National Park Reserve can take nearly five hours (excluding stops). Construction is ongoing on the main road routes that lead into the region, so check for updates and closures before you go.

BC's raw West Coast wilderness, sandy surf beaches and charming coastal communities collide in the Pacific Rim region of Vancouver Island. This area consists of a trifecta of small towns: Tofino, Canada's surf town; Ucluelet, a harbor hub for angler adventures; and Bamfield, an off-the-beaten-path inlet offering rugged outdoor fun.

The Pacific Rim National Park Reserve lies along the west coast of the area, on the traditional territories of the Nuu-chah-nulth First Nations, and is renowned for its backcountry hiking trails, cold water surfing swells and authentic Indigenous cultural sites. On its northern tip, the UNESCO-designated Clayoquot Sound Biosphere Reserve is renowned for its diverse range of ecosystems, most notably the temperate rainforest and coastal shores, and the population of around 5000 people of the Nuu-chah-nulth First Nations, whose traditional territories encompass the entire biosphere reserve.

CHASE CLAUSEN/SHUTTERSTOCK ©

Surfers, Long Beach

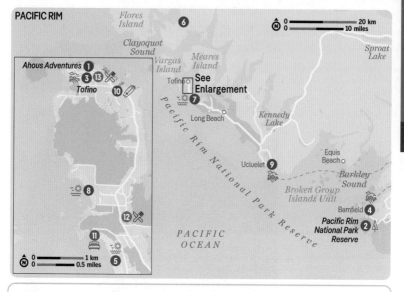

HIGHLIGHTS
1 Ahous Adventures
2 Pacific Rim National Park Reserve
3 Tofino

SIGHTS
4 Bamfield

5 Chesterman Beach
6 Clayoquot Sound Biosphere Reserve
7 Cox Bay Beach
8 Mackenzie Beach
9 Ucluelet

see 9 Ucluelet Aquarium

ACTIVITIES, COURSES & TOURS
10 Surf Sister Surf School

SLEEPING
11 Wickaninnish Inn

EATING
see 9 Pluvio
12 Tacofino
13 Wolf in the Fog

Surfing in Tofino

Canada's surf capital

Year-round swells lure surf bums of all skill levels to Tofino for unparalleled cold-water surfing along Vancouver Island's west coast. For lessons at all levels, check out **Surf Sister**, originally aimed at encouraging more women to try the sport, and now a top surf school for anyone who wants to try. **Cox Bay Beach** is Tofino's main surfing destination, where most surf competitions are held and the surf is most consistent. **Long Beach** has a long history in surf culture and is best for summer swells. **Chesterman Beach** is known for having some of the best breaks for beginners, with three different sections: North, South and Middle; **South Chesterman Beach** is the best place to start. And finally, the calm waters of **Mackenzie Beach** provide a quieter spot for beginner lessons, where

 BEST PLACES TO STAY IN TOFINO

Hotel Zed
Step into the 1970s with a stay at this retro-chic hotel, with mini disco and hidden arcade. $$

Pacific Sands Resort
Surf-in, surf-out beach houses and spacious suites situated right on the ocean. $$

Wickaninnish Inn
Storm-watching central, where luxury accommodations offer sweeping water views from a historic landmark. $$$

349

MARK CAUNT/SHUTTERSTOCK ©

Black bears, Tofino

STORM WATCHING

Along the exposed coast of Tofino, winter weather brings moody skies, wild winds and torrential downpours – conditions that would normally repel visitors during the cooler months. In 1996, after years of witnessing dramatic storms along Chesterman Beach, the McDiarmid family opened the Wickaninnish Inn hoping others would enjoy storm watching too. Now winter storm watching is one of Tofino's biggest draws, bringing visitors from around the world to try to get a glimpse of the winter weather phenomenon.

stand-up paddleboarders also prefer to play as the tidal rocks provide protection from the winds here.

Tofino Through an Indigenous Lens

Eco and cultural tours

Owned and operated by the Ahousaht Nation, **Ahous Adventures** offers authentic Indigenous tours throughout the Pacific Rim region, shared through the lens of the people who have lived on the lands and waters of the area since time

 BEST PLACES TO EAT IN TOFINO

Wolf in the Fog
Award-winning, seafood-centric food with a rustic, beach-in-the-wilderness vibe. **$$**

Tacofino
West Coast flavors meet Mexican staples at this street-food-style chain that started as a food truck in Tofino. **$**

Pluvio
Ucluelet's newest restaurant, serving sophisticated multi-course tasting menus in a warm and casual setting. **$$$**

immemorial. Explore the natural hot springs found at Hot Springs Cove, search for gray whales and humpback whales along the wild waters of Tofino on a whale-watching tour, or observe black bears in their natural habitat along the coast of Clayoquot Sound, all while learning about the history, culture, storytelling and experiences of the Ahousaht Nation.

Ucluelet Sea Life

Tide pools and touch tanks

One of Ucluelet's most popular local attractions, the **Ucluelet Aquarium** is a great family-friendly site and Canada's first catch-and-release aquarium that focuses on showcasing the marine critters found in the region's local waters of Barkley and Clayoquot Sounds. You can see everything from the alien-like sea cucumbers to squirming Pacific octopus in a fun and engaging setting on the waterfront. Touch tanks even let little ones get hands-on with the critters of the sea. The enthusiastic staff sets this place apart, educating visitors on issues of conservation in a way that's easy for kids to understand. Expect to walk away with renewed excitement about the wonders of ocean wildlife.

Hiking in Ucluelet

Wild Wilderness Walk

Take a trek along the **Wild Pacific Trail** in Ucluelet, where the temperate rainforest meets the ocean. The residents of "Ukee" have built the magnificent 10km trail that can be equally spectacular in both sunny and (stormy) rainy weather. The hike starts with a 2.6km loop that winds around the 1915 Amphitrite lighthouse and progresses northwest as far as the Ancient Cedars loop and the Rocky Bluffs beyond. The trail is well signposted with a well-marked map. To complete the whole 10km you'll need to take a couple of interconnecting pathways along quiet roads that link to several attractive beaches on the way. Various info boards provide background on the area's history and nature, and the path is dotted with benches, lookouts and artist's loops equipped with viewing platforms that are perfect for inspired artists looking to take painting stops along the way.

TACO THE TOWN

From slinging tacos from a truck in a surf shop parking lot back in 2009, to becoming an iconic West Coast brand, **Tacofino** is now a staple around Vancouver Island and the Lower Mainland, serving up the best tacos in town. Here you'll find fresh, California- and Mexico-inspired fare, like the famous fish tacos made of tempura lingcod or the seared albacore tuna taco, best enjoyed with a side of loaded tater tots.

Hit the original orange truck, which still stands in a parking lot in Tofino, or opt for a sit down at one of the 11 locations that have popped up around Vancouver, Victoria and Tofino – just be prepared to wait in line!

RUSS HEINL/SHUTTERSTOCK ©

PRACTICALITIES

For more info and to plan your visit, scan this QR code.

Clayoquot Sound

TOP SIGHT

Pacific Rim National Park Reserve

Natural wonders, cultural history and outdoor adventures amaze in this national park. Located on the traditional territories of the Nuu-chah-nulth people, the park consists of the surf beaches of Long Beach, the calm waters of Broken Group Islands and the tree-lined paths of the West Coast Trail. The protected coast of Clayoquot Sound is a UNESCO-designated site, recognized for its natural and cultural characteristics.

DON'T MISS

Clayoquot Sound

Long Beach

ʔapsčiik t̓ašii pathway

Nuu-chah-nulth Trail

West Coast Trail

Broken Group Islands

Clayoquot Sound

Found along the west-coast waters of Vancouver Island is the area known as Clayoquot Sound. The name derived from 'Tla-o-qui-aht,' the largest community of the Nuu-chah-nulth Indigenous peoples who have called this area home for thousands of years. Here, rocky ocean shores and untouched temperate rainforest (mostly ancient western hemlock) make for a choice spot for outdoor adventures and wildlife viewing. Whale-watching tours are big here, and if you can afford it, an off-grid luxury escape to Clayoquot Wilderness Lodge (accessed only by boat or air) combines wild wilderness adventures with upscale safari-style slumber.

Long Beach

Tofino is Canada's surf town and Long Beach has the swells to satisfy. It's the largest and longest beach found in the Pacific Rim National Park Reserve, stretching 16km along the coastline between Tofino and Ucluelet. Keep an eye out for passing gray and humpback whales while beachcombing, swimming, surfing or just sunbathing on its warm, sandy shores.

ʔapsčiik t̓ašii Pathway

Also found in the Long Beach area of the Pacific Rim National Park Reserve is ʔapsčiik t̓ašii (pronounced ups-cheek ta-shee, meaning 'going the right direction on the path' in Nuu-chah-nulth dialects). This paved, multi-use pathway runs 25km along the coast, connecting Tofino and Ucluelet, making the region more accessible for those who are car-free. The path invites visitors to cycle or stroll, exploring the beauty of the reserve while respecting and honoring the First Nations land and communities of the area.

Nuu-chah-nulth Trail

Formerly known as the Wickaninnish Trail, Nuu-chah-nulth Trail is the longest hiking trail in the park, connecting Long Beach to Florencia Beach. Beginning along the South Beach Trail, hikers go on a 3.8km journey through dense rainforest along raised wooden boardwalks. Along the way, look for remnants of the rich history of the land, such as old logs that run under the more modern wooden boardwalks, remaining sections of a trail that was originally used by the Nuu-chah-nulth, and later covered by logs by settlers for easy access.

West Coast Trail

A bucket-list trek for the most experienced hikers, this 75km backcountry trail consists of challenging and technical terrain, taking you up a series of ladders, through muddy bogs and along washed-out walkways. Along the trail, Tsusiat Falls is a hike highlight, with scenic, wide-spanning falls, a swimming beach and one of the more popular campsites found along the trail. The hike takes six to eight days to complete from end-to-end, with campgrounds along the way.

Broken Group Islands

A collection of over 100 tiny islands and outcrops found along calm, sheltered coastlines, Broken Group Islands has become a paradise for backcountry campers and kayakers. Gibraltar Island is a popular starting point for paddlers who make their way along the water weaving through the islets and camping along the way, with sites found on Gilbert, Clarke, Turret, Willis and Hand Islands. Many guided kayak tours through the islands are offered, which is a great way to get around without getting lost if it's your first go.

NATIONAL PARKS PASS

All visitors are required to purchase a National Parks Entry Pass (youths 17 and under gain free access to all of Canada's national parks). Adults can purchase daily passes ($10.50), annual passes ($52.25), or walk passes for select beaches ($6.50). For info visit parks.canada.ca.

TOP TIPS

- For beginner surfers, visit between June and August when the water is warmer and swells are smaller.
- For first-time surfers, skip Long Beach and consider South Chesterman Beach where most surf schools offer starter lessons.
- Visit parks.canada.ca and download the preparation guide before you tackle overnight hikes.
- When hiking overnight, pack out everything you bring with you.
- Check for sites with food poles and storage boxes when backcountry camping.
- When camping around Broken Group Islands, keep campfires below tide lines.

North Island

Go way off grid as you move further up to the North Island region of Vancouver Island, where wildlife such as eagles, whales and bears roam free among untouched landscapes, and Kwakwaka'wakw First Nations traditions, art and living culture surround you.

In this remote region of outstanding natural beauty, the infrastructure is rudimentary. Like anything north of Campbell River, it's what islanders call the 'real north.' With its tiny population, wild coastline and temperamental seas, the area is faintly reminiscent of the Scottish Highlands, but with more trees. In fact, several local landmarks are named after Scots, including the most northwesterly point, Cape Scott. Find colorful buildings set on stilts along the coast of Telegraph Cove, once a fishing village and now the launch point for ecotourism in the region. Kayak with orcas in Johnstone Strait, or immerse yourself in Kwakwaka'wakw culture here.

EB ADVENTURE PHOTOGRAPHY/SHUTTERSTOCK ©

Cape Scott

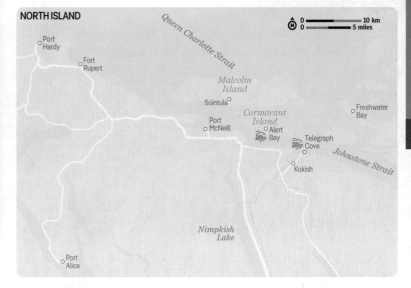

Telegraph Cove
Colorful community

Named after its beginnings as a one-shack telegraph station, Telegraph Cove evolved into a fishing village and cannery in its earlier days, and has since grown into what is now recognized as the kickoff point for ecotourism to the more remote northern regions of the island. Around 20 people call this tiny town home, but during the summer months the crowds swell, as the town floods with day-trippers looking for off-grid adventures in the wild. This town is where BC's first whale-watching company launched in 1980, and it's still famed for its aquatic adventures. The snug cove houses a series of colorful shacks that sit on stilts, creating a charming, picture-perfect harbor town.

North Island Waterways
Kayakers' paradise

Launching from Telegraph Cove, **North Island Kayak Tours**, the largest kayaking tour operator in the area, offers wildlife-watching, sea-kayak trips with guides from June to September. These range from two-hour family excursions along the coast to eight-day basecamp expeditions, all in search of humpback whales, sea lions and Indigenous cultural sites.

DRUM TRADITIONS

For the Indigenous peoples of present-day BC, the drum is used as an important tool for communication and connection. The drum symbolizes the circle, representing balance, equality, wholeness and connection. Traditional drums are made by stretching animal hide over a wooden frame and the Tsimshian and Kwakwaka'wakw also make and play box drums, which are rectangular. Some Indigenous tour operators offer drum-making classes, such as k'awat'si Tours.

BEST NORTH ISLAND WILDLIFE TOURS

North Island Kayak Tours
Go whale-watching by sea kayak and see orcas and other whales swimming by your boat.

Great Bear Nature Tours
Grizzly bear–viewing tours from Port Hardy to the river valley of the Great Bear Rainforest.

k'awat'si Tours
View wildlife from the water and roam remote beaches while listening to stories from an Indigenous guide.

TOOLKIT

The chapters in this section cover the most important topics you'll need to know about in Washington, Oregon and the Pacific Northwest. They're full of nuts-and-bolts information and valuable insights to help you understand and navigate the Pacific Northwest and get the most out of your trip.

Arriving
p358

Getting Around
p359

Money
p360

Accommodations
p361

Family Travel
p362

Health & Safe Travel
p363

Food, Drink & Nightlife
p364

Responsible Travel
p366

LGBTiQ+ Travelers
p368

Accessible Travel
p369

Gearing Up in the Pacific Northwest
p370

Nuts & Bolts
p371

Stand-up paddleboarding (p370)

THOMAS BARWICK/GETTY IMAGES ©

Arriving

The Pacific Northwest has three large international airports: Seattle-Tacoma (SEA), Portland (PDX) and Vancouver (YVR). The Pacific Northwest can also be reached by train from California and Chicago. Many visitors arrive in their own vehicles.

Visas

The US Visa Waiver Program (VWP) permits residents of 40 countries for stays up to 90 days without a visa. Other nationalities need to apply for a visa at a US embassy.

Currency Exchange

Available at all three international airports but rates are better outside the airport or from an ATM. Bring enough US currency for the first few days to cover basic needs and tipping.

Cell Phones

Ensure international roaming is enabled before departure. Local SIM cards are available at airport electronic shops or from carriers and big-box stores in the region.

ATMs

Machines linked to large banks include US Bank at Portland and Seattle airports. Vancouver has an RBC Royal Bank ATM.

Public Transport from Airport to City Center

	Seattle	Portland	Vancouver
TRAIN	$3 / 45min	$2.50 / 45min	$9 / 35min
RIDE-SHARE	$35–40 / 20min	$30–35 / 15min	$30 / 20min
TAXI	$40–45 / 20min	$35–40 / 15min	$40–45 / 20min

TO THE PACIFIC NORTHWEST BY TRAIN

Amtrak has two main routes into the Pacific Northwest from elsewhere in the US. The *Coast Starlight* travels up the West Coast from Los Angeles, with stops in Oakland and Sacramento before reaching Oregon at Klamath Falls and continuing to Eugene, Portland and Seattle. Departures are daily. From Chicago, travelers can board the *Empire Builder* and reach Seattle or Portland via St Paul. The Portland route offers spectacular scenery as it goes through the Columbia River Gorge in the final leg of the journey.

Getting Around

Using your own car (or a rental) is the quickest way to get around; bus and train travel is also available. The Northwest is a great area for cycle touring.

TRAVEL COSTS

Car rental
From $70 per day

Gas
Approx $4.30 per gallon

EV charging
$20–$40

Train ticket from Seattle to Portland
$28

Hiring a Car

Rental rates from the airport or in the city will be the same, and rates are similar across major firms. The minimum age is 25. Picking up a car in one city and dropping it off in another will increase costs. RV or trailer rental is available in most cities.

Road Conditions

Winter weather can wash out roads, cause mudslides and block roads with snow. Icy conditions can occur at higher elevations. Carry chains and check road conditions with transportation departments: Oregon (tripcheck.com), Washington (wsdot.wa.gov) and British Columbia (drivebc.ca) post road conditions.

RIGHT OF WAY

Jaywalking is common in the Northwest and bike riders often disregard rules on light changes so you'll need to stay vigilant of both bikers and pedestrians, giving them the right of way. Pull over at the sight or sound of an ambulance or fire engine, even if they are headed in the opposite direction.

TIP

Bicycles can be placed on a rack outside of public buses (they are located in front of the bus).

DRIVING ESSENTIALS

Drive on the right

65

Speed limit is 65mph on most interstate highways, 55mph on two-lane highways and 20mph in school zones during school hours

.08

Blood alcohol limit is 0.08%

Train, Bus & Ferry

The Pacific Northwest is well served by different modes of public transportation. I-5 especially has a good network of bus and train connections. Buses to rural areas are infrequent. Ferries can be used to reach cities located in Seattle's Puget Sound.

Plane

Airlines connect cities across the Pacific Northwest and travel by plane can speed up your journey; on the downside you'll miss the scenery between places. Poor weather can cause delays and cancellations. Book as early as possible for lower prices.

Public Transit Tickets

Metro areas in the Pacific Northwest have public transit cards that provide access to buses, light-rail and street cars. Portland uses the Hop Fastpass, in Seattle it's the ORCA card and Vancouver has the Compass Card.

Money

CURRENCY: US DOLLAR ($)

Credit & Debit Cards

Widely accepted for almost any purchase and essential for booking online plane tickets, car hire and hotel reservations. Visa and MasterCard are the most common. American Express and Diner's Club may not be accepted everywhere. Avoid ATM fees by getting cashback when paying at a grocery store.

Taxes

Oregon has no sales tax. Washington state sales tax is 6.5%. British Columbia sales tax is 7%. Hotel taxes are encountered across the region.

Tipping Etiquette

Tipping is standard at bars and restaurants, drivers, porters, bellhops and housekeepers will also expect a tip; 15% to 20% of the pretax bill is expected.

Using Cash

Locally owned businesses that deal in small transactions (cafes, doughnut/bagel shops) may only accept cash or will charge a fee for cards. Some gas stations also charge 10 cents more per gallon if payment is made with plastic. Have cash on hand for small purchases and tip jars.

HOW MUCH FOR A...

state parks parking ticket
$5

national park fee
$30

food-truck meal
$8–15

bridge toll
$2–4

HOW TO... **Travel on a Budget**

Buy a Northwest Forest Pass (discovernw.org), which costs $30 and grants entry to national forests in Washington and Oregon. An America the Beautiful National Parks pass (store.usgs.gov) is $80 and is good for the four national parks in the Pacific Northwest. For unlimited access to national parks in Canada, pick up a Parks Canada Discovery Pass (parks.canada.ca). A group pass costs $145.

PRICEY LIVING

Travel in the Pacific Northwest can be costly, with both Oregon and Washington among the top 10 most expensive places to live, in some rankings. Filling the gas tank in Oregon and Washington is also more expensive than any other state except California. Among Canada's most expensive cities, Vancouver is second only to Toronto. The region's high-tech industry drives up salaries, pushing up costs and real-estate prices across the board. Fortunately for visitors, most of the attractions in the Pacific Northwest are outdoorsy and either free or low-cost.

LOCAL TIP

Most cities have food cart pods where you can get low-cost meals while supporting a local business. Farmers markets are good places to pick up local organic produce at low prices.

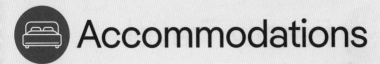

Accommodations

Old-School B&Bs

Staying at a B&B is one of the best ways to get a feel for Pacific Northwest hospitality. Accommodations are often inside a historic home, many of them tastefully restored. Hosts will cook up a hearty breakfast (frequently with locally sourced foods) and offer good advice on what to see and do in the area.

Cabins, Yurts & Tents

The Pacific Northwest is a great region for camping, provided you have your own gear. Most state parks, national forests and national parks have designated campsites with simple facilities and a camp host who can offer local advice. Private campgrounds and RV parks with tent sites are also available. Many campgrounds also offer accommodations in cabins and yurts.

Resorts Big & Small

Resorts in the Pacific Northwest come in all shapes and sizes. Some are rustic lakeside places that offer great local hospitality, such as Cultus Lake Resort (OR). Others are large, upscale places with every possible amenity, from golf to spa treatments, like Skamania Lodge (WA). Even smaller places in remote locations will have a restaurant and supply shop.

Go Modern Nomad

RV touring is growing in popularity and RV parks are popping up all over the place to serve RV needs. They range from simple places with grass and trees to more upscale resorts with swimming pools and activities. RV rentals start at around $700 a week for older models but consider that you'll be saving money by avoiding hotels.

HOW MUCH FOR A NIGHT IN...

a hostel dorm
$60–70

a campground tent site
$25–35

a B&B
From $120

Renovations Galore

Dilapidated and boarded-up hotel properties across the region are getting a second chance and being saved from the wrecking ball to accommodate tourists. Roadside motels in particular are getting a makeover, with hot tubs, pool and saunas. McMenamins has done a good job transforming old properties into swish hotels. The company now has four hotels in Washington and eight in Oregon.

HIGH SEASON & ROOM TAXES

High season in the Pacific Northwest runs from May into September. During this time hotel rooms, campgrounds and resorts can be booked out and prices skyrocket. You'll get better deals if you can visit in the shoulder season. Prices for hotels plunge in winter but many campgrounds and resorts will be closed for the season. Note that accommodations prices will spike briefly in late December for the holidays. State lodging taxes will apply for most accommodations in the region and some cities or counties add their taxes to your bill.

Family Travel

The Pacific Northwest is a great family destination with activities for all ages. Hiking, tent camping, fishing and beachcombing are a few of the adventures that await families. In urban areas, there are amusement parks, kid-friendly museums and zoos to visit. Just getting around can be fun too, with train rides and ferries that kids will love.

Prams, Strollers & Babies

Strollers will work fine in urban areas but a child carrier becomes the better option when hiking. Formula, diapers and other supplies are readily available at grocery stores, pharmacies and big-box stores. Restaurants are usually equipped with a changing table. Hotels often have a crib they can loan to families.

Car Travel

Kids must be in a car seat or booster seat, depending on their size and age. Upon landing, it can be challenging to get a taxi if you don't have a car seat (most drivers won't allow kids to sit on their parent's lap because of seatbelt laws). Rental-car companies can usually rustle up a car seat if you give them advance notice.

Kid-Friendly Restaurants

Restaurants will usually have a kids menu or can special order something. Kids are even welcome in brewpubs (but not bars). Your server may bring some crayons and paper to keep little ones busy.

Accommodations

Destination resorts are nice because of the activities to keep kids busy. Kids also enjoy spending the night in a tent so camping is a good option. Hotels with convenient parking are great if you are moving a lot of luggage.

BEST ATTRACTIONS FOR FAMILIES

Evergreen Wings & Waves Waterpark, Oregon
A year-round indoor waterslide park attached to Evergreen Aviation & Space Museum (p203) – slide out of a 747!

Science World, Vancouver (p322)
STEAM-focused museum with lots of hands-on science activities and educational exhibits.

Seattle Center (p69)
Large complex with family-friendly options including a children's museum and artists-at-play playground.

Oregon Museum of Science and Industry (p187)
Physics experiments, visit inside the human body and more.

HOLDING THE PURSE STRINGS

Family trips in the Pacific Northwest can quickly escalate in price depending on what you see and do. Fortunately, there is plenty to do that is low cost or free. Beaches are always a winning choice among kids. In the mountains, forest hikes to waterfalls and lakes are fun (as long as the trek isn't too long). Floating on tubes down streams and rivers is a kid favorite, and a one-off guided rafting trip is good value. In all Pacific Northwest cities, there are parks and playgrounds to explore. As you plan your day consider picnics in scenic areas instead of pricier sit-down restaurants.

Health & Safe Travel

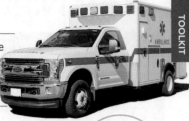

INSURANCE

Medical issues, theft and loss can occur anywhere and the Pacific Northwest is no different, so it's good to carry a travel insurance policy that can help if problems arise.

Beach Safety

Never turn your back on the ocean when beachcombing or tide pooling and don't let children go near the shore unsupervised. Sneaker waves (like a mini tsunami) are not common but can occur on the Oregon Coast without warning, knocking people down and pulling them into the sea. Heed warnings on signs posted on beaches.

Wildfire & Smoke

Wildfire has become more common in the Pacific Northwest in recent years and threatens lives and property. The associated smoke from a fire can cover cities located hundreds of miles from the actual fire. Learn about wildfire prevention when camping in forested areas and limit outdoor exposure when the Air Quality Index (AQI) goes above 150.

SUMMERS THAT BAKE

Summers can become dangerously hot. Carry lots of water, a hat and sunglasses, and always use sunscreen.

AIR QUALITY

Green
Good 0 to 50

Yellow
Moderate 51 to 100

Orange
Unhealthy for sensitive groups 101 to 150

Red
Unhealthy 151 to 200

Purple
Very unhealthy 201 to 300

Ice & Snow

Ice and snow can create hazardous driving conditions. Carry chains and rent a car with snow tires if possible, especially if you are driving east of the Cascades. When traveling in snow have extra warm clothes, food and water in case your vehicle becomes stranded. Bring a phone charger for your car. Walk like a penguin on icy sidewalks.

GO HARD, WITHIN LIMITS

Mountaineering, rock climbing, mountain biking, skiing and other outdoor adventures are all fun but inherently risky. Mountain patrols on ski slopes and search-and-rescue teams can only do so much when an accident occurs. Have fun out there but recreate within your limits, skills and experience.

Food, Drink & Nightlife

When to Eat

Breakfast Typically from 7am to 10am. Locals may just grab something to go.

Brunch Usually from 11am to 2pm on weekends. Breakfast and lunch dishes served. May include alcohol.

Lunch Served from 11:30am to 2:30pm, often for social events and business meetings.

Dinner From 5pm to 9pm. A meal with family and/or friends.

Where to Eat

Diners The best spot for breakfast and comfort food when traveling on the open road. The good ones are often in small towns and truck stops.

Brewpub Restaurant-brewery hybrids are ubiquitous in the PNW. They typically serve lunch and dinner.

Farmers markets Vendors sell produce and prepared food. Usually held just once or twice a week (and often just in summer).

Food trucks The go-to spots for quick, tasty food. Multiple trucks clustered in one area with picnic tables are called 'pods.'

MENU DECODER

Corkage You may bring your own wine bottle to a restaurant but opening it usually comes with a charge of $15 to $30.

Dungeness crab Common crab species in the Pacific Northwest. Has a slightly sweet, slightly salty taste.

Entree Another way of saying 'main course.'

Northwest cuisine Applies to dishes made with ingredients that are sourced locally and native to the area; you'll see salmon, shellfish, game meats like moose or elk, berries and wild mushrooms.

Marionberry Similar to a blackberry. These were originally bred by scientists at Oregon State University. Oregon produces 90% of them.

Sando Short for sandwich.

Tasting menu A multi-course meal that consists of several small dishes. Comes from the French tradition of *menu dégustation*.

HOW TO... Buy Seafood in the Pacific Northwest

A joy of visiting coastal areas is the opportunity to dine on freshly caught crab and fish. But seafood in the Pacific Northwest is seasonal and fishing is not allowed at certain times of the year to allow the ocean-dwelling species to breed and recover. Look at the menu boards or ask a server what is available. Dungeness crab (harvested from December to August) is served whole or the meat is put inside a sandwich. Crab fans should make a pilgrimage to Newport (OR), 'The Dungeness Crab Capital of the World.' Salmon is also seasonal. Chinook is available from April to October while coho salmon is caught from July to September. Fish and chips are a staple year-round but the fish used is often Pacific cod from Alaska. If you prefer a local fish, ask the restaurant what is available – they may be able to make it with local rockfish.

THIS IS THE ORIGINAL SINCE 1916

Dining in the Pacific Northwest

Start your day by picking up some doughnuts to go. The most unusual ones are found at Voodoo Doughnut (p208) in Oregon but most towns will have their own doughnut shop, usually opening very early.

An actual breakfast is usually old-school logging tucker – pancakes, eggs, hash browns, toast and sausage or bacon.

Come lunchtime, get fish and chips if you are anywhere near the coast. Try the Bowpicker in Astoria (but be prepared to wait in line). Alternatively, go to a food cart pod for a good meal and to support a local small business. You'll find some of the Pacific Northwest's most daring cuisine coming out of food trucks as they tend to be breeding grounds for new chefs looking to create a niche business. Taquerias are also popular and found in every town.

Dinner often means farm-to-table meals made from organic meats and veggies. The region is famed for its small ranchers producing high-quality organic meats and farmers that grow non-GMO seasonal vegetables. Wild mushrooms and fish from the Columbia River and Pacific Ocean are also important food sources. Sweets are big and locally produced ice creams, chocolates and pies will make their way to your table after a meal.

Food Trucks

Portland has around 1000 food trucks (known locally as food carts). In 2023 *Food & Wine* magazine named it Best Food Truck City in America.

HOW MUCH FOR A...

coffee
$4–6

craft beer
$6–9

burrito
$9–12

brewpub burger
$9–18

fish and chips
$13–20

plate of pasta
$16–22

large pizza
$22–28

sandwich to go
$8–12

OUT FOR A DRINK

Drinking culture has deep roots in the Pacific Northwest. Perhaps it has something to do with the cold and rainy climate and the need to stay indoors, passing the time with a beverage in one hand and a book in the other.

Seattle is home to Starbucks, over the past 50 years has become a global coffee juggernaut, but other roasters have followed. The city has 56 coffee shops for every 100,000 people so a latte is never far away. Oregon-based Dutch Bros helped start the drive-thru coffee craze and smaller roasters like Tully's have gone national.

The region is also considered the cradle of America's craft-beer scene. One reason for its success is the production of hops; the Pacific Northwest produces 98% of the US supply.

At the epicenter of this phenomenon is Bend (OR).

Sometimes called Beertown, USA, the city and its surrounding towns have around 30 breweries conjuring up everything from milkshake IPAs to British-style cask ales. But craft beer is everywhere now. Even tiny towns are churning out big-time beers – Enterprise, OR (population 2100), is home to the popular Terminal Gravity Brewing.

You won't need to go far for locally produced wine either. The Willamette, Walla Walla and Yakima valleys are major producers of wine so you'll have no trouble finding a pinot noir or chardonnay to pair with your meal. The Pacific Northwest is starting to branch out to other alcoholic beverages and you'll have a chance to visit distilleries, cideries and breweries.

Responsible Travel

Climate Change & Travel

It's impossible to ignore the impact we have when traveling, and the importance of making changes where we can. Lonely Planet urges all travelers to engage with their travel carbon footprint. There are many carbon calculators online that allow travelers to estimate the carbon emissions generated by their journey; try resurgence.org/resources/carbon-calculator.html. Many airlines and booking sites offer travelers the option of offsetting the impact of greenhouse gas emissions by contributing to climate-friendly initiatives around the world. We continue to offset the carbon footprint of all Lonely Planet staff travel, while recognizing this is a mitigation more than a solution.

Visit Rural Communities

Pacific Northwest tourism tends to concentrate around the big sights, leaving many well-deserving places without a lot of visitors. Explore some lesser-known sights and get to know the region's rural communities.

Volunteer

Opportunities for volunteering in the Pacific Northwest include supporting social services or litter-removal projects in natural areas including beaches and riverbanks. Check with nonprofit organizations, community centers and schools.

In 2020 Oregon set a goal of reducing its greenhouse gas emissions to 45% below 1990 levels by 2035 and to at least 80% by 2050.

When fishing, use catch-and-release methods and barbless hooks. If you catch an invasive species it's fine to get out the frying pan and prepare a meal.

SUSTAINABLE SEAFOOD

Pacific Northwest fishers abide by strict regulations to sustain stocks of fish and other sea creatures. Oregon State University offers a helpful guide on its website, search 'Eat Oregon Seafood.'

RESPONSIBLE HIKING

Stay on trails to avoid erosion and look for designated entry spots when getting in rivers to avoid trampling riparian areas. Leave your campsite looking better than you found it.

Leave Wildlife Alone

Lone fawn or elk calves should not be approached. Mothers often leave their young for extended periods to feed while also not drawing attention to them.

Rent an Electric Car

Cut down on your carbon footprint by renting an EV instead of a gas-powered car. Hertz has the largest fleet of EVs. Charging stations can be found all over the Pacific Northwest.

Oregon ranks 10th in the US for its green building projects based on LEED-certified gross square footage per capita.

An impressive 98% of Vancouver's energy comes from renewable sources, mostly hydropower.

Bike by the Hour

Rentable e-bikes and scooters are available in most larger cities and towns in the Northwest. It's usually pay-per-hour and you can leave your bike at a designated location.

Buying Produce

Buying local produce is a way to reduce your carbon footprint because seasonal local foods, compared to imported veggies, require less fuel to get them into the hands of consumers.

Protect Caves

Bat colonies can be harmed by white-nose syndrome, which can be transferred through clothing even if washed. If you plan to visit multiple caves during your trip, be sure to wear a different set of clothing.

Tree Canopy

Seattle is ranked seventh in the world for canopy cover, a way to measure green spaces in cities. The Emerald City has a goal of increasing its current 20% canopy cover to 30% by 2037.

RESOURCES

Downloadable cycle maps for Oregon and Washington are available on the department of transportation websites for each state.

LGBTIQ+ Travelers

The Pacific Northwest is among the most gay-friendly regions to live and travel. Portland, Seattle and Vancouver and other mid-sized cities have thriving gay communities and long histories of gay-rights activism. Rural areas in the Pacific Northwest can be fairly conservative and attitudes to the LGBTIQ+ community may be mixed.

Months to Visit

LGBTIQ+ travel is fine in any month but if you're looking to attend events then certain times of the year are better than others. The highlight is June when Pride events are held across the region, including Seattle, Bend and Spokane. Some cities hold their events later – Portland has its Pride events in July, while Vancouver and Eugene have theirs in August. Summertime is also good for visiting gay beaches, including Wreck Beach in Vancouver. In winter, head north of the border for the Whistler Pride & Ski Festival at Whistler Blackcomb.

GAY-OWNED BUSINESSES

LGBTIQ+-owned small businesses need support any time of year, not just during Pride Month. Start with Remy Wines at the Willamette Valley. This winery launched the first Queer Wine Fest in 2022; it's now an annual event.

Oregon's Pioneering Politicians

In 2022 Oregon voters sent Tina Kotek to the governor's mansion in Salem, making her one of the first two gay women governors (alongside Maura Healey of Massachusetts). In 2009 Sam Adams became the first openly gay mayor of a large US city (Portland).

CENTERS OF ATTENTION

Queer life in Seattle is concentrated in the Capitol Hill neighborhood, along a section of Pike St. In Vancouver, try Davie Village, recognizable by its rainbow-colored crosswalks. Commercial Dr in east Vancouver is popular with the city's lesbian community. There is no specific gay neighborhood in Portland although Darcelle XV Showplace is a legendary drag show. In Bend, try Turtle Island Coffee Shop downtown.

Documentaries Worth Watching

Darcelle XV was the nation's oldest performing drag queen until her death in 2023 at age 92. Her Portland cabaret is believed to be the longest-running drag revue in the country. Oregon Public Broadcasting created a 30-minute documentary about her life, available for viewing on PBS. *Queer Vancouver* and *There Goes the Gayborhood* are two documentaries worth watching on the histories of gay life in Vancouver and Seattle.

LGBTIQ+ RESOURCES

Seattle Gay News (sgn.org) Weekly newspaper that focuses on gay issues.
Proud Queer (pqmonthly.com) Online news serving Portland's gay community.
Vancouver Pride Society (vancouverpride.ca) Promotes events in the Vancouver area.
Queer Eugene (queereugene.org) Resources for Eugene's queer community.

Accessible Travel

The Pacific Northwest offers good accessibility to travelers with disabilities. The Americans with Disabilities Act (ADA) requires that public buildings are wheelchair-accessible; this includes most hotels, restaurants and museums.

Passes

The America the Beautiful Access Pass is a free, lifetime pass available to US citizens and permanent residents with a permanent disability. It provides admittance to more than 2000 recreation sites, including national parks.

Airport

Airports in the Pacific Northwest comply with ADA regulations. Airport staff will assist wheelchair users at the check-in counter but it's a good idea to let the airline know ahead of time that assistance will be needed.

Accommodations

Smaller B&Bs (especially those in historic homes) may not be able to offer comprehensive services for people with disabilities. Larger hotels are your best bet when it comes to accessibility.

TRAILS

Many trails in the Pacific Northwest are wheelchair-friendly. Traillink.com has a searchable map of trails that can accommodate wheelchair users. The website disabledhikers.com also provides good guidance for getting outdoors.

TRAINS

Amtrak trains can accommodate most types of wheelchairs but they should not exceed 27.5in wide and 48in long when occupied. Chairs should also have a minimum of 2in of ground clearance.

Buses

Lift-equipped buses are standard in the Pacific Northwest. Some municipal bus companies offer a dial-a-ride service and will pick you up at a designated location but you may need to call one day ahead.

Adaptive Sports

Adaptive sports programs are available in many areas of the Pacific Northwest. Organizations include Oregon Adaptive Sports in Bend (OR), Adaptive Sports Northwest in Portland and Seattle Adaptive Sports.

RESOURCES

Travel Oregon A great resource for accessible travel. Check the 'Plan Your Trip' page on their website.

Washington Trails Association Includes a list of accessible hikes for wheelchair users. Search 'ADA' on their website.

hellobc.com Has information on accessibility on its planning tab.

Society for Accessible Travel & Hospitality (sath. org) Useful links and general travel information.

Mobi Mats

Mobi Mats are portable, nonslip mats that roll out on beaches, allowing wheelchair users to get close to the shore. The mats are available in a few locations, including Lincoln City (OR), Alki Beach in Seattle and English Bay in Vancouver.

Gearing Up in the Pacific Northwest

A major attraction of the Pacific Northwest is the wealth of opportunities to ski, climb, bike, hike and float in its beautiful landscapes. But if you have only arrived with the boots on your feet it may be necessary to find some gear before you go and recreate.

Camping Equipment

Bringing lots of camping equipment to the Pacific Northwest may involve checking in an extra gear bag (or two), which will require you paying airline luggage fees. Airlines typically charge around $30 per bag unless you are in business class, in which case the fee is waived on most airlines. An alternative is to rent camping gear when you arrive in the region. The Mountain Shop in Portland and MTN Gear in Seattle both rent camping equipment.

Buying Equipment

Outdoor gear shops in the Pacific Northwest will usually sell gear seasonally so skis are available in winter and are put away for the summer to make room for bikes, hiking gear and camping equipment. The largest retailer in the region is REI, headquartered in Washington. MEC is the largest retailer in Vancouver. Columbia is headquartered in Oregon and concentrates mainly on winter and summer outdoor clothing.

No-Sales-Tax Shopping

There is no sales tax in Oregon so if you are planning to make any big purchases of outdoor gear you'll save a little money by shopping south of the OR–WA state line.

Bikes

Some bike shops rent bikes and other equipment for mountain-bike or cycling adventures. Bike racks for a car are also sometimes available. Fat-tire bikes, e-bikes, mountain bikes, road bikes and gravel bikes are some of the options. Prices start at around $40 and climb from there depending on the quality and type of bicycle.

Skis

Ski resorts will rent out ski equipment, of course, but prices can vary, and larger resorts tend to charge more compared to small places that cater for a local crowd. Ski shops also give good pricing and will rent skis for multiple days or the season.

FLOAT YOUR BOAT

On the coast, you shouldn't have much trouble finding kayaks and stand-up paddleboards (SUPs). Expect to pay around $20 to $25 per hour. Lakes with small resorts are dotted around the region and there is often a dock and shop where canoes, SUPs and boats can be rented. River-rafting trips are available through professional outfitters who will put a guide in the boat with you, which is a good idea if you are new to rafting and kayaking. Some companies will rent you a kayak or raft to float on your own ($160 is a typical daily fee). For additional charges, they can drop off and pick up the boat at your desired location.

Nuts & Bolts

Electricity
120V/60Hz

Cannabis & Alcohol

The legal age for buying, possessing and using cannabis is 21 in Oregon and Washington, and 19 in BC. The legal drinking age is 21 in Oregon and Washington, and 19 in BC.

Hiking Permits

Hiking permits are needed for some trails in the Enchantments in Washington and the Central Oregon Cascades.

Breastfeeding

Women breastfeed in public; some cover themselves and their baby with a thin cloth or shawl.

GOOD TO KNOW

Time Zone
Pacific Standard Time (GMT-8; GMT-7 during daylight savings)

Country Code
+1

Emergency Number
911

Population
Oregon 4.2 million, Washington 7.7 million, Vancouver 675,218

Professional Sports

Pro sports are a big deal in the Pacific Northwest. Clubs include the Seattle Mariners (baseball), Seattle Seahawks (football), Vancouver Canucks and Seattle Kraken (ice hockey), Portland Trailblazers (basketball), Portland Thorns FC and OL Reign (women's soccer), Portland Timbers and Seattle Sounders (men's soccer).

PUBLIC HOLIDAYS

New Year's Day January 1 (USA and Canada)

Martin Luther King Jr Day Third Monday in January (USA)

Easter Sunday in late March or early April (USA and Canada)

Victoria Day Monday on or preceding May 24 (Canada)

Memorial Day Last Monday in May (USA)

Juneteenth National Independence Day June 19 (USA)

Canada Day July 1, or July 2 if July 1 is a Sunday (Canada)

Independence Day July 4 (USA)

Labor Day First Monday in September (USA and Canada)

Thanksgiving Day Second Monday in October (Canada); fourth Thursday in November (USA)

Christmas Day December 25 (USA and Canada)

Boxing Day December 26 (Canada)

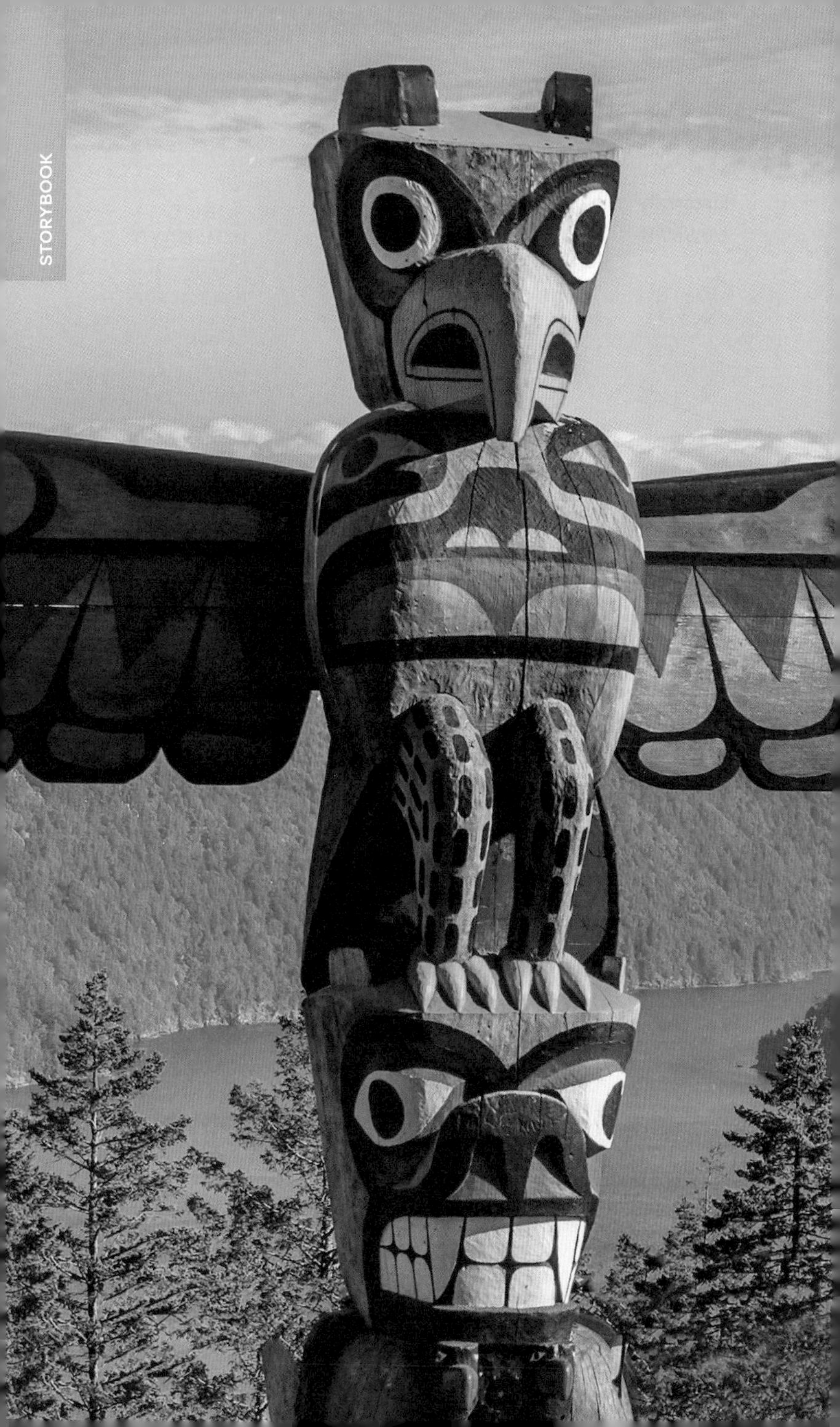

STORYBOOK

Our writers delve deep into different aspects of Pacific Northwest life

A History of the Pacific Northwest in 15 Places

Many elements have gone into making the Pacific Northwest what it is today.

Margot Bigg

p374

Meet the Oregonians

You'll find most people are big fans of their state – and its natural wonders.

Margot Bigg

p378

Fighting for Fish

Southern Oregon is the scene for the world's largest dam removal project, a costly effort to save salmon.

Michael Kohn

p380

Understanding the Seattle of Today

Exploring Seattle's evolution: navigating changes and preserving the city's essence and community spirit.

Amy Sung

p383

A HISTORY OF THE PACIFIC NORTHWEST IN

15 PLACES

Many elements have gone into making the Pacific Northwest what it is today, from early geological events that shaped its varied landscapes to the foundation of human settlements many thousands of years ago. However, it wasn't until the 19th century that the current geopolitical state of the region took form.
By Margot Bigg

ALTHOUGH INDIGENOUS PEOPLES have lived in the Northwest for at least eight millennia, it was in the 16th century that European explorers began visiting the region. Some came to chart waters, while others were interested primarily in trapping and trading for highly coveted beaver pelts. A series of successful land crossings around the turn of the 19th century set the stage for the Oregon Trail, which brought hundreds of thousands of white Americans west. This mass influx helped the US lay claim to the region – or at least everything below the 49th parallel – through the Treaty of Oregon. Everything north of it, including Vancouver Island, went to the British and later became part of Canada.

In the 1800s 'Manifest Destiny' – a belief that white Americans were bound by God to colonize the West – prevailed in US political discourse. Tragically, this led to the mass desecration of Native communities, large numbers of whom were killed or forced onto reservations.

In the grand scheme of things, all of this happened fairly recently, and the Pacific Northwest in its current incarnation is still very young. Many of the region's historic sites are less than 200 years old, a testament to the fact that a lot can change in very little time.

1. Oregon Caves National Monument and Preserve

CHANNEL YOUR INNER TROGLODYTE

In Southern Oregon's Klamath–Siskiyou region, the Oregon Caves National Monument and Preserve has around 15,000ft of serpentine tunnels and chambers decked out in stalagmites and stalactites, all formed millions of years ago. While local tribes knew about the caves for generations, they first came to the attention of settlers in 1874, when a local boy found them by accident while looking for his runaway dog, but it took years before scientists began exploring the caves in great numbers.

For more on Oregon Caves National Monument, see page 276

2. Columbia Hills Historical State Park

HIKE AMONG PETROGLYPHS

Located within the nearly-4000-acre Columbia Hills Historical State Park, Horsethief Lake has some of the best-preserved Native American pictographs and petroglyphs in the region. They're believed to date back to the 17th century. You can see a large collection of rock art by taking a hike along the Temani Pesh-Wa Trail, where you'll find dozens of examples, many depicting area fauna. If you want to see the most famous of them all – Tsagaglalal (which translates to 'She Who Watches') – you'll need to sign up for a guided tour.

For more on Columbia Hills Historical State Park, see page 225

3. Fort Clatsop
WINTER WITH LEWIS, CLARK AND SACAJAWEA

In December 1805, 31 members of the Corps of Discovery, more commonly known as the Lewis and Clark Expedition, began construction on what would be their winter abode: Fort Clatsop. Just outside of Astoria, not far from where the Columbia River meets the Pacific Ocean, this site became the first US military structure west of the Rockies. They chose the spot because it gave them easy access to a freshwater spring and was close enough to the ocean that they could set up saltworks. Today, there's a replica where the original fort once stood.

For more on Fort Clatsop, see page 250

4. Oregon City
THE END OF THE OREGON TRAIL

Oregon City first rose to prominence in the 1840s as the final stop on the Oregon Trail. The city was established in 1829 by John McLoughlin of the Hudson's Bay Company, who also built Fort Vancouver, across the Columbia River from what is now Portland. McLoughlin saw massive Willamette Falls in the Willamette River as an excellent power source for running a lumber mill, and many of the earliest settlers in Oregon filed land claims here. You can learn

more about the history of the city and of westward expansion by visiting the End of the Oregon Trail Interpretive Center and the Museum of the Oregon Territory.

For more on Oregon City, see page 203

5. Whitman Mission National Historic Site
THE MASSACRE THAT BIRTHED OREGON AND WASHINGTON

Just outside of Walla Walla, the Whitman Mission was established with the intention of converting Indigenous Americans to Christianity and, for many years, was a major stop along the Oregon Trail. However, there were tensions between white settlers and local tribes, which escalated in 1847, when roughly half of the area's Cayuse people succumbed to a measles outbreak. One of the mission's founders – Dr Marcus Whitman – was accused of poisoning the Cayuse. Soon after, Whitman and 12 others were killed in what was termed the Whiteman Massacre. When Congress caught news of the massacre, they quickly passed legislation to create the Oregon Territory.

For more on Walla Walla, see page 154

6. Victoria's Chinatown
CANADA'S OLDEST CHINATOWN

Established in the middle of the 19th century, Victoria's Chinatown is Canada's oldest and the second-oldest Chinatown in North America (San Francisco's is the oldest). Although this compact neighborhood has undergone quite a few changes over the decades, it remains a hub for Chinese culture and architecture – including Fan Tan Alley, the narrowest street in Canada. Some of its features are newer, notably the Gate of Harmonious Interest, a *paifang* (Chinese archway) that was built in 1981 in honor of the neighborhood's revitalization.

For more on Victoria's Chinatown, see page 334

7. San Juan Island National Historical Park
THE PIG WAR

In 1859, when San Juan Island was still jointly occupied by the US and the UK, American farmer Lyman Cutlar noticed a pig digging up potatoes in his garden. Cutlar shot it dead, much to the chagrin of the

Fort Clatsop (p250)

STEVE ESTVANIK/SHUTTERSTOCK ©

pig's owner, an Irishman, who demanded compensation. A kerfuffle ensued, which was soon politicized, leading to a dispute known as the Pig War, which was really more territorial than porcine. It was finally resolved peacefully in 1872, with a bit of mediation from German Emperor Wilhelm I, and though the British ultimately withdrew, the Union Jack still flies on the island to this day.

For more on San Juan Island National Historical Park, see page 105

8. Kam Wah Chung State Heritage Site
A LIVING TIME CAPSULE

The Eastern Oregon community of John Day once had a large Chinese American community, and while that's no longer the case today, a bit of the region's patrimony has been preserved at the Kam Wah Chung State Heritage Site. The site preserves a Chinese doctor's office, pharmacy and general store housed in a building dating to 1865. Stepping inside feels very much like walking into a time machine, complete with shelf upon shelf lined with old medicine bottles, many labeled in Chinese, plus furnishings that date to the structure's heyday in the 19th and early 20th centuries.

For more on Kam Wah Chung State Heritage Site, see page 297

9. Old Chief Joseph Gravesite
HERE LIES A GREAT CHIEF

Tuekakas, popularly known as Old Chief Joseph, was the main leader of the Wallowa Band for much of the 19th century and was notable in that he refused to sign a treaty that would have essentially forced him to sell his people's lands and move onto a small reservation. He was also the father of Chief Joseph the Younger, the most famous of the Nez Percé leaders to fight in the Nez Percé War. Although Tuekakas was originally buried elsewhere, his remains were exhumed and reburied at this cemetery, which is now a National Historic Site.

For more on Old Chief Joseph Gravesite, see page 296

10. Gastown
THE PRECURSOR TO MODERN-DAY VANCOUVER

Extending for 12 blocks on one side of downtown Vancouver, Gastown – the city's oldest neighborhood – is a fine example of what the city looked like back in its earliest incarnations. Most of the buildings here were built between 1886 and 1914 – in fact, only six of Gastown's buildings were constructed after 1914. Today, this cobblestoned part of the city – a National Historic Site – is full of bars, restaurants and shops, but it's an equally great place for architecture buffs to go for a wander. Just remember to look up.

For more on Gastown, see page 306

11. Cape Blanco State Park
A PARK FULL OF HISTORY

Occupying the westernmost tip of Oregon, this state park provides a snapshot of what life must have been like at the turn of the 20th century. Its Cape Blanco Lighthouse is the oldest continuously operating lighthouse on the Oregon Coast and was the first of the state's lighthouses to employ a female keeper. The park is also the site of the Historic Hughes House, which was built in 1898 as the residence of the Hughes family, who ran a massive dairy farm on the cape. The house is decked out with a mix of original and replica period furniture and functions as a museum.

For more on Cape Blanco State Park, see page 265

Dominion Building Gastown (p296)

Pittock Mansion (p181)

12. Butchart Gardens

A GLIMPSE INTO CANADIAN GARDENING HISTORY

In 1904 a woman by the name of Jennie Butchart took an old limestone quarry and began transforming it into what would later become part of one of Canada's most lauded public gardens. The quarry, now called the Sunken Garden, remains the pinnacle of the Butchart Gardens – a National Historic Site of Canada – to this day. This naturally walled expanse features elegant landscaping filled with colorful blooms that burst into color every spring. There's also a Mediterranean Garden, an Italian Garden, a Rose Garden and a Japanese Garden.

For more on Butchart Gardens, see page 338

13. The Panama Hotel

JAPANESE AMERICAN HISTORY

Designed by Sabro Ozasa, among the first Japanese architects to practice in the US, Seattle's Panama Hotel is the only place on the continent with a Japanese-style public bathhouse that's still intact. The hotel first opened in 1910 to house Japanese men who had come to Washington to find work. In 1942, when large numbers of Japanese and Japanese American people were sent to internment camps, the hotel's basement became a de facto storage area. Many never returned to collect their belongings, some of which are now on display at the hotel's cafe.

14. The Pittock Mansion

PORTLAND'S FIRST MEGAMANSION

Completed in 1914, the Pittock Mansion was commissioned by newspaper baron Henry Pittock, who was the publisher of *The Oregonian* newspaper at the time. It sits on a hill overlooking Portland, not far from the city center, and is surrounded by elegant gardens with views of Mt Hood in the distance. This gargantuan home was well ahead of its time, with unusual features such as an elevator, intercoms and a central vacuuming system. Today it operates as a nonprofit museum and provides a fascinating look into the most opulent aspect of Portland's past.

For more on the Pittock Mansion, see page 181

15. Mt St Helen's

A BLIZZARD OF ASH

On May 18, 1980, Washington's Mt St Helen's erupted, blowing off around 1200ft of its peak and killing 57 people in the process. The surrounding region was blanketed with ash, which fell like snow from the sky. Portland, less than 100 miles to the south, was hit heavily, but even far-off Spokane – a good 250 miles away – got a good dose. The mountain, which has been called 'Loowit' (smoking mountain) by local Indigenous people for generations, has had plenty of volcanic activity since, though nothing close to the magnitude of what happened in '80.

For more on Mt St Helen's, see page 144

MEET THE OREGONIANS

Oregon has a noticeable urban–rural divide, but you'll find most people are big fans of their state – and its natural wonders. Margot Bigg introduces her people.

YOU CAN TELL a lot about a place by its bumper stickers – and I'm not talking about the political variety. In Oregon, you'll often see stickers shaped like the state's outline, with big green hearts in the middle – a way of telling other motorists that no matter where you may go, your heart will always be in Oregon. While the heart-in-state sticker trend has since grown into a nationwide phenomenon, it all started in Oregon. Many Oregonians are fiercely proud of their state, whether they were born and raised here or moved to Oregon later in life.

Aside from Indigenous people and families who trace their heritage to the Oregon Trail, it seems like the bulk of people you'll meet in Oregon are not originally from the state. This is especially the case in Portland. 'Where are you from?' is a common icebreaker at potlucks and parties, and if you mention that you're Oregon-born, you'll quickly be crowned a 'unicorn,' for your apparent rareness of mythical proportions. In fact, I've found that here in Portland, I'm much more likely to meet people from California or Ohio than from Oregon.

Of course, things change quite a bit once you get away from larger urban centers such as Portland, Eugene, Bend and Salem. Nearly half of Oregonians were born in the state, and when you go beyond the

The Urban–Rural Divide

Roughly two-thirds of Oregonians live in urban areas, mostly along the I-5 corridor that connects Washington, Oregon and California. The remaining third live in rural communities or 'frontier' areas, sparsely populated spots that are mostly found in Eastern Oregon.

cities, Oregon can feel like a very different world. As a person who was born and raised in Portland, my view of the state is naturally going to be very different from that of someone who hails from a ranching community in Eastern Oregon. For example, whereas I see Oregon as a liberal place, where you're free to be your own weird self (as long as that weirdness conforms to a very strict code of Portland-acceptable weirdness), I'm not sure I'd have the same experience if I grew up on the opposite side of the state.

What we Oregonians do share, however, is an appreciation for the outdoors – in fact, I'm confident that Oregon's natural beauty is among its biggest draws, both for visitors and for those who choose to make this state their new home. Our state is big – bigger than the entire UK, even – and with so much landmass, it makes sense that we'd have a lot of ecological diversity. While Oregon has long been known for its beautiful old-growth forests and its rolling wine-growing regions, we also have huge expanses of high desert and prairie lands. Plateaus? We've got 'em. Snow-capped mountains? Ditto. Sandy beaches? Absolutely – just bring a wetsuit if you plan to swim because, as any Oregonian will be quick to tell you: we are nothing like California.

I'M NOT LIKE OTHER OREGONIANS…OR AM I?

There's an assumption that we Oregonians are an outdoorsy bunch who spent our formative years traipsing through the woods and could set up a tent before we could walk. That's certainly not the case with me. Like many who were born in the state, I'm a first-generation Oregonian, born to a father from England and a mother from New England. Camping was not part of my childhood and while I've always been fond of trees, I never saw the point in sleeping among them.

I left Portland as a young adult, and spent years living in Paris and New Delhi. When I'd come back to visit, I'd immediately notice the abundance of trees, for no matter where you are in Oregon, nature is never far away. When I finally moved back, I started spending more time exploring the outdoors – and even camping. And while I still prefer comfy hotel rooms to tents in the woods, I finally get why people appreciate Oregon so much.

FIGHTING
FOR FISH

Southern Oregon is the scene for the world's largest dam removal project, a costly effort to save salmon. By Michael Kohn

FOR NEARLY A century, four dams on the Klamath River near the Oregon–California border have quietly hummed away, producing electricity for their nearby communities. The hydroelectric power is cheap and produces zero carbon emissions. But that low-cost power has come at a cost that the builders did not fully comprehend – the collapse of an important salmon fishery. The dams they erected blocked passage to important spawning grounds upstream and led to mass fish die-offs from disease. The depletion of the Klamath fishery has had its greatest impact on the original inhabitants of the area, a group of tribes who honor salmon as a cultural and food resource. For decades the tribes fought to have the dams removed. Their tireless efforts eventually paid off and all four dams are planned to be breached by 2024 – the end of a long battle for social and environmental justice.

How the Klamath Dams Impact Fish & Indigenous Communities

Each year around 10,000 fish return to the Klamath River from the Pacific Ocean, a fraction of the one million Chinook salmon, coho salmon and steelhead trout that passed upstream before the four Klamath River dams were built in the early 20th century.

The dwindling number of salmon has been a heavy blow for Indigenous people who for a millennia had subsisted on salmon fishing in the Klamath Basin. Yurok, Karuk and other tribes consumed 450lb of salmon a year per person, a number that fell to just 5lb by the early 2000s. Indigenous people also held tremendous respect for the fish they caught, considering salmon to be a distant relative, as well as a gift of food from the creator. When salmon return from the ocean to lay eggs in their natal streams, ceremonies are held in their honor.

As the fisheries collapsed, the Indigenous people of the Klamath Basin increasingly relied on government-issued foods high in sugar, starches and fats, causing poor health and high rates of diabetes. The last straw occurred in 2002 when water diversions during a drought year caused a bacterial outbreak that killed between 33,000 and 70,000 fish in the Klamath River, the largest salmon kill in the history of the Western United States. Indigenous people, environmentalists and fishing enthusiasts joined forces and declared their intentions to remove the four dams in a campaign they called 'Un-Dam the Klamath.'

The Battle to Remove the Dams

Around that time PacifiCorp, the Portland-based company that owned the four dams, faced a new relicensing cycle. Federal agencies said new licenses were contingent on the installation of fish ladders, and as toxic algae blooms appeared in two of the reservoirs and needed to be addressed, the costs of repairing the damage were determined to be too high. PacifiCorp agreed to have the dams taken down.

Red tape stalled the project, but after 20 years of petitioning, a demolition crew armed with explosives and heavy machinery began pulling the first of the four dams down in 2023, with the others set to come down in 2024. The total cost of removal is north of $450 million, paid by taxpayers and PacifiCorp ratepayers.

WHEN SALMON RETURN FROM THE OCEAN TO LAY EGGS IN THEIR NATAL STREAMS, CEREMONIES ARE HELD IN THEIR HONOR.

The objective of freeing the river is to give fish unfettered access to more than 400 miles of important spawning area above the dams, which have been cut off for a century. Proponents say water will be cleaner as it will no longer pool and warm up in the reservoirs or collect agricultural runoff.

But the project has its share of opponents, too. Landowners near the reservoirs complained about decimated property values. The reservoirs also provided tax revenue and recreation for the nearby communities. When water was released in summer, boating companies could run rafting trips. That won't be possible when the dams go away because the natural summer flow is too low. Flooding is also a concern for residents in the area as the dams will no longer be around to control high waters.

In the end, none of those arguments held enough water to stop the dam removal.

The Klamath dams are the biggest ones to come down in the Northwest, but they aren't the first. In the early 2010s the Elwha and Glines Canyon dams in Washington were removed, opening up over 70 miles of river access for salmon on the Elwha River, most of which runs through Olympic National Park. Next on the chopping block could be four dams on the Lower Snake River, a tributary of the Columbia River.

Celilo Falls

One regional dam that is unlikely to be breached soon is the Dalles Dam on the Columbia River. Among the 10 largest hydro-producing dams in the United States, it is Dalles Dam that submerged the legendary Celilo Falls when it was completed in 1957. For thousands of years Celilo, a cauldron of white water and leaping fish, was an economic and cultural center for Native Americans and the oldest continuously inhabited settlement in North America. The roar of the water, which could be heard from miles away, was silenced in a few hours after the dam gates closed.

Native Americans living along the Columbia still dream of seeing Celilo again and using dip nets to catch salmon as they attempt to jump the falls. The US Army Corps of Engineers says taking down the Dalles Dam could happen, but that conversation is decades away.

Looking Forward

There is no guarantee that removing the Klamath dams, or any other dams in the Pacific Northwest, will restore fish populations to their historic numbers. Climate change is another factor that threatens fish, as warming temperatures in oceans can negatively impact salmon when they are out at sea. Furthermore, dam removal is also just one step in the river's recovery, and actually the easy part. Next comes the restoration of the river and its banks. Whole ecosystems need to be replanted on land that has not experienced air and sunlight for a century. But tribal members and other stakeholders have spent years gathering seeds to restore the habitat and are now eagerly awaiting their chance to help recover salmon and other fish species. The hope is one day drums will beat again, heralding the return of their relatives.

UNDERSTANDING
THE SEATTLE
OF TODAY

Exploring Seattle's evolution: navigating tech-driven changes, housing crises and tourism's impact to preserve the city's essence and community spirit. By Amy Sung

IN RECENT YEARS Seattle, just like San Francisco, has undergone a significant transformation thanks to the rise of tech companies. As the tech industry has grown, so has the city's affluent population, impacting the city's culture and residents and transforming it into something different than it was in the early 2000s and prior.

Seattle Then & Now

Before the tech boom, Seattle was a relatively laid-back city. Nirvana, Pearl Jam and Sir Mix-a-Lot were the city's claim to musical fame, happy hours came with free food, freshly shucked oysters could be had for 25¢ a pop (shout out to Elliott's Oyster House's former progressive happy hour!), and Bill Gates was our biggest name in tech. The city was known for its natural beauty, its thriving arts scene and its strong sense of community – there was a low-key pride in its unique culture and identity.

While some argue that the influx of tech companies has brought prosperity and innovation, Seattle's affordable housing crisis is now a pressing issue at the forefront of local politics. And no matter how you slice it, the city's tech industry has played a significant role in exacerbating the problem, with the influx of high-paid tech workers driving up housing prices and making it increasingly difficult for lower-income residents to find affordable housing options.

The Pitfalls of Prosperity

One of the main challenges facing policy-makers in addressing the affordable housing crisis is the tension between the need for more housing supply and the desire to preserve the city's unique character and livability. Many residents and community organizations are concerned that unchecked development will lead to gentrification and the displacement of longtime residents – and businesses – particularly in neighborhoods that have historically been home to marginalized communities. And with this gentrification comes rising prices for everything from food to transportation.

With so many people moving to Seattle and the city's growing reputation as a foodie destination, many restaurants have raised their prices to keep up with demand. While all restaurants have been forced to increase prices due to reasons like recovering from COVID-19 or the rising costs throughout the supply chain, the new – and expensive – restaurants, no matter how tasty, creative or innovative they really are, tend to be the ones to get the spotlight and the long-standing local favorites

383

are often left in the shadows, to be forgotten and pushed out of their rising rents in due time. The juxtaposition of new, pricey eateries next to the growing houseless population makes the wealth disparity all the clearer, and creates complicated feelings for longtime locals.

Then there's the growth of homeowners creating additional dwelling units (ADUs) or detached additional dwelling units (DADUs) and renting them out to travelers. Admittedly, as a traveler, there's nothing quite like the freedom and flexibility of an Airbnb or VRBO rental. The chance to live like a local, to experience a city in a more authentic way, is an undeniable draw. But as with any great innovation, there are also potential pitfalls.

On the one hand, supporters argue that Airbnb and VRBO rentals provide much-needed income for homeowners, offer a more affordable alternative to traditional hotel stays, and allow tourists to experience the city more authentically. On the other hand, opponents argue that Airbnb rentals contribute to rising housing costs and displacement of long-term residents, create noise and safety concerns in residential neighborhoods, and potentially harm the overall character of a neighborhood.

On Preservation of Culture, Community & Identity

So what can tourists do to be conscientious during their visit? The first step is to be aware of the issue and research before booking a rental. Find out if the rental is legal and properly licensed, and check if there are any restrictions on short-term rentals in the area. If you do decide to book a rental, respect the neighborhood and the neighbors.

But beyond being a conscientious tourist, there's also a larger question at play. How can we balance the benefits of tourism with the needs of long-term residents? While there are no easy answers, one potential solution to address vacation rentals is to create a regulatory framework that allows for short-term rentals while also protecting the rights of long-term residents. This could include zoning restrictions that limit the number of short-term rentals in residential neighborhoods, licensing requirements that ensure rentals meet safety and health standards, and taxes that are used to support affordable housing and other community needs.

Supporting local organizations that work toward providing affordable housing and resources for those experiencing homelessness is another way to be mindful of the homeless population and affordable housing crisis plaguing the city.

By working together, policymakers, residents and tourists can create a more sustainable and equitable approach to tourism. In the end, the controversy around vacation rentals in Seattle and the cost of eating out are just two examples of the more significant tensions that exist between the needs of residents and the demands of tourists, as well as the growing economic divide among those who live in this city.

As travelers, we have a responsibility to be respectful and conscientious, to support local businesses, artists and communities, seeking out not just what's on the best-of lists of big national magazines, but also what's being talked about as great ways to experience Seattle as it was in simpler times, glitz, glamour or fame aside – the businesses that made Seattle what it is today before it became what it is today. And while Seattle will never go back to being exactly as it was at any point in the past, it has the potential to embrace a new version of itself that respects and acknowledges the essence of what the city has always found pride in – its natural beauty, its thriving arts scene and its strong sense of community. There can still be a low-key pride in the city's unique culture and identity.

AS TRAVELERS, WE HAVE A RESPONSIBILITY TO BE RESPECTFUL AND CONSCIENTIOUS, TO SUPPORT LOCAL BUSINESSES, ARTISTS AND COMMUNITIES

INDEX

INDEX

A-E

A

accessible travel 369
accommodations 138, 361
activities 50, see
  also individual activities
alcohol 371
Anacortes 98-9, **99**
  accommodations 99
  beyond Anacortes 100-1
  food 99
animals, see individual
  species
aquariums
  Oregon Coast Aquarium
    258
  Ucluelet Aquarium 351
  Vancouver Aquarium
    310, 312
art 22-3
Ashland 269-83, 272-4
  beyond Ashland 275-8
  itineraries 33, 271
  travel within 270, 272,
    270
  walking tour 273, **273**
Astoria 250-3, **251**
  accommodations 251
  beyond Astoria 254-7
  food 253
  itineraries 32
  travel within 250
ATMs 358

B

B&Bs 361
Baker City 291-2
  accommodations 292
  beyond Baker City 293-9
  drinking 292
  food 292
  travel within 291

Map Pages **000**

bald eagles 147
Ballard Locks 81
Bandon 265-7
beaches 14-15
  Cannon Beach 255
  Olympic National Park
    114-15
beer 20-1
Bellingham 90-2, **91**
  accommodations 91
  beyond Bellingham 93-7
  drinking 91-2
  travel within 90
Bend 230-4, **231, 232**
  accommodations 233
  beyond Bend 235-43
  drinking 233
  food 234
  travel within 230
birdwatching 282
Blockbuster 232
books 37
  Twilight 121-2
breweries 20-1
  Aslan Brewing 92
  Astoria Brewing
    Company 253
  Ballard Brewery District
    80
  Chuckanut Brewery 101
  Deschutes Brewery
    Tasting Room & Beer
    Garden 233
  El Sueñito Brewing 92
  Fair Isle Brewing 80
  Fort George Brewery
    253
  Garden Path
    Fermentation 101
  Lucky Envelope Brewing
    81
  Stoup Brewing 81
  Structures Brewing 92
  Well 80 Brewhouse 125
Brownsville 211
bus travel 359

C

camping 361
  equipment 370
cannabis 371
canoeing 53

car travel 359
cell phones 358
Central Island 343-7, **344**
  food 347
  walking tour 345, **345**
Central Oregon 227-43
  itineraries 229
  travel within 228, **228**
children, travel with 13, 362
  Seattle 78-9
Chinatown (Victoria)
  334, 375
cideries
  Bale Breaker & Yonder
    Cider Taproom 80
  Fortune & Glory Cider
    Company 253
climate 34-5, 366
climbing
  Methow Valley 149
  Smith Rock 240
  South Sister 237
clothes 36
Columbia River Gorge
  212-25
  itineraries 215
  travel within 214, **214**
cooking classes 164
Coos Bay 262-3, **263**
  beyond Coos Bay 264-7
  food 263
  itineraries 28
  travel within 262
Corvallis 204-5
Coupeville 103
Crater Lake National Park
  279-80, **280**
  accommodations 280
  beyond Crater Lake
    National Park 281-3
  drinking 280
  itineraries 27, 33
  travel within 279
credit cards 360
culture 378, 383-5, see also
  Indigenous peoples
  Chinese Canadian 313,
    334
cycling 51, 52
  Camp Sherman 241
  equipment 370
  San Juan Islands 109
  Walla Walla 156

D

Dalles, the 224
dams 380-2
Darcelle XV Showplace
  176
Dayton 158
Depoe Bay 257
  itineraries 27
disabilities, travelers
  with 369
distilleries
  Big Gin Distilling 80
  Crater Lake Spirits
    Distillery Tasting Room
    234
  Pilot House Distilling 253
Drayton Harbor 94
drinking 365, see also
  individual locations

E

Eagle Cap Wilderness
  297-9
Eastern Oregon 284-99
  itineraries 287
  travel within 286, **286**
Eastern Washington
  151-65
  itineraries 153
  travel within 152, **152**
electricity 371
Elkhorn Mountains 294-5
Elwha Dam 117-18
Elwha Valley 117-18
Empress Hotel 335
entertainment 364-5, see
  also individual locations
equipment 370
etiquette 36
  wine tasting 43
Eugene 206-8, **207**
  accommodations 208
  beyond Eugene 209-11
  food 207
  itineraries 33
  travel within 206
events, see festivals &
  events

386

Map Pages **000**

Map Pages **000**

"At sunset, I serendipitously spotted four foxes in the American Camp fields on San Juan Island (p105)."

BRANDON FRALIC

"For a recent birthday, escape room-loving friends took me to the Leavenworth Escape Room (p136). We came in third. Of all time! If you see 25.12 minutes still on the leaderboard, that's us!"

ALEX LEVITON

Mapping data sources:
© Lonely Planet
© OpenStreetMap http://openstreetmap.org/copyright

THIS BOOK

Destination Editor
Sarah Stocking

Production Editor
Kathryn Rowan

Book Designer
Hannah Blackie

Cartographer
Valentina Kremenchutskaya

Assisting Editors
Janet Austin, Melanie Dankel, Michael MacKenzie, Mani Ramaswamy, Tasmin Waby

Cover Researcher
Lauren Egan

Thanks Ronan Abayawickrema, Imogen Bannister, Alex Conroy

LEFT: MICHAEL J COHEN/GETTY IMAGES ©; RIGHT: WWW.ESCAPEROOMLEAVENWORTH.COM ©

MIX
Paper from responsible sources
FSC
www.fsc.org   FSC™ C021741

Paper in this book is certified against the Forest Stewardship Council™ standards. FSC™ promotes environmentally responsible, socially beneficial and economically viable management of the world's forests.

Published by Lonely Planet Global Limited
CRN 554153
9th edition – June 2024
ISBN 978 1 78868 461 3
© Lonely Planet 2024 Photographs © as indicated 2024
10 9 8 7 6 5 4 3 2 1
Printed in China